Black Feminist Cultural Criticism

KEYWORKS IN CULTURAL STUDIES

As cultural studies powers ahead to new intellectual horizons, it becomes increasingly important to chart the discipline's controversial history. This is the object of an exciting new series, KeyWorks in Cultural Studies. By showcasing the best that has been thought and written on the leading themes and topics constituting the discipline, KeyWorks in Cultural Studies provides an invaluable genealogy for students striving to better understand the contested space in which cultural studies takes place and is practiced.

Black Feminist Cultural Criticism

Edited by

Jacqueline Bobo

BLACKWELL
Publishers

First published 2001

2 4 6 8 10 9 7 5 3 1

Blackwell Publishers Inc.
350 Main Street
Malden, Massachusetts 02148
USA

Blackwell Publishers Ltd
108 Cowley Road
Oxford OX4 1JF
UK

Library of Congress Cataloging-in-Publication Data

Black feminist cultural criticism / edited Jacqueline Bobo.
  p. cm.—(Keyworks in cultural studies; 3)
Includes bibliographical references and index.
ISBN 0–631–22239–1 (hb. : acid-free paper)—ISBN 0–631–22240–5
  (pbk. : acid-free paper)
1. Afro-American arts. 2. Feminism and the arts—United States. 3. Afro-American
women artists. 4. Feminist criticism—United States. I. Bobo, Jacqueline. II. Series.

NX512.3.A35 B625 2001
700'.82'0973—dc21

00-057916

British Library Cataloguing in Publication Data
A CIP catalogue record for this book is available from the British Library.

Typeset in Galliard 10 on 12pt
by Kolam Information Services Pvt. Ltd, Pondicherry, India
Printed and bound in Great Britain by MPG Books Ltd, Bodmin, Cornwall

This book is printed on acid-free paper.

Dedicated to the memory of Barbara Christian

Contents

Authors

Cuesta Benberry is a noted quilt historian and consultant. She was elected to the Quilter's Hall of Fame in 1983 and cited in the *Directory of African-American Folklorists*, Smithsonian Institution Office of Folklife Programs. She is the co-author of *Patchwork Pieces of Long Ago: An Anthology of Quilt Fiction*.

Jacqueline Bobo is Associate Professor and Chair of the Women's Studies Program and Associate Director of the Center for Black Studies at the University of California, Santa Barbara. She holds a Ph.D. in Film and is the author of *Black Women as Cultural Readers* (1995) and editor of *Black Women Film and Video Artists* (1998).

Arna Alexander Bontemps is a writer and historian. He is the editor of *Forever Free: Art by African American Women 1862–1980* (1980), a former editor of *Ebony* magazine, and author of numerous articles and book reviews about African American literature and history.

Barbara Christian is Professor of African American Studies at the University of California, Berkeley. She is the author of *Black Women Novelists: The Development of a Tradition, 1892–1976* (1980) and *Black Feminist Criticism: Perspectives on Black Women Writers* (1985).

Angela Y. Davis is Professor in the History of Consciousness Program at the University of California, Santa Cruz. She is the author of *If They Come in the Morning: Voices of Resistance* (1971), *Angela Davis: An Autobiography* (1974), *Women, Race and Class* (1981), *Women, Culture and Politics* (1987), and *Blues Legacies and Black Feminism: Gertrude "Ma" Rainey, Bessie Smith, and Billie Holiday* (1998).

Ruby Dee is a noted actor and author. Her recent films are *Do the Right Thing* (1989), *Jungle Fever* (1991), and the Academy Award-nominated short *Tuesday Morning Ride* (1995). Ruby Dee wrote and starred in the PBS drama *My Name Is Zora* (1989). She is the author of *My One Good Nerve* (1998) and co-author of *Of Ossie and Ruby: In This Life Together* (1998).

Jacqueline Fonvielle-Bontemps is Associate Professor of Art at Hampton University. She is curator and director of exhibitions *Forever Free: Art by African-American Women 1862–1980* and *Choosing: An Exhibit of Changing Perspectives in Modern Art and Art Criticism by Black Americans 1925–85.*

Gladys-Marie Fry, Ph.D., is Professor of Folklore at the University of Maryland, College Park. She is the author of *The Night Riders: A Study of the Social Control of the Negro* (1974) and *Stitched from the Soul: Slaves Quilts from the Ante-Bellum South* (1990).

Melody Graulich is Professor of English and Women's Studies at the University of New Hampshire. She is the editor of *Yellow Woman* (1994) and the co-editor of *Exploring Lost Boundaries: Critical Essays on Mary Austin* (1999).

C. A. Griffith is a director, writer, and director of photography. Her most recent project is the feature-length dramatic film *Del Otro Lado (The Other Side)* (1999), shot in Mexico, and the experimental short *Borderline... Family Pictures* (1996). She is currently an Assistant Professor in the Department of Film and Video at Columbia College, Chicago.

Kellie Jones is a curator and writer. She has held positions at the Studio Museum of Harlem, the Broida Museum, Jamaica Arts Center, and is adjunct curator at the Walker Art Center in Minneapolis, Minnesota. In 1989 she was the United States commissioner to Brazil's São Paulo Bienal.

Audre Lorde (1934–92) was named the State Poet of New York for 1991–3. She combined activism through her writings and speeches, participation in social justice endeavors, including Black, feminist, and gay and lesbian activism. Audre Lorde was a former Professor of English at John Jay College of Criminal Justice and at Hunter College. She was the author of numerous articles and books, including the novel *Zami: A New Spelling of My Name* (1982).

Evelyn McDonnell is a free-lance writer, editor and former music editor at the *Village Voice*. She is the co-editor of *Stars Don't Stand Still in the Sky: Music and Myth* (1998) and *Rock She Wrote: Women Write about Rock, Pop and Rap* (1999).

Deborah E. McDowell is Professor of American Literature at the University of Virginia. She is the author of *Leaving Pipe Shop: Memories of Kin* (1998), *"The Changing Same": Studies in Fiction by Black Women* (1994), the co-editor of *Slavery and the Literary Imagination* (1988), the period editor of the *Norton Anthology of African American Literature*, and the general editor of the Black Women Writers Series from Beacon Press.

Carolyn Mitchell is Professor of English and Director of the Women's Studies Program at Union College in Schenectady, New York. Her research areas are in twentieth-century American fiction, African American literature, and women writers and spirituality.

Sheri Parks is Associate Professor of American Studies at the University of Maryland, College Park. Her research covers popular aesthetics, mass media, race, gender, and family.

Tricia Rose is Assistant Professor of History and Africana Studies at New York University. She is the author of *Black Noise: Rap Music and Black Culture in Contemporary America* (1994) and co-editor of *Microphone Fiends: Youth Music and Youth Culture* (1994).

Sally Bishop Shigley is Associate Professor of English at Weber State University. She is the author of *Dazzling Dialectics: Elizabeth Bishop's Resonating Feminist Reality* (1997).

Barbara Smith is an author, independent scholar, and activist for social justice causes. She is the co-founder and publisher of Kitchen Table: Women of Color Press, the author of *The Truth that Never Hurts: Writings on Race, Gender, and Freedom* (1998), co-editor of *All the Women are White, All the Blacks are Men, but Some of Us are Brave: Black Women's Studies* (1982), editor of *Home Girls: A Black Feminist Anthology* (1983), and co-editor of *The Reader's Companion to US History* (1998).

Freida High W. Tesfagiorgis is Professor of African-American and Contemporary *African Art in the* Department of Afro-American Studies at the University of Wisconsin, Madison. She has numerous publications, including exhibition catalog essays and articles on Black artists past and present, African artists, and Black women artists. Her work has been exhibited at many galleries and museums in the United States, Senegal, and Italy.

Mara Witzling is Professor of Art and Art History and Coordinator of the Women's Studies Program at the University of New Hampshire. She is the editor of *Voicing our Visions: Writings by Contemporary Women Artists* (1991) and *Voicing Today's Visions: Writings by Contemporary Women Artists* (1994).

Preface: Bearing Witness

Jacqueline Bobo

A memorable series of images occur at the midpoint of Julie Dash's independently produced *Daughters of the Dust* (1991). The cinematic portraits depict the Peazant family gathering for a ceremonial feast commemorating their last day on the island Ibo Landing, located off the coasts of Georgia and South Carolina. Set during the turn of the twentieth century, the film portrays the lives of four generations of Black people who have lived through enslavement yet have retained memories, customs, and traditions of their African homelands.

The dinner sequence opens with a shot of a quilt spread out on the ground upon which the meal is placed. A diverse combination of traditional foods, invoking both Black people's African heritage and means of survival while enslaved, is shown in close-up: gumbo, greens, cornbread, shrimp, rice and corn. A hand-woven chair is carefully arranged as a place of honor to seat Nana Peazant, the oldest member of the family. The women appear wearing long flowing white dresses, artfully stitched, embroidered, and sewn by them. Their hairstyles, decorative, yet a regular part of the women's daily lives, form a significant aspect of the *mise-en-scène*. Layered with meaning and symbolism, the background environment becomes a canvas upon which the routine examples of Black women's creativity are displayed.

Black women's art evolved from the activities of women such as these; those who were restricted to using that which was functional and utilitarian, that which was left over to create beauty. These were women who had survived the harshness of life in bondage, yet emerged with principled dignity. Their strength, courage, and refusal to accept the dominant society's conception of them as chattel, property for which no human concerns need apply, form the essence of much of Black women's creative achievements. This perspective is fundamental to the articles selected for this volume. Writers and scholars in literature, film, television, theater, sculpture, painting, music, material culture, and other forms of cultural analysis, explicate Black women's artistic activities within the context of an activist framework. The authors are concerned with the politics of cultural production and the ways in which Black women have confronted institutional and societal barriers in their daily lives and in their creative spaces.

Black Feminist Cultural Criticism charts new directions in considerations of Black women's artistic output by expanding the contours of how we conceive of and analyze creativity. It emanates from the notion of "dry-longso," that ordinary, everyday women are the unheralded bedrock of Black feminist social, political, and cultural activism. *Black Feminist Cultural Criticism* is a *hommage*, a tribute to those women who have contributed greatly to resistance efforts against racial, sexual, and other devastating oppressions while designing for themselves and their families a better world. Immanent within this universe are the diverse manifestations of the women's artistry. Their handicrafts, quilt designs, decorations, foods and recipes, rituals and sacraments, handed down through generations, are thus integral, essential components of Black women's cultural legacy.

Legions of Black women have, historically, been artists without acknow-ledged art forms. Prohibited by law and centuries-old custom from full participation in established creative endeavors, they persevered in crafting beauty in the midst of racial carnage, community in the face of legally mandated dispossession of both their families and property. Despite being treated as manual laborers without intelligence during the slavocracy and long after, sexual repositories of rapacious plantation owners, and, in general, ravaged in mainstream cultural representations, these Black women invented their own unique aesthetic expressions. Their lifestories are not just tales of stoic endurance or mute acceptance. Historical narratives that present them simply as survivors are incomplete. Imbricated crucially in Black women's past is the manner in which their imaginative lives are part and parcel of their ability to withstand and oppose repressive circumstances.

Recent research on quiltmaking and Black folk art offers valuable correct-ives to prior theories about the myriad ways in which Black women pro-tested, fought back, and resisted over time. The passive, docile, obsequious mischaracterization, so beloved in Southern lore, does not appear in these studies. Researchers investigating material cultural artifacts have painstak-ingly recorded the presence of Black women actively involved in the struggles against enslavement using whatever mechanisms were at hand. For many women their skills as artisans were covert means of resistance. Quilt scholars Cuesta Benberry, Gladys-Marie Fry, Jacqueline Tobin, and Raymond Dobard present compelling verification that enslaved Black women used their expertise in quiltmaking, needlework, and textile production to assist those who were escaping bondage by way of the Underground Railroad and other routes to freedom.

Although there has long been a tremendous silence surrounding the contributions of Black women to American quilting traditions, documentation exists proving that Africans who were taken to the USA utilized their prior knowledge of fabric construction in making quilts for plantation households and for their own families. Together with their experience in piecing, appliqué, and embroidery, the women used their proficiency in textile design and cloth-weaving to make the transition to quiltmaking with relative ease.[1] Benberry asserts that specific pattern designs were invented by Black women. When quilts with these coded patterns were hung outside slave cabins they conveyed vital information: whether a home was a safe haven, routes with more hospitable access, directions about navigation of treacherous terrain, and various movements for safe passage.[2]

Gladys-Marie Fry, a respected scholar of quilts constructed by enslaved women, states that distinctive colors previously used in African textiles were used to encode symbolic messages for those who were fleeing.[3] In the latest research on quilts serving as subterfuge, Jacqueline Tobin and Raymond Dobard conducted extensive inquiries to establish the legitimacy of an Underground Railroad Quilt Code. Transmitted orally throughout generations, these secret codes and communication devices employed quiltmaking terminology as part of the clandestine processes used to help Black people escape to freedom.[4]

For many Black women during enslavement their labor on serviceable and practical objects, guaranteed through force, also served social and historic ends. Quilting was, according to Fry, a means for the women to gain emotional stability and spiritual sustenance.[5] In addition, their work fortuitously recorded a history for later use that was revealed through the designs, stitching, colors, and fabrics. The women told of their state of mind during difficult periods, their family lineage, and the rigors of life in bondage, among other particulars. Fry declares: "slave women cast long shadows ... they also remind us that the human mind, spirit, and talent can transcend the cruelest form of human degradation – slavery. Although slavery denied these women their physical freedom, it did not diminish their creative talent and artistic genius."[6] Quilts are visible manifestations linking Black women's cultural past to the present. Throughout generations a sense of continuity is maintained as the insurgent spirit and creative traditions established during enslavement are passed on to other Black women.

In the current renaissance of quilt appreciation situating this expressive form as high art, the work of contemporary feminist painter and sculptor Faith Ringgold is part of the reconsideration of quilts as valued commodities.

Through a combination of text, images painted on fabric, and quilting, Ringgold originated what has been categorized as the story quilt medium. In the quilts, Black women's lives are depicted in symbolic historical contexts and settings. The women's narration is the text on the quilts. They are therefore the authoritative voices of their histories. Ringgold speaks (in an interview in chapter 11 in this volume) of the importance of Black women telling their own stories: others' fabrications distort the full range of their lives while perpetuating limiting translations. Females define themselves in Ringgold's story quilts.

The recovery of the merits inherent in quilt aesthetics has guided scholarly research into other forms of creativity and self-definition in women's domestic space and private worlds. The investigations into material cultural artifacts, such as gardening and food rituals, provide insight into ways women have shaped their environments and influenced their families and culture.[7] Angela Davis writes (chapter 12 in this volume) that cultural practices have a primary role in the socialization process. She is referring here specifically to Black women and music. Extending this analysis to a range of cultural productions offers a broader understanding of art and activism, culture and agency. During periods of intense movements for social change, Davis notes, music "has helped to shape the necessary political consciousness." To understand the development of this awareness of ideo- logical forces affecting their lives, it is imperative that scholars examine the cultural forms influencing Black women, especially those to which they have themselves contributed.[8] Food is an ideal medium for examining the con- fluence of social relations, where the values, traditions, mores, and enduring historical linkages of Black life are cultivated and preserved.

Ceremonies around food have long been significant in Black people's lives. Even food choices have attained an historical and political dimension. Dur- ing enslavement Black people survived on the scraps and discards of the plantation economic system. Heritage foods, such as pigs' feet, intestines, jowls, and ribs, evolved from enslaved people using skill and creativity to produce sufficient nourishment to endure physically damaging circum- stances. Recent foodways studies probing the culture of food confirm that more than simply being peripheral to women's lives, it is a source of informa- tion about how they have contributed to cultural life. This is especially true for those with specific group affiliations, such as ethnicity, religion, nation- ality, and other relationships. Researcher Mary Douglas characterizes food practices not as static or innocuous, but "as a field of action."[9] For Black women, particularly as it relates to culture and the development of political consciousness, a further contention by Douglas is relevant. "Food choices," she writes, "support political alignments and social opportun- ities." It is on the cultural terrain that social groups make sense of their socioeconomic location and begin to understand their capacity to resist subordinate status.

The Black Family Dinner Quilt Cookbook (1993), a testimonial to Black women and food memories, presents two critical sites where essential cultural meanings are perpetuated: quilts and food. In fact, the title of the cookbook memorializes these sentiments, pointing to the revered custom of using a quilt as a table covering for ceremonial occasions. In the article (chapter 19 in this volume), "Empathy, Energy, and Eating: Politics and Power in *The Black Family Dinner Quilt Cookbook*," Sally Bishop Shigley notes that the connective tissue of quilts and food not only serves to hold the narrative together but also merges food rituals with history. Black women's public worlds and their domestic environments, through the communion of traditions of shared meal preparation, are united. As a consequence, what is perceived as ordinary and routine intersects with the symbolic in the realm of culture, underscoring its potency in community-building and group cohesion.

Agency, self-determination, recognition of systemic forces of oppression, and transformation of self and culture, are made real in Black women's cultural endeavors. These concepts are often referenced in theoretical tracts, but rendered tangible throughout the range of Black women's creative expressions, including material culture, popular representations, and other art forms. They are integral components of a cultural movement that has altered a people's awareness of their social circumstances and impelled collective actions for social change.

Black Feminist Cultural Criticism: Classic Readings

Two significant purposes are key in Black feminist criticism: to intervene strategically in privileged discourses that attempt to undervalue the merits of Black women's creative work; and to advance the causes of Black women and those of others at risk of oppression. Black feminist cultural criticism addresses concerns important to those who are usually never considered in any analysis of cultural works. Literary scholar Barbara Christian was one of the first to uncover and document a history of Black women writers that dated back to the nineteenth century. Christian categorized this body of work within the deserved stature of a tradition, thus emphasizing the expansive contours of a fertile lineage of creativity. Her initial efforts to construct a method of analyzing these writings led to a fruitful discovery about the responsibility of Black feminist critics. Christian asserts (chapter 3 in this volume) that the scholar must also be an activist seeking to substantively change Black women's lives for the better. For her the distanced stance of an objective observer is a false one, because the analyst is also a participant "in an ongoing dialogue between the writer and those who [are] reading the writer, most of whom are not academics and for whom that writing was life-sustaining, life-saving."[10]

Black Feminist Cultural Criticism is divided into five parts: "Foundations," "The Moving Image," "Art," "Music and Spoken Word," and "Material Culture." Each section contains an explanatory overview, a listing of supplementary readings, and a compilation of media resources useful as visual and audio examples to amplify the contents of the volume's chapters. The supplementary material is part of an extensive body of work on Black women's cultural history that extends back several decades. Among those that expand an understanding of the articles and supplementary readings in this volume are several landmark pieces. The most comprehensive and ambitious is the Spring 1987 "Artists and Artisans" issue of *Sage: A Scholarly Journal on Black Women*, devoted entirely to the diverse and extensive range of Black female artists. Other works include the following: Darlene Clark Hine's "To Be Gifted, Female and Black" (1982) and "The Kitchen Crisis" (1970) by Verta Mae Smart-Grosvenor. Two introductions to larger volumes are also worthy of note. Margaret B. Wilkerson wrote the ground-breaking historical overview in her collection of original plays authored by Black women, in the volume *Nine Plays by Black Women* (1986). And Beverly Guy-Sheftall offers the germinal essay "Introduction: The Evolution of Feminist Consciousness among African-American Women," laying out the background to her edited book *Words of Fire: An Anthology of African-American Feminist Thought* (1995).[11]

The majority of the films and videos referred to in the media resources listing were created by Black female artists. These add to the display of Black women's cultural productions and bring the examples referred to in the book's chapters to life. More comprehensive information on the works can be found in my edited book, *Black Women Film and Video Artists* (1998).

The first part of *Black Feminist Cultural Criticism*, "Foundations," provides three chapters laying out the early contemporary explorations into the constitution of Black feminist criticism. Activist writer Barbara Smith begins the first articulations named as such in "Toward a Black Feminist Criticism." Deborah E. McDowell, a literary scholar, critiques Smith's assertions and refines the paradigms in "New Directions for Black Feminist Criticism." Barbara Christian, in "But What Do We Think We Are Doing Anyway," gives a history of the development of Black feminist thought and offers a comprehensive assessment of the primary goals of Black feminist undertakings.

Film, theater, and television criticism are taken up in the second part of *Black Feminist Cultural Criticism*. Legendary actress Ruby Dee in "The

Tattered Queens" recalls the momentous contributions of early Black actresses who have since been forgotten. C.A. Griffith, an experienced cinematographer and director, writes of her experiences behind the camera in "Below the Line: (Re)Calibrating the Filmic Gaze." In the chapter from my book *Black Women as Cultural Readers* (1995), on Julie Dash's film *Daughters of the Dust*, I explicate the achievements of the film toward recasting Black women's history and experiences. Drama scholar Sheri Parks, in "In My Mother's House," submits that a reconsideration of the feminist aspects of Lorraine Hansberry's television adaptation of her stage play *A Raisin in the Sun* is overdue.

Four chapters focusing on art make up the third part of the book. In the first, "African-American Women Artists," art historians Arna Alexander Bontemps and Jacqueline Fonvielle-Bontemps present a historical perspective on the earliest Black female sculptors and painters, starting with those in the first part of the nineteenth century. Freida High W. Tesfagiorgis, artist and scholar, decries the marginality of Black female painters, sculptors, photographers, and performance artists, in "In Search of a Discourse and Critique/s that Center the Art of Black Women Artists." Tesfagiorgis examines the spectrum of artists, including those in the United States, Britain, and other parts of the African diaspora, who have been overlooked in mainstream art history and criticism. Innovations in photography and text art are discussed by Kellie Jones in "In Their Own Image." She looks at women who practice their craft in the United States and in Britain. Co-authors Melody Graulich and Mara Witzling selected feminist painter, sculptor, and author Faith Ringgold to interview, in part, because she consistently exercises, as the title of the chapter states, "The Freedom to Say what She Pleases."

The pivotal role of different kinds of aural expression is analyzed in the fourth part, "Music and Spoken Word." Activist scholar Angela Y. Davis formalizes music's catalytic impact in chapter 12, "Black Women and Music: A Historical Legacy of Struggle." Focusing particularly on the early blues singer Gertrude "Ma" Rainey, Davis examines how Black music has influenced other arts and shaped the development of Black people's collective social consciousness. Music historian Tricia Rose offers a sustained critical exploration of rap music in chapter 13, "Never Trust a big Butt and a Smile," asserting that Black female rappers have produced some of the most important contemporary feminist cultural criticism. Black women's dominance in an art form identified as the spoken word, an aural expression evocative of both past and present political eras, is discussed by Evelyn McDonnell in chapter 14, "Divas Declare a Spoken-Word Revolution." In the final chapter in Part IV, Carolyn Mitchell recalls the provocative effect of Ntozake Shange's choreopoem *for colored girls who have considered suicide/ when the rainbow is enuf* on diverse art forms, including theater, music, poetry, and dance. She probes the work from the perspective of its healing powers for Black women in chapter 15, "A Laying on of Hands."

Transcendence and Black females' capacity to achieve creative power and harmony in midst of oppressive circumstances informs the four chapters in the fifth part, "Material Culture." Black lesbian, activist, poet Audre Lorde's remarkable treatise "The Uses of the Erotic: The Erotic as Power" opens Part V. It is a clarion call setting forth the tenets of female empowerment that reclaims the lifeforce of creative energy within women's lives that exists on both the spiritual and political plane. Quilt historian Cuesta Benberry illustrates these sentiments in her reclamation of Black women's quilt traditions in chapter 17, "African American Quilts: Paradigms of Black Diversity." Chapter 18 examines the work of Harriet Powers, originally enslaved, later manumitted, whose Bible quilts, currently housed at the Smithsonian Institution and at the Museum of Fine Arts, were evidence that enslaved women were involved in the art of quiltmaking. Gladys-Marie Fry, quilt scholar, submits in her landmark essay, "Harriet Powers: Portrait of an African-American Quilter," that the story of Harriet Powers is a classic tale of a skilled artisan creating masterpieces of artistic expression within the harsh environment of enslavement. Black women and the transformative capacity of food rituals are taken up in chapter 19, Sally Bishop Shigley's "Empathy, Energy, and Eating: Politics and Power in *The Black Family Dinner Quilt Cookbook*."

Black Feminist Cultural Criticism takes into account the evolution of Black women's expressive culture from the struggles, sacrifices, and triumphs of those who endured a torturous existence encompassing several hundred years. This is a point too momentous to be forgotten. In fact, as Angela Davis so eloquently states: "we approach the close of the only century that people of African descent have spent on this soil which has not seen slavery."[12]

An added consideration is that legalized segregation for much of the twentieth century banned Black women from involvement in traditional art fields and excluded their work from historical and critical analyses. *Black Feminist Cultural Criticism* is thus an honorific to those Black women who pursued their creative impulses in the face of imposed constraints to produce objects of lasting value.

Alice Walker speaks of the psychic toll on those for whom there is no recognized outlet for their talents. They are, writes Walker, "driven to a numb and bleeding madness by the springs of creativity in them for which there is no release."[13] The wellsprings of Black women's creativity were kept alive in making art a part of their daily lives: in their gardens, quilts, sculptures, pottery, sewing, and other forms of creativity. Rather than minimizing these efforts, celebration is in order.

Notes

I want to express my appreciation to my research assistant Cristina Turner for her help with *Black Feminist Cultural Criticism*. Bouquets to my friends and colleagues Claudine Michel and Karen Karatsu Gundersen.

1 Cuesta Benberry, *Always There: The African-American Presence in American Quilts* (Louisville, KY: The Kentucky Quilt Project, Inc., 1992): 15.

2 Benberry, *Always There*: 25–6. The designs listed are "Jacob's Ladder," "Underground Railroad," "Phrygian Cap (or 'Liberty Cap')," and the "North Star."

3 Gladys-Marie Fry, *Stitched from the Soul: Slave Quilts from the Ante-Bellum South* (New York: Dutton Books in Association with the Museum of American Folk Art, 1990): 45–6.

4 Jacqueline L. Tobin and Raymond G. Dobard, *Hidden in Plain View: The Secret Story of Quilts and the Underground Railroad* (New York: Doubleday, 1999).

5 Fry, *Stitched from the Soul*: 1.

6 Fry, *Stitched from the Soul*: 83.

7 Anne L. Bower, ed. *Recipes for Reading: Community Cookbooks, Stories, Histories* (Amherst, MA: University of Massachusetts Press, 1997).

8 Angela Y. Davis, "Black Women and Music: A Historical Legacy of Struggle," in Joanne M. Braxton and Andree Nicola McLaughlin, eds. *Wild Women in the Whirlwind: Afra-American Culture and the Contemporary Literary Renaissance* (New Brunswick, NJ: Rutgers University Press, 1990): 3.

9 Mary Douglas, *Food in the Social Order: Studies of Food and Festivities in Three American Communities* (New York: Russell Sage Foundation, 1984): 30. Cited in Bower, *Recipes for Reading*: 10.

10 Barbara Christian, "But What Do We Think We're Doing Anyway: The State of Black Feminist Criticism(s) or My Version of a Little Bit of History," in Cheryl A. Wall, ed. *Changing Our Own Words: Essays of Criticism, Theory, and Writing by Black Women* (New Brunswick, NJ: Rutgers University Press, 1989): 68.

11 Darlene Clark Hine, "To Be Gifted, Female, and Black," *Southwest Review* 67:4 (Autumn 1982): 357–69; Verta Mae Smart-Grosvenor, "The Kitchen Crisis," in Toni Cade (Bambara), ed. *The Black Woman: An Anthology* (New York: New American Library, 1970): 119–23; Margaret B. Wilkerson, "Introduction," in *Nine Plays by Black Women* (New York: New American Library, 1986): xiii–xxv; Beverly Guy-Sheftall, "Introduction: The Evolution of Feminist Consciousness among African-American Women," in *Words of Fire: An Anthology of African-American Feminist Thought* (New York: The New Press, 1995): 1–22.

12 Angela Davis, "Black Women and the Academy," *Callaloo: A Journal of Afro-American and African Arts and Letters* 17:2 (Summer 1994): 426.

13 Alice Walker, *In Search of Our Mothers' Gardens* (San Diego, CA: Harcourt, Brace, Jovanovich, 1983): 233.

Acknowledgments

The editor and publishers wish to thank the following for permission to reprint copyright material:

Artforum for Kellie Jones, "In Their Own Image" from *Artforum* 29, copyright © *Artforum*, November 1990;

Associated University Presses for Sheri Parks, "In My Mother's House: Black Feminist Aesthetics, Television, and *A Raisin in the Sun*" from Karen Laughlin and Catherine Schuler (eds.), *Theatre and Feminist Aesthetics* (Cranburg, NJ: Associated University Presses, 1995). Reproduced by permission of the publisher;

Columbia University Press for "Daughters of the Dust" from Jacqueline Bobo, *Black Women as Cultural Readers*, copyright © 1995 Columbia University Press. Reprinted by permission of the publisher;

The Crossing Press, Inc for extracts from Audre Lorde, *Sister Outsider*, copyright 1984. Published by the Crossing Press, Freedom, CA;

Ruby Dee for Ruby Dee, "Some Reflections on the Negro Actress: The Tattered Queens" from *Negro Digest* 15 (April 1966);

Georgia Humanities Council for Gladys-Marie Fry, "Harriet Powers: Portrait of an African American Quilter" from *Missing Pieces: Georgia Folk Art 1770–1976* (Georgia Council for the Humanities, 1975). Reproduced by permission of the publisher;

Taylor & Francis, Inc./Routledge, Inc., for extracts from C. A. Griffith "Below the Line: (Re)Calibrating the Filmic Gaze," copyright © 1998 from Jacqueline Bobo (ed.), *Black Women Film and Video Artists*. Reproduced by permission of Taylor & Francis, Inc./Routledge, Inc., http://www.routledge-ny.com;

Taylor & Francis, Inc./Routledge, Inc., for Frieda High W. Tesfagiorgis, "In Search of a Discourse and Critique/s that Center the Art of Black Women Artists," copyright © 1993 from Stanlie M. James and Abena P. A. Busia (eds.), *Theorizing Black Feminisms: The Visionary Pragmatism of Black Women*. Reproduced by permission of Taylor & Francis, Inc./Routledge, Inc., http://www.routledge-ny.com;

University of Massachusetts Press for "Empathy, Energy and Eating" from Sally Bishop Shigley, *Recipes for Reading: Community Cookbooks, Stories, Histories*, copyright © 1997 by the University of Massachusetts Press;

University of Tennessee Press for Carolyn Mitchell, "'A Laying on of Hands': Transcending the City in Ntozake Shange's *for colored girls who have considered suicide/when the rainbow is enuf*" from Susan Merrill Squier (ed.), *Women Writers and the City: Essays in Feminist Literary Criticism*, copyright © 1984 by The University of Tennessee Press.

Part I

Foundations

Overview: Foundations

The three opening chapters build upon earlier works which sought to redress the glaring omission of Black women writers from mainstream scholarly and critical analyses. The authors point to the social and political activism of previous eras, including those poets and essayists agitating for women's rights during the first centuries of Black women's forced migration to the US. These efforts toward attaining "public voice" continued in the mid-twentieth century with the appearance of pivotal works showcasing Black women's social, political and cultural achievements. The publication of *The Black Woman* (1970), a collection of essays, poems, and stories edited by Toni Cade [Bambara], was generative in its impact. Both Alice Walker's *The Third Life of Grange Copeland* and Toni Morrison's *The Bluest Eye*, first novels for the writers, were published in 1970. Maya Angelou's memoir, *I Know Why the Caged Bird Sings*, adapted for television in 1974, was a 1970 bestseller and Book-of-the-Month Club selection.

Barbara Christian's study *Black Women Novelists: The Development of a Tradition, 1892–1976* (1980) substantiated the existence of a productive Black female literary tradition. Framed within this paradigm, the authors were thus rescued from the condescension of seeming to be anomalies or accidents of a particular time. That Morrison, Walker, and Paule Marshall each had at least two novels in print by the time she undertook the writing of *Black Women Novelists* legitimated Christian's assertions concerning the fecundity of Black women's literature.

The presence of Black women as powerful social and creative agents surfaced in other works of this period. Literary scholar Mary Helen Washington edited two anthologies of Black women's writings. Her introductions to these two volumes, *Black-eyed Susans: Classic Stories by and about Black Women* (1975) and *Midnight Birds: Stories by Contemporary Black Women Writers* (1980), were a revelation.

Barbara Smith, in "Toward a Black Feminist Criticism," began to formulate criteria for activist criticism, declaring that critics needed to address
the politics of sex as well as the politics of race and class as interlocking
factors affecting Black women's lives. Smith condemned the continuing
neglect of Black lesbian writers and called for critical attention to the
specifics of Black women's language and culture evident throughout a
long writing tradition. Barbara Smith applied her premises through a
reading of Morrison's *Sula* (1973) as a lesbian novel. Smith later co-edited,
with Gloria T. Hull and Patricia Bell Scott, the groundbreaking volume *All
the Women Are White, All the Blacks Are Men, But Some of Us Are Brave*
(1982). *But Some of Us Are Brave* became an indispensable sourcebook for
those studying, teaching, and writing about Black women's experiences.

Deborah E. McDowell in "New Directions for Black Feminist Criticism"
contested Smith's reading of *Sula* as a lesbian novel, noting that it was an
erroneous and incomplete assessment. Going further, McDowell sought
to refine many of Smith's ideas about the composition of feminist criticism. She submits that rigorous analysis of the text itself is imperative, but
that it must be contextualized historically and politically. Both McDowell
and Smith have contributed greatly to readers' understanding of Black
feminism and literary criticism.

Later works of significance that analyze Black feminist cultural texts are:
Black Women Writers at Work (1983), edited by Claudia Tate; *Black
Women Writers (1950–1980): A Critical Evaluation* (1984), edited by
Marie Evans; *Black Feminist Criticism: Perspectives on Black Women Wri-
ters* (1985), by Barbara Christian; *Invented Lives: Narratives of Black
Women 1860–1960* (1987), edited by Mary Helen Washington; *Recon-
structing Womanhood: The Emergence of the Afro-American Woman
Novelist* (1987), by Hazel Carby; *Changing Our Own Words: Essays on
Criticism, Theory, and Writing by Black Women* (1989), edited by Cheryl
A. Wall; and, *Wild Women in the Whirlwind: Afra-American Culture and
the Contemporary Literary Renaissance* (1990), edited by Joanne M. Braxton and Andrée Nicola McLaughlin.

In conjunction with the articles and supplementary readings, the
recommended media resources in this volume are a useful complement.
The essays in this first part analyze Black female writers for their
significance in furthering the feminist project. The novels and other
writings of Toni Morrison and Alice Walker were catalytic in the development of the underlying ideas of these initial contemporary formulations
about Black feminism. Media productions engender a closer connection
to the concepts by presenting the fiction writers themselves speaking
about what it means to be Black, female, creative, and socially
conscious.

Christian writes in "But What Do We Think We're Doing Anyway" that, had it not been for the wide publicity surrounding the publication of Morrison's *Song of Solomon* (1977), academic presses would not have been as receptive about publishing her critical study, *Black Women Novelists*. Morrison was awarded the prestigious National Book Critics' Circle Award for her third novel, *Song of Solomon*. She would later receive the Pulitzer Prize in 1988 for *Beloved* (1987) and the Nobel Prize for Literature in 1993. Even earlier, after the publication of *Tar Baby* (1981), widespread interest in Black female authors increased when Morrison was featured on the cover of *Newsweek*, the first cover story devoted to a Black woman writer in a major news magazine since that on Zora Neale Hurston in 1943.

The video *Identifiable Qualities: Toni Morrison* (1989) presents an interview with the author. Morrison is dynamic, forthright, and incisive in her comments about the influences in her background prompting the vision and provocative imagery of her novels. In her writings, Morrison states, she is interested in developing a style that is "irrevocably Black" with the identifiable qualities that Black music has. Morrison locates these aspects particularly in folklore, which has a participatory, aural quality that stresses the intimate relationship of Black people to an "enchanted world." Morrison's insights on writing, the potency of language, and the vital linkages of writers to their readers, are eloquently conveyed in her Nobel Prize Lecture of 1993, heard on the audiotape *The Nobel Lecture in Literature*.

A defining moment for Black feminist cultural analysis occurred with the publication of Alice Walker's essay "In Search of our Mothers' Gardens" in 1974. Walker situates Black female creative involvement within a tradition that includes music, quiltmaking, food rituals, and gardening. In the essay Walker calls attention to these Black women as artists who cultivated their craft without public recognition. This work of reclamation and redefinition is paramount in Walker's novels, poems, and essays. For her novel *The Color Purple* (1982), Alice Walker became the first Black woman to receive the Pulitzer Prize for Fiction. (Gwendolyn Brooks, with her volume of poetry *Annie Allen* [1949] was the first Black author awarded the Pulitzer Prize.) Walker was also accorded the American Book Award for *The Color Purple*.

The video *Alice Walker and "The Color Purple": Inside a Modern Classic* (1986) contains interviews and readings by the author. Segments include comments from Walker's family and friends, and a visit to her childhood home in Eatonton, Georgia. The final part of the video examines the impact of the film *The Color Purple* (1985), with extended interviews with Walker, director Steven Spielberg, and actor Whoopie Goldberg, who plays the part of Celie in the film. Scenes from *The Color Purple* are intercut with explanatory statements from Spielberg about the process of casting and production. Spielberg and Goldberg present their views concerning the visual treatment of the sexual relationship between the lead characters Celie and Shug. Walker concludes the discussion about the alterations from her novel in the film version with the statement, "this is why we have imaginations."

1

Toward a Black Feminist Criticism

Barbara Smith

Smith, Barbara. "Toward a Black Feminist Criticism." In Barbara Smith, *The Truth That Never Hurts* (New Brunswick, NJ: Rutgers University Press, 1998), pp. 3–21.

For all my sisters, especially Beverly and Demita

I do not know where to begin. Long before I tried to write this I realized that I was attempting something unprecedented, something dangerous, merely by writing about Black women writers from a feminist perspective and about Black lesbian writers from any perspective at all. These things have not been done. Not by white male critics, expectedly. Not by Black male critics. Not by white women critics who think of themselves as feminists. And most crucially not by Black women critics, who, although they pay the most attention to Black women writers as a group, seldom use a consistent feminist analysis or write about Black lesbian literature. All segments of the literary world – whether establishment, progressive, Black, female, or lesbian – do not know, or at least act as if they do not know, that Black women writers and Black lesbian writers exist.

For whites, this specialized lack of knowledge is inextricably connected to their not knowing in any concrete or politically transforming way that Black women of any description dwell in this place. Black women's existence, experience, and culture and the brutally complex systems of oppression which shape these are in the "real world" of white and/or male consciousness beneath consideration, invisible, unknown.

This invisibility, which goes beyond anything that either Black men or white women experience and tell about in their writing, is one reason it is so difficult for me to know where to start. It seems overwhelming to break such a massive silence. Even more numbing, however, is the realization that so many of the women who will read this have not yet noticed us missing either from their reading matter, their politics, or their lives. It is galling that ostensible feminists and acknowledged lesbians have been so blinded to the implications of any womanhood that is not white womanhood and that they have yet to struggle with the deep racism in themselves that is at the source of their ignorance.

I think of the thousands and thousands of books, magazines, and articles which have been devoted, by this time, to the subject of women's writing and I am filled with rage at the fraction of those pages that mention Black and other Third World women. I finally do not know how to begin because in 1977 I want to be writing this for a Black feminist publication, for Black women who know and love these writers as I do and who, if they do not yet know their names, have at least profoundly felt the pain of their absence.

The conditions that coalesce into the impossibilities of this essay have as much to do with politics as with the practice of literature. Any discussion of Afro-American writers can rightfully begin with the fact that for most of the time we have been in this country we have been categorically denied not only literacy but the most minimal possibility of a decent human life. In her landmark essay, "In Search of our Mothers' Gardens," Alice Walker discloses how the political, economic, and social restrictions of slavery and racism have historically stunted the creative lives of Black women.[1]

At the present time I feel that the politics of feminism have a direct relationship to the state of Black women's literature. A viable, autonomous Black feminist movement in this country would open up the space needed for the exploration of Black women's lives and the creation of consciously Black woman-identified art. At the same time a redefinition of the goals and strategies of the white feminist movement would lead to much-needed change in the focus and content of what is now generally accepted as women's culture.

I want to make in this essay some connections between the politics of Black women's lives, what we write about, and our situation as artists. In order to do this I will look at how Black women have been viewed critically by outsiders, demonstrate the necessity for Black feminist criticism, and try to understand what the existence or nonexistence of Black lesbian writing reveals about the state of Black women's culture and the intensity of *all* Black women's oppression.

The role that criticism plays in making a body of literature recognizable and real hardly needs to be explained here. The necessity for nonhostile and perceptive analysis of works written by persons outside the "mainstream" of white/male cultural rule has been proven by the Black cultural resurgence of the 1960s and 1970s and by the even more recent growth of feminist literary scholarship. For books to be real and remembered they have to be talked about. For books to be understood they must be examined in such a way that the basic intentions of the writers are at least considered. Because of racism Black literature has usually been viewed as a discrete subcategory of American literature, and there have been Black critics of Black literature who did much to keep it alive long before it caught the attention of whites. Before the advent of specifically feminist criticism in this decade, books by white women, on the other hand, were not clearly perceived as the cultural mani- festation of an oppressed people. It took the surfacing of the second wave of the North American feminist movement to expose the fact that these works contain a stunningly accurate record of the impact of patriarchal values and practice upon the lives of women, and more significantly, that literature by women provides essential insights into female experience.

In speaking about the current situation of Black women writers, it is important to remember that the existence of a feminist movement was an essential precondition to the growth of feminist literature, criticism, and women's studies, which focused at the beginning almost entirely upon investigations of literature. The fact that a parallel Black feminist movement has been much slower in evolving cannot help but have impact upon the situation of Black women writers and artists and explains in part why during this very same period we have been so ignored.

There is no political movement to give power or support to those who want to examine Black women's experience through studying our history, literature, and culture. There is no political presence that demands a minimal level of consciousness and respect from those who write or talk about our lives. Finally, there is not a developed body of Black feminist political theory whose assumptions could be used in the study of Black women's art. When Black women's books are dealt with at all, it is usually in the context of Black literature, which largely ignores the implications of sexual politics. When white women look at Black women's works they are of course ill-equipped to deal with the subtleties of racial politics. A Black feminist approach to literature that embodies the realization that the politics of sex as well as the politics of race and class are crucially interlocking factors in the works of Black women writers is an absolute necessity. Until a Black feminist criticism exists we will not even know what these writers mean. The citations from a variety of critics which follow prove that without a Black feminist critical perspective not only are books by Black women misunderstood, they are destroyed in the process.

Jerry H. Bryant, *The Nation's* white male reviewer of Alice Walker's *In Love and Trouble: Stories of Black Women*, wrote in 1973:

> The subtitle of the collection, "Stories of Black Women," is probably an attempt by the publisher to exploit not only black subjects but feminine ones. There is nothing feminist about these stories, however.[2]

Blackness and feminism are to his mind mutually exclusive and peripheral to the act of writing fiction. Bryant of course does not consider that Walker might have titled the work herself, nor did he apparently read the book, which unequivocally reveals the author's feminist consciousness.

In *The Negro Novel in America*, a book that Black critics recognize as one of the worst examples of white racist pseudoscholarship, Robert Bone cavalierly dismisses Ann Petry's classic, *The Street*. He perceives it to be "a superficial social analysis" of how slums victimize their Black inhabitants. He further objects:

> It is an attempt to interpret slum life in terms of *Negro* experience, when a larger frame of reference is required. As Alain Locke has observed, "*Knock on Any Door* is superior to *The Street* because it designates class and environment, rather than mere race and environment, as its antagonist."[3]

Neither Robert Bone nor Alain Locke, the Black male critic he cites, can recognize that *The Street* is one of the best delineations in literature of how sex, race, *and* class interact to oppress Black women.

In her review of Toni Morrison's *Sula* for the *New York Times Book Review* in 1973, putative feminist Sara Blackburn makes similarly racist comments:

> Toni Morrison is far too talented to remain only a marvelous recorder of the black side of provincial American life. If she is to maintain the large and serious audience she deserves, she is going to have to address a riskier contemporary reality than this beautiful but nevertheless distanced novel. *And if she does this, it seems to me that she might easily transcend that early and unintentionally limiting classification "black woman writer" and take her place among the most serious, important and talented American novelists now working.*[4] [Italics mine]

Recognizing Morrison's exquisite gift, Blackburn unashamedly asserts that Morrison is "too talented" to deal with mere Black folk, particularly those double nonentities, Black women. In order to be accepted as "serious," "important," "talented," and "American," she must obviously focus her efforts upon chronicling the doings of white men.

The mishandling of Black women writers by whites is paralleled more often by their not being handled at all, particularly in feminist criticism. Although Elaine Showalter in her review essay on literary criticism for *Signs* states that "the best work being produced today [in feminist criticism] is exacting and cosmopolitan," her essay is neither. If it were, she would not have failed to mention a single Black or Third World woman writer, whether "major" or "minor," to cite her questionable categories. That she also does not even hint that lesbian writers of any color exist renders her purported overview virtually meaningless. Showalter obviously thinks that the identities of being Black and female are mutually exclusive, as this statement illustrates:

> Furthermore, there are other literary subcultures (black American novelists, for example) whose history offers a precedent for feminist scholarship to use.[5]

The idea of critics like Showalter *using* Black literature is chilling, a case of barely disguised cultural imperialism. The final insult is that she footnotes the preceding remark by pointing readers to works on Black literature by white males Robert Bone and Roger Rosenblatt!

Two recent works by white women, Ellen Moers's *Literary Women: The Great Writers* and Patricia Meyer Spacks's *The Female Imagination*, evidence the same racist flaw.[6] Moers includes the names of four Black and one Puertorriqueña writer in her 70 pages of bibliographical notes and does not deal at all with Third World women in the body of her book. Spacks refers to a comparison between Negroes (*sic*) and women in Mary Ellmann's *Thinking about Women* under the index entry "blacks, women and." "*Black Boy* (Wright)" is the preceding entry. Nothing follows. Again there is absolutely no recognition that Black and female identity ever coexist, specifically in a group of Black women writers. Perhaps one can assume that these women do not know who Black women writers are, that like most Americans they have little opportunity to learn about them. Perhaps. Their ignorance seems suspiciously selective, however, particularly in the light of the dozens of truly obscure white women writers they are able to unearth. Spacks was herself employed at Wellesley College at the same time that Alice Walker was there teaching one of the first courses on Black women writers in the country.

I am not trying to encourage racist criticism of Black women writers like that of Sara Blackburn, to cite only one example. As a beginning I would at least like to see in print white women's acknowledgment of the contradictions of who and what are being left out of their research and writing.[7]

Black male critics can also *act* as if they do not know that Black women writers exist and are, of course, hampered by an inability to comprehend Black women's experience in sexual as well as racial terms. Unfortunately there are also those who are as virulently sexist in their treatment of Black women writers as their white male counterparts. Darwin Turner's discussion of Zora Neale Hurston in his *In a Minor Chord: Three Afro-American Writers and their Search for Identity* is a frightening example of the near assassination of a great Black woman writer.[8] His descriptions of her and her work as "artful," "coy," "irrational," "superficial," and "shallow" bear no relationship to the actual quality of her achievements. Turner is completely insensitive to the sexual political dynamics of Hurston's life and writing.

In a recent interview the notoriously misogynist writer Ishmael Reed comments in this way upon the low sales of his newest novel:

> But the book only sold 8,000 copies. I don't mind giving out the figure: 8,000. Maybe if I was one of those young *female* Afro-American writers that are so hot now, I'd sell more. You know, fill my books with ghetto women who can *do no wrong*. . . . But come on, I think I could have sold 8,000 copies by myself.[9]

The politics of the situation of Black women are glaringly illuminated by this statement. Neither Reed nor his white male interviewer has the slightest compunction about attacking Black women in print. They need not fear widespread public denunciation since Reed's statement is in perfect agreement with the values of a society that hates Black people, women, and Black women. Finally the two of them feel free to base their actions on the premise that Black women are powerless to alter either their political or their cultural oppression.

In her introduction to "A Bibliography of Works Written by American Black Women" Ora Williams quotes some of the reactions of her colleagues toward her efforts to do research on Black women:

> Others have reacted negatively with such statements as, "I really don't think you are going to find very much written," "Have 'they' written anything that is any good?" and, "I wouldn't go overboard with this woman's lib thing." When discussions touched on the possibility of teaching a course in which emphasis would be on the literature by Black women, one response was, "Ha, ha. That will certainly be the most nothing course ever offered!"[10]

A remark by Alice Walker capsulizes what all the preceding examples indicate about the position of Black women writers and the reasons for the damaging criticism about them. She responds to her interviewer's question, "Why do you think that the black woman writer has been so ignored in America? Does she have even more difficulty than the black male writer, who perhaps has just begun to gain recognition?" Walker replies:

> There are two reasons why the black women writer is not taken as seriously as the black male writer. One is that she's a woman. Critics seem unusually ill-equipped to intelligently discuss and analyze the works of black women. Generally, they do not even make the attempt; they prefer, rather, to talk about the lives of black women writers, not about what they write. And, since black women writers are not – it would seem – very likable – until recently they were the least willing worshippers of male supremacy – comments about them tend to be cruel.[11]

A convincing case for Black feminist criticism can obviously be built solely upon the basis of the negativity of what already exists. It is far more gratifying, however, to demonstrate its necessity by showing how it can serve to reveal for the first time the profound subtleties of this particular body of literature.

Before suggesting how a Black feminist approach might be used to examine a specific work, I will outline some of the principles that I think a Black feminist critic could use. Beginning with a primary commitment to exploring how both sexual and racial politics and Black and female identity are inextricable elements in Black women's writings, she would also work from the assumption that Black women writers constitute an identifiable literary tradition. The breadth of her familiarity with these writers would have shown her that not only is theirs a verifiable historical tradition that parallels in time the tradition of Black men and white women writing in this country, but that thematically, stylistically, aesthetically, and conceptually Black women writers manifest common approaches to the act of creating literature as a direct result of the specific political, social, and economic experience they have been obliged to share. The way, for example, that Zora Neale Hurston, Margaret Walker, Toni Morrison, and Alice Walker incorporate the traditional Black female activities of rootworking, herbal medicine, conjure, and midwifery into the fabric of their stories is not mere coincidence, nor is their use of specifically Black female language to express their own and their characters' thoughts accidental. The use of Black women's language and cultural experience in books *by* Black women *about* Black women results in a miraculously rich coalescing of form and content and also takes their writing far beyond the confines of white/male literary structures. The Black feminist critic would find innumerable commonalities in works by Black women.

Another principle which grows out of the concept of a tradition and which would also help to strengthen this tradition would be for the critic to look first for precedents and insights in interpretation within the works of other Black women. In other words she would think and write out of her own identity and not try to graft the ideas or methodology of white/male literary thought upon the precious materials of Black women's art. Black feminist criticism would by definition be highly innovative, embodying the daring spirit of the works themselves. The Black feminist critic would be constantly aware of the political implications of her work and would assert the connections between it and the political situation of all Black women. Logically developed, Black feminist criticism would owe its existence to a Black feminist movement while at the same time contributing ideas that women in the movement could use.

Black feminist criticism applied to a particular work can overturn previous assumptions about it and expose for the first time its actual dimensions. At the "Lesbians and Literature" discussion at the 1976 Modern Language

Association convention Bertha Harris suggested that if in a woman writer's work a sentence refuses to do what it is supposed to do, if there are strong images of women and if there is a refusal to be linear, the result is innately lesbian literature. As usual, I wanted to see if these ideas might be applied to the Black women writers that I know and quickly realized that many of their works were, in Harris's sense, lesbian. Not because women are "lovers," but because they are the central figures, are positively portrayed and have pivotal relationships with one another. The form and language of these works are also nothing like what white patriarchal culture requires or expects.

I was particularly struck by the way in which Toni Morrison's novels *The Bluest Eye* and *Sula* could be explored from this new perspective.[12] In both works the relationships between girls and women are essential, yet at the same time physical sexuality is overtly expressed only between men and women. Despite the apparent heterosexuality of the female characters, I discovered in rereading *Sula* that it works as a lesbian novel not only because of the passionate friendship between Sula and Nel but because of Morrison's consistently critical stance toward the heterosexual institutions of male–female relationships, marriage, and the family. Consciously or not, Morrison's work poses both lesbian and feminist questions about Black women's autonomy and their impact upon each other's lives.

Sula and Nel find each other in 1922 when each of them is 12, on the brink of puberty and the discovery of boys. Even as awakening sexuality "clotted their dreams," each girl desires "a someone" obviously female with whom to share her feelings. Morrison writes:

> For it was in dreams that the two girls had met. Long before Edna Finch's Mellow House opened, even before they marched through the chocolate halls of Garfield Primary School . . . they had already made each other's acquaintance in the delirium of their noon dreams. They were solitary little girls whose loneliness was so profound it intoxicated them and sent them stumbling into Technicolored visions that always included a presence, a someone who, quite like the dreamer, shared the delight of the dream. When Nel, an only child, sat on the steps of her back porch surrounded by the high silence of her mother's incredibly orderly house, feeling the neatness pointing at her back, she studied the poplars and fell easily into a picture of herself lying on a flower bed, tangled in her own hair, waiting for some fiery prince. He approached but never quite arrived. But always, watching the dream along with her, were some smiling sympathetic eyes. Someone as interested as she herself in the flow of her imagined hair, the thickness of the mattress of flowers, the voile sleeves that closed below her elbows in gold-threaded cuffs.
>
> Similarly, Sula, also an only child, but wedged into a household of throbbing disorder constantly awry with things, people, voices and the slamming of doors, spent hours in the attic behind a roll of linoleum galloping through her own

mind on a gray-and-white horse tasting sugar and smelling roses in full view of someone who shared both the taste and the speed.

So when they met, first in those chocolate halls and next through the ropes of the swing, they felt the ease and comfort of old friends. Because each had discovered years before that they were neither white nor male, and that all freedom and triumph was forbidden to them, they had set about creating something else to be. Their meeting was fortunate, for it let them use each other to grow on. Daughters of distant mothers and incomprehensible fathers (Sula's because he was dead; Nel's because he wasn't), they found in each other's eyes the intimacy they were looking for. (pp. 51–2)

As this beautiful passage shows, their relationship, from the very beginning, is suffused with an erotic romanticism. The dreams in which they are initially drawn to each other are actually complementary aspects of the same sensuous fairy tale. Nel imagines a "fiery prince" who never quite arrives while Sula gallops like a prince "on a gray-and-white horse."[13] The "real world" of patriarchy requires, however, that they channel this energy away from each other to the opposite sex. Lorraine Bethel explains this dynamic in her essay "Conversations with Ourselves: Black Female Relationships in Toni Cade Bambara's *Gorilla, My Love* and Toni Morrison's *Sula*":

I am not suggesting that Sula and Nel are being consciously sexual, or that their relationship has an overt lesbian nature. I am suggesting, however, that there is a certain sensuality in their interactions that is reinforced by the mirror-like nature of their relationship. Sexual exploration and coming of age is a natural part of adolescence. Sula and Nel discover men together, and though their flirtations with males are an important part of their sexual exploration, the sensuality that they experience in each other's company is equally important.[14]

Sula and Nel must also struggle with the constrictions of racism upon their lives. The knowledge that "they were neither white nor male" is the inherent explanation of their need for each other. Morrison depicts in literature the necessary bonding that has always taken place between Black women for the sake of barest survival. Together the two girls can find the courage to create themselves.

Their relationship is severed only when Nel marries Jude, an unexceptional young man who thinks of her as "the hem – the tuck and fold that hid his raveling edges" (p. 83). Sula's inventive wildness cannot overcome social pressure or the influence of Nel's parents who "had succeeded in rubbing down to a dull glow any sparkle or splutter she had" (p. 83). Nel falls prey to convention while Sula escapes it. Yet at the wedding which ends the first phase of their relationship, Nel's final action is to look past her husband toward Sula, a slim figure in blue, gliding, with just a hint of a strut, down the path towards the road . . . .Even from the rear Nel could tell that it was Sula and that she was smiling; that something deep down in that litheness was amused. (P. 85)

When Sula returns ten years later, her rebelliousness full-blown, a major source of the town's suspicions stems from the fact that although she is almost 30, she is still unmarried. Sula's grandmother, Eva, does not hesitate to bring up the matter as soon as she arrives. She asks:

"When you gone to get married? You need to have some babies. It'll settle you . . . . Ain't no woman got no business floatin' around without no man." (p. 92)

Sula replies: "I don't want to make somebody else. I want to make myself" (p. 92). Self-definition is a dangerous activity for any woman to engage in, especially a Black one, and it expectedly earns Sula pariah status in Medallion.

Morrison clearly points out that it is the fact that Sula has not been tamed or broken by the exigencies of heterosexual family life which most galls the others:

Among the weighty evidence piling up was the fact that Sula did not look her age. She was near 30 and, unlike them, had lost no teeth, suffered no bruises, developed no ring of fat at the waist or pocket at the back of her neck. (p. 115)

In other words she is not a domestic serf, a woman run down by obligatory childbearing or a victim of battering. Sula also sleeps with the husbands of the town once and then discards them, needing them even less than her own mother did for sexual gratification and affection. The town reacts to her disavowal of patriarchal values by becoming fanatically serious about their own family obligations, as if in this way they might counteract Sula's radical criticism of their lives.

Sula's presence in her community functions much like the presence of lesbians everywhere to expose the contradictions of supposedly "normal" life. The opening paragraph of the essay "The Woman-Identified Woman" has amazing relevance as an explanation of Sula's position and character in the novel. It asks:

What is a lesbian? A lesbian is the rage of all women condensed to the point of explosion. She is the woman who, often beginning at an extremely early age, acts in accordance with her inner compulsion to be a more complete and freer human being than her society – perhaps then, but certainly later – cares to allow her. These needs and actions, over a period of years, bring her into painful conflict with people, situations, the accepted ways of thinking, feeling and behaving, until she is in a state of continual war with everything around her, and usually with herself. She may not be fully conscious of the political implications of what for her began as personal necessity, but on some level she has not been able to accept the limitations and oppression laid on her by the most basic role of her society – the female role.[15]

The limitations of the *Black* female role are even greater in a racist and sexist society, as is the amount of courage it takes to challenge them. It is no wonder that the townspeople see Sula's independence as imminently dangerous.

Morrison is also careful to show the reader that despite their years of separation and their opposing paths, Nel and Sula's relationship retains its primacy for each of them. Nell feels transformed when Sula returns and thinks:

> It was like getting the use of an eye back, having a cataract removed. Her old friend had come home. Sula. Who made her laugh, who made her see old things with new eyes, in whose presence she felt clever, gentle and a little raunchy. (p. 95)

Laughing together in the familiar "rib-scraping" way, Nel feels "new, soft and new" (p. 98). Morrison uses here the visual imagery which symbolizes the women's closeness throughout the novel.

Sula fractures this closeness, however, by sleeping with Nel's husband, an act of little import according to her system of values. Nel, of course, cannot understand. Sula thinks ruefully:

> Nel was the one person who had wanted nothing from her, who had accepted all aspects of her. Now she wanted everything, and all because of *that*. Nel was the first person who had been real to her, whose name she knew, who had seen as she had the slant of life that made it possible to stretch it to its limits. Now Nel was one of *them*. (pp. 119–20)

Sula also thinks at the realization of losing Nel about how unsatisfactory her relationships with men have been and admits:

> She had been looking all along for a friend, and it took her a while to discover that a lover was not a comrade and could never be – for a woman. (p. 121)

The nearest that Sula comes to actually loving a man is in a brief affair with Ajax and what she values most about him is the intellectual companionship he provides, the brilliance he "allows" her to show.

Sula's feelings about sex with men are also consistent with a lesbian interpretation of the novel. Morrison writes:

> She went to bed with men as frequently as she could. It was the only place where she could find what she was looking for: *misery and the ability to feel deep sorrow*....During the lovemaking she found and needed to find the cutting edge. When she left off cooperating with her body and began to assert herself in the act, particles of strength gathered in her like steel shavings drawn to a spacious magnetic center, forming a tight cluster that nothing, it seemed, could break. *And there was utmost irony and outrage in lying under someone, in a position of surrender, feeling her own abiding strength and limitless power...* When her partner disengaged himself, she looked up at him in wonder trying to recall his name...waiting impatiently for him to turn away... *leaving her to the postcoital privateness in which she met herself, welcomed herself, and joined herself in matchless harmony.* (pp. 122–3; italics mine)

Sula uses men for sex which results, not in communion with them, but in her further delving into self.

Ultimately the deepest communion and communication in the novel occurs between two women who love each other. After their last painful meeting, which does not bring reconciliation, Sula thinks as Nel leaves her:

> "So she will walk on down that road, her back so straight in that old green coat...thinking how much I have cost her and never remember the days when we were two throats and one eye and we had no price." (p. 147)

It is difficult to imagine a more evocative metaphor for what women can be to each other, the "pricelessness" they achieve in refusing to sell themselves for male approval, the total worth that they can only find in each other's eyes.

Decades later the novel concludes with Nel's final comprehension of the source of the grief that has plagued her from the time her husband walked out:

> "All that time, all that time, I thought I was missing Jude." And the loss pressed down on her chest and came up into her throat. "We was girls together," she said as though explaining something. "O Lord, Sula," she cried, "girl, girl, girlgirlgirl."
>
> It was a fine cry – loud and long – but it had no bottom and it had no top, just circles and circles of sorrow. (p. 174)

Again Morrison exquisitely conveys what women, Black women, mean to each other. This final passage verifies the depth of Sula and Nel's relationship and its centrality to an accurate interpretation of the work.

Sula is an exceedingly lesbian novel in the emotions expressed, in the definition of female character, and in the way that the politics of heterosexuality are portrayed. The very meaning of lesbianism is being expanded in literature, just as it is being redefined through politics. The confusion that many readers have felt about *Sula* may well have a lesbian explanation. If one sees Sula's inexplicable "evil" and nonconformity as the evil of not being male-identified, many elements in the novel become clear. The work might be clearer still if Morrison had approached her subject with the consciousness that a lesbian relationship was at least a possibility for her characters. Obviously Morrison did not *intend* the reader to perceive Sula and Nel's relationship as inherently lesbian. However, this lack of intention only shows the way in which heterosexist assumptions can veil what may logically be expected to occur in a work. What I have tried to do here is not to prove that Morrison wrote something that she did not, but to point out how a Black feminist critical perspective at least allows consideration of this level of the novel's meaning.

In her interview in *Conditions: One* Adrienne Rich talks about unconsummated relationships and the need to reevaluate the meaning of intense yet supposedly nonerotic connections between women. She asserts:

> We need a lot more documentation about what actually happened: I think we can also imagine it, because we know it happened – we know it out of our own lives.[16]

Black women are still in the position of having to "imagine," discover, and verify Black lesbian literature because so little has been written from an avowedly lesbian perspective. The near nonexistence of Black lesbian literature which other Black lesbians and I so deeply feel has everything to do with the politics of our lives, the total suppression of identity that all Black women, lesbian or not, must face. This literary silence is again intensified by the unavailability of an autonomous Black feminist movement through which we could fight our oppression and also begin to name ourselves.

In a speech, "The Autonomy of Black Lesbian Women," Wilmette Brown comments upon the connection between our political reality and the literature we must invent:

> Because the isolation of Black lesbian women, given that we are superfreaks, given that our lesbianism defies both the sexual identity that capital gives us and the racial identity that capital gives us, the isolation of Black lesbian women from heterosexual Black women is very profound. Very profound. I have searched throughout Black history, Black literature, whatever, looking for some women that I could see were somehow lesbian. Now I know that in a certain sense they were all lesbian. But that was a very painful search.[17]

Heterosexual privilege is usually the only privilege that Black women have. None of us have racial or sexual privilege, almost none of us have class privilege; maintaining "straightness" is our last resort. Being out, particularly out in print, is the final renunciation of any claim to the crumbs of "tolerance" that nonthreatening "ladylike" Black women are sometimes fed. I am convinced that it is our lack of privilege and power in every other sphere that allows so few Black women to make the leap that many white women, particularly writers, have been able to make in this decade, not merely because they are white or have economic leverage, but because they have had the strength and support of a movement behind them.

As Black lesbians we must be out not only in white society but in the Black community as well, which is at least as homophobic. That the sanctions against Black lesbians are extremely high is well illustrated in this comment by Black male writer Ishmael Reed. Speaking about the inroads that whites make into Black culture, he asserts:

> In Manhattan you find people actively trying to impede intellectual debate among Afro-Americans. The powerful "liberal/radical/existentialist" influences of the Manhattan literary and drama establishment speak through tokens, like for example that ancient notion of the *one* black ideologue (who's usually a Communist), the *one* black poetess (who's usually a feminist lesbian).[18]

To Reed, "feminist" and "lesbian" are the most pejorative terms he can hurl at a Black woman and totally invalidate anything she might say, regardless of her actual politics or sexual identity. Such accusations are quite effective for keeping in line Black women writers who are writing with integrity and strength from any conceivable perspective, but especially ones who are actually feminist and lesbian. Unfortunately Reed's reactionary attitude is all too typical. A community which has not confronted sexism, because a widespread Black feminist movement has not required it to, has likewise not been challenged to examine its heterosexism. Even at this moment I am not convinced that one can write explicitly as a Black lesbian and live to tell about it.

Yet there are a handful of Black women who have risked everything for truth. Audre Lorde, Pat Parker, and Ann Allen Shockley have at least broken ground in the vast wilderness of works that do not exist.[19] Black feminist criticism will again have an essential role not only in creating a climate in which Black lesbian writers can survive, but in undertaking the total reassessment of Black literature and literary history needed to reveal the Black woman-identified women that Wilmette Brown and so many of us are looking for.

Although I have concentrated here upon what does not exist and what needs to be done, a few Black feminist critics have already begun this work.

Gloria T. Hull at the University of Delaware has discovered in her research on Black women poets of the Harlem Renaissance that many of the women who are considered "minor" writers of the period were in constant contract with each other and provided both intellectual stimulation and psychological support for each other's work. At least one of these writers, Angelina Weld Grimké, wrote many unpublished love poems to women. Lorraine Bethel, a recent graduate of Yale College, has done substantial work on Black women writers, particularly in her senior essay "This Infinity of Conscious Pain: Blues Lyricism and Hurston's Black Female Folk Aesthetic and Cultural Sensibility in *Their Eyes Were Watching God*," in which she brilliantly defines and uses the principles of Black feminist criticism. Elaine Scott at the State University of New York at Old Westbury is also involved in highly creative and politically resonant research on Hurston and other writers.

The fact that these critics are young and, except for Hull, unpublished merely indicates the impediments we face. Undoubtedly there are other women working and writing whom I do not even know, simply because there is no place to read them. As Michele Wallace states in her article "A Black Feminist's Search for Sisterhood":

> We exist as women who are Black who are feminists, each stranded for the moment, working independently because there is not yet an environment in this society remotely congenial to our struggle – [or our thoughts].[20]

I only hope that this essay is one way of breaking our silence and our isolation, of helping us to know each other.

Just as I did not know where to start I am not sure how to end. I feel that I have tried to say too much and at the same time have left too much unsaid. What I want this essay to do is lead everyone who reads it to examine *everything* that they have ever thought and believed about feminist culture and to ask themselves how their thoughts connect to the reality of Black women's writing and lives. I want to encourage in white women, as a first step, a sane accountability to all the women who write and live on this soil. I want most of all for Black women and Black lesbians somehow not to be so alone. This last will require the most expansive of revolutions as well as many new words to tell us how to make this revolution real. I finally want to express how much easier both my waking and my sleeping hours would be if there were one book in existence that would tell me something specific about my life. One book based in Black feminist and Black lesbian experience, fiction or nonfiction. Just one work to reflect the reality that I and the Black women whom I love are trying to create. When such a book exists then each of us will not only know better how to live, but how to dream.

Notes

1   Alice Walker, "In Search of our Mothers' Gardens," in *Ms.* (May 1974), and
    in *Southern Exposure* 4, no. 4, *Generations: Women in the South* (Winter 1977):
    60–4.
2   Jerry H. Bryant, "The Outskirts of a New City," *The Nation*, November 12,
    1973, p. 502.
3   Robert Bone, *The Negro Novel in America* (New Haven, CT: Yale University
    Press, 1958), p. 180. *Knock on Any Door* is a novel by Black writer Willard
    Motley.
4   Sara Blackburn, "You Still Can't Go Home Again," *New York Times Book
    Review*, December 30, 1973, p. 3.
5   Elaine Showalter, "Literary Criticism," Review Essay, *Signs* 1 (Winter 1975):
    460, 445.
6   Ellen Moers, *Literary Women: The Great Writers* (Garden City, NY: Anchor
    Books, 1977); Patricia Meyer Spacks, *The Female Imagination* (New York:
    Avon Books, 1976).
7   An article by Nancy Hoffman, "White Women, Black Women: Inventing an
    Adequate Pedagogy," *Women's Studies Newsletter* 5 (Spring 1977): 21–4, gives
    valuable insights into how white women can approach the writing of Black
    women.
8   Darwin T. Turner, *In a Minor Chord: Three Afro-American Writers and Their
    Search for Identity* (Carbondale and Edwardsville: Southern Illinois University
    Press, 1971).
9   John Domini, "Roots and Racism: An Interview with Ishmael Reed," *Boston
    Phoenix*, April 5, 1977, p. 20.
10 Ora Williams, "A Bibliography of Works Written by American Black Women,"
    College Language Association Journal 15 (March 1972): 355. There is an
    expanded book-length version of this bibliography: *American Black Women in
    the Arts and Social Sciences: A Bibliographic Survey* (Metuchen, NJ: Scarecrow
    Press, 1973; rev. and expanded ed., 1978).
11 John O'Brien, ed., *Interviews with Black Writers* (New York: Liveright, 1973),
    p. 201.
12 Toni Morrison, *The Bluest Eye* (1970; reprint ed., New York: Pocket Books,
    1972, 1976) and *Sula* (New York: Alfred A. Knopf, 1974). All subsequent
    references to this work will be designated in the text.
13 My sister, Beverly Smith, pointed out this connection to me.
14 Lorraine Bethel, "Conversations with Ourselves: Black Female Relationships in
    Toni Cade Bambara's *Gorilla, My Love* and Toni Morrison's *Sula*," unpublished
    paper written at Yale University, 1976, 47 pp. Bethel has worked from a premise
    similar to mine in a much more developed treatment of the novel.
15 New York Radicalesbians, "The Woman-identified Woman," in *Lesbians Speak
    Out* (Oakland, CA: Women's Press Collective, 1974), p. 87.

16 Elly Bulkin, "An Interview with Adrienne Rich: Part I," *Conditions: One* 1 (April 1977): 62.

17 Wilmette Brown, "The Autonomy of Black Lesbian Women," manuscript of speech delivered July 24, 1976, in Toronto, Canada, p. 7.

18 Domini, "Roots and Racism," p. 18.

19 Audre Lorde, *New York Head Shop and Museum* (Detroit: Broadside Press, 1974); *Coal* (New York: W. W. Norton, 1976); *Between Our Selves* (Point Reyes, CA: Eidolon Editions, 1976); *The Black Unicorn* (New York: W. W. Norton, 1978).

Pat Parker, *Child of Myself* (Oakland, CA: Women's Press Collective, 1972 and 1974); *Pit Stop* (Oakland, CA: Women's Press Collective, 1973); *Womanslaughter* (Oakland, CA: Diana Press, 1978); *Movement in Black* (Oakland, CA: Diana Press, 1978).

Ann Allen Shockley, *Loving Her* (Indianapolis: Bobbs-Merrill, 1974).

There is at least one Black lesbian writers' collective, Jemima, in New York. They do public readings and have available a collection of their poems.

20 Michele Wallace, "A Black Feminist's Search for Sisterhood," *Village Voice*, July 28, 1975, p. 7.

2

New Directions for Black Feminist Criticism

Deborah E. McDowell

McDowell, Deborah E. "New Directions for Black Feminist Criticism," *Black American Literature Forum*, 14(4) (Winter, 1980): 153–9.

What is commonly called literary history," writes Louise Bernikow, "is actually a record of choices. Which writers have survived their times and which have not depends upon who noticed them and chose to record their notice."[1] Women writers have fallen victim to arbitrary selection. Their writings have been "patronized, slighted, and misunderstood by a cultural establishment operating according to male norms out of male perceptions."[2] Both literary history's "sins of omission" and literary criticism's inaccurate and partisan judgments of women writers have come under attack since the early 1970s by feminist critics.[3] To date, no one has formulated a precise or complete definition of feminist criticism, but since its inception, its theorists and practitioners have agreed that it is a "corrective, unmasking the omissions and distortions of the past – the errors of a literary critical tradition that arise from and reflect a culture created, perpetuated, and dominated by men."[4]

These early theorists and practitioners of feminist literary criticism were largely white females who, wittingly or not, perpetrated against the Black woman writer the same exclusive practices they so vehemently decried in white male scholars. Seeing the experiences of white women, particularly white middle-class women, as normative, white female scholars proceeded blindly to exclude the work of Black women writers from literary anthologies and critical studies. Among the most flagrant examples of this chauvinism is Patricia Meyer Spacks's *The Female Imagination*. In a weak defense of her book's exclusive focus on women in the Anglo-American literary tradition, Spacks quotes Phyllis Chesler (a white female psychologist): "I have no theory to offer of Third World female psychology in America.... As a white woman, I'm reluctant and unable to construct theories about experiences I haven't had."[5] But, as Alice Walker observes, "Spacks never lived in nineteenth-century Yorkshire, so why theorize about the Brontës?"[6]

Not only have Black women writers been "disenfranchised" from critical works by white women scholars on the "female tradition," but they have also been frequently excised from those on the Afro-American literary tradition by Black scholars, most of whom are males. For example, Robert Stepto's *From Behind the Veil: A Study of Afro-American Narrative* purports to be "a history... of the historical consciousness of an Afro-American art form – namely, the Afro-American written narrative."[7] Yet, Black women writers are conspicuously absent from the table of contents. Though Stepto does have a token two-page discussion of Zora Neale Hurston's *Their Eyes Were Watching God* in which he refers to it as a "seminal narrative in Afro-American letters,"[8] he did not feel that the novel merited its own chapter or the thorough analysis accorded the other works he discusses.

When Black women writers are neither ignored altogether nor merely given honorable mention, they are critically misunderstood and summarily dismissed. In *The Negro Novel in America*, for example, Robert Bone's reading of Jessie Fauset's novels is both partisan and superficial and might explain the reasons Fauset remains obscure. Bone argues that Fauset is the foremost member of the "Rear Guard" of writers "who lagged behind," clinging to established literary traditions. The "Rear Guard" drew their source material from the Negro middle class in their efforts "to orient Negro art toward white opinion," and "to apprise educated whites of the existence of respectable Negroes." Bone adds that Fauset's emphasis on the Black middle class results in novels that are "uniformly sophomoric, trivial and dull."[9]

While David Littlejohn praises Black fiction since 1940, he denigrates the work of Fauset and Nella Larsen. He maintains that "the newer writers are obviously writing as men, for men," and are avoiding the "very close and steamy" writing that is the result of "any subculture's taking itself too seriously, defining the world and its values exclusively in the terms of its own restrictive norms and concerns."[10] This "phallic criticism,"[11] to use Mary Ellman's term, is based on masculine-centered values and definitions. It has dominated the criticism of Black women writers and has done much to guarantee that most would be, in Alice Walker's words, "casually pilloried and consigned to a sneering oblivion."[12]

Suffice it to say that the critical community has not favored Black women writers. The recognition among Black female critics and writers that white women, white men, and Black men consider their experiences as normative and Black women's experiences as deviant has given rise to Black feminist criticism. Much as in white feminist criticism, the critical postulates of Black women's literature are only skeletally defined. Although there is no concrete definition of Black feminist criticism, a handful of Black female scholars have begun the necessary enterprise of resurrecting forgotten Black women writers and revising misinformed critical opinions of them. Justifiably enraged by the critical establishment's neglect and mishandling of Black women writers, these critics are calling for, in the words of Barbara Smith, "non-hostile and perceptive analysis of works written by persons outside the 'mainstream' of white/male cultural rule."[13]

Despite the urgency and timeliness of the enterprise, however, no sub-stantial body of Black feminist criticism – either in theory or practice – exists, a fact which might be explained partially by our limited access to and control of the media.[14] Another explanation for the paucity of Black feminist criti-cism, notes Barbara Smith, is the lack of a "developed body of Black feminist political theory whose assumptions could be used in the study of Black women's art."

Despite the strained circumstances under which Black feminist critics labor, a few committed Black female scholars have broken necessary ground. For the remainder of this essay I would like to focus on selected writings of Black feminist critics, discussing their strengths and weaknesses and suggest-ing new directions toward which the criticism might move and pitfalls that it might avoid.

Unfortunately, Black feminist scholarship has been decidedly more prac-tical than theoretical, and the theories developed thus far have often lacked sophistication and have been marred by slogans, rhetoric, and idealism. The articles that attempt to apply these theoretical tenets often lack precision and detail. These limitations are not without reason. As Dorin Schumacher observes, "the feminist critic has few philosophical shelters, pillars, or guide-posts," and thus "feminist criticism is fraught with intellectual and profes-sional risks, offering more opportunity for creativity, yet greater possibility of errors."[15]

The earliest theoretical statement on Black feminist criticism is Barbara Smith's "Toward a Black Feminist Criticism." Though its importance as a groundbreaking piece of scholarship cannot be denied, it suffers from lack of precision and detail. In justifying the need for a Black feminist aesthetic, Smith argues that "a Black feminist approach to literature that embodies the realization that the politics of sex as well as the politics of race and class are crucially interlocking factors in the works of Black women writers is an absolute necessity." Until such an approach exists, she continues, "we will not even know what these writers mean."

Smith points out that "thematically, stylistically, aesthetically, and con-ceptually Black women writers manifest common approaches to the act of

creating literature as a direct result of the specific political, social, and economic experience they have been obliged to share." She offers, as an example,
the incorporation of rootworking, herbal medicine, conjure, and midwifery
in the stories of Zora Neale Hurston, Margaret Walker, Toni Morrison, and
Alice Walker. While these folk elements certainly do appear in the work of
these writers, they also appear in the works of certain Black male writers, a fact
that Smith omits. If Black women writers use these elements differently from
Black male writers, such a distinction must be made before one can effectively
articulate the basis of a Black feminist aesthetic.

Smith maintains further that Zora Neale Hurston, Margaret Walker, Toni
Morrison, and Alice Walker use a "specifically black female language to
express their own and their characters' thoughts," but she fails to describe
or to provide examples of this unique language. Of course, we have come
recently to acknowledge that "many of our habits of language usage are sex-
derived, sex-associated, and/or sex-distinctive," that "the ways in which
men and women internalize and manipulate language" are undeniably sex-
related.[16] But this realization in itself simply paves the way for further
investigation that can begin by exploring some critical questions. For example, is there a monolithic Black female language? Do Black female high
school dropouts, welfare mothers, college graduates, and Ph.Ds share a
common language? Are there regional variations in this common language?
Further, some Black male critics have tried to describe the uniquely "Black
linguistic elegance"[17] that characterizes Black poetry. Are there noticeable
differences between the languages of Black females and Black males? These
and other questions must be addressed with precision if current feminist
terminology is to function beyond mere critical jargon.

Smith turns from her discussion of the commonalities among Black
women writers to describe the nature of her critical enterprise. "Black
feminist criticism would by definition by highly innovative," she maintains.
"Applied to a particular work [it] can overturn previous assumptions about
[the work] and expose for the first time its actual dimensions." Smith then
proceeds to demonstrate this critical postulate by interpreting Toni Morrison's *Sula* as a lesbian novel, an interpretation she believes is maintained in
"the emotions expressed, in the definition of female character and in the way
that the politics of heterosexuality are portrayed." Smith vacillates between
arguing forthrightly for the validity of her interpretation and recanting or
overqualifying it in a way that undercuts her own credibility.

According to Smith, "if in a woman writer's work a sentence refuses to do
what it is supposed to do, if there are strong images of women and if there is a
refusal to be linear, the result is innately lesbian literature." She adds,
"because of Morrison's consistently critical stance toward the heterosexual
institutions of male–female relationships, marriage, and the family," *Sula*

works as a lesbian novel. This definition of lesbianism is vague and imprecise; it subsumes far more Black women writers, particularly contemporary ones, than not into the canon of Lesbian writers. For example, Jessie Fauset, Nella Larsen, and Zora Neale Hurston all criticize major socializing institutions, as do Gwendolyn Brooks, Alice Walker, and Toni Cade Bambara. Further, if we apply Smith's definition of lesbianism, there are probably a few Black male writers who qualify as well. All of this is to say that Smith has simultaneously oversimplified and obscured the issue of lesbianism. Obviously aware of the delicacy of her position, she interjects that "the very meaning of lesbianism is being expanded in literature." Unfortunately, her qualification does not strengthen her argument. One of the major tasks ahead of Black feminist critics who write from a lesbian perspective, then, is to define lesbianism and lesbian literature precisely. Until they can offer a definition which is not vacuous, their attempts to distinguish Black lesbian writers from those who are not will be hindered.[18]

Even as I call for firmer definitions of lesbianism and lesbian literature, I question whether a lesbian aesthetic is not finally a reductive approach to the study of Black women's literature which possibly ignores other equally important aspects of the literature. For example, reading *Sula* solely from a lesbian perspective overlooks the novel's density and complexity, its skillful blend of folklore, omens, and dreams, its metaphorical and symbolic richness. Although I do not quarrel with Smith's appeal for fresher, more innovative approaches to Black women's literature, I suspect that "innovative" analysis is pressed to the service of an individual political persuasion. One's personal and political presuppositions enter into one's critical judgments. Nevertheless, we should heed Annette Kolodny's warning for feminist critics to

> be wary of reading literature as though it were polemic.... If when using literary materials to make what is essentially a political point, we find ourselves virtually rewriting a text, ignoring certain aspects of plot or characterization, or over-simplifying the action to fit our "political" thesis, then we are neither practicing an honest criticism nor saying anything useful about the nature of art (or about the art of political persuasion, for that matter).[19]

Alerting feminist critics to the dangers of political ideology yoked with aesthetic judgment is not synonymous with denying that feminist criticism is a valid and necessary cultural and political enterprise. Indeed, it is both possible and useful to translate ideological positions into aesthetic ones, but if the criticism is to be responsible, the two must be balanced.

Because it is a cultural and political enterprise, feminist critics, in the main, believe that their criticism can effect social change. Smith certainly argues for socially relevant criticism in her conclusion that "Black feminist criticism would owe its existence to a Black feminist movement while at the same time contributing ideas that women in the movement could use." This is an exciting idea in itself, but we should ask: What ideas, specifically, would Black feminist criticism contribute to the movement? Further, even though the proposition of a fruitful relationship between political activism and the academy is an interesting (and necessary) one, I doubt its feasibility. I am not sure that either in theory or in practice Black feminist criticism will be able to alter significantly circumstances that have led to the oppression of Black women. Moreover, as Lillian Robinson pointedly remarks, there is no assurance that feminist aesthetics "will be productive of a vision of art or of social relations that is of the slightest use to the masses of women, or even one that acknowledges the existence and struggle of such women."[20] I agree with Robinson that "ideological criticism must take place in the context of a political movement that can put it to work. The revolution is simply not going to be made by literary journals."[21] I should say that I am not arguing a defeatist position with respect to the social and political uses to which feminist criticism can be put. Just as it is both possible and useful to translate ideological positions into aesthetic ones, it must likewise be possible and useful to translate aesthetic positions into the machinery for social change.

Despite the shortcomings of Smith's article, she raises critical issues on which Black feminist critics can build. There are many tasks ahead of these critics, not the least of which is to attempt to formulate some clear definitions of what Black feminist criticism is. I use the term here simply to refer to Black female critics who analyze the works of Black female writers from a feminist or political perspective. But the term can also apply to any criticism written by a Black woman regardless of her subject or perspective – a book written by a male from a feminist or political perspective, a book written by a Black woman or about Black women authors in general, or any writings by women.[22]

In addition to defining the methodology, Black feminist critics need to determine the extent to which their criticism intersects with that of white feminist critics. Barbara Smith and others have rightfully challenged white women scholars to become more accountable to Black and Third World women writers, but will that require white women to use a different set of critical tools when studying Black women writers? Are white women's theories predicated upon culturally specific values and assumptions? Andrea Benton Rushing has attempted to answer these questions in her series of articles on images of Black women in literature. She maintains, for example, that critical categories of women, based on analyses of white women characters, are Euro-American in derivation and hence inappropriate to a consideration of Black women characters.[23] Such distinctions are necessary and, if held uniformly, can materially alter the shape of Black feminist scholarship.

Regardless of which theoretical framework Black feminist critics choose, they must have an informed handle on Black literature and Black culture in general. Such a grounding can give this scholarship more texture and completeness and perhaps prevent some of the problems that have had a vitiating effect on the criticism.

This footing in Black history and culture serves as a basis for the study of the literature. Termed "contextual" by theoreticians, this approach is often frowned upon if not dismissed entirely by critics who insist exclusively upon textual and linguistic analysis. Its limitations notwithstanding, I firmly believe that the contextual approach to Black women's literature exposes the conditions under which literature is produced, published, and reviewed. This approach is not only useful but necessary to Black feminist critics.

To those working with Black women writers prior to 1940, the contextual approach is especially useful. In researching Jessie Fauset, Nella Larsen, and Zora Neale Hurston, for example, it is useful to determine what the prevalent attitudes about Black women were during the time that they wrote. There is much information in the Black "little" magazines published during the Harlem Renaissance. An examination of *The Messenger*, for instance, reveals that the dominant social attitudes about Black women were strikingly consistent with traditional middle-class expectations of women. *The Messenger* ran a monthly symposium for some time entitled "Negro Womanhood's Greatest Needs." While a few female contributors stressed the importance of women being equal to men socially, professionally, and economically, the majority emphasized that a woman's place was in the home. It was her duty "to cling to the home [since] great men and women evolve from the environment of the hearthstone."[24]

One of the most startling entries came from a woman who wrote:

> The New Negro Woman, with her head erect and spirit undaunted, is resolutely marching forward, ever conscious of her historic and noble mission of doing her bit toward the liberation of her people in particular and the human race in general. Upon her shoulders rests the big task to create and keep alive, in the breast of black men, a holy and consuming passion to break with the slave traditions of the past; to spurn and overcome the fatal, insidious inferiority complex of the present, which . . . bobs up ever and anon, to arrest the progress of the New Negro Manhood Movement; and to fight with increasing vigor, with dauntless courage, unrelenting zeal and intelligent vision for the attainment of the stature of a full man, a free race and a new world.[25]

Not only does the contributor charge the Black woman with a formidable task, but she also sees her solely in relation to Black men.

This information enhances our understanding of what Fauset, Larsen, and Hurston confronted in attempting to offer alternative images of Black women. Moreover, it helps to clarify certain textual problems and ambiguities of their work. Though Fauset and Hurston, for example, explored feminist concerns, they leaned toward ambivalence. Fauset especially is alternately forthright and cagey, radical and traditional, on issues that confront women. Her first novel, *There Is Confusion* (1924), is flawed by an unanticipated and abrupt reversal in characterization that brings the central female character more in line with a feminine norm. Similarly, in her last novel, *Seraph on the Swanee* (1948), Zora Neale Hurston depicts a female character who shows promise for growth and change, for a departure from the conventional expectations of womanhood, but who in the end apotheosizes marriage, motherhood, and domestic servitude.

These two examples alone clearly capture the tension between social pressure and artistic integrity which is felt, to some extent, by all women writers. As Tillie Olsen points out, the fear of reprisal from the publishing and critical arenas is a looming obstacle to the woman writer's coming into her own authentic voice. "Fear – the need to please, to be safe – in the literary realm too. Founded fear. Power is still in the hands of men. Power of validation, publication, approval, reputation...."[26]

While insisting on the validity, usefulness, and necessity of contextual approaches to Black women's literature, the Black feminist critic must not ignore the importance of rigorous textual analysis. I am aware of many feminist critics' stubborn resistance to the critical methodology handed down by white men. Although the resistance is certainly politically consistent and logical, I agree with Annette Kolodny that feminist criticism would be "shortsighted if it summarily rejected all the inherited tools of critical analysis simply because they are male and western." We should, rather, salvage what we find useful in past methodologies, reject what we do not, and, where necessary, move toward "inventing new methods of analysis."[27] Particularly useful is Lillian Robinson's suggestion that "a radical kind of textual criticism...could usefully study the way the texture of sentences, choice of metaphors, patterns of exposition and narrative relate to [feminist] ideology."[28]

This rigorous textual analysis involves, as Barbara Smith recommends, isolating as many thematic, stylistic, and linguistic commonalities among Black women writers as possible. Among contemporary Black female novelists, the thematic parallels are legion. In Alice Walker and Toni Morrison, for example, the theme of the thwarted female artist figures prominently.[29] Pauline Breedlove in Morrison's *The Bluest Eye*, for example, is obsessed with ordering things:

Jars on shelves at canning, peach pits on the step, sticks, stones, leaves.... Whatever portable plurality she found, she organized into neat lines, according to their size, shape or gradations of color.... She missed without knowing what she missed – paints and crayons.[30]

Similarly, Eva Peace in *Sula* is forever ordering the pleats in her dress. And Sula's strange and destructive behavior is explained as "the consequence of an idle imagination."

Had she paints, clay, or knew the discipline of the dance, or strings; had she anything to engage her tremendous curiosity and her gift for metaphor, she might have exchanged the restlessness and preoccupation with whim for an activity that provided her with all she yearned for. And like any artist with no form, she became dangerous.[31]

Likewise, Meridian's mother in Alice Walker's novel *Meridian* makes artificial flowers and prayer pillows too small for kneeling.

The use of "clothing as iconography"[32] is central to writings by Black women. For example, in one of Jessie Fauset's early short stories. "The Sleeper Wakes" (1920), Amy, the protagonist, is associated with pink clothing (suggesting innocence and immaturity) while she is blinded by fairy-tale notions of love and marriage. However, after she declares her independence from her racist and sexist husband, Amy no longer wears pink. The imagery of clothing is abundant in Zora Neale Hurston's *Their Eyes Were Watching God* (1937). Janie's apron, her silks and satins, her head scarves, and finally her overalls all symbolize various stages of her journey from captivity to liberation. Finally, in Alice Walker's *Meridian*, Meridian's railroad cap and dungarees are emblems of her rejection of conventional images and expectations of womanhood.

A final theme that recurs in the novels of Black women writers is the motif of the journey. Though one can also find this same motif in the works of Black male writers, they do not use it in the same way as do Black female writers.[33] For example, the journey of the Black male character in works by Black men takes him underground. It is a "descent into the underworld,"[34] and is primarily political and social in its implications. Ralph Ellison's *Invisible Man*, Imamu Amiri Baraka's *The System of Dante's Hell*, and Richard Wright's "The Man who Lived Underground" exemplify this quest. The Black female's journey, on the other hand, though at times touching the political and social, is basically a personal and psychological journey. The female character in the works of Black women is in a state of becoming "part of an evolutionary spiral, moving from victimization to consciousness."[35] The heroines in Zora Neale Hurston's *Their Eyes Were Watching God*, in

Alice Walker's *Meridian*, and in Toni Cade Bambara's *The Salt Eaters* are emblematic of this distinction.

Even though isolating such thematic and imagistic commonalities should continue to be one of the Black feminist critic's most urgent tasks, she should beware of generalizing on the basis of too few examples. If one argues authoritatively for the existence of a Black female "consciousness" or "vision" or "literary tradition," one must be sure that the parallels found recur with enough consistency to support these generalizations. Further, Black feminist critics should not become obsessed in searching for common themes and images in Black women's works. As I pointed out earlier, investigating the question of "female" language is critical and may well be among the most challenging jobs awaiting the Black feminist critic. The growing body of research on gender-specific uses of language might aid these critics. In fact, wherever possible, feminist critics should draw on the scholarship of feminists in other disciplines.

An equally challenging and necessary task ahead of the Black feminist critic is a thoroughgoing examination of the works of Black male writers. In her introduction to *Midnight Birds*, Mary Helen Washington argues for the importance of giving Black women writers their due first:

> Black women are searching for a specific language, specific symbols, specific images with which to record their lives, and, even though they can claim a rightful place in the Afro-American tradition and the feminist tradition of women writers, it is also clear that, for purposes of liberation, black women writers will first insist on their own name, their own space.[36]

I likewise believe that the immediate concern of Black feminist critics must be to develop a fuller understanding of Black women writers who have not received the critical attention Black male writers have. Yet, I cannot advocate indefinitely such a separatist position, for the countless thematic, stylistic, and imagistic parallels between Black male and female writers must be examined. Black feminist critics should explore these parallels in an effort to determine the ways in which these commonalities are manifested differently in Black women's writing and the ways in which they coincide with writings by Black men.

Of course, there are feminist critics who are already examining Black male writers, but much of the scholarship has been limited to discussions of the negative images of Black women found in the works of these authors.[37] Although this scholarship served an important function in pioneering Black feminist critics, it has virtually run its course. Feminist critics run the risk of plunging their work into cliché and triviality if they continue merely to focus on how Black men treat Black women in literature. Hortense Spillers offers a more sophisticated approach to this issue in her discussion of the power of language and myth in female relations in James Baldwin's *If Beale Street could Talk*. One of Spillers's most cogent points is that "woman-freedom, or its negation, is tied to the assertions of myth, or ways of saying things."[38]

Black feminist criticism is a knotty issue, and while I have attempted to describe it, to call for clearer definitions of its methodology, to offer warnings of its limitations, I await the day when Black feminist criticism will expand to embrace other modes of critical inquiry. In other words, I am philosophically opposed to what Annis Pratt calls "methodolatry." Wole Soyinka has offered one of the most cogent defenses against critical absolutism. He explains:

> The danger which a literary ideology poses is the act of consecration – and of course excommunication. Thanks to the tendency of the modern consumer-mind to facilitate digestion by putting in strict categories what are essentially fluid operations of the creative mind upon social and natural phenomena, the formulation of a literary ideology tends to congeal sooner or later into instant capsules which, administered also to the writer, may end by asphyxiating the creative process.[39]

Whether Black feminist criticism will or should remain a separatist enterprise is a debatable point. Black feminist critics ought to move from this issue to consider the specific language of Black women's literature, to describe the ways Black women writers employ literary devices in a distinct way, and to compare the way Black women writers create their own mythic structures. If they focus on these and other pertinent issues, Black feminist critics will have laid the cornerstone for a sound, thorough articulation of the Black feminist aesthetic.

Notes

1 Louise Bernikow, *The World Split Open: Four Centuries of Women Poets in England and America, 1552–1950* (New York: Vintage Books, 1974), p. 3.
2 William Morgan, "Feminism and Literary Study: A Reply to Annette Kolodny," *Critical Inquiry* 2 (Summer 1976): B11.
3 The year 1970 was the beginning of the Modern Language Association's Commission on the Status of Women, which offered panels and workshops that were feminist in approach.
4 Statement by Barbara Desmarais quoted in Annis Pratt, "The New Feminist Criticisms: Exploring the History of the New Space," in *Beyond Intellectual Sexism: A New Woman, A New Reality*, ed. Joan I. Roberts (New York: David McKay, 1976), p. 176.

5   Patricia Meyer Spacks, *The Female Imagination* (New York: Avon Books, 1976),
    p. 5. Ellen Moers, *Literary Women: The Great Writers* (Garden City, NY: Anchor
    Books, 1977) is another example of what Alice Walker terms "white female
    chauvinism."

6   Alice Walker, "One Child of One's Own – An Essay on Creativity," *Ms.*, August
    1979, p. 50.

7   Robert Stepto, *From Behind the Veil: A Study of Afro-American Narrative*
    (Urbana: University of Illinois Press, 1979), p. x. Other sexist critical works
    include Donald B. Gibson, ed., *Five Black Writers* (New York: New York Uni-
    versity Press, 1970), a collection of essays on Wright, Ellison, Baldwin, Hughes,
    and Leroi Jones, and Jean Wagner, *Black Poets of the United States: From Paul
    Lawrence Dunbar to Langston Hughes*, trans. Kenneth Douglas (Urbana: Uni-
    versity of Illinois Press, 1973).

8   Stepto, *From Behind the Veil*, p. 166.

9   Robert Bone, *The Negro Novel in America* (1958; reprint ed., New Haven, CT:
    Yale University Press, 1972), pp. 97, 101.

10 David Littlejohn, *Black on White: A Critical Survey of Writing by American
    Negroes* (New York: Viking Press, 1966), pp. 48–9.

11 Ellman's concept of "phallic criticism" is discussed in a chapter of the same
    name in her *Thinking about Women* (New York: Harcourt, Brace & World,
    1968), pp. 28–54.

12 Introduction to *Zora Neale Hurston: A Literary Biography* by Robert Hemen-
    way (Urbana: University of Illinois Press, 1976), p. xiv. Although Walker makes
    this observation specifically about Hurston, it is one that can apply to a number
    of Black women writers.

13 Barbara Smith, "Toward a Black Feminist Criticism," in this volume,
    pp. 7–23.

14 See Evelyn Hammonds, "Toward a Black Feminist Aesthetic," *Sojourner* (Octo-
    ber 1980), p. 7, for a discussion of the limitations on Black feminist critics. She
    correctly points out that Black feminist critics "have no newspapers, no mass-
    marketed magazines or journals that are explicitly oriented toward the involve-
    ment of women of color in the feminist movement."

15 Dorin Schumacher, "Subjectivities: A Theory of the Critical Process," in *Fem-
    inist Literary Criticism: Explorations in Theory*, ed. Josephine Donovan (Lex-
    ington: University Press of Kentucky, 1975): 34.

16 Annette Kolodny, "The Feminist as Literary Critic," Critical Response, *Critical
    Inquiry* 2 (Summer 1976): 824–5. See also Cheris Kramer, Barrie Thorne, and
    Nancy Henley, "Perspectives on Language and Communication," *Signs* 3
    (Spring 1978): 638–51, and Nelly Furman, "The Study of Women and Lan-
    guage: Comment on Vol. 3, no. 3," *Signs* 4 (Fall 1978): 152–85.

17 Stephen Henderson, *Understanding the New Black Poetry: Black Speech and
    Black Music as Poetic References* (New York: William Morrow, 1973), pp. 31–46.

18 Some attempts have been made to define or at least discuss lesbianism. See
    Adrienne Rich's two essays, "It Is the Lesbian in Us..." and "The Meaning
    of Our Love for Woman Is What We Have," in *On Lies, Secrets and Silence* (New

York: W. W. Norton, 1979), pp. 199–202 and 223–30, respectively. See also
Bertha Harris's "*What We Mean to Say*: Notes Toward Defining the Nature of
Lesbian Literature," *Heresies* 1 (Fall 1977): 5–8, and Blanche Cook's " 'Women
Alone Stir My Imagination': Lesbianism and the Cultural Tradition," *Signs* 4
(Summer 1979): 718–39. Also, at least one bibliography of Black lesbian writers
has been compiled. See Ann Allen Shockley's "The Black Lesbian in American
Literature: An Overview," *Conditions: Five* 2 (Fall 1979): 133–42.

19 Annette Kolodny, "Some Notes on Defining a 'Feminist Literary Criticism,' "
Critical Inquiry 2 (Fall 1975): 90.

20 Lillian S. Robinson, "Working Women Writing," *Sex, Class, and Culture*
(Bloomington: Indiana University Press, 1978), p. 226.

21 Robinson, "The Critical Task," *Sex, Class, and Culture*, p. 52.

22 I am borrowing here from Kolodny, who makes similar statements in "Some
Notes on Defining a 'Feminist Literary Criticism,' " p. 75.

23 Andrea Benton Rushing, "Images of Black Women in Afro-American Poetry,"
in *The Afro-American Woman: Struggles and Images*, ed. Sharon Harley and
Rosalyn Terborg-Penn (Port Washington, NY: Kennikat Press, 1978), pp. 74–
84. She argues that few of the stereotypic traits which Mary Ellman describes in
Thinking About Women "seem appropriate to Afro-American images of black
women." See also her "Images of Black Women in Modern African Poetry: An
Overview," in *Sturdy Black Bridges: Visions of Black Women in Literature*, ed.
Roseann P. Bell et al. (New York: Anchor Books, 1979), pp. 18–24. Rushing
argues similarly that Mary Ann Ferguson's categories of women (the submissive
wife, the mother angel or "mom," the woman on a pedestal, for example)
cannot be applied to Black women characters, whose cultural imperatives are
different from white women's.

24 *The Messenger* 9 (April 1927): 109.

25 *The Messenger* 5 (July 1923): 757.

26 Tillie Olsen, *Silences* (New York: Delacorte Press, 1978), p. 257.

27 Kolodny, "Some Notes on Defining a 'Feminist Literary Criticism,' " p. 89.

28 Lillian S. Robinson, "Dwelling in Decencies: Radical Criticism and Feminist
Perspectives," in *Feminist Criticism*, ed. Cheryl Brown and Karen Olsen (Metu-
chen, NJ: Scarecrow Press, 1978), p. 34.

29 For a discussion of Toni Morrison's frustrated female artists see Renita Weems,
"Artists Without Art Form: A Look at One Black Woman's World of Unrevered
Black Women," *Conditions: Five* 2 (Fall 1979): 48–58. See also Alice Walker's
classic essay, "In Search of our Mothers' Gardens," *Ms.*, (May 1974), for a
discussion of Black women's creativity in general.

30 Toni Morrison, *The Bluest Eye* (New York: Pocket Books, 1970), pp. 88–9.

31 Toni Morrison, *Sula* (New York: Bantam Books, 1980), p. 105.

32 Kolodny, "Some Notes on Defining a 'Feminist Literary Criticism,' " p. 86.

33 In an NEH Summer Seminar at Yale University in the summer of 1980, Carolyn
Naylor of Santa Clara University suggested this to me.

34 For a discussion of this idea see Michael G. Cooke, "The Descent into the
Underworld and Modern Black Fiction," *Iowa Review* 5 (Fall 1974): 72–90.

35 Mary Helen Washington, *Midnight Birds: Stories of Contemporary Black Women Writers* (Garden City, NY: Anchor Books, 1980), p. 43.
36 Ibid., p. xvii.
37 See Saundra Towns, "The Black Woman as Whore: Genesis of the Myth," *The Black Position* 3 (1974): 39–59, and Sylvia Keady, "Richard Wright's Women Characters and Inequality," *Black American Literature Forum* 10 (1976): 124–8, for example.
38 Hortense Spillers, "The Politics of Intimacy: A Discussion," in Bell et al., eds, *Sturdy Black Bridges*, p. 88.
39 Wole Soyinka, *Myth, Literature and the African World* (Cambridge: Cambridge University Press, 1976), p. 61.

3

But What Do We Think We're Doing Anyway:

The State of Black Feminist Criticism(s) or My Version of a Little Bit of History*

Barbara Christian

Christian, Barbara. "But What Do We Think We're Doing Anyway: The State of Black Feminist Criticism(s) or My Version of a Little Bit of History." In Cheryl A. Wall, ed. *Changing Our Own Words: Essays on Criticism, Theory, and Writing by Black Women* (New Brunswick, NJ: Rutgers University Press, 1989), pp. 58–74.

In August 1974, a unique event occurred. *Black World*, probably the most widely read publication of Afro-American literature, culture, and political thought at that time, used on its cover a picture of the then practically unknown writer Zora Neale Hurston.[1] Under Zora's then unfamiliar photograph was a caption in bold letters, "Black Women Image Markers," which was the title of the essay by Mary Helen Washington featured in the issue. Alongside the Washington essay were three other pieces: an essay now considered a classic, June Jordan's "On Richard Wright and Zora Neale Hurston: Notes Towards a Balancing of Love and Hate," an essay on major works of Zora Neale Hurston, "The Novelist/Anthropologist/Life Work," by poet Ellease Southerland, and a short piece criticizing the television version of Ernest Gaines's *The Autobiography of Miss Jane Pittman*, by Black psychologist Alvin Ramsey. It was not particularly striking that the image of a Black woman writer graced the cover of *Black World*; Gwendolyn Brooks's picture, for example, had appeared on a previous *Black World* cover. Nor was it especially noteworthy that literary analyses of an Afro-American woman writer appeared in that journal. That certainly had occurred before. What was so striking about this issue of *Black World* was the tone of the individual pieces and the effect of their juxtaposition.

Mary Helen Washington's essay sounded a strong chord – that there was indeed a growing number of contemporary Afro-American women writers whose perspective underlined the centrality of women's lives to their creative vision. June Jordan's essay placed Hurston, a relatively unknown Afro-American woman writer, alongside Richard Wright, who is probably the best known of Afro-American writers, and illuminated how their apparently antithetical worldviews were *both* necessary ways of viewing the complexity of Afro-American life, which Jordan made clear was not monolithic. Ellease Southerland reviewed many of Hurston's works, pointing out their significance to Afro-American literature and therefore indicating the existence of major Afro-American women writers in the past. And in criticizing the television version of *The Autobiography of Miss Jane Pittman*, Ramsey objected that that commercial white medium had omitted the message of struggle in Ernest Gaines's novel and turned it into an individual woman's story – a foreshadowing of criticism that would be repeated when, periodically, images of Black women from literature were translated into visual media.

What the configuration of the August 1974 *Black World* suggested to me, as I am sure it did to others, was the growing visibility of Afro-American women and the significant impact they were having on contemporary Black culture. The articulation of that impact had been the basis for Toni Cade's edition of *The Black Woman* in 1970.[2] But that collection had not dealt specifically with literature/creativity. Coupled with the publication of Alice Walker's "In Search of our Mothers' Gardens," only a few months before in the May issue of *Ms.*,[3] the August 1974 *Black World* signaled a shift in position among those interested in Afro-American literature about women's creativity. Perhaps because I had experienced a decade of the intense literary activity of the 1960s, but also much antifemale Black cultural nationalist rhetoric, these two publications had a lightning effect on me. Afro-American women were making public, were able to make public, their search for themselves in literary culture.

I begin my reflections on the state (history) of Black feminist criticism(s) with this memory because it seems to me we so quickly forget the recent past. Perhaps some of us have never known it. Like many of us who lived through the literary activism of the sixties, we of the eighties may forget that which just recently preceded us and may therefore misconstrue the period in which we are acting.

Less than 20 years ago, without using the self-consciously academic word *theory*, Mary Helen Washington articulated a concept that was original, startling even, to many of us immersed in the study of Afro-American literature, among whom were few academics, who knew little or cared less about this literature. In "Black Women Image Makers" Washington stated what for me is still a basic tenet of Black feminist criticism: "We should be about the business of *reading, absorbing,* and giving *critical* attention to those writers whose understanding of the black woman can take us *further*" (emphasis mine).[4] The names of the writers Washington listed, with the exception of Gwendolyn Brooks, were then all virtually unknown; interestingly, after a period when poetry and drama were the preeminent genre of Afro-American literature, practically all of these writers – Maya Angelou, Toni Cade Bambara, Paule Marshall, Toni Morrison, Alice Walker – were practicing fiction writers. While all of the writers were contemporary, Washington implied through her analysis that their vision and craft suggested that previous Afro-American women writers existed. Hence Zora Neale Hurston's picture on the cover of this issue connoted a specific meaning – that of a literary foremother who had been neglected by Afro-Americanists of the past but who was finally being recognized by her daughters and reinstated as a major figure in the Afro-American literary tradition.

It is important for us to remember that in 1974, even before the publication of Robert Hemenway's biography of Hurston in 1977 or the reissuing of *Their Eyes Were Watching God*, the articulation of the possibility of a tradition of Afro-American women writers occurred not in a fancy academic journal but in two magazines: *Ms.*, a new popular magazine that came out of the women's movement, and *Black World*, a long-standing Black journal unknown to most academics and possibly scorned by some.

Walker's essay and *Black World*'s August 1974 issue gave me a focus and are the recognizable points that I can recall as to when I consciously began to work on Black women writers. I had, of course, unconsciously begun my own search before reading those pieces. I had spent some portion of the late sixties and early seventies asking my "elders" in the Black arts movement whether there were Black women who had written before Gwendolyn Brooks or Lorraine Hansberry. Younger poets such as Sonia Sanchez, Nikki Giovanni, Carolyn Rodgers, June Jordan, and Audre Lorde were, of course, quite visible by that time. And by 1974, Morrison and Walker had each published a novel. But only through accident or sheer stint of effort did I discover Paule Marshall's *Brown Girl, Brownstones* (1959) or Hurston's *Their Eyes Were Watching God* (1937) – an indication that the contemporary writers I was then reading might too fade into oblivion. Although in the sixties the works of neglected Afro-American male writers of the Harlem Renaissance were beginning to resurface, for example, Jean Toomer's *Cane*, I was told the women writers of that period were terrible – not worth my trouble. However, because of the conjuncture of the Black arts movement and the women's movement, I asked questions I probably would not have otherwise thought of.

If movements have any effect, it is to give us a context within which to imagine questions we would not have imagined before, to ask questions we might not have asked before. The publication of the *Black World* August 1974 issue as well as Walker's essay was rooted in the conjuncture of those two movements, rather than in the theoretizing of any individual scholar, and most emphatically in the literature of contemporary Afro-American women who were able to be published as they had not been before, precisely because that conjuncture was occurring.

That the development of Black feminist criticism(s) is firmly rooted in this conjuncture is crystal clear from a pivotal essay of the 1970s: Barbara Smith's "Toward a Black Feminist Criticism," which was originally published in *Conditions II* in 1977. By that time Smith was not only calling on critics to read, absorb, and pay attention to Black women writers, as Washington had, but also to write about that body of literature from a feminist perspective. What *feminist* meant for Smith went beyond Washington's emphasis on image making. Critics, she believed, needed to demonstrate how the literature exposed "the brutally complex systems of oppression"[5] – that of sexism, racism, and economic exploitation which affected so gravely the experience and culture of Black women. As important, Smith was among the first to point out that Black Lesbian literature was thoroughly ignored in critical journals, an indication of the homophobia existent in the literary world.

Because the US women's movement had begun to extend itself into academic arenas and because women's voices had been so thoroughly suppressed, by the middle seventies there was a visible increase of interest among academics in women's literature. Yet despite the existence of powerful contemporary Afro-American women writers who continued to be major explorers of Afro-American women's lives – writers, such as Bambara, Jordan, Lorde, Morrison, Shange, Walker, Sherley Anne Williams (the list could be much longer) – little commentary on their works could be found in feminist journals. In many ways, they continued to be characterized by such journals as Black, not women, writers. Nor, generally speaking, were critics who studied these writers considered either in the Afro-American or feminist literary worlds – far less the mainstreams literary establishment – to be working on an important body of literature central to American letters. By 1977, Smith knew that the sexism of Afro-American literary/intellectual circles and the racism of white feminist literary journals resulted in a kind of homelessness for critical works on Black women or other Third World women writers. She underlined this fact in her landmark essay: "I think of the thousands and thousands of books which have been devoted by this time to the subject of Women's Writing and I am filled with rage at the fraction of these pages that mention Black and other Third World women. I finally do not know how to begin, because in 1977 I want to be writing this for a black feminist publication."[6]

At that time, most feminist journals were practically all white publications; their content dealt almost exclusively with white women as if they were the only women in the United States. The extent to which the mid-twentieth-century women's movement was becoming, like its nineteenth-century predecessor, infected by racism seemed all too clear, and the split between a Black and a white women's movement that occurred in the nineteenth century seemed to be repeating itself.

Smith seemed to believe that the lack of inclusion of women-of-color writers and critics in the burgeoning literature on women's voices was due, in part, to "the fact that a parallel Black feminist movement had been slower in evolving," and that that fact "could not help but have impact upon the situation of Black women writers and artists and explains in part why during that very same period we have been so ignored."[7] My experience, however, suggests that other factors were more prominently at work, factors Smith also mentioned. In calling for a "body of Black feminist political theory," she pointed out that such a theory was necessary since those who had access to critical publications – white male and, increasingly, Black male and white female critics – apparently did not *know how* to respond to the works of Black women. More accurately, I think these critics might have been resistant to this body of writing which unavoidably demonstrated the intersections of sexism and racism so central to Afro-American women's lives and therefore threatened not only white men's view of themselves, but Black men and white women's view of themselves as well. Smith concludes that "undoubtedly there are other [Black] women working and writing whom I do not know, simply because there is no place to read them."[8]

I can personally attest to that fact. By 1977 I was well into the writing of the book that would become *Black Women Novelists: The Development of a Tradition* (1980) and had independently stumbled on two pivotal concepts that Smith articulated in her essay: "the need to demonstrate that Black women's writing constituted an identifiable literary tradition" and the importance of looking "for precedents and insights in interpretation within the works of other Black women."[9] I found, however, that it was virtually impossible to locate either the works of many nineteenth-century writers or those of contemporary writers, whose books went in and out of print like ping-pong balls. For example, I xeroxed *Brown Girl, Brownstones* (please forgive me, Paule) any number of times because it simply was not available and I wanted to use it in the classes I had begun to teach on Afro-American women's literature. At times I felt more like a detective than a literary critic as I chased clues to find a book I knew existed but which I had begun to think I had hallucinated.

Particularly difficult, I felt, was the dearth of historical material on Afro-American women, that is, on the contexts within which the literature had evolved – contexts I increasingly saw as a necessary foundation for the development of a contemporary Black feminist perspective. Other than Gerda Lerner's *Black Women in White America* (1973), I could not find a single full-length analysis of Afro-American women's history. And despite the proliferation of Afro-American and women's history books in the 1970s, I found in most of them only a few paragraphs devoted to Black women, the favorites being Harriet Tubman in the Black studies ones and Sojourner Truth in the women's studies ones. As a result, in preparation for my book, I, untrained in history, had created a patchwork quilt of historical facts gathered here and there. I remember being positively elated when Sharon Harley and Rosalyn Terborg Penn's collection of historical essays – *The Afro-American Woman* (1978) – was published. But by then, I had almost completed my manuscript. If Afro-American women critics were to turn to Black women of the past for insights, their words and works needed to be accessible and had to be located in a cogent historical analysis.

As well, what was stunning to me as I worked on *Black Women Novelists* was the resistance I experienced among scholars to my subject matter. Colleagues of mine, some of whom had my best interest at heart, warned me that I was going to ruin my academic career by studying an insignificant, some said nonexistent, body of literature. Yet I knew it was fortunate for me that I was situated in an Afro-American studies rather than in an English department, where not even the intercession of the Virgin would have allowed me to do research on Black women writers. I also found that lit crit journals were not interested in the essays I had begun to write on Black women writers. The sustenance I received during those years of writing *Black Women Novelists* came not from the academic/literary world but from small groups of women in bookstores, Y's, in my classes and writers groups for whom this literature was not so much an object of study but was, as it is for me, life-saving.

Many contemporary Afro-American critics imply in their analyses that only those Afro-Americans in the academy – college faculty and students – read Afro-American literature. I have found quite the opposite to be true. For it was "ordinary" Black women, women in the churches, private reading groups, women like my hairdresser and her clients, secondary school tea-chers, typists, my women friends, many of whom were single mothers, who discussed *The Bluest Eye* (1970) or *In Love and Trouble* (1973) with an intensity unheard of in the academic world. In fact most of my colleagues did not even know these books existed when women I knew were calling these writers by their first name – Alice, Paule, Toni, June – indicating their sense of an intimacy with them. They did not necessarily buy the books but

often begged, "borrowed," or "liberated" them – so that book sales were
not always indicative of their interest. I had had similar experiences during
the 1960s. Postal clerks, winos, as well as the folk who hung out in
Micheaux's, the Black bookstore in Harlem, knew Baldwin's, Wright's,
Ellison's works and talked vociferously about them when many of the folk
at CCNY and Columbia had never read one of these writers. Ralph Ellison
wrote an extremely provocative blurb for *Our Nig* when he pointed out that
Harriet Wilson's novel demonstrated that there is more "free-floating"
literacy among Blacks than we acknowledge.

No doubt we are influenced by what publishers say people should read or
do read. When I began sending out sections of *Black Women Novelists*,
practically all academic presses as well as trade presses commented that my
subject was not important – that people were not interested in Black women
writers. Couldn't I write a book on the social problems of Black women?
Affected by the rhetoric à la Moynihan, most of these presses could hardly
believe Black women were artists – a point we might remember as some of us
today minimize the craft and artistry of these writers in favor of intellectual or
social analysis. In response to these comments I could not point to any
precedents, for in 1978 there had not been published a full-length study of
Black women writers. I believe if it were not for the incredible publicity that
Toni Morrison's *Song of Solomon* received in 1978, and that fact that one of
my chapters was devoted to her work, I would not have been able to publish
Black Women Novelists when I did. Smith was right on target when she
suggested that there might be other Black women critics writing and working about whom she did not know because there was no place to read them.

That situation began to change by 1980, however. And I think it is
important for us to recall some of the major signs of that change. One
such sign was the Black sexism issue of the *Black Scholar* published in May/
June of 1979 which grew out of Black sociologist Robert Staples's extremely
critical response to Ntozake Shange's play *for colored girls who have considered
suicide/when the rainbow is enuf* and Michele Wallace's critique of the sexism
in the civil rights movement – *Black Macho and the Myth of the Superwoman*
(1979).[10] In his critique of Shange and Wallace, Staples insinuated that Black
feminists were being promoted by the white media – a stance that would be
reiterated years later by some critics in the *Color Purple* debate. Although the
debate among the Afro-American women and men on the issue was not a
specifically "literary" debate, its very existence indicated the effect Afro-
American women's literature was having on Afro-American intellectual circles. What was also interesting about the debate was the intense involvement
of Afro-American women writers themselves who unabashedly responded to
Staples. Audre Lorde put it succinctly: "Black feminists speak as women and
do not need others to speak for us."[11]

Such speaking had certainly ignited the literary world. In the 1970s Black women published more novels than they had in any other decade. Some, like Morrison and Walker, were beginning to be acknowledged as great American novelists. Poets such as Lorde, Jordan, Sherley Williams, and Lucille Clifton, to mention a few, were clearly literary/political activists as well as writers in the Afro-American and women's communities. And many of these writers, most of whom were not academicians (e.g., Walker in "One Child of One's Own," Lorde in "The Uses of the Erotic"), were themselves doing Black feminist criticism. Increasingly even academicians could not deny the effect this body of literature was having on various communities in American life. Simultaneously, critical essays and analysis began to appear in literary academic as well as in more generalized intellectual journals.

That a Black feminist criticism was beginning to receive attention from the academic world was one basis for Deborah McDowell's essay "New Directions for Black Feminist Criticism," which originally appeared in an academic journal, *Black American Literature Forum*, in 1980.[12] In responding to Smith's call for a Black feminist criticism, McDowell emphasized the need for clear definitions and methodologies, a sign as well of the increasing emphasis on theory surfacing in the academic world. She asked whether Black feminist criticism was relegated only to Black women who wrote about Black women writers. Did they have to write from a feminist/political perspective to be Black feminist critics? Could white women/Black men/white men do Black feminist criticism? a question which indicated that this literature was beginning to attract a wider group of critics.

McDowell's questions continue to have much relevance as more and more critics of different persuasions, genders, and races write critical essays on Afro-American women writers. Just recently, in April 1988, Michele Wallace published a piece in the *Village Voice* which seemed almost a parody of the August 1974 *Black World* issue.[13] The piece was advertised in the content listing with the titillating title "Who Owns Zora Neale Hurston: Critics Carve up the Legend," and featured on the first page of its text was a big photograph of Zora, who had become the darling of the literary world. Wallace counterpointed the perspectives of Black women, Black men, white women, even one prominent white male critic who had written about Hurston. Everyone apparently was getting into the act, though with clearly different purposes, as Wallace insinuated that Hurston had become a commodity. Wallace's own title for her piece, "Who Dat Say Who Dat When I Say Who Dat?" spoken as if by Hurston herself, underlined the ironic implications of the proliferation of Hurston criticism, much of which, Wallace implied, was severed from Hurston's roots and most of which ignored Hurston's goddesslike mischievousness.

"Who Dat Say Who Dat When I Say Who Dat?" took me back to
McDowell's essay and her suggestions of parameters for a Black feminist
criticism. In addition to the ones articulated by Washington in 1974 and
Smith in 1977, McDowell emphasized the need for both contextual and
textual analysis – contextual, in that the critic needed to have a knowledge of
Afro-American history and culture, and women's situation within it, and
textual, that is, paying careful attention to the individual text. If one were to
combine Washington's, Smith's, and McDowell's suggestions, few of the
critical works cited by Wallace would even come close to doing Black feminist
criticism. Wallace acceded that "Black literature needs a rainbow coalition,"
but she wondered if some critical approaches did not silence Hurston. While
Hurston's and other Afro-American women's writing are deep enough, full
enough to be approached from any number of perspectives, their work
demands rigorous attention as does any other serious writing.

The question as to who the critic is and how that affects her/his
interpretation was very much on my mind when I put together *Black
Feminist Criticism* in 1983–4.[14] In thinking about my own attempts to do
such criticism, I increasingly felt that critics needed to let go of their
distanced and false stance of objectivity and to expose their own point of
view – the tangle of background, influences, political perspectives, training,
situations that helped form and inform their interpretations. Inspired by
feminist discussions about objectivity and subjectivity, I constructed an
introduction to my volume that, rather than the usual formal introduction
found in most lit crit books, was intended to introduce me in my specific
context. It was a personalized way of indicating some of my biases, not the
least of which was the fact that the literature I chose to study was central to
an understanding of my own life, and not *only* an intellectual pursuit. Such
exposure would, I thought, help the reader evaluate more effectively the
choices I had made about the language I used, the specific issues I
approached, the particular writers I emphasized. By then I realized I did
not want to write about every contemporary Afro-American woman writer –
some did not speak to me – and that the extent of my own personal
involvement with the writer's work was one aspect of my doing Black
feminist criticism.

But even more to the point, I thought that Black feminist criticism needed
to break some of the restricted forms, personalize the staid language associated with the critic – forms that seemed opposed to the works of the writers
as well as the culture from which they came – and forms that many readers
found intimidating and boring. In the introduction dialogue I used call and
response, jazz riffs, techniques found in writers like Hughes and Hurston, as
well as the anecdote, a device I had found so effective in the essays of Jordan
and Walker, as ways of reflecting on my own process.

In fact the form of the book was based on the idea of process as a critical aspect of an evolving feminist approach – that is, a resistance to art as artifact, to ideas as fixed, and a commitment to open-endedness, possibility, fluidity – to change. These qualities were significant characteristics of the writers I studied. Inspired by Jordan's adroit use of headnotes in *Civil Wars*, I compiled a collection not of every essay I had written between 1975 and 1985 but examples of writing events I considered necessary to doing Black feminist criticism – most of which were not essays written originally for academic outlets. For me, doing Black feminist criticism involved a literary activism that went beyond the halls of academe, not because I had so legislated but because in practice that is what it often, happily, had to be.

I also intended the book to be a tracing of that journey some of us had been making since 1974, a journey guided by what I considered to be another important element of doing this type of criticism, that is, on being a participant in an ongoing dialogue between the writer and those who were reading the writer, most of whom were not academics and for whom that writing was life-sustaining, life-saving. As the race for theory began to accelerate in 1984, I became concerned that the dialogue was drying up as critics rushed to construct theories in languages that many writers abhorred and which few readers understood or enjoyed or could use. In particular I was struck by a talk I had had with one major writer who told me she had gone to a lit crit panel on her work but could not comprehend one word, nor could she recognize her work in anything that was said. To whom, she asked, were we critics speaking?

Finally, I used the phrase *Black Feminist Criticism* as the title of my book because it seemed to me, in 1984, as it still does that few Black women critics were willing to claim the term *feminist* in their titles. *Women* was an acceptable term, but the political implications of the term *feminist* meant that it was fast giving way to the more neutral term *gender*. I believed it was important to place the term on the Black literary map, so to speak, even if it were only a reminder of an orientation no longer in vogue.

My introduction was an appeal to practice as one decisive factor in defining a Black feminist criticism. In 1985 Hortense Spillers contributed another point of view. Along with Marjorie Pryse, she edited a volume entitled *Conjuring: Black Women, Fiction and Literary Tradition*,[15] which included essays by Black and white women as well as Black men. The subtitle was particularly striking to me since the volume privileged fiction, as had the majority of such collections, including my own. And I began to wonder why, in this rich period of Afro-American women's poetry, that genre was being so summarily ignored.

Spillers's afterword, entitled "Cross-currents, Discontinuities: Black Women's Fiction," made it clear that "the community of Black women

writing in the US can be regarded as a vivid new fact of national life." She
defines this community as "those composed of fiction writers, as well as
writers of criticism who are also teachers of literature."[16] In emphasizing the
overlapping of these categories, she saw that the academy was fast becoming
the site of this community and pointed to one reason why perhaps criticism
had taken the direction it had. She might have added as well that new
development might be one reason criticism had become so focused on
fiction. Perhaps intellectual analysis is more suited to fiction and the essay
than it is to poetry and drama – genres that insist on the emotions, the
passions, the senses as well as the intellect as equally effective ways of
knowing.

In characterizing Afro-American women's fiction as a series of discontinuities and relating these discontinuities to other American writing – to
Faulkner, Dreiser, Wright – Spillers constructed a picture of American
literature unthinkable in the academic world of 1974. And by using
language associated with "new" critical approaches, she demonstrated how
an overview of Afro-American women's fiction converged with the more
conventional American literary tradition. Her essay extended the perimeters
of Black feminist criticism(s) in that they could now be situated in the
study of American letters as an entirety. Spillers was clearly responding
to the impetus for revised canons by showing how Afro-American women's
fiction intersected with the currents of other literatures in the United
States.

Canon formation has become one of the thorny dilemmas for the Black
feminist critic. Even as white women, Blacks, people of color attempt to
reconstruct that body of American literature considered to be *the* literature,
we find ourselves confronted with the realization that we may be imitating
the very structure that shut our literatures out in the first place. And that
judgments we make about, for example, the BBBs (Big Black Books) are
determined not only by "quality," that elusive term, but by what we academicians value, what points of view, what genre and forms we privilege.

We finally must wonder about whether this activity, which cannot be
value free, will stifle the literatures we have been promoting. For while few
white male American critics feel compelled to insinuate "white" literary
works into *our* characterizations of American history and culture, we are
almost always in a position of having to insinuate our works into their
schema.[17] Spillers concludes her afterword with a provocative statement:
"The day will come, I would dare to predict, when the Black American
women's writing community will reflect the currents of both the New new
critical procedures and the various literatures concurrent with them."[18] One
might also turn that statement around. We might wonder, given that Afro-
American women's writing is so clearly at the vortex of sex, race, and class

factors that mitigate the notion of democracy at the core of "traditional" American literatures, whether one might want to predict the day when other literatures will reflect the currents of the Black American women's writing community.

While Spillers was still concerned with Afro-American women's literature as a recognizable literary tradition, Hazel Carby, in the introduction to her *Reconstructing Womanhood* (1987), was positively negative about the use of the term *tradition*. In "Rethinking Black Feminist Theory," Carby insisted that Black feminist criticism has "too frequently been reduced to an experiential relationship that is assumed to exist between Black women as readers and Black women as writers who represent Black women's reality" and that "this reliance on a common or shared experience is essentialist and ahistorical." Her book, she stated, "does not assume the existence of a tradition or traditions of Afro-American intellectual thought that have been constructed as paradigmatic of Afro-American history."[19]

In what frame is her book situated? Carby tells us that her inquiry "works within the theoretical premises of societies – 'structured in dominance' by class, by race, and by gender and is a materialist account of the cultural production of Black women intellectuals within the social relations that inscribed them."[20] As Valerie Smith pointed out in her review of Carby's book in *Women's Review of Books, Reconstructing Womanhood* signals a new direction in Black feminist criticism in that Carby is not as much interested in Afro-American women writers as she is in constructing a Black female intellectual history.[21]

Ironically, in reconstructing that history, Carby turns to creative writers/novelists. Perhaps that is because Afro-American writers, female and male, are central, pivotal, predominant figures in Afro-American intellectual history. Why that is so would take volumes to investigate, but one explanation might be that the usual modes of European/American intellectual production were not accessible to or particularly effective for Afro-Americans. That is, the thoroughly rationalist approach of European intellectual discourse might have seemed to them to be too one-dimensional, too narrow, more easily co-opted than narratives, poetry, nonlinear forms where the ambiguities and contradictions of their reality could be more freely expressed and that in these forms they could address themselves to various audiences – their own folk as well as those readers of the dominant culture. In any case, a large number if not the majority of those considered intellectuals in the Afro-American world, female or male, were or attempted to be creative writers – which might account for some of the focus Afro-American intellectual critics have had on creative literature.

No doubt Carby's emphasis on the reconstruction of a Black female intellectual history is needed. And that history can now be imagined and

speculated about by her and others, as it could not have been even a decade
ago, because the words and works of Afro-American women of the past are
more accessible. Yet Carby's approach, as she articulates it, does not seem to
allow for other emphases within the arena of Black feminist criticism, and the
work she can now do is possible because others pursued different orienta-
tions from her own. Twenty years ago, scholars who used the language and
approach she uses (and it is indeed a primarily academic language) were
completely opposed to the inclusion of gender as central to their analyses
and in fact called that term "essentialist." Nor could Carby be doing the
work she is doing unless a space for it was created by a powerful contemporary Afro-American women's literature which in part comes out of the
very paradigm she denies. What, I wonder, would Frances Harper or Pauline
Hopkins think of her denial of the possibility of Afro-American literary
history?

In addition, as my and other overviews of the development of Afro-
American literature suggest, there is more of an inclination in the academic
and publishing worlds (and we might ask why) to accept sociological/poli-
tical analyses of Black writers – female, male – whether they be from a
materialist or bourgeois point of view, than to conceive of them as artists
with their own ideas, imagination, forms. This seems to be a privilege
reserved for only a few selected white men. Finally one must ask whether
the study of an intellectual tradition necessitates the denial of an imaginative,
creative one? Who is to say that the European emphasis on rational intellectual discourse as the measure of a people's history is superior to those
traditions that value creativity, expression, paradox in the constructing of
their historical process?

Carby's introduction brings the debate as to what Black feminist criticism
is full circle, back to Mary Helen Washington's essay in the August 1974
Black World in that Washington's assumptions about the relationship
between Black women's writings and the reality of a shared experience
among Black women are held suspect – a question worth pursuing. What is
so riveting to me is that the term *Black feminist criticism* continues to be
undefinable – not fixed. For many that might seem catastrophic; for me it is
an indication that so much still needs to be done – for example, reading
the works of the writers, in order to understand their ramifications. Even as
I cannot believe all that has been accomplished in the last 15 years –
a complete revision of, conceptualization of nineteenth-century Afro-
American literature, and a redirecting of definitions in contemporary life
about women's sexuality, motherhood, relationships, history, race/class,
gender intersections, political structures, spirituality as perceived through
the lens of contemporary Afro-American women – there is so much yet
to do.

So – what do we think we're doing anyway? More precisely, what might we have to do at this juncture, in 1990?

For one – we might have to confront the positives and negatives of what it means to become institutionalized in universities.

Does this mean we will no longer respond to the communal/erotic art that poetry and drama can be because it is so difficult to reduce these forms to ideological wrangling? As Audre Lorde has so profoundly expressed, it is often in poetry that we imagine that which we have been afraid to imagine – that poetry is an important source of imagining new ideas for change.

Does our emphasis on definitions and theories mean that we will close ourselves to those, the many, who know or care little about the intense debates that take so much of our time in universities? Can we conceive of our literary critical activities as related to the activism necessary to substantively change Black women's lives?

Does our scholarly advancement mean that more and more of us will turn to the study of past writers as a safer pursuit in the university which apparently has difficulty engaging in the study of present-day literatures? As necessary as the study of the past is, it is just as important to be engaged in the history that we are now making – one that has been so powerfully ignited by the contemporary writers.

In spite of the critical clamor, how many of us have actually produced sustained readings, critiques?

Can we ignore the fact that fewer and fewer Blacks are receiving Ph.Ds? In fact, only 820 in 1986. Although Black women are not the only ones who can do feminist criticism, it would be a significant loss if they were absent from this enterprise.

Do we assume that this orientation will be here even at the turn of the century?

To whom are *we* accountable? And what social relations are in/scribing us?

Does history teach us anything about the relationship between ideas, language, and practice? By 2000 will our voices sound like women's voices, Black women's voices to anyone?

What do we want to do anyway and for whom do we think we're doing it?

Notes

The title of this chapter is a riff on Gloria T. Hull's title, "What It Is I Think She's Doing Anyhow," in Barbara Smith, ed., *Home Girls: A Black Feminist Anthology* (New York: Kitchen Table: Women of Color Press, 1983), pp. 124–42.

1   *Black World* 23, 10 (August 1974).
2   Toni Cade, *The Black Woman* (New York: New American Library, 1970).
3   Alice Walker, "In Search of our Mothers' Gardens," *Ms.* 2, 71 (May 1974).
4   Mary Helen Washington, "Black Women Image Makers," *Black World* 23, 10 (August 1974): 10–19; quote, 11.
5   Originally published as Barbara Smith, "Toward a Black Feminist Criticism," *Conditions II* 11 (October 1977): 25–44. Cited from Judith Newton and Deborah Rosenfelt, eds., *Feminist Criticism and Social Change* (New York: Methuen, 1985).
6   Ibid., 3–4.
7   Ibid., 5.
8   Ibid., 16.
9   Ibid., 8–9.
10   "The Black Sexism Debate," *Black Scholar* 10, 8–9 (May/June 1979): 14–67.
11   Audre Lorde, "The Great American Disease," *Black Scholar* 10, 8–9 (May/June 1979): 17.
12   Deborah E. McDowell, "New Directions for Black Feminist Criticism," *Black American Literature Forum*, no. 14, 1980.
13   Michele Wallace, "Who Dat Say Who Dat When I Say Who Dat?" *Village Voice Literary Supplement* (April 12, 1988): 18–21.
14   Barbara Christian, *Black Feminist Criticism: Perspectives on Black Women Writers* (New York: Pergamon Press, 1985).
15   Marjorie Pryse and Hortense Spillers, eds., *Conjuring: Black Women Fiction and Literary Tradition* (Bloomington: Indiana University Press, 1985).
16   Hortense Spillers, "Afterword: Crosscurrents, Discontinuities: Black Women's Fiction," in Pryse and Spillers, *Conjuring*, 249–61.
17   For a current overview of canonical issues in American literature see Frederick Crews, "Whose American Renaissance," *New York Review of Books* (October 27, 1988) 68–81. For an alternate view on the dangers of canonical formation in Afro-American literature, see Theodore D. Mason, Jr., "Between the Populist and the Scientist: Ideology and Power in Recent Afro-American Literary Criticism" or "The Dozens as Scholarship," *Callaloo* 11, 3 (Summer 1988): 606–15.
18   Spillers, "Afterword," 259.
19   Hazel Carby, "Woman's Era: Rethinking Black Feminist Theory," *Reconstructing Womanhood: The Emergence of the Afro-American Woman Novelist* (New York: Oxford University Press, 1987), p. 16.
20   Ibid., 17.
21   Valerie Smith, "A Self-Critical Tradition," *Women's Review of Books* 5, 5 (February 1988): 15.

Supplementary Readings and Media Resources

Supplementary Readings

"Artists and Artisans" (entire issue) *Sage: A Scholarly Journal on Black Women*, 4:1 (Spring 1987).

Christian, Barbara, "The Race for Theory," *Feminist Studies*, 14:1 (Spring 1989): 67–79. (Revised from earlier article in *Cultural Critique* 6 (Spring 1987): 51–63.)

Hull, Gloria, Patricia Bell Scott and Barbara Smith, eds. *All the Women Are White, All the Blacks Are Men, But Some of Us Are Brave: Black Women's Studies* (Old Westbury, NY: Feminist Press, 1982).

Smith Barbara, ed. *Home Girls: A Black Feminist Anthology* (New York: Kitchen Table: Women of Color Press, 1983).

Media Resources

Bridglal, Sindamani, *Identifiable Qualities: Toni Morrison*. 30 minutes, color, video, 1989. (Women Make Movies.)

Morrison, Toni, *The Nobel Lecture in Literature* (New York: Random House Audio Publishing, 1994), 30 minutes.

Osman, Samira, *Alice Walker and "The Color Purple": Inside a Modern Classic*. 60 minutes, video, color, BBC documentary, 1986. (Films for the Humanities.)

Part II

The Moving Image

Overview: The Moving Image

Part II, on the moving image, presents four articles analyzing popularized manifestations of Black women over time in various media. "The Tattered Queens," written by actress Ruby Dee in 1966, begins with a lament over the scarcity of substantial roles for Black women in film and theatre. However, the article is not a complaint but a call for concerted efforts to alter the circumstances, both in front of and behind the camera, in training programs to support playwrights and to maintain repertory companies. It is a prescient piece, a reminder that art can be utilized as a vital tool to bring about progressive changes in Black people's lives. Dee stresses that Black people must become "proficient in every phase" of image construction, lobbying for inclusion at every level of media production.

Ruby Dee is known to contemporary audiences for her roles in *Do the Right Thing* (1989) and *Jungle Fever* (1991). She has long been revered for her portrayal of Ruth Younger in Lorraine Hansberry's *A Raisin in the Sun*, both the 1959 stage play and the 1961 film adaptation. In 1989 Dee produced and starred in the Public Broadcasting Service television play *My Name is Zora*, based upon the life of novelist Zora Neale Hurston. M. Neema Barnette, an experienced Black female filmmaker, directed the program.

Mainstream cultural representations of Black women, as Ruby Dee accurately chronicled, have indeed been persistently negative. Images perpetuated throughout generations are: the sexual siren; the rotund, full-bosomed nurturing mother figure; the dominating matriarch incarnate; eternally ill-tempered wenches; and wretched victims.

Recasting dominant representations of Black women is a major goal of the writers in Part II. In the chapter from my book *Black Women as Cultural Readers* on director Julie Dash's *Daughters of the Dust*, I examine its success reconstructing a cultural history. The film, the first created by a Black woman to be released in commercial distribution, is a benchmark in its widespread public recognition. Although Black females have been making films since the early part of the twentieth century, the overwhelming response from audiences impelled critical attention to *Daughters of the Dust*. Its themes of empowerment, resistance, and collective action are enacted by four generations of Black women seeking to reconcile past tribulations from enslavement with a heritage of survival and triumph derived from their own inner resources. *Daughters of the Dust* is a foundational text, for it portends a break from both mainstream white representations and Black, male-directed films in its progressive and subversive presentation of a new cinematic reality for Black women.

Cinematographer, filmmaker, and writer C. A. Griffith emphasizes the importance of analyzing every phase of film construction in "Below the Line: (Re)Calibrating the Filmic Gaze." Griffith writes from the perspective of a veteran who worked as a camera assistant on music videos, feature films and as director of photography for the independent documentary *A Litany for Survival: The Life and Work of Audre Lorde* (1995), directed by Ada Gay Griffin and Michelle Parkerson. Insightful guidelines are applied in Griffith's examination of her own video *Border Line... Family Pictures* (1996).

Television's hybrid nature and potent effects in circulating meanings throughout society are interrogated in the final article. Communication scholar Sheri Parks reexamines the significance of Hansberry's *A Raisin in the Sun* through its various transmutations: from stage play, film adaptation, to its PBS presentation in 1989. The television version marked the thirtieth anniversary of the play's Broadway première, reinserting originally deleted material considered at the time too controversial for either theater or film. "In My Mother's House: Black Feminist Aesthetics, Television, and *A Raisin in the Sun*" is provocative. Parks submits that Hansbery has been too cavalierly dismissed from the feminist canon. She repositions the play and Hansberry within an activist paradigm, celebrating the playwright for her conscientiously nuanced elucidation of Black women confronting the debilitating constraints of race, caste, and gender oppression.

Stock characterizations of Black women have been criticized in each of the articles in this section on the moving image. Visual evidence is provided in the documentary *Color Adjustment* (1991), directed by Marlon Riggs, narrated by Ruby Dee. Clips from well-known television shows include those from early 1950s situation comedies "Amos 'n' Andy," and "Beulah." Later programs from the 1960s and 1970s were severely criticized though popular with mainstream audiences. Examples in the documentary of the most familiar are "Julia," "Good Times," and "All in the Family." Scholars, television actors and producers comment on the production history and possible effects of these shows.

Screenings of Dash's film *Daughters of the Dust* and the accompanying video *Cinematic Jazz of Julie Dash* (1992) are particularly beneficial in understanding how images of Black women can be celebratory rather than a caricature. The short video *Cinematic Jazz* presents an interview with Dash and clips from her body of work, including *Four Women* (1975), *Diary of an African Nun* (1977), *Illusions* (1982), and *Praise House* (1991), in addition to scenes from *Daughters of the Dust*.

Lorraine Hansberry was as famous for her play *A Raisin in the Sun* as Alice Walker became for her novel *The Color Purple* and Toni Morrison for *Beloved*. In May 1959 Hansberry received the Drama Critics' Circle Award, becoming the youngest person, the fifth woman, and the only Black person up to that time to receive the award. The honor was not lightly given, for the competitors included Archibald MacLeish's *JB*, Eugene O'Neill's *A Touch of the Poet*, and Tennessee William's *Sweet Bird of Youth*. The documentary *Lorraine Hansberry: The Black Experience in the Creation of Drama* (1976) contains interviews with the playwright and scenes from several of her creative works. The body of work includes *A Raisin in the Sun*, the television play *The Drinking Gourd* (1960), *What Use Are Flowers* (1961), *The Sign in Sidney Brustein's Window* (1964), and *Les Blancs* (1964).

4

Some Reflections on the Negro Actress:
The Tattered Queens

Ruby Dee

Dee, Ruby. "Some Reflections on the Negro Actress: The Tattered Queens." (*Negro Digest*, 15 April, 1966): 32–6.

I maintain that we actresses must concern ourselves more with the fate of each other and of the younger actresses coming along, by helping to find material and getting it produced, by promoting scholarships for intensive training.

When I first learned about the death of Dorothy Dandridge, a tremendous sadness came over me. I'd known her slightly only, really – over the years; our paths had never crossed in work – occasionally socially; but I had seen her, mostly as an actress and remembered with joy her beautiful performance as Carmen Jones in the movie *Carmen Jones*. I felt I knew her as well as I knew myself.... What, as a young performer, she aspired to, what she had to settle for – the active search for opportunities, the sporadic success, the long periods of nothing to look forward to, the deliberate pretense of indifference, the deep self-doubt; a major role – then waiting, waiting...

She was lucky, for her career as an actress began with a head start as a singer, and between the betweens, she could fill club dates. (How fortunate not to be "Just an actress.")

I wondered if the tragedy of Dorothy was not indeed the tragedy of all Negro actresses.

I worked with an actress once in a huge theatre in the Bronx, in a play – *Arsenic and Old Lace*. I had vaguely known of her. "What style she had," I recall thinking, "what grace." I wondered where she had been trained. There was something about her personality – distinctly royal, profoundly human. She might have played any role from a queen to a peasant, representing any race or country. Her name was Abbie Mitchell. She had worked with some of the leading talents of the early 1900s, she had been acclaimed here, but mostly in Europe, an extraordinary soprano, a *prima donna*. I felt fortunate that our lives had touched. At the time of our meeting I was quite young and coming along well "for a colored girl" at the time. I believe that often young performers lacking a continuity of experience, lacking knowledge of history of entertainment, of the tradition and great contribution that our people have made to the theatre, may tend to feel that a whole new world begins with each newcomer. Not so.

Inspired by Abbie Mitchell, I began to read books about and by Negro performers. I am deeply grateful to such people as James Weldon Johnson, Tom Fletcher, and Edith Isaacs for having written on the subject. It was through their books that I began to feel a sense of belonging somewhere as an actress . . . as part of a tradition. I'd almost missed knowing Abbie Mitchell. Where was her scrapbook? Where was there a more complete description of her life? Couldn't my husband, Ossie Davis, write her story as a play? Why didn't I talk to her more, ask her what it is like to reach the top? Is there a top for Negro actresses? Why wasn't she as well known and as frequently employed as the leading white performers of the time? Retired? Why? What would she play next? It was some years later by then. After talking about her, after asking older performers who "came out of retirement" about her, I finally wrote her asking for an appointment. The letter came back unanswered, unopened. It was marked, "Deceased."

Rose McClendon and the famous walk down those stairs (even Ethel Barrymore complimented her on it, with kindness that comes only from being white, regularly employed, and nationally recognized), who was she? Had she worked in more than a half dozen plays I'd seen referred to? Where was there a record of her accomplishments? I remember tall, sensitive, Edna Thomas. Why don't I see her on television sometimes – or Broadway – on or off? Retired now, perhaps; but because she wants to be?

It seems that Negro actresses enjoyed a fuller creative life in the old community theatre: e.g. the all-Negro Lafayette Players. Such actresses as Edna Thomas, Hilda Offley, Evelyn Ellis, and Laura Bowman knew and benefited from working in stock companies. They had a chance to more fully explore the depths of their talent. They were not primarily restricted to plays about Negroes. One may be extremely talented, *but only constant exposure makes a performer stage-worthy and camera-worthy.* I never heard of a Negro starlet with a seven-year contract, learning the ropes in B movies and studio schools. Quite a few moderately talented white actresses have blossomed into fame and fortune under such attention. What might have happened to Dorothy Dandridge with a seven-year contract? And the security that goes with it?

We actresses are so accustomed to the fact that performers such as Ethel Waters, Lena Horne, Beah Richards, Pauline Myers, Jane White, Hilda Simms, and Claudia McNeil have no part in television, or work regularly in stock, that we stop trying. We hear talk of integration and things getting better, and indeed there are some marvelous integrated commercials, and more Negroes actors appearing in incidental parts, and every now and then racially mixed leads, and an occasional all-Negro show, but these are isolated instances, not a trend indicating that things may be somewhat better in an individual sense. Group participation in the creative life of the country is less than ever.

We cannot grow in isolation. The Negro actress is still acting on the fringes, not really a part, only occasionally let in, better off portraying the prostitute, the second – roles written with not enough imagination and truth. We can point to no one of us who has remotest chance of reaching the prominence of Helen Hayes, Ethel Barrymore, Bette Davis, etc. No one with that kind of economic opportunity either. We dream, we scream, we pretend, we picket. Or like some other of our most gifted – Mildred Joan Smith, Muriel Smith, Marion Douglas – we quit. Will the newer names on the horizon – like Cicely Tyson and Diana Sands and Gloria Foster – escape the paucity of opportunity that always seems to follow occasionally spurts of comparative good fortune for "colored stars"?

When we talk or write about ourselves and our place in American society so much is necessarily a lament. But perhaps a look at stark reality may help clarify and make objective our grievances, indicate alternatives to despair through some program of action. I fully realize the cultural poverty that is abroad in the land. Leading white actresses are afflicted by some of the same ills that affect the Negro actress. (Their lowest level of employment is, however, often commensurate with our highest.) There are many more parts written for men than for women, white and Black. But my concern here is with the Negro actress, who faces double discrimination – that of sex and that of race. What must we do – we Negro actresses – to be saved?

We must, most certainly, make a determined effort to encourage our playwrights – particularly female – to write for all media. There is a kind of autocracy about an entertainer – each one sort of spinning around in a personal orbit, on individual momentum. I maintain that we actresses must concern ourselves more with the fate of each other, and of the younger actresses coming along, by helping to find material and getting it produced, by promoting scholarships for intensive training. We must also see to it that the new theatres springing up over the country include Negro actors as basic and intrinsic parts of their companies. Indeed, the future of the theatre may lie in repertory companies, and on the road.

In the past, musicians – singers and instrumentalists – fared better in relation to their art than we have. They have been for the most part innovators and pace-setters. (Top money and opportunity, however, still go to their white imitators.) Innovators in song, dance, and language. Theirs is a development springing from the soul roots of our people. But that same "soul roots" truth of the lives of our people has yet to be explored in drama. We know best on stage and screen the prostitute. The Negro Maid (as a person rather than a stereotype), the Negro Mother, the Average Woman, and the Middle-class Woman have for the most part yet to be dealt with in depth.

This holds true of the heroines of our history also. We must ask our playwrights to do better by us. We do have, as a people, an address to life, a cry, a joy, that is particularly ours, that has yet to be fully and unselfconsciously put forward. Women must become producers – pioneering and prospecting among our own for backing. (I am particularly gratified at the work done in this connection by Maria Cole and Juanita Poitier.) We must see to it that our young people consider the very important backstage and off-camera roles as technicians. More people see films than ever go to the theatre. If one of the purposes of art is to effect change, we must make every effort to become proficient in every phase of filmmaking, working for inclusion in American films at every possible level. The reality is that we are but 10 percent of a population which is geared to segregate and to discriminate – improving, I believe, but desperately in need of artistic effort to help change the image of the Negro and so effect social change more quickly. As art not only reflects life but also influences it, we must dedicate ourselves to the improvement of life and its truths – about women, about Negroes.

The Negro actress cannot afford to be isolated from this effort. We must not evade the fact that in today's America most Negro "stars" are at best tattered queens, haunted always by an aura of tragedy, failure, and defeat. But we must not be defeated. With a sober look at what is happening with us today, we must make every effort to make things better for those who will come after us.

And I would especially encourage those young women of my race most likely to be overlooked – the very black, the very Africanesque – to study and to work. I believe they have shied away from theatre because their particular kind of beauty has not only not been encouraged, but has been heretofore too often rejected. But how else can a people know its own beauty except that those artists most representative of it come forth and tell it? The fair-skinned, those nearer to Caucasian in appearance and manners, have always fared better in our theatre. But are we not, basically, of African descent? In the better times to come, there will be equal place on our stage and screens for all shades, all types, all colors. We must see to it that this is so.

5

Daughters of the Dust

Jacqueline Bobo

"Daughters of the Dust." In Jacqueline Bobo, *Black Women as Cultural Readers* (New York: Columbia University Press, 1995), pp. 133–65, 214–15.

When a work is so densely seeded within black culture, a lot of people who are not from the culture will say that they find the film inaccessible or they find it is not engaging. What they are saying is that they do not feel privileged by the film. So they choose not to engage or allow themselves to become engaged.
                                                    – Julie Dash, in an interview with the author

From the slow, leisurely pace of the film's unfolding to the strategic place-ment of visual references to earlier Black artists, director Julie Dash estab-lishes the creative provenance of *Daughters of the Dust*. It is a film deeply saturated in Black life, history, and culture and is intended to honor those traditions from which it is spawned. By very conscious tributes to the photographs of Harlem photographer James Van derZee, the religious folk dramas of early Black filmmaker Spencer Williams, and the unorthodox cinematic vision of Black director Bill Gunn in *Ganja and Hess* (1973), Dash constructed a work that places Black people at the center of the story.

Van derZee's portraits were first "discovered" by the public at large during an exhibition of photographs entitled "Harlem on My Mind" at the Metropolitan Museum of Art in 1968. Van derZee was 83 at the time and had lived and worked in Harlem since the turn of the century. A self-taught photographer, Van derZee trained himself through experimentation with the use of different kinds of cameras as well as with the varieties of developing and printing methods. Although the pictures that Van derZee took were a means to earn a living, he exhibited such care in the composition of each individual portrait that the photos were later considered to be works of art. One of the techniques he used was multiple imaging, in which, through double printing, one photograph was superimposed on another. A striking example of this technique is the now famous funeral photograph of the daughter of the minister of the largest Black church in New York. Blanche Powell, daughter of Adam Clayton Powell, Sr., and the older sister of the man who would become the first Black elected United States congressman from New York, died when she was not yet 30. Van derZee had previously taken a photograph of Blanche Powell as a young girl, and this he superimposed on the one of her lying in her coffin.[1]

Dash emulated Van derZee's multiple-image technique in the composition of her film. Through lap dissolves that end with one shot superimposed on another – what Dash terms "layered dissolves" – she re-creates a technique that has its origins in the work of one of the first, if not the first, Black photographers. The beginning of the film is an example of this superimposition: through the careful composition of individual shots, and through editing in such a way that the scenes become iconic portraits, the images resonate beyond their duration on the screen.

As the film opens, after the initial credits are shown, a prologue explains that the setting of the story is the Sea Islands located off the mainland of South Carolina and Georgia. The inhabitants are descendants of Black people captured from Africa who have chosen to live in isolation and have retained much of the culture that was brought by the earlier Africans. The island people are called Gullah. On this, their last day on Ibo Landing before their migration north, there is a family gathering in celebration of the move. The feast is conceived as a Last Supper before the family takes its leave of the island. The time is 1902.

After the prologue there is a series of slow dissolves over a background sound of the wind blowing and then a close-up of a pair of hands covered with soil that is being blown away by the wind. Toward the end of the dissolve the hands begin to spread apart, and their image is superimposed on that of a fully clothed woman washing herself in a river. That image is held for a time before the start of the next dissolve, over what appears to be a nightstand in a bedroom. There is a slow pan left, to a bed with gossamer netting over it. Two people are lying in the bed. There is another slow dissolve to a wide-angled shot of the mouth of a very large river, where a boat appears very small in the distance. The next dissolve ends in a shot of a woman standing majestically in a boat that is maneuvered by three men, and is followed by a dissolve to an extreme close-up of a St. Christopher medal worn around the woman's neck. After the fade to Black the title of the film appears.

The changing of the scenes is accomplished precisely and is synchronized so that the images at the end of each dissolve correspond to the words spoken in the voice-over. The person who is speaking, we later learn, is the one standing in the boat. The voice-over timed to the shot of the woman bathing in the river begins with these words: "I am the first and the last, I am the honored one and the scorned one." There is a period of silence until the voice-over of the bedroom scene states: "I am the whore and the holy one; I am the wife and the virgin; I am the barren one, and many are my daughters." After a quiet interlude the voice-over accompanying the image of the woman standing in the boat reveals: "I am the silence that you cannot understand; I am the utterance of my name."

For Dash, each dissolve means something; it is more than a transition device signaling the passage of time. The dissolves are used to convey important information, such as in the opening of the film. They are also a homage to Van derZee and the method he used to compose his photographs featuring the Black inhabitants of Harlem during the early decades of this century.

The words spoken during the dissolves are taken from the collection of Gnostic scriptures in the volume *Nag Hammadi Library*. The passage is entitled "Thunder: Perfect Mind." It is used to introduce the audience to the fact that this is a Black woman's story, telling of the fate of Black women since their journey across the sea. The juxtaposition of the images noted earlier with "Thunder: Perfect Mind" invokes the symbolism of this passage. Parallelism, antithesis, and paradox are conveyed by the contrasting phrases: first, last; honored, scorned; barren, multiple progeny; silence, utterance. "Thunder: Perfect Mind" is interpreted as a revelation discourse that is unique in its use of a female figure as the speaker. It is understood as encompassing the active, intelligent element in all things. Through reason, the female figure is able to provide instruction, to those who listen, about the course of true life.[2]

The hands covered with soil serves as a play upon the title of the film, which Dash took from a passage in the Bible. Although the words from the book of Ezekiel refer to "ye sons of the dust" Dash paraphrased it as "daughters of the dust."[3] The old woman bathing in the river symbolizes rebirth and the integral connection of the old with the new. Later the theme will be expanded upon with the introduction of the Unborn Child, who has been beckoned from the "otherworld" by the matriarch of the family as a way of healing the growing dissensions among the people of the island.

The sleeping couple are at odds because the husband, Eli, is uncertain that the child carried by the wife, Eula, is his. He wants her to reveal the name of the man who raped her; Eula refuses. The woman in the boat represents those Black women who have lived life as it has been handed to them yet have not lost contact with their past or been broken or bowed. For this reason she stands proudly in the boat. The dissolve to the close-up of the

St. Christopher medal recalls old photographs of Black women at the turn of the century. It shows that every culture has its talisman, whether it be "scraps of memory" contained in a tin can, as for the great-grandmother, or charms worn around the neck, as for the worldly granddaughter. The old woman, Nana Peazant, will later ask her granddaughter, Yellow Mary, in a tone tinged with skepticism, what she is wearing around her neck. She queries her, "What kind of belief that is?" She then asks her with concern, "Do it protect you?" as she leans her forehead against Yellow Mary's while her hands are placed lightly on her shoulders.

Later in the film an additional layer of information is added when the woman who was standing in the boat, Yellow Mary, tells Eula, the character who has been raped by a white landowner and is now pregnant: "At the same time, the rape of a colored woman is as common as the fish in the sea." This is the first and only time the word *rape* is used to describe what has happened to Eula. Not only is the word not spoken but the action is deliberately concealed. Dash states that the historical facts of the sexual carnage of Black women by white men is a story that has been referred to so many times that it has lost its potency and its ability to enrage. For this reason, she felt it was important to deal with the aftereffects of the rape, to show how the couple and the family handle it; therein lies their demonstration of the strength needed to survive.[4]

To further enhance the horrors of enslavement and lift the images from the mundane and the ordinary, Dash felt it was necessary to show the family's hands permanently stained from the poisonous indigo dye that was the source of riches for those who had captured the people on the island. Dash reveals that she knew the permanent imprint of the dye was historically inaccurate, but she felt it was imperative to reconstruct the familiar symbols of enslavement – the scars on the backs and the chains around the hands and feet – and recast the images to re-create the shock associated with the enormity of the acts of enslavement.[5]

The baptismal procession to the river is another cinematic reconstruction that has a dual purpose – both to honor the religious "passion plays" of early Black filmmaker Spencer Williams in his films *Go Down Death* (1944) and *The Blood of Jesus* (1941), which feature similar processions, and to provide a contrast and comparison of religious beliefs between the people on the island. The Black people in the procession are following the new mores of Christianity learned from their sojourn in this country and are antagonistic to the beliefs of the Islamic religion practiced by Bilal Muhammed, the last Black person brought over from Africa, who still maintains his African traditions and practices.

In the final third of the film two scenes are intercut to reveal this blending of the past and present and its significance for the future of the people of the island. The scenes involve Yellow Mary and Eula sitting under an umbrella on the beach and Bilal Muhammed walking past a line of Baptist worshipers as they follow their leader in a baptismal procession to the river.

Yellow Mary is lying down in such a way that Eula can lean back comfortably against her under the umbrella. She tells Eula about a pink satin case that she saw once on her travels. The case had a handle on one side that could be turned so that music played. Yellow Mary tells Eula that even though she could not afford the case, in her mind she possessed it and put all her bad memories in the case and locked them there. She said: "So I could take them out, look at them when I felt like it, and figure it out, you know. But I didn't want them inside of me. I don't let nothing in that case or outside that case tell me who I am or how I should feel about me." After Yellow Mary finishes talking she and Eula turn their heads to the right, and that image is held in a medium shot before a cut to the Christians walking to the river.

The people in the procession are dressed in white robes. The lead person is cradling a Bible in both hands. The shot is framed so that the worshipers walk straight toward the camera and out of the frame just as there is a cut to an old man passing, holding a prayer rug. The leader of the Christians says the man's name three times – "Bilal, Bilal, Bilal Muhammed" – and enjoins the man to come with them to the river. As the leader raises his hand in a gesture of entreaty, he says to Bilal, "Come wash away your sins in the blood of the lamb Jesus." As Bilal completely ignores the procession and continues on his way, two other men in the group respond to his actions angrily, making sarcastic comments to his back: "Let him go, Deacon. Bilal's a 'salt water, Negro.' He has no shame." The other man replies in kind, "He's the master of the sun and the moon." After the taunts and jeers at Bilal the procession continues on its way out of the frame, and a long shot of open space is held until there is a cut back to Yellow Mary and Eula under the umbrella. They have now been joined by Trula, Yellow Mary's lover.

Yellow Mary tells Eula that it is time for her to depart from the island to go to Nova Scotia. She feels it is an appropriate time for her to leave; she shares her plans in a veiled reference to her life as a prostitute: "I never had too much trouble making a dollar, you know. Never needed nobody to help me do that. I can't stand still, got to keep moving, new faces, new places. Nova Scotia will be good to me." There is a cut back to the baptismal party at the river as a woman is dunked under the water. Another cut shows the other Christians standing on the banks of the river with their hands held high, rejoicing as the woman is baptized.

The scenes of the baptism hold particular significance in the film for they both refer back to the films of Spencer Williams, especially *The Blood of Jesus*, and rework a worn-out tradition first used in the film *Hallelujah* (1929). The baptismal scene in *Hallelujah* was commented upon by a *New York Times* reviewer as a faithful rendering of "the peculiarly typical religious hysteria of the darkies and their gullibility... their hankering after salvation, the dread of water in the baptism."[6] In the film the director, King Vidor, has the Black actors jump around hysterically, as if they were overcome by religious frenzy after their encounter with the water.

The opening scenes of *The Blood of Jesus* follow a procession of worshippers walking slowly behind a minister flanked by two women as the group advances toward the water. Those who are a part of the ceremony are dressed somberly in dark clothing, while the people who are to be baptized are in white gowns. Gospel singing provides an accompaniment to the march to the river. When the baptismal ritual begins, one of the women begins to line out a hymn with the others following her lead as the minister and a deacon lower a woman into the water. Williams's film exhibits a fidelity and dignity to the proceedings that had not been shown in films directed by white people. According to cultural scholar Adrienne Lanier-Seward in "A Film Portrait of Black Ritual Expression: *The Blood of Jesus*," Williams's work set a precedent as a model example of Black cultural expression in film.[7] Lanier-Seward feels that Williams deserves to be remembered for the way in which his film "employed structures and themes from Afro-American folk drama and religious expression to simultaneously entertain Black audiences and acknowledge the culture's expressive style" (p. 198).

The baptismal sequence in *Daughters of the Dust* is an acknowledgment of Williams's contribution to the history of Black films. In Dash's tribute the same formal style is used as the baptismal party heads toward the water. There is an additional quality in *Daughters of the Dust*, for it is clear that the Christian believers are under scrutiny (by the filmmaker) as they reverently adhere to the tenets of their new religion. There is also a subtle commentary on contemporary Black people who likewise disparage those who would practice a religion much older than Christianity. That the baptismal procession is intercut with the scenes of Yellow Mary and Eula on the beach is indicative of the director's sentiment that everyone handles the crossing over to the "new" world, with its harshness and brutality, in whatever manner they can and still retain their sense of themselves and their integrity; therein lies their solace and comfort. As Yellow Mary re-creates her grandmother's tin can of memories in her vision of the pink satin case holding her demons until she is ready to handle them, so too does Bilal Muhammed exist in a land not of his choosing but in possession of his own traditions, principles, and beliefs.

As Dash discovered during her research for the film, Bilal Muhammed was an actual person who lived on the Sea Islands in the 1800s. He practiced his Islam religion and prayed five times daily. His papers and diaries are still on permanent exhibition at the Smithsonian.[8] In 1902, the time of *Daughters of the Dust*, Bilal's five daughters were still living on the islands, practicing their religion. Dash featured the character Bilal Muhammed in the film because the historical person had never been acknowledged in any other film produced by a Black person, and she felt he needed to be remembered.

The way in which we are first introduced to the character provides a continuity in the overall construction of the film. Just as Bilal is employed as a contrast to the religious fanaticism of the people attending the baptism, so too does he link up with Dash's goal of utilizing cinematic techniques practiced by Black filmmakers from the past as a way to honor and remember them. Thus, she juxtaposes Bilal Muhammed's scenes with those of the young women on the beach.

The women grouped together are seen earlier in the film with Yellow Mary and Trula sitting in a large tree as Eula gazes up at them. The scenes in the tree are influenced by the work of Black director Bill Gunn in *Ganja and Hess*. Gunn's film now holds something of a cult status among film aficionados, but it was suppressed for many years because the distributors did not feel that Gunn had made the film for which he was contracted. The film was made during the boom period of the Black action adventure films, and the distributors wanted to exploit that market while it was being made. The instructions were to make a film about blood. Blood there is in *Ganja and Hess*, but Gunn's project is more than that, for the film concerns an anthropologist, Dr. Hess Greene, who has contracted a rare blood ailment from an artifact he collected on one of his field trips to Africa. Dr. Greene becomes a vampire who survives by sucking blood stolen from blood banks or taken from human beings. Dr. Greene's assistant is George Meda, played by Bill Gunn, an artist who has been institutionalized and is still fighting madness. Meda's estranged wife, Ganja, comes to look for him at Dr. Greene's estate, but George has died, either by successfully committing suicide or being killed by Hess Greene. After Ganja arrives and finds George's body, she joins Dr. Greene in his life as a vampire, and continues it even after Dr. Greene repents and dies.

Gunn's film is an unconventional one that challenges the traditional tenets of filmmaking and the routine understanding of cinema. According to Manthia Diawara and Phyllis Klotman in "*Ganja and Hess*: Vampires, Sex, and Addictions," one of the attractions the film holds for contemporary Black film critics and filmmakers is Gunn's questions regarding the Black artists' responsibilities in a white-controlled art environment and the artists' desire to utilize the resources found within Black life.[9]

The scene from *Ganja and Hess* that resonates in *Daughters of the Dust* concerns George Meda sitting in a tree with a rope looped over a branch of the tree and loosely tied around his neck. The tree is in Dr. Greene's yard. When he goes to look for George and finds him sitting in the tree he is concerned that George will commit suicide on his property and the police will be summoned to interrogate him, the only Black resident of the neighborhood, and thus make him vulnerable because of his vampire secrets. In the scene Hess Greene is looking up at George in the tree, and all we see are George's legs swinging slowly back and forth as he shares his anguish with Dr. Greene.

In the tree sequence in *Daughters of the Dust* both Yellow Mary and Eula tell of their troubles as we see Trula's legs hanging down from the tree, swinging slowly back and forth. As the sequence begins, Yellow Mary and Trula are in the tree, while Eula gazes up at them as they share a cigarette and laugh merrily. There is a cut to a close-up of Eula, who says to Yellow Mary: "As much as I like to fish, I'll never put a pole in that water." Eula tells the story of the young "salt-water girl" who was drowned by her owner. Yellow Mary chides Eula for her parochial ways, saying, "I thought this was supposed to be *Ibo* Landing" – a reference to one of the sustaining myths of the island, according to which the captured Africans, after their arrival on land, walked on water back to their homeland.

Although Eula looks puzzled by Yellow Mary's gentle jibes at the backwardness of the people on the island, she does not seem offended. She tells Yellow Mary of her experience the night before, in which her long-dead mother came to her and took her by the hand. She speaks of the Gullah custom of placing a letter under a glass of water under the bed to summon forth the spirit of those who have died. Eula says that because she needed to talk to her mother, she came to her.

Even though Yellow Mary exclaims over the superstitions of the isolated people on the island, she is still in the grip of Eula's need to find a resolution for her problem with Eli. She eventually questions Eula about whether she has told Eli who raped her. After Eula shakes her head, Yellow Mary tells her she has done the right thing: "There is enough uncertainty in life without having to sit at home wondering which tree your husband's hanging from." Yellow Mary reiterates her charge: "Don't tell him anything."

As the three women remain by the tree Yellow Mary explains to Eula how she came to be "ruint," as she is labeled by the other women on the island. The other people know she is a worldly woman who has earned her keep through prostitution, and they also sense that she and Trula are lovers. Of both relationships the people of the island disapprove. In a remarkable moment in the film, as Yellow Mary sits in the tree there is a close-up of her in profile as she tells Eula how she happened on the life she lived. She shares with Eula the story of her baby being born dead – "And my titty was full of milk. We needed money, so I hired out to a wealthy family." Yellow Mary nursed their baby, even after they moved to Cuba, and they refused to let her return home. She tells Eula, "That's how I got ruint. I want to go home, and they keep me. They keep me. So I fixed a titty. They sent me home."

Yellow Mary's treatment by the family in Cuba parallels Eula's rape by the white landowner. Although she doesn't talk about it, and it is absent from the film, Yellow Mary was herself raped by the husband of the family for whom she worked. This led to her becoming a prostitute to earn the money to leave the family. In the eyes of the people of the island this is part of her depravity, as is her relationship with Trula, the woman she brings home to the island. It is indeed a sexual relationship; the women are lovers. Dash based the relationship between the women on research that she undertook for the film. According to her studies, many of the prostitutes at that time were lesbians or bisexual, and the women traveled together, perhaps as a means of protecting themselves from the hazards of their profession.

Trula also served another purpose in the film: the introduction of her character added additional tension to Yellow Mary's homecoming and provided insights into the character of the people on the island. It wasn't simply that Yellow Mary is a prostitute coming home to her family; and it wasn't just that she was with another woman, or that this woman was truly light-skinned, whereas Yellow Mary has worn that nickname all her life, until she finally wears the name with pride. By bringing someone not from the island into the islanders' midst, Yellow Mary revealed aspects of their recidivist natures. For as much as the ancient African traditions, folkways, and principles of the people on the island are celebrated in the film, their insularity, their pettiness, and their obstinate holding on to many destructive ways are also examined.

The Myth of Ibo Landing

The setting of the film derives its name from three stories, or myths, that have been handed down since the arrival of the inhabitants of the island. The three myths about Ibo Landing – or, as Dash states, two myths and one reality[10] – relate to the fact that the African captives from the Ibo tribe refused to live enslaved. One account of the myth has the captives walking on top of the water all the way back to Africa; another describes how the captives flew over the water back to Africa; the third account, which Bilal Muhammed substantiates in the film, is that the captives walked back into the water, shackled and chained, and drowned themselves. Thus, although the name of the island is a mythical one, every inlet on the Sea Islands is labeled Ibo Landing because they are all seen as the place where the captives, one way or another, resisted. According to Dash, the myth of Ibo Landing provides sustenance for a tradition of Black resistance.

In *Daughters of the Dust* the myth of Ibo Landing is used to bring resolution to the trauma between Eli and Eula. The elements involved in the resolution are the myth, the Unborn Child, and the wooden figurehead of the torso of an African warrior floating in the river, whose function in the film is to symbolize the loss of status of the African people in this country and of all that was sacred to them in their homeland. It is a replica of a figurehead used on the prow of a slave ship, and Dash utilized it as an unspoken reminder that this was the first thing the African captives saw as they were being led onto the boat that would carry them away from their land. Fifty years after enslavement, the figurehead lies floating and rotting in the water as a constant relic of that time.[11]

The Unborn Child symbolizes the belief in the connection between the "otherworld" of those who have lived before and are now dead, and life in the present. During the flashback of the earlier inhabitants of the island working as slaves on the indigo plantation, there are scenes of the workers pounding the indigo solution and dipping the fabric in vats of hot, steaming dye. The Unborn Child is among them, trailing her finger among the containers of blue dye. In a voice-over she talks about the nobility of her ancestry and her beckoning to Ibo Landing: "We were the children of those who chose to survive. Years later, my ma told me she knew I had been sent by the old souls."

After the flashback to the indigo plantation the Unborn Child returns to the present of the family picnic, looking through a wish book with Myown and tracking the objects in the book with her blue-stained finger. The Unborn Child notes whimsically, "I was travelling on this very true mission. But sometimes I would get distracted." There is a charmingly quixotic quality to this part of the film, in which the sacred belief that those who reside in the realm of the spiritual are vitally connected to the people in the present is symbolized by a 5-year-old girl who is knowingly caught up in the normal activities of a child that age. This ambience is enhanced as she remains the same throughout the film, costumed in the same white dress with the same blue ribbon in her hair, as she travels between both worlds.

After the sequence between past and present there is a cut to a group of children running in slow motion up a path, followed by the Unborn Child, who scampers along behind them. After a cut to a close-up of the river the camera tilts slowly up over the water. At the completion of the dissolve Eula enters the frame from the left, looking back wistfully over her shoulder. In a voice-over the Unborn Child reveals: "My ma said she could feel me by her side." There is a cut to a bird circling in the sky, then another to a medium shot of Nana Peazant breathing deeply and looking out over the land. In a voice-over the Unborn Child tells how she came to Eula and Eli: "I remember the call of my great-grandmother. I remember the journey home." A cut takes us to a long shot of the graveyard, adorned with the bottles, pots and pans, seashells, broomsticks, twisted metal, and other grave markers that were the personal effects of those who died. In a voice-over the Unborn Child says, "I remember the long walk to the graveyard, to the house that I would be born in..." There is a slow dissolve to a superimposition of the graveyard with a man riding a bicycle along the beach, moving leftward across the screen. The voice of the Unborn Child continues, "... to the picnic site." She begins to speak more slowly, and her words become more drawn-out at a slow dissolve to a superimposition of Nana Peazant leading a group of children, carrying chairs upside-down on their heads, over the sand dunes and onto the picnic area. During the overlap the voice of the Unborn Child says, "I remember. And I recall," as the waves seen in one shot become a part of the background for Nana Peazant's leading the children over the land.

In *Daughters of the Dust* references to the past are usually made through scenes in which a character travels left across the screen or looks off to the left.[12] In this sequence the boy on the bicycle riding left across the screen emphasizes a gesture toward the past as Nana Peazant enters the frame. With the waves forming a backdrop to the scene the intent was to symbolize the Middle Passage, in which the captured Africans were brought on slave ships to the land of their captivity. The chairs carried by the children upside-down on their heads symbolize crowns and are emblematic of the grand and glorious civilization that once was Africa. As the Unborn Child states that she remembers and recalls, the significance is that the past is fused with the present moment, for she is a new member of the Peazant family, summoned by one who was an active participant in that past. The suggestion is that it is necessary to cling to the parts of the past that are vital to understanding the present and that there is knowledge to be gained from those who have lived before.

This intertwining of the wisdom learned from the past with its influence in the present is again visible as Eli follows the Unborn Child to the graveyard. There is a cut to a close-up of Eula pensively watching Eli enter the graveyard and become seized by emotion as he falls to his knees at his mother's grave, then another to an extreme close-up of Eli bent over before the grave. The camera pans slowly over his body as there is a dissolve to the figurehead floating in the water and then a dissolve to Eula facing left with her arms raised as her body undulates to receive the Unborn Child, who comes skipping along in slow motion, merging with Eula's body. After a cut to two figures on a bicycle traveling across the sand to the left of the screen, there is another cut to a medium shot of the Ibo Landing sign on the bank of the river, then another to a close-up of Eula's shoes, as the camera tilts slowly up her body and she begins to recite the Ibo Landing tale.[13]

Eula is passing the tale along to the Unborn Child. The version of the myth she uses is the one in which the Ibo walk back across the water to Africa. As Eula tells the story Eli returns from his sojourn with the spirit of his mother at the graveyard, walking slowly and deliberately toward the river. In the distance the figurehead is visible, resting in the water. Eula relates how the Ibo departed from the ship and took a look around, studying the place carefully: "And they saw things that day that you and I don't have the power to see. Well, they saw just about everything that was to happen around here." The Ibo foresaw the coming war and what was to happen to their descendants there on the island. As Eula speaks we see Eli begin to walk out in the shallow water toward the figurehead. A shot of Eula in the foreground, Eli standing in the water in the middle distance, and the figurehead resting in the water in the background is held for a time. Eula continues relating the myth: "When those Ibo got through sizing up the place real good and seeing what was to come, my grandmother said they turned, all of them, and walked back into the water. Every last man, woman, and child." There is a cut to a close-up of Eula as she smiles proudly and looks down as if she were in the company of a small child. Intercut with shots of Eula speaking are shots of Eli kneeling down by the figurehead, cradling it in his arms, then pushing it farther out into the water. There is a dissolve to a moving camera shot of Eula watching the figurehead as it floats down the river, followed by another dissolve that ends in a close-up of the figurehead, and then a cut back to Eli walking, with his back to the camera, toward where Eula is standing. He kneels down in front of her, grasps her around the waist, and clutches her tightly.

At the beginning of the film, Eli's great-grandmother, Nana Peazant, advises him to contact the spirit of the ancestors, so that they may guide him during his turmoil over the rape and pregnancy of Eula. She tells him that he won't ever have a child that wasn't sent to him – that "the ancestors and the womb, they one and the same." Even though he was not ready to heed Nana's words, she makes the connection for him: he comes to see for himself, through Eula's retelling of the myth, the present-day entrance of the Unborn Child and the force of the figurehead and its poignant history. Nana tells Eli: "There's a thought, a recollection, something somebody remembers," as a signal that her story will invoke a contemplation from the past. She continues: "We carry these memories inside of we. Do you believe that those hundreds and hundreds of Africans brought here on this other side would forget everything they once knew? We don't know where the recollections come from. Sometimes we dream them. But we carry these memories inside of we." Nana provides Eli with a benediction when she tells him she is trying to help him contact the spirit of the ancestors, that if he could learn to beckon them they would come at unexpected moments to guide him. She tells him, "Let them feed your head with wisdom that ain't from this day and time." Nana Peazant reminds Eli: "Those in this grave and those what across the sea, they with us. They all the same, the ancestor and the womb."

"God's My Witness..."

Nana Peazant's "recollection" is enacted earlier in the film when we first hear the voice of the Unborn Child telling us that her story is older than she is: "My story begins on the eve of my family's migration North. My story begins before I was born. Nana prayed, and the old souls guided me into the New World." But Nana's belief that the spiritual exists in the living present is contested by two of the women: Haagar and Viola, each of whom has a clearly defined function in the film.

Haagar is first seen running the tip of her toe through the broken bottles on the ground. The bottles are from one of the bottle trees beside each house, each bottle of which represents someone who has died. The bottle trees provide protection and goodwill for the inhabitants of the homes. Eli has smashed this particular tree, after his conversation with Nana in the graveyard. He is frustrated because his lifelong belief in the power of Nana's charms is being challenged by his inability to come to grips with Eula's rape. While Haagar is out near the destroyed bottle tree the Unborn Child enters the frame and tugs at her dress. She gazes wistfully up at Haagar, waiting for her to acknowledge her spirit. Haagar's disbelief is so strong and so willfully held that she makes no contact with the Unborn Child, who turns around and runs merrily on to the rest of her mission.

Haagar gazes up to the top of a huge tree, and as the camera tilts slowly down from the top of the tree to a long shot of Haagar, she beats her hand against her chest, proclaiming grandly, "God's my witness. When I leave this place I'm never again gonna live in your land."

This particular moment in the film is reminiscent of the famous penultimate moment in *Gone with the Wind* in which, after the South had lost the war and those who formerly were living grandly are now left without even the bare necessities, Scarlett O'Hara falls down at the foot of a gigantic tree and vows that, as God is her witness, she will never be hungry again. Scarlett's declaration in one of the most heralded films of all time is a declaration of the tenacity of those who would stop at nothing, even to the point of feeling appointed as "owners" of other human beings, in the service of their belief in an innate superiority. In *Daughters of the Dust*, Dash reverses Scarlett's declaration: it is a repudiation of the antebellum South and all that it represented.

The film is constructed around such moments, with all the grandeur and pomp usually devoted to those securely lodged within mainstream culture. A radical reversal takes place as Black people form the center of the story instead of being used as background window dressing for the chronicle of others' lives. When Haagar displays her strength of will at the foot of the tree and issues her challenge to all, she stands as a symbol for those whose stories have never been told. As her particular history unfolds throughout the film it echoes previous Black women's lives – specifically her speech to the women gathered at the picnic site preparing the food for the celebration feast.

After scenes of Iona and St. Julian Last Child, the last Cherokee nation-born child remaining on the island, talking and embracing on the beach, there is a cut to a medium shot of the Newlywed Woman leaning back against a tree, gazing off into the distance. Haagar begins to glance around and call out for Iona. She turns away, frustrated at Iona's absence, and then begins to criticize Nana Peazant in front of Viola, Nana Peazant's granddaughter, who is lying on a blanket reading her Bible, and the Hairbraider, who is shucking ears of corn. Haagar tells them that Nana needs to stop going off by herself contemplating the objects from the past in her tin can of memories. She follows up with the thought that perhaps Nana Peazant is not in her right mind. Viola defends her grandmother, chastisting Haagar, "You're laughing at an old woman, Haagar Peazant." Viola reminds Haagar, "Just like Eula, you married into this family. But she's our grandmother. Ain't nothing wrong or harmful in that tin can she carries." After Haagar and the Hairbraider mimic what seems to them to be a familiar chant about Nana's "scraps of memories," Viola tells them that she is aware that Nana is carrying a lot of baggage from the past and that she needs to put "her soul in the hands of the Lord. But she built her life around this family. She's old, and she's frightened. What does Nana know about the world outside? Nothing. Nana was never educated. All she knows are simple things, things people told her a long time ago."

The Hairbraider insists that Nana must go with them to the North. At this point Haagar becomes even more agitated and states adamantly that Nana and her old ways need to remain on the island. Haagar walks defiantly toward the other two women, one hand on her hip and the other grasping a carrot that she is preparing to cook, jabbing the air with the carrot to emphasize her point. She states, "I might not have been born in this family, but I'm here now. And I say, Let Nana Peazant stay behind. That's what she wants. We moving into a new day. She's too much a part of the past." The Hairbraider responds that Daddy Mac, Nana Peazant's son, had better not hear Haagar saying what she just said. Haagar becomes even more belligerent, telling them, "I'm a fully grown 'oman and I don't have to mind what I say. I done born five children into the world and put two of them in the ground alongside they daddy. I work all my life and ain't got nothing to show for it. And if I can't say what's on my mind, then damn everybody to hell."

Haagar is mired in the same parochial mentality as the other residents of Ibo Landing. She is naive in her optimism that there is a much better life for them away from the island. She is as frightened of new things as Nana Peazant is, as we witness in her treatment of Yellow Mary when Yellow Mary returns from her world travels with her can of "store-bought" biscuits. But Haagar stands tall for her rights and is fiercely protective of what is hers. For that reason her children are named Myown and Iona. She tells the other women, "My children ain't gonna be like those old Africans, fresh off the boat." She feels it is a new world that they are moving toward: "I want my daughters to grow up to be decent somebodies. I don't want my girls to have to hear about all that mess." Haagar issues a warning: "I'll lock horns with anything and anybody that tries to hold me back." Because of these sentiments – that the old ways are harmful to her children – she is determined to stop them from joining the others in kissing the "hand" that Nana has prepared as a charm to protect them on their journey to the North. Haagar demonstrates her sense of commanding all that is hers at the end of the film, when Iona runs off to join St. Julian Last Child and they ride away on the horse. Haagar protests loudly to everyone that she owns the child and thus can dictate what her actions should be.

Haagar also displays a strength of purpose and a toughness of will that reveals how she was able to survive the tortures of life there on the island. In her declaration at the foot of the tree and her speech to Viola and the Hairbraider on the beach she is reminiscent of such Black women as Sojourner Truth, who demonstrated the same courage and endurance as she told of her life under slavery. Sojourner Truth also spoke of bearing children who later died under the rigors of slavery, and of working hard and feeling the lash of the whip. In *Daughters of the Dust* Haagar and the other Black women answer affirmatively and proudly Truth's centuries'-old question – "And ain't I a woman?"

Each of the women in the film also serves to represent the full scope of black women's lives and experiences. In contrast to the limited depictions of Black women formerly available in mainstream cultural forms, *Daughters of the Dust* presents the varieties within Black womanhood. Nana Peazant places her faith in her ancestors and the relics from their past lives; Yellow Mary clings to her St. Christopher charm and her strong conviction that she can always make her way in the world; and Eula sets a letter beneath a glass of water under her bed to summon the spirit of her mother to guide her. Haagar believes firmly in herself and doesn't need any of what she terms "that hoodoo mess." Viola, more than anyone else, has entrusted her life to the belief systems of the dominant culture.

Viola has moved away from the island and become a devout Baptist missionary. Viola's style of dress and coiffure reveal that she is a tightly corseted woman with not a hair out of place. Her stern visage as she constantly interjects her religious homilies – "Mind now, the Lord is a-listening" – is a mask behind which she hides her self-doubts, her fears of abandoning her traditional mores, and her womanhood. At the end of the film, when it becomes evident that those who are leaving for the North are truly parting with Nana Peazant and the home of their birth, Viola begins to unravel. Her hair comes undone, and her blouse pulls halfway out of her skirt. She protests that old folks are supposed to die and go to heaven, not be left behind grieving for their lost kin. When Viola realizes the value of her grandmother's traditions and folk beliefs, she finally kisses the "hand" that her grandmother has fixed as a gesture of reconciliation of her past with her future.

Viola's burgeoning understanding and reevaluation of her past is accompanied by Mr. Snead's appreciation of his African background. Mr. Snead is a photographer and an anthropologist who has come with Viola to document the Peazants' last day on Ibo Landing. He has an ulterior motive, however, of assembling an exhibition of his photographs when he arrives back in the North, to showcase his collection of photographs of "primitive" people. For Dash, he represents the viewing audience – those who perceive the people and the culture she has depicted as exotic, foreign, and something to be looked at under a microscope.[14]

But Mr. Snead undergoes a transformation during his sojourn with the people on the island. His sense of superiority and his scientific outlook are eclipsed as he reaches an awareness that these are the people and traditions that are part of his heritage. After Mr. Snead takes a series of photographs and talks with several people, he appears overjoyed and grabs Viola in a hug and whirls her around in a circle. She reproaches him, saying sternly, "Mr. Snead!" while pulling her arms from his grasp and attempting to put herself back together. Mr. Snead asks Viola if he may talk with Bilal Muhammed; he wants to know if he is family. Viola desists, however, for she sees no value in talking to Bilal Muhammed: "That old heathen. He's not important." She goes on to explain to Mr. Snead that everyone on the island is family in some way, but, she adds, "Unfortunately, so many like Bilal are so backward. They believe everything that happens is caused by conjure, magic, or their ancestors." Viola inserts her own religious sentiments self-righteously: "They don't leave nothing to God." Mr. Snead finally talks with Bilal Muhammed and learns the true story of the Ibo and how they drowned themselves rather than live enslaved. While he takes the portrait of the entire assembled group of Peazants, Mr. Snead is so overcome that he shouts to them, "Look! Look up! And remember Ibo Landing!" Later, Daddy Mac adds his recollections to those of Bilal about what he learned from his elders. In the scene the men sit spread out along the beach. Present are Eli, lying down looking around contentedly; Bilal Muhammed, standing by a tree and gazing out at the water; and Daddy Mac, kneeling on one knee as he leans in to talk with Mr. Snead, who sits spread-legged on the sand, having given up his studies of the people to really learn from them. Daddy Mac tells Mr. Snead he was taught that "woman is the sweetness of life." Daddy Mac describes the beauty of Black women and their "lovely" voices and repeats his assertion that "woman is the sweetness of life." He concludes the litany of instructions from his elders, telling Mr. Snead, "And that's what I remember." After his conversation with the men, Mr. Snead readily joins in the ritual kissing of Nana's "hand" and then walks quickly over to Viola, grabs her, and kisses her on the mouth.

In the film Mr. Snead becomes a changed person. He is no longer a voyeur stationed outside the community, minutely examining the people and their assumed backward ways, wanting only to exploit them under the guise of scientific studies. Rather, Mr. Snead becomes a true believer. His transformation is matched by that of Viola, who formerly interacted with her family with a bemused tolerance. She appeared to be harboring a secret desire to convert them from their heathenism to a better appreciation of the finer points of "civilization" – evident as she demonstrates through the scenes in which she tries to teach the young girls the "proper" way to sit and comport themselves gracefully. Although Viola chastises Haagar for demeaning Nana Peazant's supposedly pagan practices, Viola is just as disdainful of Bilal Muhammed's religion. Her strict, tight-laced dress and demeanor suggest that she is rigidly holding herself in. Viola suppresses not only her background but her sexual self as well, displacing it onto her strict religious beliefs.[15]

Viola's attempts to restrain her sexual feelings were not unusual, for many Black women of that era attempted to present themselves as refined and genteel in response to the pervasive sentiment that Black women were loose, untameable sexual creatures. The Club Movement initiated by Black women at the turn of the century worked to counter these historical misrepresentations. Literary works such as *Iola Leroy* (1892) by Frances Harper and *Contending Forces* (1900) by Pauline Hopkins are two examples of fictional works engaged in the effort to eradicate this false image of Black women.

Daughters of the Dust is the first film to explore the issue of Black women and the ways they responded to images of themselves as sexually immoral. The presentation of Viola and her starched, restrained, religious countenance provide a stark contrast to Eula's rape and to Yellow Mary. Their two stories, coupled with Nana Peazant's history, are a dramatic reconstruction of one of the most devastating myths about Black womanhood.

" . . . We Never Was a Pure 'Oman"

Dash talks about the process of taking historical moments and depicting them in a different way, of "showing Black families, particularly Black women, as we have never seen them before."[16] In this way events come to have more meaning than they would in a strictly conventional presentation of the story. There are two scenes in which Dash had planned to depict the reality of slavery that were different from their routine presentations. One was actually shot but not included in the final edit; the other, written but not shot.

The first scene is a flashback to Nana Peazant as a baby who has been taken from her mother and sold to another plantation. Nana's mother had cut off a lock of her own hair and sewn it into a baby's blanket to send along with the young girl, so that when she was old enough she could take the lock of hair out and remember her mother. The image that was to be used to convey the mother's feelings of loss, of the need to maintain a connection with the child who had been taken from her, was the milk that flowed from her engorged breasts. After a baby is born the mother produces milk, even in the absence of the child. To show the mother's grief, Dash constructed a scene in which the milk seeps from the mother's breasts through her dress and drips to the ground. In place of tears the milk flowing from her breasts was to serve as a symbol of the mother mourning the baby that was taken from her.

The second scene revolves around Yellow Mary and her experiences with the white family in Cuba, where she worked as a nursemaid. There is a flashback to the Cuban bedroom, where Yellow Mary nurses a white baby as the baby's father fondles her other breast. At the point where Yellow Mary talks to Eula about the rape, as she is sitting in the tree, there was to be continual cross-cutting with the Cuban bedroom scenes.[17]

It was a conscious decision not to show the rape of Eula, because that segment of history has been graphically presented many times. With Yellow Mary the parallel editing accomplishes a different purpose, a stark Black and white contrast that amplifies her predicament of having faced the personal trauma of losing her child and needing to escape what has been forced upon her. That Yellow Mary becomes a prostitute to gain her independence emphasizes that she is the one in control of her life rather than at the mercy of those who felt they had a divine right to the use of her body.

Although the two proposed scenes were not part of the finished film, they are present as a subtext, underscoring the need to remember the specific details of Black women's history. As Dash relates, "It is the specifics that are so important, that add resonance to what we as Black filmmakers do. And we have to be very careful that we don't lose our original voice in the writing, in the editing, and in the final cut. We have to be very careful because what to us reads as resonance, to others can be read as an error."[18]

In the finished film the original voice of Black women and their life histories is seen in the final moments, when Nana Peazant, Yellow Mary, and Eula demonstrate the ways in which Black women cope, survive, and, most important, triumph despite centuries of abuse.

After Bilal Muhammed and Daddy Mac share with Mr. Snead their teachings about Black women, there are loud cries from Nana Peazant as she sits among the women. She is distraught, pressing her hands against her breasts and shaking her head from side to side. Everyone becomes alarmed, trying to determine the cause of her anguish. Nana stands and begins to run away from the group. Yellow Mary clasps her in an embrace as they rock back and forth on the sand, and tries to comfort Nana by assuring of her need for her and her desire to be among the people who realize who she is. She tells her, "I need to know I can come and hold on to where I come from. I need to know that the people know my name. I Yellow Mary Peazant, and I a proud 'oman, not a hard 'oman." Yellow Mary tells Nana, "I want to stay. I want to stay with you here."

Yellow Mary has been out in the world that the others of the island are so eager to enter – been in it and found it wanting. Although, as it becomes increasingly clear, staying on the island means separation from Trula, who will travel on to Nova Scotia, Yellow Mary remains with her grandmother and takes solace in the familiarity of her past.

Nana Peazant herself is confused about the others' need to leave the island. She asks them, "How can you leave this soil? This soil, this what our loved ones – they here in this soil." Even though they persist in going, Nana tells them, "I love you 'cause you mine. You the fruit of an ancient tree."

As the people are gathered around them, Eula takes up the charge that Yellow Mary and Nana Peazant began. She has heard the not-so-subtle comments about Yellow Mary's being "ruint"; she has seen the way they have treated her since her return to the island. Eula reminds them that Yellow Mary was responsible for providing the money that kept one of their kin from jail. Eula probes further into the prejudices and biases of her family. She asks, "You so ashamed of Yellow Mary 'cause she got ruint. Well, what do you say about me?" She then makes a statement that is the overarching theme of the film: "As far as this place is concerned, we never was a pure 'oman. Deep inside we believe they ruin our mothers and their mothers what come before them." Eula speaks passionately of the routes Black women have taken to protect themselves, of their battle for a sense of their own importance, and of their value to themselves and their families. She says,

"And we live our lives always expecting worse, 'cause we feel we don't deserve no better. Deep inside we believe that even God can't heal the wounds of our past or protect us from the world that put shackles on our feet." She reaffirms for the women that their past was forced on them and that their future may not be as soiled. She tells them to let go of that past while holding on to the resources from their ancestors: "We are the daughters of those old dusty things that Nana carries in her tin can." Eula reassures them that they deserve whatever good comes from the roads they take in life, "because we all good 'oman."

Eula's soliloquy is as much directed to those members of the family surrounding her as it is a tribute to the Black women who have not let their inheritance from enslavement rob them of their heritage of resistance and survival. Eula talks about the sustenance Black women gain from the support of other Black women and reminds them that this is a necessary part of their survival: "If you love yourselves, then love Yellow Mary, because she a part of you. Just like we a part of our mothers."

Black Women in Otherworlds

"As a Black woman," states Julie Dash, "you take for granted that you are never going to see certain moments – certain private moments – on the screen."[19] For this reason she makes a conscious effort to bring the audience into the film, to convey a closeness, rather than try to distance the audience from the film. Three sequences in particular illustrate Dash's assertions. The first example of the intimacy, of the subtle shadings provided by a director who is part of the culture being portrayed, involves Yellow Mary and Nana Peazant. The careful attention to the choice of words spoken, the positions taken by the actors as Yellow Mary crouches on her haunches before Nana Peazant in her regal chair, the contrasts of the women's styles of dress, and the familiar manner in which they touch and stroke one another – all are intricate aspects of a mise-en-scène that places the viewer within the midst of the women's emotional moment. The motion from two-shot to close-up and the poise and control of the actors in the reaction shots all blend together to create an aura of warmth and poignancy as Yellow Mary tells her grandmother, "I wanted to surprise you, Nana." The weight of years is heard in Nana Peazant's gentle reply: "No surprises here, Yellow Mary." Without censure, without expectations, without judgment, Yellow Mary's grandmother strokes her hair and gazes affectionately into her face, making sure that her excursion to the New World has not destroyed her inner being. When she is satisfied that all is well, Nana Peazant leans in toward Yellow Mary and places their foreheads softly together.

The second example contains a series of shots of Yellow Mary with Eula or interacting with Trula that culminate in the three of them sitting together on the beach under an umbrella. After Yellow Mary recalls for Eula her experiences in Cuba, there are shots of her and Trula walking along the edge of the water. The music accompanying them is soft and soothing, providing a gentle background as Yellow Mary touches Trula's hair and bows her head to look up at her face, then the two embrace and gently rock back and forth. In the next shot Trula walks off by herself as Eula and Yellow Mary enter the frame, trailing along behind her. The three of them find an old, discarded umbrella lying disintegrating on the shore. The music continues as they twirl and spin the umbrella. After a dissolve we see the three of them sitting on a fallen tree. The image is held as the camera slowly pulls back.

It is a remarkable moment in cinema when all these elements converge – the music, the cinematography, the editing – to create a loving portrait of three Black women. The moment resumes as Yellow Mary and Eula sit under the umbrella while Yellow Mary gives Eula an example of shutting off the demons in her mind until she is prepared to cope with them.

The closing scenes of *Daughters of the Dust* are an epiphany, providing coherence and balance to the opening scenes of the film. In the beginning the female voice-over speaks of being the first and the last: "Many are my daughters." At the end of the film, the lingering evocative shots of four generations of Black women walking along the water's edge are a fitting conclusion. Nana Peazant has lived to see the birth of the newest member of the family.

Daughters of the Dust is not simply a tale of Black women reclaiming their past. As a work deliberately conceived as a film about Black women, with Black women intended as its primary audience, it intervenes strongly in a tradition of derogatory portrayals of Black women in dominant cinema. It is thus a powerful component of a cultural movement toward the empowerment of Black women.

Notes

1 Jim Haskins, *James Van DerZee: The Picture Takin' Man* (Teaneck, NJ: Africa World Press, 1991).
2 The interpretation of the passage "Thunder: Perfect Mind" in the Gnostic scriptures is given by Douglas M. Parrott and George W. MacRae. See their interpretation in James M. Robinson, ed., *The Nag Hammadi Library* (San Francisco: Harper and Row, 1988), pp. 295–6.
3 From an interview with Black independent filmmaker Zeinabu irene Davis. See "Daughters of the Dust," *Black Film Review* 6, no. 1 (1990–1): 12–17, 20–1.

4   Personal interview on March 3, 1992, in Los Angeles.
5   Taken from interview with Houston A. Baker, Jr. See his article "Not Without My Daughters," *Transition: A International Review* 57 (1992): 164.
6   Quoted in Donald Bogle, *Toms, Coons, Mulattoes, Mammies, and Bucks* (New York: Continuum, 1989), p. 30.
7   Adrienne Lanier-Seward, "A Film Portrait of Black Ritual Expression: *The Blood of Jesus*," in Geneva Gay and Willie L. Baber, eds, *Expressively Black: The Cultural Basis of Ethnic Identity* (New York: Praeger, 1987), pp. 195–212.
8   Interview with bell hooks in the book by Dash, *Daughters of the Dust: The Making of an African-American Woman's Film* (New York: New Press, 1992), p. 36.
9   See their article "*Ganja and Hess*: Vampires, Sex, and Addictions," *Black American Literature Forum* 25, no. 2 (Summer 1991): 299–314.
10 Interview with bell hooks in Dash, *Daughters of the Dust*, p. 29.
11 Interview with Houston A. Baker, Jr., "Not Without My Daughters," p. 165.
12 Personal interview with author on March 3, 1992.
13 The actual words are used in the film with the permission of the author Paule Marshall, from her book *Praisesong for the Widow* (New York: Putnam, 1983).
14 Interview with bell hooks in Dash, *Daughters of the Dust*, p. 38.
15 Literary scholar Deborah McDowell notes Black women's transference of their sexuality to their religion: "It has long been a stereotype that the church has provided Black women a 'safe' and controlled release of unexpressed sexual desires." McDowell points to the work of Jewelle Gomez, who describes how Black women have "hidden from their sexuality behind a church pew." See McDowell's endnote in her introduction to two novels by Nella Larsen, *Quicksand* (1928) and *Passing* (1929) (New Brunswick, NJ: Rutgers University Press, 1986), p. xxxv.
16 Interview with bell hooks in Dash, *Daughters of the Dust*, p. 32.
17 Personal interview with the author on March 3, 1992.
18 Ibid.
19 Ibid.

6

Below the Line:
(Re)Calibrating the Filmic Gaze

C. A. Griffith

Between a Rock and a Hard Place

Boston. 1989. I can't shake this chill, and the roar of a second chopper over my head forces me to hunch over and curse under my breath. I watch a ghostly pale Mick Jagger dash out from the helicopter before he is swallowed by a swarm of thick-necked security forces as the crowd screams and lurches forward. I flash my ALL ACCESS stage pass and duck into a side door. The camera room is full of enough equipment to start a small camera rental shop. Eight or ten of the best ACs (Camera Assistants[1]) in the business are setting up for tonight's shoot and trading war stories. The testosterone levels are way past the legal limit for safety, and I have to make sure my kit and all of my operator's (Camera Operator[2]) gear made it off the plane safe and sound. As I work, I whisper a mantra to keep the walls from closing in one me: "Any set is just a set and the camera's just a tool to process film. The camera's just an expensive blender." I introduce myself to the guys, and keep a mental note of the few who are surprised but friendly enough, and the rest who look at me with distrust and perhaps a bit of envy.

We're walking backstage. Anastas (Tass) Michos is about 35 with the build and grace of a dancer. He also has one Black woman on each arm. One is me, a woman who has been called attractive or intimidating – it all depends on the context, but one description usually outweighs the other. The other is a stunningly beautiful young woman, his girlfriend, the model. Even backstage among all the jaded paparazzi, fans, and film and music biz people, we cause heads to turn. The director comes up to us, greets Tass warmly, and we all exchange names and niceties. He's busy briefing Tass on the shoot when he stops suddenly and asks, "Tass, where's your man?" "She's right here," Tass responds as we keep walking. "No. Really. Where's your man?" I stop and look at him. "I'm right here." He looks at Tass. Tass smiles. I look him straight in the eye and re-introduce myself. "Crystal Griffith. First AC." He looks uncomfortable. "So what are we talking about here?" Tass says, getting right back to business. "You want the whole concert or just a few cuts?" "At least two cuts, plus the new one – 'Rock and a Hard Place.' We'll get you a list for tonight's shoot."

I hadn't really eaten since Tass called me two days ago. He had to convince me why I was the best person for the job before I accepted it: "You do docs, and crazy Rock and Rap videos where there's no time for tape measures, depth of field charts, walk-throughs, or fear." He'd hired me over a long list of others because I pulled focus, stayed calm and easy going, and didn't have time to be afraid. But I was afraid. At dinner, the model, an Australian roadie, and I are the only Blacks in sight. I can't stomach the massive lobster staring at me on my plate. We'll be shooting mostly to playback, except for the live footage tomorrow night at the concert. And the camera we're using is an Arri III.[3] It's lightweight, so it's perfect for steadicam. The only problem is that on an Arri III, if the loop is two or three perfs too long, the emulsion will hit the screw inside the camera body and scratch the emulsion right down the center. If the loop is too short, the camera will jam, or if it's cold enough (this is September in Boston), the film may break. That means the loaders have to be right on the nose. That means that if they're not, I'm in serious trouble for not noticing it, rethreading the mag, and correcting the problem. Of course, AC's make mistakes all the time; the trick is catching them before they're noticed and before they cause any problems – otherwise it's my head.[4] It's Tass's head for hiring an AC that messed up the shoot (but the fact that he trusted a Black woman First AC with their film will be all they'll talk about). And it'll be the director's and DP's[5] nightmare, and the producer's tens of thousands of dollars for film that can't be used.

This is my first big steadicam job as a First and I'm understandably anxious. Fortunately, Tass keeps that magical distance that instills confidence in my ability, yet is close enough to see and alert me to any trouble. Just before we're up, he helps me double-check everything once again, correct problems, and make sure we show no seams and no sweat.

We shoot for hours under incredible stress that night. All eyes are on us. I don't take out my tape measure enough, so they're not sure it's really in focus, although everything looks good in the director and DP's video tape monitor.[6] They ask Tass if it's good for camera and he tells them yes, the composition is good, but they'll have to tell him about focus.[7] The producers do a rush on the film and have it processed and flown back in from New York for screening the next day. Tass calls his friends at the lab for a negative report and we get a message at the hotel a few hours later saying that everything's fine. Still, I don't sleep. I act loose, cool, and copacetic. My jeans are getting looser and my stomach is a tight, tight knot. I exude confidence.

At dusk the next day, during a sound and tech run-through, they throw this amazingly smooth, hot, and impossibly sharp footage up on the giant concert stage screen. Everyone stops what they're doing to watch as the camera holds a long shot on Keith Richards, moves in for a close up, whip pans over to an extreme long shot of Jagger at the edge of the stage, and holds him in sharp, clear focus as he runs directly up to the lens to purse and pucker those famous, thick, juicy lips, all of two inches from the lens. I hear an audible gasp from Tass, from myself, and all around us. I'm thinking, whoever this guy is, he's good. And I'm in trouble. On such a huge screen, the slightest miscalculation, or hesitation in camera movement, the slightest, most trivial loss of focus will look terrible. And they're impossibly flawless. Take after take. I ask Tass if they're going to cut this footage in with what we shot last night and he looks at me, truly stunned. "That's our work up there, Crystal. That's us." I don't recognize it, and I'm not sure how to absorb this information. The reel is over and suddenly, the entire crew, including the roadies who've taken this tour up and down around the world, applaud us. The producer, director, DP, and Tass are pounding my back and shaking my hand. But years later, I still ask this question: what if I'd made a mistake?

Adventures in the Land of Supertech

ACs are expected not to make mistakes, to be machinelike in attention to detail, yet still perform duties machines cannot perform – and, of course, be a "good fellow" throughout. I was very good at what I did. I walked a tightrope called ARROGANT BLACK BITCH SUPERTECH NOIR. The special, limited-engagement show: how to be one of the few professional Black DP/Camerawomen. The price of the ticket on 15 October 1991: two slipped and herniated disks, a neck that curved the wrong way, and severe nerve damage. I left New York that December. It took my friend and DP, Juan Cobo, over ten excruciating minutes to help me down three flights of stairs, across the treacherous sidewalk, and into a waiting cab. It had rained the night before and the streets were covered with a thin, dangerous coat of ice that told me it really was time to go.

I live in California with my partner of six years. My recovery has been slow, yet somehow, I've been as productive (maybe more) during these five years in California as I was in New York. I'm a published author, I've directed

three video narratives, and twice made the finals at Sundance for my first
feature-length screenplay. H.T.L. Quan and I are codirecting/producing
The Angela Davis Project (working title), a documentary series on women
of color as cultural workers. We shot the first segment, which includes a
conversation between Angela Davis and 75 year-old political activist Yuri
Kochiyama, in May 1996. A month later, I completed an MFA at the
University of California, Santa Barbara. I've also had the honor and privilege
to work and study with leading Black intellectuals like Dr. Cedric J. Robinson and Isaac Julien, who demand excellence, and challenge you to excel.
Writing this article has meant revisiting what I now refer to as my past
life.

I will argue that filmmaking is essentially a blue-collar industry with a
glossy but thin veneer of mystique and prestige that makes it appear impene-
trable. It is also a highly hierarchical yet collaborative process with artificial
boundaries existing above and below the line. By above the line, I mean the
producers, directors and lead actors – the handful of people whom audiences,
academic cultural critics, and the popular presses reify. Straddling the space
between these lines, officially, part of one world, but outside of it in many
ways, are the writer and DP. By below the line, I mean the filmmakers that we
call the crew, who compose 98 percent of the film production unit, the
forgotten, invisible names that roll by in the credits long after the audience
have left their seats. I have been a PA, AC, and DP; and the film world looks
very different above and below the line.

Grand Expectations

> *At all times, Cameramen ... shall be responsible for doing their work to the utmost
> of their ability, artistry, and efficiency, and strive to uphold the best traditions of
> the photographic profession. Bearing in mind that upon their efforts rests the
> ultimate responsibility for reproducing in artistic and visible form the results of
> the great expenditures undertaken by the Producer, they shall also strive to perform
> their work efficiently, rapidly, and as excellently as possible, seeking to heighten
> their efficiency and that of the Production unit with which they work.... Before a
> person can call himself a Cameraman, he must know and be able to perform the
> duties of each classification. This knowledge separates the professional from the
> amateur.[8]*

Sexist language aside, this description of the cameraman's responsibilities, a
kind of preamble to the responsibilities of the profession, clearly establishes
the following: that the producer, and not the director is the site of power and
control on set;[9] that the importance of the camera department is critical not
only in technical but also artistic terms; and that the profession is intensely

exclusive in its pedagogy. By relating a series of experiences – of how I circulated within the independent film-making industry/community – and by attempting to analyze critically their meanings, I seek to address the complexity of filmmaking within the framework of race, class, gender, and sexuality. It is critical to our understanding of film theory and film practice to re-situate and re-address what happens below the line in order to understand the entirety of the filmmaking process.

As Director of Photography Steven Bernstein points out, "film production is an expensive business and mistakes are not happily tolerated. It is also a high-pressure trade, and pressure naturally leads to mistakes."[10] One might argue that the position called Camera Assistant functions as a kind of gate – the proverbial "weak link" and also the site of a great deal of underexplored power and knowledge. As a professional AC, I not only learned my trade but also that of almost every member of the cast and crew except perhaps the editors, simply by virtue of standing by and working on the camera during shooting or between setups. While a lot of "action" takes place behind closed doors, a great deal happens at and around the camera. Further, the AC is one of few people privy to the conversations, creative machinations, and decision-making processes of the producer, writer, director, DP, and the talent. While working in the film industry, I learned firsthand what worked and what didn't, why and why not. It was an invaluable education for which I was paid very generously.

Generally, however, the AC's role is recognized on set as a site of under-explored power, one that demands the utmost professionalism, technical knowledge, and perfection. For example, the AC's job is so important that Bernstein devotes the majority of two chapters to detailing these responsibilities. In *The Professional Cameraman's Handbook*, which is principally used as a technical reference guide (on film stocks, filtration, exposure, and camera equipment, etc.) for filmmakers, the description of the AC's responsibilities exceeds that of the DP's and Camera Operator's combined. It is not an exaggeration to state that the First AC has one of the most critical jobs on set; the best performance and work by the entire cast and crew can be destroyed by small, immediate, or not immediately detectable mistakes by the AC. One of the AC's primary duties is to keep the filmed image in focus. If the image is "soft" (out of focus), off-speed, improperly exposed, or if the film is accidentally "fogged" (exposed to direct light before or after it has left the camera), the image is lost. And if the image is lost, then so is all the time, money, and effort of everyone involved. Such a loss could include irreplaceable or impossibly expensive reshoots of locations and performances. Because the First AC is so important, this site of power is closely and very jealously guarded with signs that read "no mistakes," "no women," and "no people of color allowed."

From the beginning of film production in this country, and still today, filmmakers recruited from the dominant society employed biological essentialist arguments to justify their exclusive, nondemocratic practices. It is, of course, highly problematic to argue that only a certain race (white) and gender (male) is capable of performing certain duties, or that directing and producing a so-called Black film must be done only by Blacks themselves. In the case of a woman doing "a man's job," it is generally argued and believed that women cannot take the pressure and long hours involved with filmmaking. Women are presumed to be too small and too weak to carry heavy camera equipment for the usual 12+-hour-day. It is also argued that more Blacks and women are needed to challenge or subvert racist or sexist film images and ideologies. To all of this, I respond with the following, greatly abbreviated list of insights as a counter-intuitive challenge to such problematic claims:

A small toddler who insists upon being carried (30–60 lbs).

A Panavision with a loaded 400 foot rear-slung mag (film magazine), 50 mm lens, follow focus attachments, video tap, hand-held brace (about 40 lb).

The stress of working full time and raising two children as a single parent.

The stress of a 5-day, 14–16 hours per day production schedule with not enough turn around and a switch to shooting nights at mid-week.

White/Male filmmaker John Sayles's *Brother from Another Planet*.

Black/Male filmmaker Mario Van Peebles's *New Jack City*.

Black/Female filmmaker Julie Dash's *Daughters of the Dust*.

White/Female filmmaker Martha Coolidge's *Fast Times at Ridgemont High*.

Black/Female filmmaker Leslie Harris's *Just Another Girl on the IRT*.

Black/Male filmmaker Charles Burnett's *To Sleep with Anger*.

Black/Male filmmaker Bill Duke's *The Cemetery Club* and *Deep Cover*.

A backpack full of textbooks for a research paper on a crowded bus (15–30 lb).

A case full of Panavision prime lenses (20–35 lb).

PMS.

Male ego (masked insecurities).

A full-time career and intimate relationship, perhaps with a few sexist assumptions that women should cook, clean, and raise children (14–16 hours per day).

A 6-day-week of 12–14-hour-days on a low budget feature under high stress in a remote location with the only other woman/gay/person of color as your nemesis and a director who can't make up their mind.

Living, working, and giving 110+ percent for only 60 percent of the salary as compared to equally qualified men.

Down-loading, loading, and threading a Panavision (under 1 minute).

Threading a spool and bobbin on a sewing machine (about 1 minute).

Excelling in your career of choice and being dismissed or devalued as an oversensitive minority or unqualified affirmative action hire.

Five hundred years of resistance.

The erosion and erasure of thirty years of civil rights gains.

The bag of cotton my grandmother Lily James picked and carried alone to the scale when she was 24 years old (100 lbs).

The Arri BL IV with a loaded 1,000 foot mag, 10–1 zoom lens and attachments, mini Worral geared head, matte box, filter, follow focus, video tap, extended eye-piece and tripod that I moved by myself – there was no grip available to carry it for me so I squatted underneath the tripod legs, set the shoulder pad at the curve of my neck, held onto the rods and the legs, and in correct form, lifted the entire camera smoothly, with absolute confidence and relative ease across the room because the DP and director kept barking for the camera – and inadvertently won the respect and awe of most every man and woman on set (100 lb).

And finally, when compared to even the most convincing biological essentialist argument, I do not know what compares to living, working, surviving, resisting, and ABOVE ALL, MAINTAINING YOUR SANITY AND SENSE OF HUMOR in an amerika.

Redefining the Lines

Most cultural scholarship tends to focus on film content through an analysis of how meaning is conveyed by the above-the-line personnel and how ideology and emotion are perceived by the audience. This assumes a myopic and problematic binary of film production: that only the above-the-line filmmakers are worthy of analysis, and that an audience is definable. Completely absent from this academic and popular discourse are the below-the-line personnel. I believe this discussion needs to include, and more thoroughly examine, the physical, intellectual, and artistic contributions of these filmmakers generally marginalized by the strict borderlines of film theory and film practice, above and below the lines.

Regarding the analysis of the audience and the filmmaker, as much as individual, group, and cultural identity politics do play a role in audience and filmmaker perspectives, audience and demographic analysis will always be problematic. A "Black audience perspective" or a "female audience perspective" and perhaps even a "Black film aesthetic" do not exist except within an all too conveniently narrowed scope that does not approach or reflect the complex realities of those existences. Such diverse and conflicting groups should not be so easily categorized. I will use these terms and group designations with full awareness that they are contested terrains. Therefore, it is with some hesitation that I begin this investigation into New York's independent filmmaking industry and community during the late 1980s to early 1990s.

Many of the cultural critics who research and write on film have attempted to define the Black aesthetic and the role of film as art and ideology, but remain focused solely on the actors and directors (auteur theory), or producers and film costs (production, marketing, and distribution). Such analysis overlooks the highly collaborative nature of filmmaking and remains stuck above the line. Film genre, technical and creative innovation or reproduction, aesthetics and film as art, and ideological formation also remain stuck on the above-the-line film practitioners.

We must interrogate why academic film criticism and the popular press are so heavily invested in reporting on how a handful of directors, actors, and producers[11] create a body of work over time, how they communicate their artistic vision, and how that vision is infused with traceable intellectual and political agendas. Such hierarchical and exclusive approaches to a medium that is so influential and multifaceted beg a more thorough and democratic analysis – particularly given the hierarchical and nondemocratic nature of filmmaking itself. And while cultural scholars Manthia Diawara, Tommy Lott, and others have attempted to bridge the gap between film theory and film praxis, I believe that it is equally critical to expand the scope of what it means to be a filmmaker to include and more accurately represent the reality of the filmmaking process. The process is highly stratified yet collaborative, and it is embedded with mystique and prestige. Films are achieved by a highly specialized elite core of what I call "neon blue-collar workers." Finally, it is a process where both above-and below-the-line personnel are filmmakers, making artistic interventions and contributing skill and labor to the film.

More important perhaps, the usual Marxist thinking that differentiates mental labor from physical labor and posits that the "real" work in society is the result of manual laborers does and does not hold true here. For example, on any given film set, one is likely to find enough electricians (lighting department), carpenters (set builders), riggers (grip department), painters and draftspersons (art department/production designers), specialized technicians (special effects, sound and camera departments), construction supervisors (assistant directors, production managers, and continuity/script supervisors), jacks of all trades (production assistants, a.k.a. PAs), real-estate specialists (location scouts), developers and architects (directors and producers), to design and construct a small apartment complex. Interestingly, when film work slows down, many grips and electrics moonlight doing construction work.

That most filmmakers who are defined as film technicians do not describe themselves or understand themselves to be blue-collar workers is due to the mystique and prestige of working in the film industry. This makes class conflict unusual in that the worker is not envisioned as part of a mass unionization effort, but as an elite core. For example, in 1990, union membership for a First AC cost $3,500 and did not guarantee rights for all. Rather, it guaranteed rights for a highly selective (read: generally nepotistic, racist, sexist, homophobic) few. Union membership is a perk obtained through apprenticeship and seniority, criteria that have systematically excluded anyone not part of the inner circle. This could mean other white males, but principally it means excluding women and people of color. In the early 1970s, Alicia Weber became the first woman camera operator in New York's IATSE.[12] The man who sponsored her membership refused to yield to threats and intimidation. In 1991, I became an IATSE First AC while doing *Juice* (1992) and became the first Black woman focus puller in the union, and one of the few Black people to enter the union as a First AC.[13] In addition to learning from the top ACs in the business and receiving my training at General Camera Corporation,[14] which at the time was the top camera rental house on the East Coast, it took the intervention of Larry Banks, Robert Shepard (African American DPs), Bruce MacCallum (an Irish American First AC), Alicia Weber (a British Cameraperson), and others to help get me in at IATSE

The intersections of race and gender within a profession that is almost exclusively white and male were often the cause of tension and conflict. It was frustrating to challenge constantly bigots and sexists and still function professionally with my character and will intact – day after day. It was also confusing and exhausting to counteract the weight of negative stereotypes about women and people of color, weather the abuse, and then find myself fiercely supported by many of those who had made working so difficult. For example, some white men who initially gave me absolute hell (initiation by fire) sometimes became my staunchest allies or fiercest protectors. The same guys that hurled every racist, sexist joke, and jab to see how much I could take, then chastised me for not being able to "take it like a man" and fit in with the guys, or who dismissed the pain they inflicted as part of "paying dues, just like the rest of the guys," later got me hired on top jobs. They also shared with me the benefits of their experience and mistakes.

Ironically, some women and men who initially responded warmly to me when I was a "lowly PA" became predatory and threatened when I expressed interest in working in the camera department. Some Black independent filmmakers who espoused more open and inclusive hiring practices seemed resistant to hiring a Black woman as their First AC until they learned that I'd AC'd first for white filmmakers and production companies such as MGMM, Mark (MTV) Pellington, or Pennebaker and Associates. Black and white directors, producers, and DPs alike hesitated entrusting their film to a woman – who also happened to be Black – until they double-checked my rep, or learned that the crew and talent responded well or more favorably to me as a person and film professional.

Most interesting, however, were the cases where Black women directors and actors dismissed me by nature of my position as a film technician. Overall, however, significantly more Black women mentored, challenged, and helped me to reach my goal of becoming a top-notch documentary DP/Cameraperson. They also encouraged me to find whatever it was that would intrigue me emotionally, artistically, and financially. Grace Blake, Ada Gay Griffin, Michelle Parkerson, and Kathe Sandler were among the Black women who gave me my first and best breaks. In sum, manifestations of paternalism and institutional racism and sexism at times blurred with more manageable rites of passage such as mainstream society coming face to face with "the other," who happened to be me.

In addition to the complex intersections of race and gender, I must add class (formerly upper middle, but during college and on my own in Manhattan, I barely made rent), education (elite and private), and sexuality (gay). I moved to New York in 1991, having been blessed by finding a share in a huge, rent-controlled, raggedy three-bedroom apartment with a living room, dining room, foyer, two bathrooms, and a magnificent view of the river and bridge. It was in Washington Heights, on Haven Avenue between 174th and 175th Streets, and I shared it with two other women. We split the $560-a-month rent three ways. The reason I mention all of this is that had it not been for this unheard of rent, I would never have survived on the $6K I made doing film work as a PA that first year. This is very important. New York is an expensive city and because, like most cultural work, film work is freelance, there is no job security. Very few can consider, let alone attempt and overcome such obstacles.

It is ironic that most perceive filmmakers as wealthy and glamorous. I had moved to New York with literally only one connection – producer Grace Blake – $200 for the next month's rent and utilities, and only $50 to spare for food and transportation (often, I couldn't afford subway fare and had to jump the turnstiles, risking a $50 fine). A "good daughter" is not supposed to graduate from Stanford University and then turn down a full ride for graduate school at Howard University (and lose an opportunity to work with Haile Gerima), only to move to one of the highest crime rate areas of New York in order to try and do camera work in the film business. It was "critical" that I succeed without any help from home.

In 1987, at the age of 23, I didn't know that I had chosen a career in which very few women, few Blacks, and perhaps no other Black woman at that time had achieved "success." I was in a field dominated by neon blue-collar white males who might have gone to college, but few had attended top institutions because it was not a priority when being an "A-list" AC or DP was the "family business." I was a curiosity and a threat. And I learned quickly that I had to hide my educational background, my parents' class status and professions, my sexuality, and to try to be as asexual as possible. This was not easy.

I am the child of a first-generation American whose parents emigrated from Panama, and a Southerner who grew up in Jim Crow amerika. Both were raised in extreme poverty, excelled in their careers, and raised the three of us children never to forget where they, or we, had come from, what it would take to move on, and, most of all, that we must always "reach back" to help others along. They saw this as one of the best ways to move forward as individuals, as a society, and as a people. In New York, I was fortunate to meet people who "reached back" for me: complete strangers, new friends, and colleagues looked out for me, trained me, and hired me. With dedication, skill, finesse, and perhaps the odd luck of being the "wrong" color and sex at the "right" time (resistance to Reagan and Bush's destructive and divisive policies), I found allies in the strangest of places. Most people spend almost five years in each subfield before moving on to the next career step. However, an odd combination of timing, education, people, values, apprenticeships, and luck made it possible for me to move incredibly rapidly from PA, to Second AC, to First AC, to Camera Operator and DP – in five short years.

By interning at General Camera Corporation, I was able to network with some of the top ACs in the business while learning how to pre-pare, operate, troubleshoot, and, if needed, do on-the-set repairs of almost every type of motion picture camera, lens, or accessory. With General Camera credentials, and excellent mentors, I not only became a "top-notch" film professional but also someone able to "reach back" for others as well.

I brought in, hired, and trained as many "outsiders" – women, people of color, and poor whites – as possible. Sometimes, this meant bringing some-one along on a camera check out, going by Spike Lee's office and talking to Monty Ross or the Production Office Coordinators (POCs) to lobby for someone. Sometimes this meant introducing people at parties, getting some-one on set as a PA and then helping them move up or over to where they really wanted to be, and once, it meant telling a little lie to a director.[15] These are some of the same things others did for me. And I returned "the favor" in the way they requested, my parents expected, and the only way I knew how: by doing the same for someone else.

A Neon Blue-collar Artist?

We're in Washington, DC, filming Billy Jackson's *Didn't We Ramble On: The Roots of Black Marching Bands*. The crew is ready to go and the talent has fallen asleep in the middle of his interview. Nobody moves. We look at each other, afraid to wake him. The man is 72 years old and still on the road. He's one of the greatest living musicians in the world. Right now, with his chin tucked down on his chest like a large, beautiful owl, he could be my grand-father, or father to any one of the men on the crew. He's now a weary old man, but he once took Miles Davis under his wing. He helped to invent bebop. Mr. Dizzy Gillespie snores gently and we watch him sleep. After almost ten minutes, he startles awake, embarrassed.

"Was I out long? Damn."
"I don't know," Billy says as we all take our places, pretending that we just now got ready. "Camera ready? Sound ready?" We nod. Gillespie yawns through most of the interview. When we pause to change mags, he gets up from the chair.
"Billy. I'm beat. We'll do this another time, okay. No more. I'm tired."

The director is crushed. There is no more time. It's got to happen. He tries everything he can to convince him. "Fifteen, twenty minutes max," he promises. But Gillespie isn't hearing him. He's shaking hands with the crew. I look to Bobby Shepard, my DP, not sure what to do. Billy tells him to turn off the lights. That's as good as calling it a wrap.

I'm one of the last to say good-bye to Gillespie. I cup his hand in mine and tell him what a pleasure it was to meet him after listening to him since I was "this high." He doesn't believe me so I tell him how I found all these moldy 78s while cleaning my parent's house the summer I turned 13. I had discovered a whole new world – Ray Charles, Dinah Washington, Billie Holiday, Harry Belafonte, Sarah Vaughan, and Dizzy Gillespie.

"And your favorite?" he asked. I've never had much of a poker face so I had to tell him the truth. At 13, with a major case of adolescent blues, it had to be Lady Day. He tells me little stories about her as the rest of the crew packs up. And I tell him what wonderful stories he told today, during the breaks, and how much I'd enjoyed them. I tell him it's a shame that touring keeps him so busy and so exhausted. I tell him that there are so many people who would love to just sit and listen to him talk, hear his stories, and learn about the history of jazz and its roots.

"It's been so wonderful today I have to pinch myself. I feel really honored to be here and learn from you."
He grins like a school boy, flattered, incredulous.
"Really, now?"
"Yeah. Really."
"Oh, I'm just full of air."
"Oh, no you're not Mr. Gillespie."
"Call me Diz, child."

Somehow, he's sitting back in the interview chair. I kneel beside him, chatting, and being my mother's child. I have to tell you that my mother possesses a good old, genuine, Southern charm, and is a beautiful, big-boned, heavy-hipped, preacher's daughter, whose warmth is irresistible. And that same charm, when used sparingly and potently by me, her daughter, got Dizzy Gillespie to do what no one in that room could do – get him to feel a little younger, a little more bold, and more like the distinguished older gentleman of the world that he was.

He knew what an awkward spot the director was in. He knew this tour was packed and the chances of Billy catching up with him on the East Coast were slim to none. He knew that we were a tight crew and it would be hard to find a better one. He knew that the history of the Black marching bands and their Mardi Gras and African roots were a crucial and underexplored link to the development of jazz and blues as cultural art forms. Independently produced documentaries can take years, sometimes a decade or more, to complete. And he knew that a little more of his time, right here and now, would make all the difference in the world. But as he straightened his clothes and cleared his voice, he said, "Okay. I'll do it for Crystal."

Obviously, this is not a story about how charming I am. Rather, this story demonstrates how respect for the subject, collaborative work, and a non-voyeuristic, nonsensationalist approach is critical to filmmaking. This story also makes the case that interventions by film technicians can not only make or break a shoot but also can and do have real artistic impact. This example is not an exception, and more attention needs to be devoted to studying the roles of film technicians as filmmakers.

(Re)Calibrating the Filmic Gaze

Like most women of color, I have not had the luxury to be mono-issued. My sexual orientation was a "nonissue" compared to proving myself as a Black woman technician and filmmaker in a white, hyper-heterosexual, male-dominated field. My larger concern was subverting the sexual tension and sexual harassment that appeared to be an occupational hazard of being the only woman in the camera department, often with zero female representation or support in the sound, lighting, and grip departments.

Having and maintaining a comfortable professional and social relationship with the majority of the men I worked with for a minimum of twelve hours a day, under extreme stress and pressure, was difficult on many levels. My identity as a Black, gay, female, college-educated, middle-class woman working with both Black and white independent filmmakers raised eyebrows and caused tension that had to be constantly renegotiated and dissipated. The fact that my job as First AC often required me literally to be responsible for keeping the image focused on women and people of color in a very male/objectified gaze was problematic. What was most troubling, however, was that in order to keep the images focused and perform my job well, I had to participate in creating these same problematic constructions of race and gender identities, rehearse and anticipate the "action." At times, I was at liberty to discuss or even challenge these constructions. These were rare pleasures.

However, having to remain silent as I helped maintain a problematic gaze was all too often the norm. For example, while working with DP/Operator Bill Dill during a music video for Guy's hit song, "I Like," I had to mount the camera on a dolly with a jib arm which Bill swept over the lingerie-clad bodies of several beautiful women lying on satin sheets. Cinematically, I learned that pale rose satin (awful) looked marvelous under deep chocolate (surprise) gelled lights. But as one of the few women on the crew, it was difficult for me to take part in a production which totally objectified these women as interchangeable sexual toys and morsels of flesh to be admired, revealed, and consumed for the camera and male gaze.

These women were quite literally made delicious. The women were told to seduce the camera, and Bill hovered above them, one knee resting on the "bed" or straddling them in order to sweep the camera over the landscape of their bodies. The sensual music guided his movements. And my job required absolute concentration on seminude body parts so that I could determine that the lenses, which seemed more phallic than usual, did not accidentally hit these women in the Camera Operator's zeal for a close shot. I had to make sure that the full, moist cleavage of their breasts (it's hot under the lights) was kept in sharp focus from about 7'1" to 6.3" from the film plane (which is behind the lens, an inch or so into the camera body). I have helped shoot love scenes also. My embarrassment for the talent and for myself was acute on a closed or open set – either way, it was claustrophobic, voyeuristic, sexy, and mechanical at the same time. It was very difficult to turn off my raging mind to do what I must do: lose myself in the moment, abandon myself to the sensual, and stay focused.

As a woman, and as a filmmaker who wishes to resist issues of power/ dominance implicit to the male gaze, I find myself perplexed as to how I will communicate the erotic scenes and sensuality embedded in my writing, films, and videos. For example, my MFA project, a video installation entitled *Border Line...Family Pictures*, is the first of a four-part series on the contested terrain of biography and history in four urban cities: East Palo Alto, Los Angeles, Washington, DC, and New York City. Like much of my recent work, the story on which the installation is based addresses issues of agency and resistance, but it also explores the sensual and non-traditional modes of filmmaking. The video juxtaposes a fictionalized story about a poor Black woman within an elite university and her experiences of loss, and secrecy regarding her sexuality, with memories of her grandfather, who was a member of the Brotherhood of Sleeping Car Porters. The video incorporates original footage, historical footage, and images from the bloody history of the California Railroads and Stanford University. Most importantly, by having four diverse women of color portray a single main character, the project challenges essentialized identity while creating a democratic space for shared experience.

In my own work, and in the films that I seek out as a member of the audience, I value films that destabilize the dominance and power of a gaze that devalues gender, sexuality, and race. How I will evoke the erotic as powerful and woman centered without the visual and theoretical baggage of oppression, voyeurism, and objectification is still something with which I am grappling. But I will use the sensual, inclusive, democratic lens of Julie Dash's and Arthur Jafa (A. J.) Fielder's *Daughters of the Dust* (1991) as a guide. In this film, lighting and movement caressed and elevated the multi-faceted nature of Black female identity and form like no film I have seen before or since.

How do we situate the works of established and upcoming independent filmmakers who are attempting to innovate and redefine the so-called Black film aesthetic in a creative manner? Where are the voices and perspectives of women?

My experiences working on *Juice* demonstrate some of the concerns regarding how to define the Black aesthetic, and the limitations of identity politics or biological essentialist arguments. This was an independently produced film, written, directed and performed by Black men, and coedited by a Puerto Rican American woman. Yet however much the film attempted to challenge mainstream constructions of public enemy number one, the Black male youth, it instead reproduced a genre that ghettoized, demonized, and pitted young Black and Puerto Rican men against each other. It failed to address faithfully the real enemies: poverty, police brutality, economic apartheid, and poor education. Further, *Juice* ended up replicating the archetypal, dangerously narrow, male gaze of *Boyz 'N the Hood* (1991), where the lives and struggles of Blacks were reduced to a typical mainstream construction of Black life through Black boys who saw most women as oppositional to their "homies," caretakers, or sex objects. Unfortunately, the interventions of the women on set, in the cutting room, and the women in these Black men's lives did little to alter this nonliberating cinematic construction. *Juice*, like many films situated in the "hood" by Black male or Black female directors, sacrificed or devalued women for the "larger good" of the race/class/culture/nation. This is a serious problem that permeates government policies, personal politics, spectacles like the Million Man March, and films.

As a filmmaker and film consumer, I look forward to the creation and distribution of more positive, liberational films. However, I do not think that only Blacks can make these films. Like many, I believe that such biological essentialist aruguments are ahistorical and inherently flawed. My thinking is more in line with cultural critic Tommy Lott, who argues for a "no-theory theory" of Black film, which addresses the "complexity of meanings we presently associate with the political aspirations of Black people . . . a theory which is designed to be discarded when those meanings are no longer applicable."[16] Lott's theory suggests some hope that we will see an end to this most recent wave of blaxploitation films by bad Black boyz and girlz in the director's chair. It also suggests that, like filmmaking, film criticism may also take on a different form. Lott maintains that "when a film contributes ideologically to the advancement of Black people, within a context of systematic denial, the achievement of this political objective ought to count as a criterion of evaluation on a par with any essentialist criterion."[17] Lott seeks to disrupt Hollywood's "master narrative" of Black self-hate and oppression while recognizing that films have tremendous power.

Political scientist and film critic Cedric Robinson concurs with Lott's call for a pluralistic, liberational "political theory of Black cinema"[18] and insists that we need "oppositional voices and images which are redemptive of Black images on film and the society in which they are made."[19] Such models of film culture are instructive, necessary, and attainable. For Robinson, the film that best fits his model for redemptive, democratic, and liberational filmmaking is *Daughters of the Dust*. For me, it is seeing and wishing to emulate *Daughters of the Dust* and being a part of making *A Litany for Survival: The Life and Work of Audre Lorde* (1995).

There is always a moment of transition between the lines of one path and the lines of the next. In this case, the line from AC to DP/Operator took an unexpected detour and became the line that led to directing, writing, and academic life. I had begun turning down AC jobs because the only way to move into the next stage was to begin doing it and not look back. If finances demanded it, or a friend needed me, I'd AC. Twice, I was ready to AC for people I would do anything for, and was stunned and honored when they reached back and brought me up to the next stage. The first was D. A. Pennebaker, who asked me to be a Cameraperson for a documentary on Branford Marsalis. The second, and the last, were Ada Gay Griffin and Michelle Parkerson, who asked me to DP/Operate *A Litany for Survival*. I DP/Operated for this documentary not knowing exactly what was wrong with me, only knowing that I was in too much pain. I shot the Barbara Smith interview and Audre's New York State Poet Laureate awards ceremony, with Michelle and Ada refusing to let me carry anything, even my own bags. They took the camera off my shoulder as soon as the shot was over.

My experience filming Smith's interview was challenging on many levels. The decisions I made in terms of lighting and composition were the sum of my own aesthetic, heavily influenced by Bobby Shepard, Larry Banks, and A. J. Fielder. We were filming in the tiny, ground-floor apartment of her home. It was so small that she had to step through a simple lighting set-up that turned into an obstacle course in the claustrophobic space we shot in: the Kitchen Table Press office. I was stunned by what had been before my eyes all along: literally, a kitchen and a few tables. This is the only women of color press in the United States and it's been around for almost 30 years. That this small organization had made such an impact on the world from such a modest and tiny space was indeed mind-boggling.

Ada and Michelle have always made every member of the crew feel valued for their skill, expertise, and artistry. Audre's opinion, their opinion, the PA's opinion, the DP's opinion, were all critical to their process. Theirs was the most truly democratic, warm, and affirming set I have ever had the privilege to be a part of. When Ada called and asked me to go with her and Michelle to St. Croix to film Audre, probably for the last time before she died, I was touched and honored, but my body and spirit were still too broken. That I could not join my sisters, and say good-bye to Audre, is one of my great regrets. And although I worked on the film, when I finally saw it I found myself so moved, I was unable to restrain my tears. I was unprepared for the emotional force of this film that took them almost a decade to complete. I was utterly devastated by this film on Audre's life – its poignancy, grief, indomitable spirit, and life-affirming joy. For a change, no one moved from their seats until the last of the credits rolled by. And for a long moment afterwards, there was absolute silence, then the deafening thunder of applause. Ada and Michelle could not be there to present it at the Los Angeles International Gay and Lesbian Film Festival. They asked filmmaker Dawn Suggs and me to introduce it for them. We did, and tried our best to answer audience questions, to accept thanks for everyone who made the film possible. After the Q & A, as my partner and I were leaving, a woman came up to me and shook my hand. But she didn't thank me. She said, "Thank you all."

Above and below the line may always need to exist in film credits – it's a way for filmmakers to get known and get work, and it's how the popular media and cultural critics site and track films and filmmakers. But as soon as you separate the tasks of some of the filmmakers with the tiny little word "by" – as in "directed by..." or "cinematography by..." – and then list the rest of the crew without this distinction, a clear line is drawn. Ideally, I would like to do a film and have the credits make no distinction between above and below the line. But this is not entirely possible and perhaps it is not really important. My goal is to blur these artificial boundaries in the credits and to eradicate them on the set. This is the way we worked on *Litany.* On the set, above and below the line didn't really exist. But what about the artistic temperament and all of the tender egos, you ask? Perhaps my friend has the answer: "I see big egos every day. Humility is more grand."

Checking the Gate[20]

We need to make more and clearer connections between film scholars in the academy and filmmakers in the industry. Open dialogues between these parties at every stage of film production – writing, filming, and editing – would benefit both sides. Filmmakers would benefit from years of research by scholars, from an opportunity to receive critical feedback, and from having the platform and time to make important changes if needed. Film scholars would benefit from seeing and learning first-hand the many-faceted issues, concerns, and limitations of the filmmaking process. They would also provide more informed knowledge on the meaning and realities of the entirety of film production.

In sum, before calling a wrap to this discussion I must stress that I have barely explored the surface of a complex and profound subject. I have suggested that a "clearer" vision is critical to our understanding of film culture, and this article is really just a beginning. On set, a long lens is often used to capture images up close. Unfortunately, many film historians and theorists have thus far mimicked, reified, and adapted to viewing film culture through this same lens. Let us not mimic the hierarchical traditions of dominant film culture. Let us recalibrate the filmic gaze by employing a more democratic lens. Let us now pan, tilt, and track with a long lens, and intercut the scene with a wide-angle lens as well. In that way, we can interrogate and capture the complexities and spaces above and below the line.

In order to begin this task of recalibrating the cinematic gaze, more integrative and critical writing and research on a whole set of crucial problems needs to be explored. The complex dynamics that reside above and below the line need to be explored in academia, the film industry, and the film community. Problems of power need to be explored as well. In particular, we need to reconsider the problematics of "show biz mystique" and the reification of cinematic and cultural icons. Filmmaking and the prestigious/mystical world it creates for itself are already hierarchical. As cultural critics, filmmakers, and audiences, we must consider what roles we play in perpetuating the power and mystique of an industry and medium of socialization that systematically excludes and demonizes women, people of color, and oppositional/liberational independent filmmakers who reside in the tenuous boundaries above and below the line.

FADE TO BLACK
ROLL END CREDITS
"THE BEGINNING"

Notes

1   According to *The Professional Cameraman's Handbook*, "the Assistant Camera-man must be familiar with and able to: check camera equipment and accessories to determine they are in working order and that no items are missing; inventory and record all raw stocks assigned him; load magazines; assemble and prepare the camera at the photographic site; make hand tests; run the tape, set marks; check parallax, handle the slate; make camera reports; set lens aperture; regulate all focus changes; record meter readings; execute use of filters, gauzes, mattes, and diffusion discs; change lenses; check gate; change magazines; thread camera; disassemble and store camera equipment and accessories; charge batteries; unload and reload magazines; label, pack, and ship exposed stock to the laboratory; reinventory film supply; present duplicate camera, raw stock, and exposed stock reports to the Production Manager; any further necessary and incidental duties that may be required." However, in my experience, ACs were also required to perform the following duties, those designated in this "industry bible" as the Camera Operator's responsibilities, such as to "set the ground-glass focus; ascertain the parallax, regulate all shutter changes, note footage count; and assure the security of the mounted camera." Verne and Sylvia Carson, *The Professional Cameraman's Handbook* (London and Boston: Focal Press, 1981), 17–18.
2   According to the same text, "the Camera Operator (Second Cameraman) must be completely familiar with and able to: execute smooth and efficient camera movements; maintain the composition(s) prescribed by the Director of Photography; and certify each 'take' as it relates to camera operation" (ibid., 17).
3   "Arri" is short for "Arriflex," a German camera.

4 An AC cannot, under any circumstances, even utter the word "OOPS" anywhere on set, and particularly near the camera. One of the best ACs in the business had told me this. He'd said the dangerous word when he dropped a pen and suddenly, ten sets of panicked eyes were upon him. "If you make people nervous, you don't get called again," he said. "Your rep is everything."

5 Also according to *The Professional Cameraman's Handbook*, "the Director of Photography (First Cameraman) must be completely familiar with and able to: light studio and location settings; compose scenes; take [light] meter readings; select lenses; determine the use of filters, gauzes, mattes, and diffusion discs; call attention to and solve any photographic problem pertaining to the production which may arise. Whenever requested by the Producer, he shall advise the Producer; attend story conferences, give advice and suggestions in connection to the designs and selection of sets, costumes, and locations as they relate to photography; and generally render assistance in simplifying production, in heightening production values, and affecting economies" (Carson and Carson, *Cameraman's Handbook*, p. 17).

6 The First AC pulls focus directly on the lens barrel without looking through the camera by judging the distance between the object filmed and the film plane – except with steadicams, where a remote control unit is used to adjust the focus, adjust zoom, and aperture settings, and even to turn the camera off and on.

7 When you shoot steadicam, the eyepiece is dead weight, so it's removed if possible. If not, it's closed and taped over to prevent light leaks. The operator looks at a small on-board monitor.

8 Carson and Carson, *Cameraman's Handbook*, p. 17.

9 After all, in most film festivals, it is the Producer, not the Director, who receives the award for Best Picture.

10 Steven Bernstein, *Film Production* (Oxford: Focal Press, 1994), p. 76. Bernstein was the DP for *Like Water for Chocolate* (1993).

11 Missing from this "short list" is the writer, who must begin with the blank page. S/he is rarely credited with originating this vision, or made central to the critical discourse.

12 The International Association of Theatrical Stage Employees.

13 I was hurt while working on a feature and did not have the opportunity to pay off the balance of my membership and receive my official union card. Fortunately, as a union member, I was eligible for disability payments for a full year. Had it not been for IATSE coverage, the first 16 to 20 months I spent literally on my back would have landed me in the poor house. Workman's Compensation is insufficient and is in many ways a contradiction in terms.

14 Film equipment is prohibitively expensive. Thus, filmmakers usually rent the cameras, lighting, and grip equipment. Also, there are essentially three routes to becoming a DP: being a DP's child, working in the electric/lighting department, or working in the camera department. Like everything, it takes connections to get on set and through the door of a rental house. There are simply too many people ahead of and behind you. I used connections, incessant but friendly phone calls, and one day of sitting in the lobby with a copy of Richard Wright's

The Outsider (1953) for company until someone would see me. I'd just finished working in Spike's New York production office while they were in Atlanta shooting *School Daze* (1988) and was feeling bold. After several hours, the West Indian receptionist who'd had to tell me that the person I needed to see "was in a meeting" for the past three months picked up her phone and said (and I still can't believe it), "I don't care what you tell me. I'm sending her up right now." Thank you, sister! I must add that there were perhaps five women, all clericals, that worked there. The only other woman to work on the camera-rental floor had sued for sexual harassment and discrimination. I got in the door and was told they'd try it out with me there for a week. I stayed six months.

15   I am proud to say that I told a littey bittey lie to St. Clair Bourne. St. had asked me to recommend a DP and I suggested several. He chose Juan Cobo, but seemed a little anxious that Juan seemed a little young. St. said that it didn't matter, because Juan's reel was fantastic, but he ended his sentence with an inarticulate "but..." So I looked him in the eye and said that Juan just had a baby face but he was really in his mid-thirties. Actually Juan was my age, about 24. We did *The Making of Do the Right Thing* (1989) with St. Clair. His producer, Dolores Elliot, was so impressed that she hired him to DP *Portrait of Max Roach* (still unreleased). I often wonder if some of the people who got me on jobs "forgot" to mention that I was Black or female, because I certainly got some surprised expressions on people's faces.

16   Tommy Lott, "The No-Theory Theory of Contemporary Black Cinema," *Black American Literature Forum* 25, 2 (September 1991): 223.

17   Ibid., 231.

18   Ibid., 232.

19   Author's interview with Dr. Cedric Robinson, Chair of the Department of Black Studies (UC Santa Barbara) and author of *Terms of Order: Political Science and the Myth of Leadership* (Albany: SUNY Press, 1980), and *Black Marxism: The Making of the Black Radical Tradition* (London: Zed, 1983).

20   Before filming ends for the day and we call it a wrap, the film gate is checked one last time to insure that the film emulsion has not been scratched, or that a "hair" (dust, or other debris) is not caught in the gate – which could render the image shot unusable.

7

In My Mother's House: Black Feminist Aesthetics, Television, and *A Raisin in the Sun*

Sheri Parks

Parks, Sheri. "In My Mother's House: Black Feminist Aesthetics, Television, and *A Raisin in the Sun*." In Laughlin, Karen and Catherine Schuler, eds. *Theatre and Feminist Aesthetics* (Cranburg, NJ: Associated University Presses, 1995), pp. 200–28.

The Public Broadcasting Service's television production of Lorraine Hansberry's *A Raisin in the Sun* was first aired in 1989 to mark the thirtieth anniversary of the play's Broadway opening. The television production, currently available on videotape, was an ambitious one, particularly by public television standards, and tested the network's ability to deliver demanding material to a large audience. The PBS presentation was also truer to Hansberry's original message, marking the first time that a professional production of the uncut script was made available to an audience. By closely following Hansberry's directions and reinserting information that was considered too controversial for American audiences in 1959, the directors placed the play back into the center of Black women's concerns for the continuity of the culture and survival of self and family. By presenting the play to a mass audience, PBS recaptured Hansberry's original aim of art designed for large-scale social utility. The issues of Black traditional female power that Hansberry presented in 1959 remain central to the lives of Black women, perhaps providing evidence of the historical significance and intrinsic nature of those issues. The production also suggests that the medium has an ability to convey Black feminist theatre to millions more viewers than can even the most successful stage production. A television production of the play provides a discussion of the lives of Black women in a form that is aesthetically attractive and available to Black women, many of whom do not have regular access to the more elite form of live stage theatre.

Culture and Consciousness

A Raisin in the Sun is a play already put to many cultural uses by both Black and white audiences. Originally produced in 1959, it showed white American audiences the intimacies of Black life and validated the daily existences of its Black audiences. The play also heralded the arrival of the Black Arts Movement as well as the Civil Rights Movement as a part of the national agenda but later, Black male critics would use its fame to lambaste "integrationist" works. Meanwhile, the play was popular enough to warrant a film version, which won an award at Cannes, and a Broadway musical version, which won a Tony. Buried beneath all the racially related criticism was the fact that the author was a Black feminist and the play bespoke a particular brand of feminism, that practiced by women within the family in traditional Black culture. Hansberry biographer Anne Cheney writes that Hansberry was a feminist only in the most general sense,[1] but if the play is put in the context of its time and place, Hansberry appears to be a feminist in a most specific sense, that of Black women coping simultaneously with issues of race, caste, and gender.

Hansberry's cultural message was heavily influenced by the person and the works of W. E. B. Du Bois. He was a frequent visitor to the Hansberry family home, and Lorraine later studied African culture and philosophy under him. Hansberry's husband, Robert Nemiroff, told Cheney that Lorraine was particularly influenced by Du Bois's *The Souls of Black Folk*, originally published in 1903. The influence of Du Bois is most evident in *Raisin* in the concepts of double and merged consciousness. Du Bois wrote that the consciousness of imprisoned people might take one of three main forms: a state of rebellion and revenge; a state of double consciousness, in which one tries to adopt the consciousness of the ruling people; and merged consciousness, in which one successfully mixes one's cultural history and one's present situation to achieve self-realization.[2] Double consciousness is a result of trying to recontextualize oneself, to lose one's own history, which is impossible, and to adopt, wholecloth, someone else's history and culture without any opportunity for complete entry and privilege in that culture. It is, in a sense, cultural limbo:

> It is a peculiar sensation, this double consciousness, this sense of always looking at one's self through the eyes of others. . . . One ever feels his twoness, – an American, a Negro; two souls, two thoughts, two unreconciled strivings; two warring ideals in one dark body, whose dogged strength alone keeps it from being torn asunder.[3]

Merged consciousness allows the person to reach a new equilibrium, bringing the past into one's journey through the present; it is described by Du Bois as a tool for an imprisoned people:

> The history of the American Negro is the history of this strife, – this longing...to merge his double self into a better and truer self. In this merging he wishes neither of the older selves to be lost. He would not Africanize America....He would not bleach his Negro soul in a flood of white Americanism...He simply wishes to make it possible for a man to be both a Negro and an American.[4]

Culture is an important element of the Black feminist message. Black women have always been concerned with the multidimensional character of their disenfranchisement. Angela Davis, historian Paula Giddings, and others provide evidence that Black women have been hesitant to address issues of gender apart from issues of race. Giddings argues that if either had to come first for political reasons, race consistently emerged as the definitive issue. As a result, much of what might be considered prefeminist or feminist has been defined as Black rather than feminist. A common theme in the writings of Black women and, more recently, in Black feminist criticism is that of cultural duality and double racial consciousness. Gwendolyn Brooks and Toni Morrison, among others, have written about Black women in cultural limbo. Maud Martha, Brooks's protagonist in her autobiographical novel of the same name, sees herself through a white culture's gaze and proclaims herself ugly and worthless. Toni Morrison's *The Bluest Eye* is the story of a Black woman in cultural limbo. Morrison is also concerned with maintaining Afro-American heritage once relationships to the Black rural South have been stretched thin over distance and time. Michael Awkward, Barbara Christian, Mary Helen Washington, and Susan Willis have all examined various aspects of double racial consciousness in the works of Black women writers.[5]

Hansberry took the concept of double consciousness and feminized it to reflect the multifaceted roles of Black women by expanding the concept into two other spheres of double consciousness. While various characters move from holding dichotomous and paradoxical conceptualizations of race, they also move from the dichotomy of individual identity versus group identity to the merged position of individual within a family group, and from the gender dichotomy of male versus female to the merged role of an adult. Hansberry's women encounter or experience all three forms of double consciousness: race, family, and gender.

Reconciliation of double consciousness is portrayed in form as well as content. In *Raisin*, Hansberry appears to use blues music as a background sound of merged consciousness. The blues are a culturally merged aesthetic form, an amalgam of African descendent, rural Southern Black sound transported to the urban North to give voice to urban problems. The music evokes the emotionality of the Black micro-experience, and the Youngers listen to it almost constantly. When one character temporarily rejects Hansberry's symbol of merged state, Hansberry makes clear in her notes that we are not to regard blues in the same way that Beneatha does. "(*She promenades to the radio and, with an arrogant flourish, turns off the good loud blues that is playing.*) Beneatha says, 'Enough of this assimilationist junk!' "[6]

Group identity with the culture and the family are historically significant tools of survival for Black people. While assimilation is a cornerstone of American society, African Americans have never been allowed full access to mainstream institutions and remain largely alienated from the dominant culture. The adoption of mainstream American consciousness is emotional orphanage for a Black American. However, failure to adapt somehow to current living conditions is to endanger one's physical survival. The reconciliation of cultural dichotomy is itself a tool of survival. *Raisin* is a story of family members in different stages of racial double consciousness moving toward cultural reconciliation. At the beginning of the play, Mama and Walter form the endpoints of a racial consciousness continuum. Walter, played by Danny Glover, exhibits the most extreme manifestations of double consciousness. He overvalues a capitalistic American dream of power and wealth, and his dream of money has led to his attempt to break with the cultural group and the history that he blames for his difficulties. He is bitter with frustration, seeing himself as trapped with "the world's most backward race of people" (p. 26). Mama, played by Esther Rolle, recognizes Walter's ahistorical perspective:

> You something new, boy. In my time we was worried about not being lynched and getting to the North if we could and how to stay alive and still have a pinch of dignity too. . . . You ain't satisfied or proud of nothing we done. I mean that you had a home; that we kept you out of trouble till you was grown; that you don't have to ride to work on the back of nobody's streetcar – You my children but how different we done become. (p. 61)

Mama's emotional survival is based upon culturally contextualized and reconciled strategies: religion and a sense of historical interrelatedness. Her spirituality is so strong as to be visible. "She has, we can see, wit and faith of a kind that keeps her eyes lit and full of interest and expectancy. She is in a word, a beautiful woman" (p. 27). Her spirituality, while heavily laced with Christianity, also has a strong Afrocentric element of cultural and familial ancestry. The mother as link to cultural history is quickly established. "Her

bearing is perhaps most like the women of the Hereros of Southwest Africa –
rather as if she imagines that as she walks she still bears a basket or a vessel
upon her head" (p. 27). Mama remembers a cultural and familial past that
the others do not. As she speaks of the early family history, she is "seeing
back to times that only she can see," when furnishings "were selected with
care and love and even hope – and brought to this apartment and arranged
with taste and pride. That was a long time ago" (p. 33). A significant part of
Mama's memory of the past is her memory of Big Walter, her dead husband.
Big Walter is still very present in the family. He and Mama shared the dream
of a better home, and he literally worked himself to death for a house of the
sort that the family is about to acquire. The television production makes Big
Walter's spiritual presence very visible. There is a large, framed photograph
of him, positioned strategically in the living room so that he is present for
family discussions and events. Often characters are placed so that, just for a
moment, Big Walter's face is actually between them. Mama is not dependent
upon Big Walter or his memory; rather, his memory is one part of her past
and a source of her strength. Hansberry was a student of African history and
philosophy and probably was familiar with prominent cross-tribal conceptualizations of the past as part of the present and future and of the spiritual
presence of dead ancestors.[7]

Her link to a pastoral Southern history is also a central spiritual theme
for Mama. She has "a feeble little plant, growing doggedly in a small pot
on the window sill." She worries that it does not get enough sun in the
almost sunless apartment (pp. 27–8) as she remembers lusher gardens
"down home" (p. 41). Mama's plant expresses both her personality
(p. 191) and her dream of a place to garden, and her children give her
gardening tools and a gardening hat before the family moves to the new
house (p. 11). The historical role of flower gardening in Black women's
creativity and spiritual survival has been deeply explored in Alice Walker's *In
Search of our Mothers' Gardens*, in which Walker remembers her own
mother's gardens . . .[8]

In Black traditional culture, spiritual life is an amalgam of Christianity and
folk belief that is practiced in a less ritualized and fractionalized manner than
"church" religion often is. God and spirituality have been popularized and
reconstructed to meet the spiritual needs of Black people, and so it is
common to hear religious references on the street corner and in popular
secular Black music. Mama Younger's spirituality reflects a Black merged
religious experience.

Beneatha and Ruth are at different places on the continuum. Ruth's
behavior suggests a double consciousness that is less extreme than Walter's.
She is less concerned with cultural continuity than is either Mama or
Beneatha and affects the polite distance of white, bourgeois manners with

George Murchison and Karl Lindner. Beneatha is just beginning to have a merged consciousness, with a few traces of double consciousness remaining. She is an educated Black woman with more access to the dominant cultural institutions than her mother, but she retains some cultural traits.

The potential poles of Beneatha's consciousness are represented by the men she dates. George Murchison is the son of a wealthy Black businessman and is heavily invested in the consciousness of the white upper class. He believes that Beneatha's (and his) cultural heritage is best forgotten. He tells her, "Let's face it, baby, your heritage is nothing but a bunch of raggedy-assed spirituals and some grass huts" (p. 68). She resists him, telling her family, "The only people in the world who are more snobbish than rich white people are rich colored people" (p. 37).

In contrast to Mama, who is deeply invested in the recent cultural past, Beneatha is relearning her African past from another, more favored man. Asagai, a Yoruba from Nigeria, is deeply invested in his own culture. He brings Beneatha gifts of Yoruba music and robes. He teases her about looking for her identity and encourages her to make decisions and learn her own heart (p. 50). Then, he presents her with the robes of a Nigerian woman, his sister (p. 47), and questions the texture of her straightened hair. "Assimilationism is so popular in your country," he says, telling her that she really more closely resembles a queen of the Nile than a Hollywood queen (p. 49). At first, Beneatha responds to the robes in a manner closer to romanticized Western feminine images than to actual African women. When she wears them for the first time, "She is coquettishly fanning herself with an ornate oriental fan, mistakenly more like Butterfly than any Nigerian that ever was" but she quickly "remembers" (p. 63). In the robes, listening to the music, "a lovely Nigerian melody, she listens, enraptured, her eyes far away – 'back to the past'" (p. 64). In the 1989 television production, Beneatha sees the aesthetic inconsistency of her hair and the robes and has her hair cut into an Afro. When she eventually takes off the robes, the hairstyle remains and she appears as a merged, African American woman. When Mama meets Asagai, the African American past confronts and becomes comfortable with the African present. He is respectful of an elder. Mama smiles, repeats what Beneatha has told her about Africa and begins to mother him. Asagai is moved (pp. 51–2).

It is left to Beneatha to merge her own past with the present, but she has to confront and become comfortable with her personal past as well. Beneatha's education has cost her. She is having trouble finding her bearings, for she has come to distrust the spiritual anchors so useful to her mother. Beneatha thinks Ideas are Life, that life is simply a question of which ideas to incorporate, a spiritual betrayal which leads to a pivotal confrontation. Beneatha says she is "sick of hearing about God. . . . What has He got to do with anything?

Does he pay tuition?" Mama warns her off. Ruth agrees that Beneatha has overstepped her limits, but Beneatha insists:

> Mama, you don't understand. It's all a matter of ideas, and God is just one idea I don't accept. It's not important. I am not going out and be immoral or even think about it. It's just that I get tired of Him getting credit for all the things the human race achieves though its own stubborn effort. There simply is no blasted God – there is only man and it is he who makes miracles! (p. 39)

The conflict between Mama's spiritualism and Beneatha's humanism had been foreshadowed early in the play when Beneatha and her mother argue over her reciting scripture "in vain" (p. 34). With this more serious transgression, Mama moves swiftly to reestablish her dominance of person and ideas.

> (MAMA *absorbs this speech, studies her daughter and rises slowly and crosses to* BENEATHA *and slaps her powefully acroos the face. After, there is only silence and the daughter drops her eyes from her mother's face, and MAMA is very tall before her.*) MAMA Now – you say after me, in my mother's house there is still God. (*There is a long pause and* BENEATHA *stares at the floor wordlessly.* MAMA *repeats the phrase with precision and cool emotion.*) In my mother's house there is still God.
> BENEATHA   In my mother's house there is still God. (*A long pause.*) [In the television production, Beneatha is looking into her mother's eyes with a mixture of hurt and respect as she says the words.]
> MAMA   (*Walking away from* BENEATHA, *too disturbed for triumphant posture. Stopping and turning back to her daughter.*) There are some ideas we ain't going to have in this house. Not long as I am the head of this family.
> BENEATHA   Yes ma'am. (*MAMA walks out of the room.*) (p. 39)

Beneatha appears to her mother to be tossing aside the tools of her emotional survival. Beneatha is experimenting with many ideas, and her "flitting" from idea to idea has heretofore been tolerated by her family. This time she has, perhaps, ventured too far into European relativism, and her mother must act to curb the potentially dangerous wandering. Given Hansberry's extensive knowledge of African life and philosophy, the importance of this scene may go well beyond Christianity and childish rebellion. Hansberry was fond of puns and there are several different interpretations of "In my mother's house there is still God." Mama did not say, "God is alive," or "There is a God." She said that in her house there is God. In African spiritualism, the gods are literally with you, in your house, and for them to leave is a very unusual and dangerous thing. The spirits of the dead are also with you; a person is not really dead as long as somebody remembers him or her. God could be the abstracted Christian God, the African deities, or the soul of Big Walter. The line may be interpreted in one of the several ways or, in keeping with reconciliation of culture, in a mixture of the three.

Differences of caste and race force a wide gap between the concerns of Black women and those of elite, white feminism. I use the term *caste* rather than *class* to capture the permanence of Blacks' marginalization in the United States. Class membership is perceived as relatively fluid and subject to individual initiative. Class mobility is at the heart of American mythology. All of the Youngers are trying to change their class status. However, for Blacks, caste membership is assigned at birth and does not change in the face of class mobility. Although Hansberry was raised in affluence, she realized that affluence does not change caste membership, that her family's relative wealth did not bring privilege or protection. She was born in a ghetto because of racial housing covenants and soon learned that her race made her more vulnerable to sexual harassment by white men. She wrote in the autobiographical play *To Be Young, Gifted and Black*, "The white boys in the streets, they look at me and think of sex. . . . Baby, you could be Jesus in drag – but if you're brown they're sure you're selling."[9]

Raisin is set "somewhere between World War II and the present," a relatively affluent period in US history, but it is immediately established that the Youngers have not shared in the nation's affluence (p. 11). Their home is a poor one, showing the ravages of "too many people for too many years" (p. 11). A previously deleted bit of material reemphasizes the amalgam of race, caste, and gender issues that are of concern to Black women. The original stage production, which deemphasized the issue of the Youngers' poverty, excluded a short speech by Travis in which he describes seeing a rat as large as a small dog in the street. Witnessing this small but graphic detail of daily urban poverty lends new urgency to the family's move to a healthier neighborhood and adds new context to statements such as Beneatha's "We've all got acute ghettoitis" (p. 47).

Previous productions also downplayed the danger of the move and the warnings of the potential for white racial violence in the new white neighborhood. Another previously deleted scene makes it clear that the Youngers (and the audience) know the chance they are taking. Mrs. Johnson, a neighbor with whom the Youngers are on cordial, but not intimate terms, warns of racial violence by showing them a Black newspaper account of violence directed toward another Black family who moved into a white neighborhood. The Younger family had not known of the violence, which adds further concern regarding their own move. The reintroduction of the speech

changes the ending of the play, in which the family happily moves to their
new home, to an emotionally charged and ambiguous one. Staying with the
original script, the television production did not include additions written by
Hansberry for the 1961 movie, which added a safe arrival at the new home
and so diffused some of the original dramatic tension of the play.

While *Raisin* was not autobiographical, Hansberry did draw from figures
and events in her own life. The wealth of Hansberry's father, Carl, was
accrued through real estate investments, and the family lived in several
predominantly white neighborhoods where she and her family experienced
racial violence in the forms of vandalism and physical threat. When Carl
Hansberry purchased a house in a particularly hostile neighborhood, an
angry crowd gathered outside the home and someone threw a brick, narrowly missing 8-year-old Lorraine's head. Racially restrictive covenants kept
them out of some neighborhoods altogether, but Carl Hansberry fought and
eventually won a celebrated United States Supreme Court case against
covenants.

Hansberry seemed aware that class mobility was a precarious step for
members of a lower caste, who might never gain full membership into the
dominant society. Mrs. Johnson, the Youngers' neighbor, also warns of the
dangers of class mobility and education, of leaving that which one knows for
an uncertain future. "Education has spoiled many a good plowhand," she
quotes, and she attributes the line to Booker T. Washington. Hansberry's
intellectual mentor W. E. B. Du Bois was an intellectual and political advers-
ary of Washington, and wrote that "Mr. Washington represents in Negro
thought the old attitude of adjustment and submission."[10] Mama Younger
responds to Mrs. Johnson by calling Washington a fool. It is significant that
Mama, a lover of the pastoral past and so, one might think, a potential
admirer of Washington, should call him a fool, but Mama is particularly
interested in education and upward mobility for her children.

The Younger family has invested its collective dreams of upward mobility
in the daughter rather than the son, a dramatic portrayal which has a certain
verisimilitude. Education, rather than commerce, has historically been a
common class mobility strategy for Blacks. It has also been historically
common for families to give priority to educating their girls, since boys
could earn as much money through skilled labor as they might have through
college-related job fields. Black families have traditionally sent more women
than men to college and continue to do so.[11] Mama Younger is determined
that nothing will stand in the way of Beneatha's education (p. 32), while
nothing is said about the elder male child's education. Education, however,
does not bring about a change in family members' status. Although Mama is
uneducated, she retains her status as head of the family and will act to
reinforce her status if necessary.

Traditional Black Female Power and Family Consciousness

Mama Younger is a Black Mother, an example of a prominent traditional Black feminist role. A very strong and pervasive female culture has survived within Black communities, but its role has been disguised by negative "matriarchy" arguments of white and Black men. While Black, middle-class, male critics continue to decry the "mammy" as a negative Black stereotype, the Black Mother continues to be a strong, historically based symbol of Black feminism for working-class Black women. The Black Mother situates Black feminism in the place where it is ordinarily and traditionally practiced by Black women, in the home. While part of the mainstream, academic feminist agenda has deemphasized mothering as an important part of women's lives, to do so with Black women would be to dismiss a traditional locus of Black female power. The two older Younger women are the backbone of the family, as interested in the long-term emotional survival of their family as they are in its short-term physical survival. Their caretaking as well as their income enable the Younger family to survive. As a result of their position vis-à-vis men and the family, Black women shoulder much responsibility for day-to-day family life. The Black-traditional definition of the family means that children, and often extended family, are of primary concern to Black women. Having a child in the Black community is a rite of passage to womanhood; it connotes status that a permanent relationship to a man does not. The definition of motherhood and the Black Mother's relationship to her children are Black feminist issues.

The Younger women cannot depend upon Walter to keep the family intact. While Walter has dreams that are consistent with American capitalism, the women make him go to work so they can pay the rent. The women work to keep the family alive. Because the structural relationships between African American men and women are fundamentally different from those intergender relationships in the dominant culture, any feminism that professes to represent Black women must confront those differences. Black men have never been in a position to completely disenfranchise Black women; theirs is an equality of powerlessness in relation to the dominant culture.

Black women often assume or share primary responsibility for their own survival and that of their families regardless of class. A reconstruction of the role of women in the Black community may find that the artificially easy dichotomy between male and female is even more problematic here than it is in the dominant culture. A dominant historical and theoretical theme in mainstream American feminism is the modern dichotomization of private and public life. The privatization of the American home marks the point at which the popular feminine ideal became that of a nonproductive consumer whose daily work produced no capital and came to be undervalued. It is also at this point that a poignant difference between Black women and white women emerged. All American homes were not privatized. Like Mama and Ruth Younger, the vast majority of Black women never stopped producing capital. Although the same is true of poor women of all races, Black women in the middle class continued to work and still do. Many Black households also have "side hustles," the postmodern equivalent of Ruth's laundry service, operated out of the home. The home as a locus of capital production has continued to be an economic reality for Black America. The Black home and the Black community are not easily dichotomized for other social reasons; like Mrs. Johnson, community members who are not blood kin are likely to be somewhat more active in Black homes than in white homes.

The entire play occurs in the domestic arena, so that all of the interaction is under the leadership of Mama. Domestic stories are prevalent among Black female writers, perhaps as a commentary upon the centrality of Black Mothers. More than a blind following of tradition, domestic story lines are a commentary upon the importance of family to the political orientation of Black women since outside events are filtered through their effect upon the family. So it is with the Youngers. Information about racial violence, of interest to the larger Black community, is filtered through its immediate meaning for the family. The information is delivered to the home in a way that dictates this application; a relationship with a neighbor woman, based upon the borrowing of domestic supplies and the serving of pie and coffee, becomes the entry point of the politically charged information and reframes it as information pertinent to the survival of the family. The "women's room" in this family is the kitchen; it is literally the source of the light, a small, determined light: "The sole natural light the family may enjoy in the course of a day is only that which fights its way though this little window" (p. 12). The women wage war on the ravages of poverty but "weariness, has in fact, won in this room. Everything has been polished, washed, sat on, used scrubbed too often" (pp. 11–12). The fight to stay in touch with the hopeful past has been a feminine one – cleaning is mentioned more often than use, indicating the sheer energy needed for survival. The audience sees only the women participating in domestic labor...

The women work hard in this family and they know that it is for their family that they work. Mama tells Walter that although he has never understood it, she "ain't got nothing, don't own nothing, ain't never really wanted nothing that wasn't for you" (p. 86). When Mama tells Walter about Ruth's planned abortion, Walter objects that Ruth would not have an abortion. Mama instructs him, "When the world gets ugly enough – a woman will do anything for her family. *The part that's already living*" (Hansberry's emphasis, pp. 61–2). Illegal abortion becomes an act of family survival perpetuated by women for women; the fact that the doctor is a "she" makes Mama "immediately suspicious."

The Youngers are a whole family and Mama is the head of it. Despite all the current discussion of the crisis in the Black family, Black people, particularly working-class Black people, have long considered a female-headed home to be a family. Niara Sudarkasa has produced a body of anthropological work which presents the female-centered household as the Afrocentrically traditional form.[12] The physical absence of a Black father does not mean that the family has been destroyed. Given the arrival of the insurance money, Mama must be a fairly recent widow, yet there is no sense of this. She does not seem the helpless widow new to heading her family. Despite the cries of middle-class Black men and well meaning but culturally ignorant whites, the traditional form of Black family is female oriented. Clearly then, the gender-based definition of the Black family and of Black family leadership are feminist issues.

The cultural message is that the children are more central to the definition of the woman than is the traditional husband. Children are the focus of the Younger family. Ruth's pregnancy and possible abortion sparks a running theme of the value of children. The dialogue is arranged so that the audience hears Mama remember the death of one of her infant children before Ruth actually says she is pregnant. Ruth says, in sympathy for Mama and perhaps for herself, "Ain't nothin' can tear at you like losing your baby" (p. 33). Despite the obvious emotional and financial difficulties, Mama expresses "grandmotherly enthusiasm" at the news of Ruth's pregnancy, hoping for a girl, because Travis needs a sister (p. 45). Indeed, Ruth must fight Mama to be Travis's primary mother (pp. 28, 76). Mama includes Ruth when she refers to "my children" (p. 31), often calling her "child." Ruth in turn often calls the older Mrs. Younger "Mama." The primacy of Ruth as the biological mother is asserted by Ruth but not always allowed by Mama.

Mama nurtures everybody and keeps tabs on most of the activity in the apartment, even that of Travis, who has another mother, and the resistant Beneatha and Walter. She has a habit of "listening vigorously" to others' conversations. (p. 44). Mama is the economic and ideological head of the family, and she controls the ideas and the actions within it. Her children deviate from her teaching only with her benign permission and risk her anger if they stray too far; twice she strikes her children when she thinks they are pursuing courses that endanger their own or the family's physical or emotional survival. Yet Mama's strength and the power which it garners within her family are usually carried with gentleness. "Her speech . . . is as careless as her carriage is precise – she is inclined to slur everything – but her voice is perhaps not as much quiet as simply soft" (p. 27). This is not a romantic

caricature of the old Black mammy with her little Black brood. Both biological children are trying desperately, each in his or her own way, to break
away from Mama and the familial–cultural collective history that she represents even as each acknowledges his or her continuing dependency. Mama
compares them to the little plant in the kitchen window; neither has had
enough sunshine or anything else – they have spirit but are twisted.

The power held by Black women in the family makes the domestic role
fundamentally different from the more passive, ideal mother-wife in mainstream American society, whose life is consumed by a family in which she has
little power. The responsibility that Black women traditionally hold in the
family suggests that the family is a traditional locus of Black female power
which demands a particular leadership style. Rather than a traditional leader,
what Antonio Gramsci calls an inorganic leader who assumes power through
heredity, wealth, or military might, Black mothers are organic leaders who
naturally emerge to facilitate group survival and gain power though responsibility and history. An organic leader knows and cares for the concerns of the
group.[13]

Through the characterizations of the Youngers, Hansberry demonstrates
levels of family group consciousness that are analogous to Du Bois's states of
racial consciousness. One state, demonstrated by Walter and Beneatha, is
that of individual consciousness, in which a person is concerned only with
him- or herself to the detriment of the group. The second state, demonstrated by Ruth, is that of total family consciousness, in which one is focused
upon the concerns of the group to the detriment of the self. The third state,
that of the individual with group consciousness, is a reconciliation of the first
two states and facilitates survival of the self and the family. The third state is
best demonstrated by Mama. Although the racial messages of the play took
precedence in earlier interpretations of the work, the timing and emphasis of
the television play allow as much attention to be paid to the lives of the Black
women who are central to the Younger family and to the Black feminist ideas
contained within the work itself. Mama Younger is the family's and the play's
central character. As if to make her more regal, she is introduced last. Her
presence provides a stark contrast to the unrest of the adult children. Although
Ruth bears the closest resemblance to Mama, Ruth shows that biological
motherhood alone does not make a viable Black Mother. While much older
than Ruth, Mama has none of Ruth's weariness of spirit. Loosely based upon
Hansberry's own mother, she is "full bodied and strong. She is one of those
women of a certain grace and beauty who wear it so unobtrusively that it
takes a while to notice … Being a woman who has adjusted to many things
in life and overcome many more, her face is full of strength" (p. 27). In
a more general sense she is based upon the archetypical Black Mother,
whom Hansberry, quoting Langston Hughes's poem "Washerwoman,"

described as the "the Black matriarch incarnate...who scrubs floors of a nation in order to create Black diplomats and university professors."[14]...

Ruth, the "good" and long-suffering wife who is not as strong or as spiritually supported as Mama, most closely approximates the role of the completely family-oriented wife-mother who tries to get through life without a sense of self. About 30, she "was a pretty girl, even exceptionally so...Now disappointment has already begun to hang in her face" (p. 12). Hansberry notes that in a few years she will be a "settled woman," which on its surface, simply means a married, middle-aged woman. But here marriage and middle age also carry a weariness and disappointment that comes with settling for less than one had hoped. Ruth is so tired of this life that she wakes up sleepy. Hansberry's notes direct the actress to play the role of Ruth with a strong undertone of weariness. She speaks "like someone disinterested and old" (p. 25). While Hansberry describes Ruth's weariness, she also immediately shows her dogged determination and pained energy with her son and her anger at her husband as she tries to jumpstart them for the day.

Ruth constantly thinks in terms of family. What is Ruth's personal dream? Where does *her* rage go? We never know. She seems to live for her family and, unlike Mama, *through* her family. (Mama does not fear Walter's disapproval or change her actions to the point that all her plans are lost.) Although Ruth has a job, she is the only character who seems to almost never leave home, the exception being her preliminary visit to the abortionist. Her only creations are two children, and she almost loses both. Travis is quickly gaining a life of his own and is testing the limits of his autonomy, and she comes close to aborting the baby, despite her own wishes. Involvement without power or personal strength is an emotionally draining experience. Although Ruth is capable of gentleness and motherly humor with Travis and with Walter, her moods also change rapidly, from humor to brusqueness, perhaps because she is struggling to maintain the appearance of emotional equilibrium without the supports that are useful to her mother-in-law (p. 18). She speaks of her life as a burdensome one, "I got too much on me this morning" (p. 16)...

Beneatha, Mama's daughter, is based upon a younger Lorraine Hansberry; the name is a pun, for there was a time in Hansberry's life when she felt superior to all things.[15] Nevertheless, Hansberry describes Beneatha as less beautiful than Ruth or Mama, perhaps because of her youth and lack of wisdom. Beneatha is really a woman-child, and the name may actually be a double pun – she is beneath her mother. Although 20 years old, she is seen by the other women as a "fresh" child (p. 34), as a little girl (p. 36), and as childish (p. 40). She is self-centered, more individualistic than the other women, and an unreliable source of strength.

Walter, Mama's son and Ruth's husband, is still a man-child, a "lean, intense young man," as opposed to Ruth, who is actually younger but

seems older and more tired (p. 13). He behaves in almost stereo-
typically shifty ways, "inclined to quick nervous movements and erratic
speech habits" (p. 13). Walter loves to pontificate in a distracted philosophical style, giving vent to long romantic speeches, full of "hysterical
promise" (p. 89). He is childish and lacks group survival skills. Ruth's
humor is motherly; Walter's is boyish (p. 27). Since he is played by
Danny Glover in the television version, this Walter is in striking contrast
to Sidney Poitier's characterization in the original stage production and
film. While Poitier was lean and skittish so that the childishness was
almost fitting, Glover is big and powerful so that the childishness is an
aberration.

Because he is the male lead, directors may have assumed that Walter is the
central character of the play, that it is his dream deferred that had dried up,
but there are many dreams in this play and they are all at one point deferred
or dead. Walter is an artificial center of attention in a female-headed
household. Like a child, he commands an enormous amount of attention
with his louder-than-life actions and temper tantrums that other family
members try to rein in, but his "acting out" is destructive to the family
and himself. Walter actually adds little to the family. He appears to be a drain
– emotionally and, after he stops going to work and gets conned by a close
associate, financially. If he were gone, the family would be calmer and
steadier.

Walter is childish because he is selfish. Mama and Ruth are still trying
to raise him, emotionally, morally, financially, and familially. Ruth is trying to
teach him to spend money wisely, to go to work, to stop drinking so much,
to stop trusting conmen, to get off the furniture, to be polite to guests.
Mama tries to teach him how to handle large sums of money, to set up
his own bank account (with Mama's money), and to stop yelling at his wife.
Walter's selfishness and lack of group identification manifests itself in
an extreme lack of cooperation with, or sympathy for, family members.
He is alone and blames everyone else – the family, the race, the family as
race – for his life situation; "always in his voice there is a quality of indict-
ment" (p. 13)...

Although Walter wants what his mother and wife cannot give him, he does
not accept that which they can give him. He asks Ruth, "Why you always
trying to give me something to eat?" Ruth "(*Standing and looking at him
helplessly*)" responds, "What else can I give you, Walter Lee Younger?" (p.
74). Even when Walter speaks of family concerns, he sees them from an
idiosyncratic point of view. *He* thinks that only he suffers when the women
have to work to provide for the family; he complains, "Everytime we need a
new pair of curtains and I have to watch you go out and work in somebody's
kitchen" (p. 58). More often, his selfishness leads him away from family

relationships. He has left the family, betraying the group dream in his "quest". He sees no benefit in his relationship with Ruth since it brings him no financial reward. When Mama warns Walter about his treatment of Ruth, he asks, "Why – what she do for me?" Mama answers, "She loves you." Walter responds by leaving the house to be alone, but not before Mama suggests that it is dangerous for a man to go outside his home to look for peace (pp. 59–60)....

For Walter, male adulthood is defined in outside, extracultural terms, in the taking over and running the world, in the bossing of secretaries, and he is frustrated that he cannot have the sort of power which he assumes will guarantee his manhood (pp. 70, 89)....

Walter achieves his adulthood in very domestic terms through the family issues of financial crisis and abortion. The type of adult he becomes is in keeping with the kind Mama and Ruth value – cooperative, sensitive to the effects of his actions upon the family, and aware of his historical context. The instruments of his transformation are twofold. One is the threatened logical extreme of a family with a diseased member, that of the desperate drama of his wife willing to risk a back alley abortion to insure the family's survival in the face of an irresponsible, terminally angry husband. The other is the temporary and artificial patriarchal restructuring of the family through which he is shown that the dominant culture's traditional patriarchal system and extrafamilial orientation will not work in this family – because of the type of man, the type of women, and the world in which they and all African Americans live...

Despite Walter's passage into adulthood, it is clear that the family is not restructured because of it....As an adult he will share power with Mama, Ruth, and Beneatha and is positioned, not as a would-be-patriarch, but as one adult among several in the family. His double gender consciousness is resolved. Mama and Ruth share a proud moment, for his "coming into his manhood" (p. 130). His double racial consciousness is also resolved: he becomes a person-with-history. He has looked back to the past, both culturally and familially, and has contextualized himself. His consciousness of race, group, and gender is reconciled. In the PBS production, the audience last sees Walter as he proudly takes Big Walter's portrait from the wall to move it to the new home. One of the last shots of the play is the wallpaper where Big Walter's portrait hung.

The potential of television as a beneficial Black feminist forum is particularly significant since the form can reach women who are the backbone of a traditional, popularist Black feminism that operates in the Black family and community, away from the more privileged centers of feminism.

Notes

1   Anne Cheney, *Lorraine Hansberry* (Boston: Twayne, 1984), p. 17.

2   W. E. B. Du Bois, *Souls of Black Folk* (Millwood, NY: Kraus-Thomson, 1973), pp. 1–2.

3   Ibid., p. 3.

4   Ibid., p. 4.

5   See Michael Awkward, *Inspiriting Influences: Tradition, Revision and Afro-American Women's Novels* (New York: Columbia University Press, 1989); Barbara Christian, *Black Feminist Criticism: Perspectives on Black Women Writers* (New York: Pergamon, 1985); Mary Helen Washington, "Taming All That Anger Down: Rage and Silence in Gwendolyn Brooks's *Maud Martha*," in *Black Literature and Literary Theory*, ed. Henry Louis Gates (New York: Methuen, 1984), pp. 249–62; Susan Willis, "Eruptions of Funk: Historicizing Toni Morrison," in *Black Literature and Literary Theory*, pp. 263–322.

6   Lorraine Hansberry, *A Raisin in the Sun* (New York: Signet, 1966), p. 63. All subsequent quotations are cited parenthetically within the text.

7   See John Mbiti, *African Religions and Philosophy* (Garden City, NY: Anchor, 1970).

8   See Alice Walker, *In Search of our Mothers' Gardens: Womanist Prose* (San Diego: Harcourt Brace Jovanovich, 1983).

9   Lorraine Hansberry, *To Be Young, Gifted, and Black: Lorraine Hansberry in Her Own Words*, ed. Robert Nemiroff (New York: New American Library, 1970), p. 78.

10 Du Bois, *Souls*, p. 50.

11 See Bart Landry, *The New Black Middle Class* (Berkely: University of California Press, 1987).

12 See Niara Sudarkasa, "African and Afro-American Family Structure: A Comparison," *The Black Scholar* 11.8 (November–December 1980): 37–60.

13 Antonio Gramsci, *Prison Notebooks*, trans. Joseph A. Buttigieg and Antonio Callari, ed. Joseph A. Buttigieg (New York: Columbia University Press, 1992), p. 133.

14 Cheney, *Lorraine Hansberry*, p. 60–1.

15 Ibid., p. 60.

Supplementary Readings and Media Resources

Supplementary Readings

Bobo, Jacqueline, *Black Women as Cultural Readers* (New York: Columbia University Press, 1995).

Bobo, Jacqueline, *Black Women Film and Video Artists* (New York: Routledge, 1998).

Dates, Jannette, "From 'Beulah' to 'Under One Roof': African American Women on Prime-Time Commercial Television," in Alan Wells and Ernest Hakanen, eds. *Mass Media and Society* (Greenwich, CT: Alex Publishing Corp., 1997), pp. 527–40.

Nelson, Angela M. S., "The Objectification of 'Julia': Texts, Textures, and Contexts of Black Women in American Television Situation Comedies," in Devoney Looser and E. Ann Kaplan, eds. *Generations: Academic Feminists in Dialogue* (Minneapolis, MN: University of Minnesota Press, 1997), pp. 237–49.

Media Resources

Dash, Julie, *Daughters of the Dust*, 120 minutes, 35 mm (also available in 16 mm and video), color, 1991 (Kino).

Riggs, Marlon, *Color Adjustment*. 87 minutes, video, color, 1991 (California Newsreel).

Tangney, Ralph J., *Lorraine Hansberry: The Black Experience in the Creation of Drama*. 35 minutes, video, color, 1976 (Films for the Humanities).

Welbon, Yvonne, *Cinematic Jazz of Julie Dash*. 26 minutes, video, color, 1992 (Third World Newsreel).

Part III

Art

Overview: Art

Contemporary Black women artists preserve cultural traditions and originate meaningful forms of visual expression. Sculpture, painting, photography, mixed media, installation, and performance are placed in historical context in the four articles on art in Part III. "African-American Women Artists: A Historical Perspective," by Arna Alexander Bontemps and Jacqueline Fonvielle-Bontemps, gives an indispensable lineage of Black female artists from the early nineteenth century through the Harlem Renaissance of the 1920s. Among the artists investigated are the first known Black female sculptors, Mary Edmonia Lewis (1845–1911), May Howard Jackson (1877–1931), and Meta Vaux Warrick Fuller (1877–1968), and the first Black person to become established as a major painter, Laura Wheeler Waring (1887–1948).

Black female artists have produced major innovations in style and aesthetic choices over a long period of time. *Forever Free: Art by African-American Women, 1862–1980*, an exhibition catalogue by Jacqueline Fonvielle-Bontemps, extends the reach of the first article in Part III. (It is listed in the supplementary readings). Artists examined in this chronicle include many contemporary sculptors and painters, and those who work in fiber, prints, and other mixed media. These include Elizabeth Catlett, Barbara Chase-Riboud, Betye Saar, Faith Ringgold, and Varnette Honeywood.

In spite of venerable contributions of Black women to the art world, they remain, for the most part, overlooked. Freida High W. Tesfagiorgis, in "In Search of a Discourse and Critique/s that Center the Art of Black Women Artists," presents compelling arguments stressing the need to recognize the history, skill, and talents of female artists of African descent throughout the world. Tesfagiorgis discusses the work of Black American artists Adrian Piper and Howardina Pindell, both of whom have criticized the dominant art establishment for its exclusionary practices in art history, criticism, and exhibition. Black women artists have, however, persevered to produce art objects that cannot be ignored. Examples analyzed include the works of British painter Libaina Himid, Ugandan painter Therese Mosoke, and Sokari Douglas Camp, a Nigerian artist who lives and works in London. Camp's metal sculptures are a declaration of her self-determination and resistance to imposed constraints, for metal is generally thought of as the province of African males who have historically worked as blacksmiths and bronzecasters. Tesfagiorgis is persuasive, stating that female artists throughout the African diaspora "produce convincing works of art with eloquence and integrity." She cites noted Black art historian Leslie King-Hammond, who insists that Black women worldwide have created a body of work worthy of inclusion in art history and the global art world.

Kellie Jones, in "In Their Own Image," makes a similar case for Black American and Black British females involved in the medium of photography and text art. Jones shows how these artists of African, Asian, or Caribbean descent living or born in America or Britain have enlarged the context of photography in their artistic creations. Jones looks at Americans Lorna Simpson, Clarissa Sligh, Pat Ward Williams, and Carrie Mae Weems and British photographers Zarini Bhimji, Roshini Kempadoo, Ingrid Pollard, and Mitra Tabrizian. The women recapture a history in their texts that challenges fixed meanings in dominant culture. They engage in intercultural and international dialogues offering alternate perspectives to different audiences.

The final chapter in Part III is an interview with sculptor, painter, mixed media, and performance artist Faith Ringgold. Melody Graulich and Mara Witzling, in "The Freedom to Say What She Pleases: A Conversation with Faith Ringgold," examine in depth the artist's latest creations. *The French Collection, Part I* portrays one of the central themes of Ringgold's art: feminist interpretations of the past. *The French Collection, Part II* goes further in one quilt "Dinner at Gertrude Stein's." This gathering of historical figures depicted on the quilt has Zora Neale Hurston as its central character. The authority to determine who is or is not among the pantheon of "great artists" is investigated in Ringgold's story quilts. Ringgold also discusses, among other things in the interview, the influences on Black female artists and the need to consider all forms of art as important.

The recommended videos in Part III convincingly visualize the creative processes of these artists. The earliest known Black female painters and sculptors are included in *Against the Odds: The Artists of the Harlem Renaissance* (1993). Sculptor Augusta Savage (1892–1962) is seen interacting with students in her classes in Harlem. Many of the arts and artists discussed in the opening chapter are also shown, including painter Laura Wheeler Waring, sculptor Elizabeth Prophet (1890–1960), and textile artist and painter Lois Mailou Jones (1908–98).

Nigerian Art: Kindred Spirits (1990), narrated by actress Ruby Dee, presents the work of leading Nigerian artists. It explores the constructs of tradition and belief, colonialism and independence, the lure of tradition and the seduction of other environments. Sculptor Sokari Douglas Camp, discussed in Tesfagiorgis's article, is one of the many who aspire to illuminate the many cultures of Nigeria.

Three of the suggested videos focus on individual artists working in their studios and discussing their creative processes. Sculptor and printmaker Valerie Maynard, in *Valerie: A Woman, an Artist, a Philosophy of Life* (1975), demonstrates how her art is vitally connected to her political impulse. Faith Ringgold constructs her remarkable renditions of history with the cameras rolling in *Faith Ringgold: The Last Story Quilt* (1991). Scenes of the artist at work in her studio are interwoven with her narration in *The Work of Elizabeth Catlett* (1976).

8

African-American Women Artists: An Historical Perspective

Arna Alexander Bontemps and Jacqueline Fonvielle-Bontemps

Bontemps, Arna Alexander and Jacqueline Fonvielle-Bontemps, "African-American Women Artists: An Historical Perspective." *Sage*, 4(1) (Spring, 1987): 17–24.

Black women, by virtue of their statistical presence and economic importance in the New World, but more importantly by virtue of the character of their struggle to endure the unendurable – the way she nurtured and reared her children, supported her family, maintained and sustained her own sense of worth and well-being – were undeniably essential to the ultimate survival of the Black community. It follows, therefore, that Black women – through the intellectual and aesthetic choices they made and the traditions they helped preserve – played a vital role in developing those meaningful forms of self-expression by which Black people in America have managed to survive two-and-a-half centuries of chattel slavery and nearly half a millenium of racial oppression.

But what are the specifics of her contributions to that culture? And what was the nature of the intellectual process through which she sought self-realization and self-respect both for herself and for those she loved? Unfortunately, the answers to these questions are sadly lacking, due to the dearth of scholarly research devoted specifically to the history of Black women's cultural contributions in America. This essay will examine the experiences and artistic expressions of African-American women from the early nineteenth century through the Harlem Renaissance. It was from a small group of relatively privileged African-Americans that the first Black women to paint or sculpt in a western tradition achieved public prominence in America.

The Beginnings: Edmonia Lewis

Edmonia Lewis, like most other American sculptors of her time, was not a great artist – there are too many unresolved, conflicting impulses in her work, and her technical proficiency, though solid and promising, was never fulfilled – yet she is nevertheless an important figure in the history of American and African-American art. It is not clear where she was born – either near Albany, New York, or in an Ohio town (Greenhigh) that no longer exists – or when she was born – either in 1843 or 1845.[1] She said, however, that her mother was a Chippewa Indian and her father was a Black man and a gentleman's servant. Thus, as a female American of African and Native American descent, she was subject to a myriad of possible socio-economic, intellectual and cultural influences.

For Edmonia Lewis, as for a growing number of free Black people in the North, the profound transitions that were occurring in American society in the middle decades of the nineteenth century meant that she was able to receive a formal education. In 1859 she entered the preparatory department of Oberlin College in Oberlin, Ohio. Founded in 1832, the college was a direct outgrowth of the sort of reform-minded Protestant, evangelical revivalism that motivated many of the nation's most fervent abolitionists and crusaders for other human rights causes in the first half of the nineteenth century. It is not entirely clear how she managed to go to Oberlin – either on an "abolitionist scholarship" or because of the assistance of a "thrifty brother" who lived in California – but it is certain that she did attend the school from 1859 to 1863, and that she followed the prescribed literary course while there. The significant feature of Edmonia's intellectual and academic life at Oberlin, however, was not that she followed the prescribed liberal arts curriculum or that she was an average, above, or below average student, but that her interest in the fine arts began to develop. It is not clear to what extent she was influenced by the crafts traditions of her Ojibwa ancestors, but her background in that regard was fairly extensive. She made moccasins as her mother did, and it is possible that she had also been influenced by her exposure to other Ojibwa crafts. One of her statues, for instance, is of an *Old Indian Arrow Maker and his Daughter.* The daughter is making moccasins and the father is making arrows.

Regardless of the possible source of her artistic inspiration, she had, by September 9, 1862, produced at least one pencil drawing of a sculpted figure, sculpted in the neo-classical tradition that prevailed in America for the first three-quarters of the nineteenth century.[2] This fact, coupled with those relating to the possible Ojibwa influences on her artistic development, are significant because most scholars, until fairly recently, assumed that

Edmonia's artistic inclinations were entirely untapped before she arrived in Boston in 1863 and was exposed to the monumental statuary there.

Edmonia Lewis, though generally thought to have followed Reason's pattern, never sculpted a Black figure, though many of her statues dealt with racial or sexual repression as a theme. She glorified abolition as a movement and individual abolitionists, but not Black people. More than 250 Black students attended Oberlin prior to the Civil War, but her friends were all white. Her father lived until she was a teenager, but all her memories are of her mother and her mother's people. When she found herself in deep trouble – accused of poisoning two of her closest friends – the Black community in Oberlin pronounced her guilty in advance of her trial because, her Black lawyer recalled, "of all her easy and rather unusual social relations with the whites." Irate local whites attacked and nearly killed her before her trial, undoubtedly because she was Black, but the people who comforted, consoled, and tried to protect her were the white liberals (and Blacks like her lawyer who shared their ideals), whose spirit and commitment to religious revival and social reform were the foundations on which Oberlin was built. And it was to those friends that Edmonia gave her trust and affection, and it was into their world that she fled when her life at Oberlin was finally over – after she was accused and acquitted, the following year, of stealing brushes and paints from a local art teacher. A decade later, however, Edmonia recalled rather matter-of-factly that "after I finished what little schooling I had in Ohio, I thought I would go to Boston and learn a little music. I went."[3]

Fortunately, when she left Oberlin, she was given a letter of introduction and recommendation to the radical abolitionist leader William Lloyd Garrison, and he in turn was willing to make it possible for her to meet and study under Edmund Brackett, a local sculptor. Within a year she opened her own studio and by January of 1865, she had received enough encouragement and support for her work to go to Rome where she immediately began to study and attempt original sculpture. According to all accounts of her life and career, she was so impressed by the statuary she encountered in Boston, especially a life-sized statue of Benjamin Franklin by Horatio Greenough, that she decided she would rather study sculpture than music.

The two works that made her career in Boston (both done in 1864) were a medallion of the head of John Brown, of which she sold several copies, and a bust of Colonel Shaw. The Colonel, as leader of the 54th Massachusetts Regiment, had achieved a degree of immortality, along with 247 of his men, at the siege of Fort Wagner on Morris Island, South Carolina, July 18, 1863. Lewis sold nearly 100 plaster replicas of the Colonel's bust, and his family bought the original. The money she earned from the sale of these works and the recognition and interest they inspired among her circle of friends and their associates in Boston made it possible and desirable for her to go to Rome in 1865. There she quickly joined, or was absorbed into, what Henry James called "a white marmorean flock," by which he meant "that strange sisterhood of American 'lady sculptors' who at one time settled upon the seven hills (of Rome)."[4] The "marmorean flock" gathered around Harriet Hosmer – "the best known sculptor of her generation" – and Charlotte Cushman, an actress to whom most of the leading women sculptors in Rome were devoted.[5] Hosmer, in fact, sailed to Rome with Cushman in 1852.

Male American sculptors had begun to go to Italy for inspiration and training as early as 1825, when Horatio Greenough made the journey. Hiram Powers, one of the best known sculptors of the nineteenth century, also settled in Florence in 1837. Both men, as did all other academically oriented American sculptors of that era, male or female, inherited or adopted the European tradition of neo-classicism as exemplified in the works of Antonio Canova and Bertel Thorvaldsen.

When Lewis arrived in 1865, "Charlotte took her up as a personal project," because, she said, she "has more than anybody else to fight." Both Hosmer and Cushman were devoted feminists with abolitionist sympathies. Most of Edmonia's friends and associates at Oberlin and afterward were similarly disposed. Her pencil drawing in 1862 was, in fact, a gift for Clara Steele Norton, an ardent feminist, and the drawing itself may have had a meaning related to their shared commitment to the feminist movement of their day. In Boston, Garrison and Henry Wadsworth Longfellow, and others like them, came generously to her aide; in Rome it was Cushman and Hosmer and William Wetmore Story, a "lawyer turned poet and sculptor" and "the doge of the New England expatriates in Rome."[6] To such people, women sculptors were looked upon as heroes, not social deviants or misfits, and Black female sculptors seemed especially blessed. Thus Edmonia was inspired to give her loyalty to these supporters and friends, just as she did to her Indian relatives and ancestors. Her loyalties, however, did not extend very far toward her father's people; her work, in fact suggests that she sought to avoid the central fact of her life. Yet in doing so she reflected one of the strongest impulses in Black art: the compelling and compulsive urge to declare one's humanity in individual rather than racial terms.

Whatever its motivation, however, her work is full of social commentary about the central human rights issues of her day and it is marked by a degree of naturalism – often too emotional and sentimental – that distinguishes it stylistically from that of many of her contemporaries. In this respect she, like John Adams Ward, must be credited for having helped lead the way toward greater realism in her field, though technically she remained a neo-classicist. She was a relatively prolific sculptor during the first decade or so of her artistic career. There was very little by way of thematic originality in her work, even her best and most skillfully rendered pieces, but she did manage on occasion to transcend the hackneyed themes and subject matter that dominated American sculpture during most of the nineteenth century and to realize a degree of emotional sensibility and interpretive insight that was lacking in the work of lesser artists.

Illustrative of her creative potential was, perhaps, her most controversial work, *The Death of Cleopatra*, which was exhibited during the 1876 Centennial Exposition in Philadelphia. The only description of the work emphasized its realistic depiction of the effects of death, which the observer suggested indicated a lack of taste on the part of the artist. Little is known of Edmonia's life, either professionally or privately, after this date. Consequently, it has been generally assumed that she was unable to respond to the changing artistic tastes of the late nineteenth century.[7] This, however, is an unlikely suggestion considering her stylistic history as a sculptor and considering the modest nature of the changes in American sculpture prior to World War I. A more telling factor, undoubtedly, was the decline of interest, among white liberals, in racial issues, reform movements, and the careers of Black, Ojibwa, female sculptors.

The Torturous Transition: Black Art in the Late Nineteenth and Early Twentieth Centuries

Edmonia's sincerity of expression and realistic approach to art was vindicated in the work of subsequent American sculptors, including her sister sculptors, May Howard Jackson and Meta Vaux Warrick Fuller, both of whom were born in Philadelphia in 1877. It is interesting to note, though the comparison is seldom made, that Fuller's early work picks up where Edmonia's left off in 1876, with the vivid depiction of sombre and macabre subject matter. It is equally suggestive to note that the eras that followed, known as the Gilded Age and the Progressive era in American history, are known to Black Americans as an age of betrayal or the nadir of Black life, a time of retrenchment and fear, of "compromise . . . compliance and conformity," "of legalized segregation and disfranchisement," of cultural isolation and continued social and economic discrimination.[8]

Caught in the backlash of a nation turned topsy-turvy by the twin forces of modernism – urban and industrial growth – Black Americans sought to defend and protect themselves by stressing the ideas of self-reliance and self-help. In such an atmosphere, as during the long nightmare of slavery, art based or strongly rooted in the Black Folk Tradition flourished and matured, but the fine arts suffered, due largely to the lack of interest in, or the patronizing and condescending attitude white intellectuals had toward Black life and the creative capacity of Black people.

May Howard Jackson "was one of the first Black sculptors to reject popular European tastes and to deliberately use America's racial problems as a thematic source of their art."[9] Born in Philadelphia, as was Henry Ossawa Tanner, the most distinguished Black painter of this era, and Fuller, she studied at Professor J. Liberty-Tadd's art school and the Pennsylvania Academy of Fine Arts. Described as having been "temperamental, withdrawn," and reclusive, her professional life was apparently quite tragic.[10] It would, of course, be interesting to know the full dimensions of her tragedy, but its general outline is an all-too-familiar story. The rebuffs she received in her attempts to study art, for example, were faced by all Black artists then, as well as by most white women artists, although they were somewhat more privileged in this regard than Blacks.[11] Similarly, the lack of exhibition outlets was a major obstacle to the development of Black artists throughout the nineteenth and early twentieth centuries and continues to be one of the most significant impediments to the growth and maturity of Black art in America. Prior to the end of World War I, state fairs and other such expositions were practically the only places Black artists had to publicly display their art.[12]

Most students of Jackson's art have acknowledged her extraordinary talent as a modeller; they generally allow as well that she frequently achieved a degree of lyrical expressiveness that imbued her work with a distinctiveness worthy of special merit. At the same time, however, critics have tended to dismiss her as a sculptor of "forthright portraits of forthright men," an apt but incomplete assessment. A more telling criticism was that her art exhibited "no great originality... and [that] she made no noteworthy departure from the American pictorial tradition in sculpture as exemplified in the cognate styles of St. Gaudens and Charles Grafly." Of course, the same judgment could have been applied to many other very fine American sculptors of Jackson's era, although that fact alone does not exempt her from criticism. Indeed, she, perhaps more than anyone else, was aware of her artistic limitations, of how much more she could have achieved if given the opportunity and encouragement. Within those limitations, the most important of which were psychological and thus perhaps unappreciated by her, she achieved an admirable level of technical proficiency and creative expressiveness. Her portrait busts were often very strong yet sensitive character studies, which is what she obviously intended them to be, facts acknowledged by the *Washington Star*'s art critic in 1913 and again in 1916.[13] Moreover, she sculpted several groups that strongly suggested that she was capable of realizing more ambitious and complex thematic conceptions, as for example her *Mulatto Mother and Her Child*. More importantly, perhaps, her *Head of a Negro Child* established a sensitive and intensely humanistic approach to the portrayal of Black folk types that Black sculptors have followed and refined ever since, a preoccupation that some Black art critics and historians privately regret but a compelling and entirely understandable one nonetheless. Portraiture, after all, was the most direct means available to those Black artists who wanted to respond to the demeaning and distorted images of Black life and character that white America has nourished so carefully for nearly four centuries, a racist tradition that gathered renewed intensity in the quarter of a century preceding World War I.

Jackson's intense racial pride represented a central feature of a growing Black reaction to the sort of unrestrained racial injustice and bigotry that had gained legal sanction in post-Reconstruction America. Fuller's career, however, is perhaps more expressive of the full breadth and development of that reaction than Jackson's. Unlike Jackson, who was unable to continue her studies after graduating from the Pennsylvania School of Industrial Art in 1897 and the Philadelphia College of Industrial Art in 1898, she studied at the Ecole des Beaux Arts in 1899 and at the Académie Colarrossi from 1899 to 1902. On her return to America, she entered the Pennsylvania Academy of Fine Arts (1903), graduating four years later in 1907.[14]

Both women apparently "married well," Jackson to a mathematics professor and high school principal,[15] and Fuller to a distinguished Black physician.[16] Both apparently came from similar socio-economic backgrounds and faced the same sorts of color-caste prejudices that tormented so many other near-white Black women in post-Reconstruction America. Thus as archetypes they may have very well reflected strong undercurrents of self-hatred and personal guilt symptomatic of a kind of racial schizophrenia and motivated by a powerful, perhaps, irrational, assimilationist dream. As individual artists, however, they were considerably more complex, representing most of the main currents of Black intellectual life prior to World War I. Indeed, Samella Lewis has suggested that as a transitional figure in the history of Black art, "Warrick expressed ideals that are more in accord with the Black Renaissance of the generation that followed hers than with the prevailing artistic views of her own period."[17]

Thematically, Fuller's work does not seem to exhibit the same clearly articulated social focus as that by Jackson, but Fuller's work was so much more extensive and diverse than Jackson's that such comparisons are meaningless. Her career, in fact, has been generally divided into two very distinct phases: "the romantic and the social." Stylistically, she was an impressionist in the manner of the great French master Auguste Rodin. Porter noted, however, that she also reflected Edmonia Lewis's desire to evoke a sense of "emotional realism or romanticism."[18] Her early work has been termed "macabre and gruesome" because it dealt with powerful subject matter – themes of death, war, despair, and human anguish. Her subsequent sculpture, however, "demonstrated a social interest and included sentimental ethnic pieces such as *Water Boy*."[19]

The source of her early thematic concerns, according to Fuller's friend Velma J. Hoover, "was her racial experience," her rejection, first, by white society in general, and later by the American art world, which disdained her work even though it had been acclaimed in Paris. "At the turn of the century in the United States," Hoover explained, "most Black persons were afraid to publicly verbalize the pain, sorrow, and despair of the Black experience, and a woman was seldom expected to voice any opinion at all. Meta Fuller found creative expression of these feelings through her sculpture, and her works were 'powerful' because she was expressing very real pain, sorrow and despair."[20]

In another context, Fuller explained that she "acquired her bent for horrors" from ghost stories her brother and her grandfather used to tell her when she was a child: "Ghost stories and that characteristic type of Negro folklore which is never separated from the fearful, the weirdly super-stitious." Oddly, she said, the stories did not frighten her as they were intended to; instead she was fascinated by them. "Maybe some faint vibra-tions in my spiritual self," she speculated, "carried along through the blood of generations from the wilds of Africa, where my great-great grandmother was captured into slavery – maybe this, too, had something to do with my predilections. Anyway, the horror bent came naturally."

Marked by such a promising beginning. Fuller's subsequent career is often viewed with varying degrees of regret. Her thematic focus was somewhat narrowed yet at the same time her work became more socially relevant. Stylistically, she reverted to a more conventional orientation, that is, as con-ventional as her extraordinary imagination would allow. Hoover suggested that part of the explanation for this transition in her approach to art was due to the great sense of disappointment she felt when American critics did not accept her art with the same warmth and enthusiasm as had Parisian observers. Also in 1910 much of her early work was destroyed by fire, thereby greatly adding to her general sense of frustration. Thus, Hoover argued, Fuller accommodated herself to expected norms regarding the role of women and Blacks in pre-World War I society. Her creative genius, Hoover explained, was "restricted to expressions of helpful religious fantasy, instead of depicting the reality of life." In 1909 she married Dr. Solomon Fuller and they moved to Framingham, Massachusetts, where she bore three sons and "her work turned more and more to portraiture and traditional themes, thereby losing the qualities which had caused Rodin to describe it as 'powerful'."[21]

This assessment may be too extreme, though clearly relevant, for it was through the latter phase of her career that Fuller makes her most forceful commitment to the social needs and concerns of Black people, and it is through that concern that post-war artists take their lead. Moreover, the shift in her approach to art was not as complete and definite as Hoover suggests. She continued to be one of the most imaginative Black artists of her generation, and she never entirely relinquished her "bent for horrors." For example, in 1937 she not only sculpted *Richard B. Harrison as De Lawd*, an example of "the sculptural monumentality she often achieved," but she also created *The Talking Skull*, which reflected her earlier stylistic and thematic concerns. In either case, Fuller's work, like Jackson's, prefigured a greater preoccupation with ethnic or racial themes and images and a more direct and forceful approach to social issues by African-American artists. By contrast, the work of contemporary Black painters, most of whom were men, tended to avoid such themes and issues. Annie E. Walker, one of the very few Black women to receive recognition as a painter during the prewar era,[22] strongly reflected this trend.

Born in Alabama in 1855, she studied at the Cooper Union (1892–5) and was admitted to the Art School of the Corcoran Gallery in Washington, DC, on the basis of her work, though she was later refused admittance because of her color and despite the protests of leaders such as Frederick Douglass. At the Cooper Union she studied under Eakins, the quintessential American realist, and John Henry Twachtman, a leading American impressionist who represented an effort by some American artists to combine "visual realism and esthetic sensitivity" in their work. She received her diploma in drawing and portrait painting from the Union and earned enough money while there to study in Paris at the Académie Julien in 1896. More conventional, stylistically, than Tanner, who followed Eakins' example in the use of subtle control of light but who moved ahead of him in the direction of Van Gogh as a colorist, she rejected the admonition of her gifted mentor to explore the American scene for appropriate artistic themes; nor did she or any of her immediate African-American contemporaries follow the lead of the Eight, founders of the so-called Ash Can School of American art, to plumb the depths of American society for meaningful subject matter, which is not to say that Eakins, Homer, Thomas Hovenden, Eastman Johnson, the Eight and other American artists, who had begun to develop "the Negro subject and theme as a fresh and fascinating new province of native American material," did not have a significant and lasting influence on the subsequent development of Black art in America.[23]

The Harlem Renaissance

Among Black painters, the transition from the sort of social perspective reflected in the work of Tanner and Walker to that which characterized the age of the New Negro, an age inspired by a "new sense of self and race" – the age of Anne Spencer and Gwendolyn Bennett, of Florence Mills and Josephine Baker, of A'Lelia Walker and Mary McLeod Bethune, of Ethel Waters and Bessie Smith, Nella Larsen and Zora Neale Hurston – can be conveniently observed in the career of Laura Wheeler Waring, who, notwithstanding Walker's promise, was the first African-American to establish herself as a major painter in Black America. She was a truly fine and prolific artist, but unfortunately, she is known almost exclusively for her portraiture, when, in fact, she was equally productive as a painter of still lifes, landscapes and genre scenes. She also sculpted at least two figures in clay – "A Dance in the Round" (1935) and "Nude in Relief" (1937). Oil was her preferred medium, but she also produced numerous water-colors, one of which ("Heirlooms") won a highly competitive prize at the New York Watercolor Club exhibit in 1917.[24]

Born in Hartford, Connecticut, in 1887, she entered the Pennsylvania Academy of Fine Arts in 1906. In 1914 she was awarded the Cresson Traveling Scholarship as a reward for her work as a student illustrator at the Academy, and between 1924 and 1925 she studied at La Grande Chaumière in Paris. Stylistically, she evolved, accordingly to Professor Porter, from an early preoccupation with chromatic modulations of color and an almost voracious appetite for the planar painting of value. The distinctive nature of her work, however, does not come from its stylistic influences, which reflect a conscious and studied preference for the programmatic European approach to impressionism as opposed to the less self-conscious American attitude, but from the personal perspective she brought to her work, the visual impact of "her scrupulous objectivity," and the corresponding warmth and affection with which she regarded her subjects. Thus, she frequently reflected an expressionistic impulse in her art. Her interest in Black subjects and themes, meanwhile, accurately reflected the prevailing intellectual sentiment among Black artists during the Harlem Renaissance, as well as the general trend in American realism established during the first decade of the twentieth century by the Eight.

Like Aaron Douglas, who spent most of his post-Renaissance career teaching art at Fisk University, Waring spent nearly all of her adult life, beginning in 1917, doing the same thing at Cheyney State College near Philadelphia. Both artists shared many other artistic inclinations in common. They were both obsessed with matters of technique and fascinated by the craft of painting, due undoubtedly to the rigorous nature of their training both in America and in Paris, and as a consequence of their long careers as art teachers. Both experimented with other, more modern approaches to their art, but they remained primarily devoted to impressionism; and therein lay the crux of their dilemma as Black artists in a swiftly changing art world.

Both recognized a need and felt a responsibility to explore native themes more fully in their art and to try and realize the aesthetic implications of African art and the African past for Black art in general; indeed, few Black artists have ever been more dedicated to such aims than was Douglas, and the corpus of Waring's work suggests that she possessed a similar sensitivity. Neither Douglas nor Waring apparently had any difficulty in accepting the idea of a socially relevant art, or in Douglas' case, an art inspired by African rather than European aesthetic traditions. Their continued commitment to impressionism, however, suggests that they were reluctant at the same time to abandon the aesthetic idealism that Black artists had traditionally associated with European traditions in the fine arts. Such reservations, though implied and obscure, caused both artists to become increasingly isolated from the mainstream of Black art following the decline of the Renaissance; and although both have continued to be admired as pioneers in their field they have been grossly under-recognized in terms of their overall commitment to technical excellence, the constancy with which they sought to pursue their art, their humanistic approach to Black life as an artistic theme and the enormously important transitional role they played in the evolution of modern Black art.

No other Black woman achieved the distinction that Waring did as a painter during the Renaissance. Vivian Schuyler Key, from New York City, received the Amy E. Spingarn Award as a promising young painter/illustrator in 1927. She exhibited in the Harmon Foundation exhibits in 1930 and 1931 and she continues to paint and sculpt today, but economic pressures and domestic responsibilities have kept her from pursuing her art with the necessary intensity and concentration that continued development requires. Thus, she has only recently begun to realize the extraordinary promise she displayed in paintings such as "Study in Yellow" (oil, 1931). Indeed, the technical skill and imaginative design of "God Bless the Child that's Got his Own" (oil, 1976) – a tribute to Billie Holiday – shows clearly that she is an artist who deserves greater recognition and encouragement.

Thus, the Renaissance belonged to Waring, Fuller, and Jackson, and to two young sculptors – Nancy Elizabeth Prophet and Augusta Savage.

Prophet was born in Warwick, Rhode Island, on March 19, 1890. Her mother was Black, or, as she described herself, a "mixed negro," and her father, a city employee, was a Narragansett Indian.[25] It is doubtful that they would have been able to help or encourage her artistic aspirations if they had wanted to but thinking such dreams impractical they sought to discourage or distract her ambitions; thus Prophet had not only to struggle against obvious economic and racial disadvantages but against the will of her parents and their friends. Without hesitation, however, she set herself against these considerable odds, paying her own tuition to the Rhode Island School of

Design from which she graduated in 1918. She also managed to save enough money to pay her own way to Paris in 1922. There she studied at the Ecole des Beaux Arts, exhibited in the Salon d'Automne (1924, 1927) and the Salon des Artistes Français (1929), received warm and even glowing reviews in the Paris press, and was befriended by Henry Ossawa Tanner. She remained in France for a full decade, returning to America once or twice to exhibit her work. The poet, Countee Cullen, met her in Tanner's studio in 1930, and described her as a well-focused young artist, happy in her surroundings and content with her life.

She swept into the studio, he wrote, with unequalled éclat, wearing "a flowing black cape and a broad, black felt hat." Apparently, he said, she did not live or work in luxury, describing her studio on rue Broca as being set "deep back in a passage that conjured up a picture of vanished dreams, but she seemed to be at peace with herself, content with the direction of her life and her art..."[26] He also said that while in Paris she kept herself well-informed regarding cultural affairs in Black America, and that she maintained a strong sense of racial pride and identity. Her work, however, does not appear to be self-consciously racial as was Jackson's. She died, her passing little noted, in 1960, the same year in which Cedric Dover reported in his book, *American Negro Art*, that she had declined inclusion on the basis that she was "not a negro."[27] Her career, meanwhile, had declined much earlier. She taught art at Spelman College and Atlanta University for a number of years, beginning in 1934, but after 1939 her work was apparently not exhibited again during her lifetime.

Augusta Savage's life was equally troubled and difficult, but her response to adversity was much different than Prophet's. Both were strong, determined, and ambitious women, but whereas Prophet lived a very private, lonely, and reclusive life, Savage lived a more public and socially active existence, often marching ahead of others in the struggle to combat racism and bigotry in American society and in the modern art world as well: as when she was denied an opportunity to study in Paris in 1922 because program officials feared the reaction of southern students;[28] or when she sought and received a $1,500 grant from the Carnegie Foundation during the early days of the Depression to open her studio classes to any Harlem youngster who wanted to study with her; or when she led other Black artists in their efforts to partipate more fully in the WPA art projects; or when she organized the Vanguard, a club designed to "develop among black artists an awareness of the issues and a solidarity in their struggles"; or when she helped to organize the Harlem Artists Guild of which she became the second president.[29]

Her work does not possess a singular aesthetic personality in the way that Prophet's does, but Prophet did not possess Savage's greater skill at characterization. More importantly, perhaps, she was a gifted and inspirational teacher. Indeed, she discovered or helped to train a number of the best-known and most talented Black artists of the past half century, including painters Norman Lewis, Ernest Crichlow, Jacob Lawrence, and sculptor William Artis. Thus her significance in African-American art history is manifold. In addition to the intrinsic merit of her art, she established a tradition of cultural leadership as an educator, administrator, organizer and promoter of Black art and Black artists that persists today in the work of such women as Samella Lewis and Margaret Burroughs.

Born in Green Cove Springs, Florida, on February 29, 1892, her artistic interests developed at an early age, as did her teaching career and her fighting spirit.[30] Like Prophet, but for different reasons, her parents – Edward and Cornelia Fells – did not encourage her artistic interests. Her father, who was a carpenter and an itinerant Methodist minister with little other than his intense religious faith to sustain him and his large family (including 14 children of whom Augusta was the seventh), even opposed and tried to suppress her early enthusiasm for sculpting or modeling clay images of small animals, especially ducks. He thought that they were somehow "graven images" and thus sacrilegious. She finally won him over at the age of 15 with an "eighteen-inch statue of the Virgin Mary," which she modelled from clay she "begged" from a small pottery factory in West Palm Beach. Thereafter, her life-long struggle to break free of other sorts of narrow-mindedness and to pursue her artistic interests vacillated wildly between great moments of triumph and failure, between periods of buoyancy and sombre despair. In West Palm Beach, for instance, she managed to earn nearly $175 at a local fair in which she displayed some of her sculpture, but when she tried to use the money to establish herself as a sculptor, seeking commissions to do busts of prominent Black people in Jacksonville, she lost most of that money and with it her dream of founding an art center there.

Thus she arrived in New York City in 1920 with $4.60. Miraculously, however, she managed to enroll at the Cooper Union, but within three months she had to quit school and go to work. Later she was able to return to the Union and continue her studies on a working scholarship, but she nonetheless spent most of the Renaissance living from hand to mouth, clerking, working in laundries, and ironing. Meanwhile, her determination to persevere and her undeniable talent impressed many prominent people in Harlem and through their help she managed to survive the whirlwind of difficulties that plagued her progress throughout the Renaissance and the Depression. In 1922, for example, friends and well-wishers helped her get commissions to sculpt busts of Dr. Du Bois and Marcus Garvey, splendid portraits in the noble tradition of May Howard Jackson. Similarly, in 1923, the Harlem community rallied to her aid when she was denied a fellowship to study in France, an award she was granted on merit but which the white American selection committee withdrew when it discovered that she was Black. The international controversy that ensued made her a hero of sorts in Harlem, but she was branded a "trouble-maker" downtown. "No one knows," her biographers wrote, "how many times she was excluded from exhibits, galleries, and museums on this score."

And so it went throughout the Renaissance. In 1925, Dr. Du Bois managed to secure a scholarship for her to study at the Royal Academy of Fine Arts in Rome but she could not raise enough money to pay her traveling expenses. And thus she was forced to continue to work in factories and laundries until 1929, when, through the efforts of John E. Nail and Eugene Kinckle Jones of the National Urban League, she was granted a Julius Rosenwald Fellowship to study in Europe for two years.

In Paris she studied under Felix Beuneteaux at La Grande Chaumière. Later she was able to study with Charles Despiau. Both experiences evidently helped refine, though not control, her considerable technical facility, thereby allowing her to explore a greater range of themes in her art, including an unsuccessful atavistic impulse (e.g., "African Savage" and "The Tom Tom"). Her major works, in addition to her portrait busts, include "The Abstract Madonna," "Envy," "A Woman of Martinique," and "Lift Every Voice," a "Sculptural interpretation of American Negro Music," commissioned by the New York World's Fair in 1939 and destroyed by bulldozers at the end of the Fair because she could not afford to have it cast in metal and the Fair did not offer to do so. Through photographs, however, it became her most famous as well as her last major work. She died on March 27, 1962, nearly two decades after she entered a long period of virtual retirement as an artist and a teacher.

Conclusion

In the interim – that is, during the two decades following the end of the Renaissance – May Howard Jackson died (1931), Meta Fuller entered a long period of semi-retirement, Prophet faded from prominence, and Laura Wheeler Waring began a valiant struggle to continue her career despite the pain she suffered from a recurring illness. The nascent careers of nearly twenty other Black female artists, initially highlighted by the Harmon Foundation exhibits, flared and then quickly dissolved. Indeed, in many ways, the Great Depression appeared to mark the demise of the "New Negro," especially the "New Negro Woman," who dreamed of becoming a painter or sculptor.

Certainly, among the masses of Black people in America the glow of the Renaissance was quickly dimmed. The Renaissance, in fact, had served to obscure a pattern of urban decay that had been spreading throughout northern Black communities since the late nineteenth century. Meanwhile the shockwaves of economic depression that rocked Wall Street in 1929 greatly exacerbated Black America's traditional economic woes during the fabled Renaissance. Indeed, by 1926 thousands of Black people who had found jobs in Northern industries before World War I "were on the turf" where they were joined by nearly a million other unemployed Black men and women before the decade was over. Forty-eight thousand of the pre-World War I industrial workers who were fired during the "Jazz Age" were Black women. Moreover, the competition for domestic work intensified during the Depression, thereby threatening the livelihood of nearly a million more Black women and lowering the benefits for all.

In a broad cultural sense, however, the Depression did not so much mark the demise of the Renaissance as it signified a profound shift in emphasis and perception among Black artists. Clearly, the Depression shattered a great many naive racial illusions, but the Renaissance was more than an illusion, more than a fad that suddenly lost its appeal among a fashion-conscious intellectual elite. Nonetheless, it very definitely had its voguish dimension. Fed by the romantic racialism of certain white Americans and the racial chauvinism of many Black Americans, the Renaissance of myth and legend was, simultaneously, abandoned by its panic strickened white patrons and admirers and rejected by Black artists and intellectuals, who had become embittered by the condescending nature of white interests in Black culture and who had grown disillusioned by the realization that their cultural achievements had not materially improved the life of most Black Americans or significantly altered the nature of race relations in American society.

Over the next several decades, Black women continued to demonstrate their ability to forge a world of their own in which they were able to give greater reign to their need for self-expression based on freely chosen aesthetic preferences. Obviously the work of contemporary Black women artists, like the age in which they live, is too fluid and diverse to summarize here; nor is it possible to predict what directions art by Black women in America will take in the future. It is clear, however, that the role of Black women in the development of Black art has increased rather than diminished in recent years and that more and more their vision of Black reality will shape the visual imagery of Black life in America. She has also begun to reveal more and more of herself in her art, thereby increasing its complexity and meaning, its power to captivate and inspire – to disturb and challenge – all of us.

Notes

1   The most reliable biographical information on Lewis is in James A. Porter's entry on her in *Notable American Women, 1667–1950* (Cambridge, MA.: Belknap Press, 1971), pp. 397–8. This essay says she was born near Albany, NY, in 1845; Eleanor M. Tufts, "Edmonia Lewis, Afro-Indian Neo-Classicist," *Art in America* (July–August, 1974), 64–70, reported that Lewis was born in Greenheigh, Ohio, in 1843.

2   Marcia Goldberg and W.E. Bigglestone, "A Wedding Gift of 1862," *Oberlin Alumni Magazine* (January–February, 1977): 11.

3   Phillip M. Montesano, "The Mystery of the San José Statues," *Urban West* (March–April 1968): 25.

4   William H. Gerdts, *The White, Marmorean Flock: Nineteenth Century American Women Neo-Classical Sculptors* (New York: Merchants Press, 1972), p. 1.

5   Ibid., p. 5.

6   Cedric Dover, *American Negro Art* (New York: Graphic Society, 1960), p. 28.

7   Tufts, "Edmonia Lewis," pp. 71–2.

8   Arna Bontemps, *Free at Last: The Life of Frederick Douglass* (New York: Dodd, Mead & Company, 1971), pp. 278–9; Saunders Redding, *The Lonesome Road: The Story of the Negro's Past in America* (Garden City, NY: Doubleday & Company, Inc. 1958), p. 150.

9   Samella Lewis, *Art: African American* (New York: Harcourt Brace Jovanovich, Inc., 1978), p. 52; Alain Locke, *Negro Art: Past and Present* (New York: Arno Press, 1969), p. 30.

10   *The Crisis* (September 1927): 231.

11   The enormous obstacles faced by women artists in America are detailed and interpreted in Ann Sutherland Harris and Linda Nochlin, *Women Artists: 1550–1950* (an exhibition catalogue published by Alfred A. Knopf, 1978), pp. 50–67; and in Germaine Greer's article, "Repression of Women Artists: Why are there so few great female painters?" *The Atlantic* (September, 1979): 68–77.

12   Writing in his *Two Centuries of Black American Art*, p. 78, about the decades between 1930 and 1950, Professor David Driskell made a perceptive point that is as applicable today as it was in Jackson's era: "No viable aesthetic," he said, "was developed among black artists... because black leaders and intellectuals did not take the artists nor their art seriously." See also Romare Bearden's article, "The Negro Artist's Dilemma," in *Critique: A Review of Contemporary Art*, edited by David Lashak (November 1946), pp. 16–22.

13   Dover, *American Negro Art*, p. 29; James A. Porter, *Modern Negro Art* (New York: Arno Press and the *New York Times*, 1969, 1942), pp. 92–3; The *Crisis* (July 1916): 115.

14   Benjamin Brawley, "Meta Warrick Fuller," *The Southern Workman* (January 1918), pp. 25–6.

15   Samella Lewis, *Art: African American*, p. 78; *The Crisis* (June 1912): 67.

16 Born in Monrovia, Liberia (1872), Dr. Fuller was a neuropathologist, who became "the first Black psychiatrist in the world"; Velma J. Hoover, "Meta Vaux Warrick Fuller: Her Life and Art," *Negro History Bulletin* (March/April 1977): 679.

17 Lewis, *Art: African American*, p. 55.

18 Porter, *Modern Negro Art*, p. 77.

19 Elsa Honig Fine, *The Afro-American Artist: A Search for Identity* (New York: Hacker Art Books, 1982), p. 75.

20 Hoover, "Meta Vaux Warrick Fuller," p. 679.

21 Ibid.

22 Lowery Sims, "Nineteenth Century Black Women Artists," *Easy: The Black Arts Magazine* (January 1978): 32; and Porter, *Modern Negro Art*, pp. 78–9; also lists Pauline Powell of Oakland, California, and Fannie Hicks of Louisville, Kentucky, as gifted painters during this era.

23 Alain Locke, *The Negro in Art: A Pictorial Record of the Negro Artist and of the Negro Theme in Art* (New York: Harker Art Books, Inc., 1940, 1969, 1971), pp. 9–10. See also his discussion of this topic in *Negro Art: Past and Present*, chapt. 6.

24 *The Crisis* (February, 1917): 189.

25 Leslie King Hammond, "Prophet, Nancy Elizabeth," in the exhibition catalogue, *Four from Providence: Black Artists in the Rhode Island Social Landscape* (Providence, RI: a joint project of Rhode Island College and The Rhode Island Black Heritage Society, 1978), p. 9.

26 Countee Cullen, "Elizabeth Prophet: Sculptress," *Opportunity* (July, 1930): 205.

27 Dover, *American Negro Art*, p. 56.

28 *Opportunity*, (June 1923): 25.

29 Romare Bearden and Harry Henderson, *Six Black Masters of American Art* (Garden City, NY: Doubleday & Company, Inc. 1972), pp. 95–6.

30 Ibid., pp. 76–7.

9

In Search of a Discourse and Critique/s that Center the Art of Black Women Artists

Freida High W. Tesfagiorgis

A Critical Call: An Introduction

Black women artists in the USA confront the attitude and practice of negation and marginalization in conventional art history and criticism,[1] the cornerstone discourses of the dominant art world Euro-patriarchy.[2] However, beyond the hegemonic utterances of art writing[3] and art world practice,[4] their largely dismissed voices and unexhibited works evince a pervasive presence that intimates the longevity and complexity of their lives, works, and interventions within their diverse contexts.[5] The art history and criticism of African-Americanists prioritize the lives and works of African-American men while inscribing women as complements, those of Euro-American feminists center the work and issues of Euro-American women while marginalizing American women of color. Black women artists, in the last decade of the twentieth century, remain semi-muffled, semi-invisible and relatively obscure.[6]

For Black women artists the contradiction between their material culture and their configured negation, complementarity and/or marginality in discourses on art constitutes the crisis they consistently resist: one that must be vehemently confronted in the 1990s and beyond if history's given course is to be altered. A discourse that would prioritize the lives and concerns of Black women artists is urgently needed.

Without a discourse of their own, Black women artists remain fixed in the trajectory of displacement, hardly moving beyond the defensive posture of merely responding to their objectification and misrepresentation by others. The severity of this predicament is clearly evident in the agency of protest consistently registered in their voices, a sign of the need not only for a drastic change but also for a specific discourse wherein that change can be seriously initiated...

Dispersed Voices of Resistance and Self-determination

Black women artists on both sides of the Atlantic ocean acknowledge and respond to their historical crises of victimization, defiance, and self-determination. The breadth and depth of their crises are implicated in the unifying character of dissent in their voices and actions. Though this chapter focuses on the USA, Black women artists globally are diachronically and synchronically linked through colonialism, slavery, racism, and capitalism, and in their various countries confront the international transgressive art network that is characterized by Eurocentrism, sexism, elitism, imperialism, and capitalism.

In the USA, American artist/philosopher Adrian Piper challenges what she identifies as the "triple negation" of "Colored Women Artists" in Eurocentric discourses, a problem that she describes as discrimination against them because of their race, gender, and profession (Piper, 1990b: 16). Delineating specific "strategies" that Euro-patriarchists and Euro-feminist/women employ to dismiss the work of "colored women artists," Piper observes that such art critics and art historians: (1) exoticize/objectify women of color, thus investigating the psychosociological self of the speaker rather than the presumed subject of discussion, which is rendered silent; (2) deflect away from the meaning in the art object by raising "Euroethnic homogeneity" questions of "otherness"; and (3) make generalizations about Black women artists based on "gender and race stereotypes."[7] Such approaches, rather than describing, interpreting and evaluating concrete works of art or offering art-critical insight, alternatively obscure the subject, thus failing to serve properly either the work under consideration, the audience to whom the critic speaks, or the artist, who is rendered unimportant by the misinterpretation or dismissal of her work.

Overlaying Piper's critique, New York painter Howardina Pindell challenges the negation and marginalization of all people of color in the dominant art world, particularly in major museums in New York and elsewhere which almost exclusively exhibit works by men of European descent (Pindell, 1989: 32–6). Pindell encourages people of color to work together to open "closed doors"; the visual arts are emphatically not a "white neighborhood"

(Pindell, 1989: 36). Pindell's activism interpenetrates that of various people of color including the African-American cultural nationalist patriarchy; the different cultural groups operating from their particular ideological positions to counteract art world racism (as well as sexism in the case of feminists) (Failing, 1989: 124–31). For example, Pindell's critique overlays that of African-Americanist art historian/artist David Driskell (not regarded as a cultural nationalist) which confronts the contradictions in the actions of Eurocentrists who attack Black art exhibitions, supposedly on the basis of their objections to segregated shows and group privilege, while they simultaneously offer "group" privilege of various types to "white males," including "all white male exhibitions" (Driskell, 1987: 13–15). But though Pindell's activism, in her various contexts, coalesces with that of Driskell in opposing art world exclusionism, it also diverges from it by underscoring the specific professional problems encountered by Black women artists, thereby concurring more so with Piper's challenge of the multiple oppressions of Black women artists. The given perspectives and problems articulated by Piper, Pindell, and other Black women artists demonstrate the need for a discourse wherein their work, lives, and other concerns can be critically investigated.

Black women artists in other parts of the African diaspora and Africa engage in similar dialectics. In her catalogue introduction to an exhibition by Black women artists at the Institute of Contemporary Art in London in 1985, British painter Libaina Himid, for example, remarks: "We are claiming what is ours and making ourselves visible. We are eleven of the hundreds of creative Black Women in Britain today. We are here to stay" (quoted in Parker and Pollock, 1990: 67). Do not Himid's rebellious remarks resemble those of American Blacks, including males such as Driskell who adamantly reaffirm the here-to-stayness of Black artists, their works, and exhibits in the face of racism and sexism? Is it not evident that Black women artists on both sides of the Atlantic utilize resistant speech indicative of a shared determincy to self-inscribe a visibility that is absent in the dominant art world? And is there any doubt that their oppression and their resistance to it are interrelated?

Moreover, in what other ways beyond speech of resistance do Black women artists register their thoughts and acts of self-determination? One answer to this latter question lies in the character of their work, particularly in their choices of form and subject-matter which often encode specific aesthetic and moral values that resist dominant modernist styles or are beyond dominant tendencies in postmodernist pluralism/s. For example, New York artist Faith Ringgold like most artists produces work with expressive content that represents her individual aesthetic taste, imagination and social interests.[8] Having departed from "conventional" European oil-on-canvas techniques since the early 1970s, before that became fashionable, Ringgold insists on redefining art by innovatively synthesizing "crafts" (sewing) and "fine arts" (painting), thus subverting the separation between so-called "low" and "high" art that is paramount in dominant discourses on art. Such a practice not only contributes to the artist's distinctive style that displays dynamic tactile qualities, but also explicitly illustrates the fundamental connection between the "low" and "high" arts in African-American traditions whether visual (spatial) or ephemeral phenomena. Ringgold's forms synthesize academic painting techniques with colorful, high-contrast, multi-rhythmic, textural materials, aesthetic qualities that are evident in folk-quilting traditions.

In recognizing the importance of both the ordinary taken-for-granted knowledge and skill developed in African-American cultural traditions, and the knowledge and skill derived from more formal academic settings, novelist and critic Alice Walker calls attention to the varied manifestations of the creative spirit as she laments the limited viewpoints employed by those in search of artists and artistic production and admonishes the searchers: "We have constantly looked high, when we should have looked high – and low" (Walker, 1983: 239). She recalled a quilt nearly a century old hanging at the Smithsonian Institution in Washington, DC, that was identified as the product of "an anonymous Black woman in Alabama," "an artist who left her mark in the only materials she could afford, and in the only medium her position in society allowed her to use" (ibid.).

Art historians, historians, anthropologists and philosophers, especially African-Americanists, have recovered hundreds of vernacular forms that were utilized in everyday life, art/artifacts that are both aesthetically pleasing and functional, and that have vitally contributed to American culture since the period of forced migration and slavery. Such objects, part of a much larger corpus of art works that have developed over a 400-year period, can be seen today in places ranging from the Old Slave Mart Museum in Charleston, South Carolina (quilts, baskets, metalwork, woodcarvings, etc.), and the Boston Museum of Fine Arts (Harriet Powers's quilt) to, say, something found on your grandmother's bed or in a relative's barn in Mississippi. Because of their formal structure, media and utilitarian purpose, these works, consciously or unconsciously valued by their communities for both their intrinsic and extrinsic significance, are identified by Eurocentric scholars as crafts or "low" arts and are de-legitimated by the discipline of art history because they are outside of Eurocentric definitions of art. These very forms contribute to the "cultural memory" of African-American/American life and history discussed by such scholars as John Blassingame, Robert Thompson, Reginia Perry, and John Vlach. It is apparent in such scholars' works that the crafted/vernacular forms, the so-called "low" entities of material culture, vitally inform the aesthetic tastes of many Black and other Americans today, and that there is an obvious connection between them and the so-called "high" or fine arts produced by many African-Americans whose aesthetic judgments are informed by vernacular cultural traditions inherited within families and communities, as well as by judgments introduced and reinforced in lecture halls and studios of institutions where African-Americans and others are socialized to recognize/accept/adopt European-derived canons, many of them reinforced by cultural institutions such as fine art museums or the popular media industry; the former exclude African-American art, the latter manipulate and distort African-American imagery.

That Ringgold dares, as many African-American artists do, to retain or reclaim aesthetic values of African-American traditions, knowing that such qualities will be rejected and/or marginalized by the dominant art establishment, is the most immanent indication of her self-determination. She is often discussed in terms of her feminist ideology, and her work in association with the reclamation of women's work; thus emphasis is placed on the rebellious character of artist and work alike. However, the employing of material cultural theory situate the art object and better understand its extrinsic values, particularly associated beliefs, perspectives, expressions which can offer deeper insight into the contextual significance of the work (Prown, 1982: 1–18), makes clear that Ringgold and her work are in fact rather conventional though innovative within African-American traditions. Intertextual readings of folk art, fine art, performance, dress, music, sculpture, and folklore among other works reveal the continum consequent on the inextricable relationship between the "low" and "high" aspects of culture in African-American traditions,[9] a factor fundamental to Ringgold's production. However, within the context of the dominant art world, which separates folk art from fine art, Ringgold's work is interpreted as revolutionary, rebellious, political feminist production because it defies form, meaning, technique, aesthetics, and function that are encoded in European-derived canons. Formalist, iconographical, and feminist interpretations limit our understanding of the complexity of Ringgold and her work. Whether she is conventional or rebellious depends on the canon utilized to make that determination. Interpretation of her work in relation to her feminist ideology needs to be expanded with greater depth to substantially consider its intertextual and contextual cultural grounding.

The Ugandan painter Therese Mosoke, one of the few known African women artists, utilizes mixed media (dye and ink on canvas) to render her own truth and imagination in subject-matter that might be perceived as catering to a tourist audience: wildlife in Kenya. Despite the controversial nature of the subject-matter, however, she nevertheless continues to paint it, in an expressive style that bears her distinct signature. Her evocative compositions stimulate emotional responses perhaps not too dissimilar from her own special feelings for the wildlife that offers her "almost an inexhaustible kind of subject matter."[10] Mosoke has achieved the status of a successful independent artist whose work is her art; i.e. she lives off her work, so to speak. Given her position, however, she does confront the polemical challenge of being "true" to one's self and the consistent pressure of tourism and the limited exhibition opportunities in Kenya. Her determination to simultaneously strive for individuality and work successfully with popularized subject-matter is an indication of her independence.

Also from Africa (Nigeria), but living in London, Sokari Douglas Camp produces sculpture in metal, a material that within African conventions is restricted to the masculine sphere of production (Blacksmiths, bronzecasters, etc.).[11] Camp's persistence in working with materials and subject-matter of her choice indicates her self-determination; she has placed herself in an environment where she can freely produce what she chooses without experiencing the limitations imposed on her by Kalabari or other traditions.[12] Drawing heavily on themes of masquerade and associated symbolic forms, colors, textures, and sounds, Camp generally constructs spiritual and human figures and objects in welded metal, utilizing processes of accumulation (and reduction) to achieve the desired effect. These forms are often juxtaposed in display to reconstruct ritual and context. Her style is impressionistic with a characteristic interplay of dynamic mass and voids. Paramount in her structures are rhythmic geometricized and curvilinear designs that are harmoniously enhanced by luminous mono-, bi-, or polychromatic surfaces. Mirrors, feathers, paint, nails, and other details contribute to the imaginative presentment of each figure, which resonates with a dynamic quality that is heightened by kinetics (movement, sounds, etc.). Camp's work, in form and subject matter, is heavily influenced by Kalabari traditions. Yet the artist, like Ringgold and Mosoke, demonstrates a distinctive personal vision that is recognizable in her individual style. Her representation of women is a particularly distinctive mark in contemporary African art, for unlike the prevailing stereotypical prototypes – ritualized puberty figure, mother, youthful beauty, etc. – Camp's impressionistic representation of the female subject effectively evokes character, power and action (see her "Woman, part of Audience Ensemble," 1986, steel and paint, 75.5"), a sign of the provocative imagination, skill, subjective knowledge and experience that give rise to the basic assumption of women's differences in personalities and roles, as well as her desire to deploy those assumptions in her dominant themes. Camp's work cannot be divorced either from her identity as a Kalabari woman or from the individual freedom with which she works as a contemporary sculptor. Her work and life stimulate both greater thought about the divergent identities of women artists of African descent – the stylistic and thematic differences in our works of art, and the complexities scholars will encounter in developing the critical art history that must synthesize conventional and new art-historical methods – and also further investigation of the appropriate histories and cultures that will allow us to get beyond the mystification surrounding the artistic products of Black women in art history and art world practice.

Ringgold, Mosoke, and Camp are among the many Black women artists who produce convincing works of art with eloquence and integrity. Most of them remain unrecorded in the dominant discourses on art and largely unknown either to the professional art world or to the public audience, because of the controlling institutional biases of the art world and its canonized scholarly proclivities.

The persistence of these artists, African-American and African, is perhaps partially derived from the strength retained, reclaimed, and synthesized in cultural and ideological patterns extant in their various communities, factors to which they and many other Black artists had been exposed in their material conditions prior to, and during, their academic training. Paradoxically, the determinacy implicit in such influence inheres an expressive freedom leading to the kind of imaginative and dynamic works discussed, yet it is also weighted by the canon problematic in prevailing discourses that negates the artists' importance to conventional and even postmodern art history and criticism.

Interestingly, some Black women artists observe that their "outsider" status in Eurocentric discourses, with its critical distance from the mainstream, stimulates a greater sense of independence and creative freedom. Piper finds joy and freedom in the margins, in the company of artists who are doing "much of the really advanced, exciting, [and] original work," with a clear view of "the narrow range of aesthetic options validated by the mainstream" (Piper, 1990a: 12–13). Ringgold, too, emphasizes that since she is on the outside anyway, she can do what she wants.[13] Sociologist Pat Hill Collins uses the term "outsider within" to identify this distanced marginal placement and the special viewpoint that some Black women say they acquire within the construct of Eurocentric exclusionism, and surmises that it provides "a special perspective on self, family and society" which contributes to "distinctive analyses" (Collins, 1991: 40). It is not surprising that the voices of the artist and sociologist interpenetrate in exposing the specific inclusion/exclusion dichotomy/advantage that is experienced by Black women within the contexts of systems dominated by the Euro-patriarchy.

Any interpretation of such remarks as acceptance of the given status would be naive. In any case, who is to say that a similar joy and freedom might not exist for the "outsider within" if she were positioned more centrally within the currents of the dominant art (or other) world/s with the full benefits of such placement? In the area of art in particular, Piper and Ringgold are among the most vocal American women who continue to resist established boundaries in the art world that exclude people of color, especially women. Ringgold herself has for some 25 years addressed the interests and problems of Black and other women (and men) in various discourses, often articulating her own personal narrative to underscore the reality of Black women's subjugated identities and experiences. She most recently commented, "Everything about my life has to do with the fact that I am a Black woman. The way I work has everything to do with that, because I am struggling against being a victim which is what Black women become in this society" (Flomenhaft, 1990: 14).

Sociologist Deborah King identifies the shared distinctive circumstances of Black women in general as the phenomenon of "multiple jeopardy," a quality that she describes as socially constructed by the simultaneity and multiplicative relationships among their race, gender, and class, and to which she attributes a shared "multiple consciousness."[14] In support, sociologist Pat Hill Collins specifies that the commonalities among Black women are grounded in two major interlocking factors: (1) Black women's "political and economic status that provide[d] them with a distinctive set of experiences" and (2) distinctive Black feminist consciousness stimulated by the experience derived from their material realities.[15] Though their discussions refer specifically to the circumstances and awareness of Black women in the USA they are applicable to the shared realities of Black women artists globally, for, regardless of where they live, Black women artists inherit a common devalued (though different) status that has major adverse economic, political, and cultural implications for their lives and production.

Only the rare art historian, critic or theorist offers substantive interpretations of works and thoughts of Black women artists. Among them, art historian Leslie King-Hammond reconstructs empirical facts, the basis of art criticism,[16] art history and theory, in her quest to make justifiable aesthetic judgments of the art objects and performances of Black women artists. King-Hammond stresses production over the victimization in her analyses, concluding that in spite of their material conditions, "these artists speak eloquently of the vision and presence of a people long overdue for inclusion in the art world of this country." Based on the material evidence that I have seen in the USA, London, and various countries in Africa, I must add that Black women artists (and all people of color) throughout the world are long overdue for inclusion in art history and in the systematic operations of the global art world.[17]

With a self-activated and sustained discourse characterized by the knowledge and conviction of self-determination evident in the fragmented voices of Black women artists, art historians, and others, a major shift in the focus on Black women artists can be implemented. Most importantly, that shift could transform defensive discussions to more insightful interpretative exchanges that would lead to the construction of a critical art history.[18] In addition, more effective strategies for dismantling the exclusionary devices of the dominant art establishment could conceivably be constructed. Such objectives, in their entirety, could be identified as a Black feminist art project that would be both academic and political in character, its monumentality beyond my scope here. But it must begin with a distinctive discourse that would center Black women artists for such a discourse would circulate and debate facts, critiques, and theories while inscribing them into history. . . .

. . . Black feminist theorizing to date has given minimal attention to art and where it has, the focus is on popular art and culture; i.e. film, video and music.[19] Michele Wallace and bell hooks are the most prominent scholars, particularly in film criticism. Their theories intersect with the art writing of historians, curators, artists, and others who have given particular attention to visual and/or performing art by Black women.[20]

Given the precedent that Black feminist theorizing has established in subjectivizing the thought and challenges of Black women, and given its analytical approach, it is evident that a discourse and critique that center the art of Black women artists would benefit tremendously from its perspective/s.

A Working Black Feminist Critique of the Visual Arts

The critique within the proposed Black feminist art-historical discourse would constitute a significant component of a critical art history. Because of the differences between art history and criticism, the former concerned with the reconstruction of the history of the art objects and the latter with an evaluative response to the art objects that are recovered by art history, the two disciplines are recognized as separate yet interrelated (Ackerman, 1963: 162). However, art historians necessarily make critical evaluation that goes beyond basic art-historical methods, and critics significantly contribute to the development of art history; hence the boundary is sometimes problematic. Within the proposed discourse, criticism must be developed along with Black women's art history (African-American, British, Nigerian, etc.) since the latter is hardly known. Pre-eminent is the archeological recovery of buried art objects and lives, and the description and systematization of relevant empirical data both diachronically and synchronically. This project includes the discovery, description, and attribution of art works to artists and their particular historical periods among other problems. The fundamental task is to locate and organize a vast body of data for study, interpretation, and evaluation. Essentially, the significance of this beginning phase for Black women artists would mean the systematic recovery and historicizing of their work, little of which has been done to date. Most of what has been written lies within the history of African-American art, is secondary to male production, and for the most part is without critiques of class, gender and sexuality, though racial and aesthetic difference are traditionally considered in discussions of style, historical periods, and cultural and political movements.

Inextricably bound to the task of historicism is the formulation of analytical methods that would contribute to an understanding of the polyvalent production of Black women artists and to other scholarly/social interests of the Black feminist imagination/s. As art historian Michael Pondro expounds, the archeological question requires us to "provide answers on diverse matters of fact, on sources, patronage, purposes, techniques, contemporaneous responses and ideals"; while the critical history itself requires us to examine questions of sustained purposes and interests that are "both [irreducible] to the conditions of their emergence as well as [inextricable] from them" (Pondro, 1989: xviii). Hence a careful balance of formal and extra-formal investigations must constitute a significant element in the proposed critique. Analyses of form, iconography, and iconology, engaged in that critique, should consider integrally the simultaneity-multiplicative construct of race, class, gender, and sexuality, a consideration beyond conventional criticism which is largely formalist in its focus on the intrinsic qualities of the art object, though new art history and criticism both include and move beyond formalism (Flemming, 1991: 8).

Art educator Paulette Flemming criticizes the conventional art critics who "in vernacular and academic settings arbitrate meaning, significance, and value of art forms, stabilizing meaning or offering new insight into those forms with which they are familiar and explaining and evaluating those with which they are unfamiliar" (Flemming, 1991: 9). She calls attention to the inadequate perspectives in existing art criticism, attributing them to the lack of research and theory development in its fundamental teaching. Her critique of enthroned models of criticism in the educational system such as E. Feldman's "critical performance" (description, analysis, interpretation, and evaluation) and H. S. Broudy's "aesthetic scanning" (discussions of sensory, formal, expressive, and technical qualities) and others (Flemming, 1991: 9) reveals the limitations of those approaches, as does her interrogation of criticism's claim of universality based on the belief that "the aesthetic experience, formal qualities of the art object, and pansocial human activities" are universally accessible (Flemming, 1991: 9). Flemming's rejection of the cultural elitism and legitimacy given to "certain artworlds" overlays that of Black feminist theory in general as does her reiteration of the need to recognize cultural difference and the subjective response to aesthetic experience; qualities in which art criticism must engage if it is to be pluralistically valid.

Functionalist and contextualist theories are important to the proposed Black feminist critique, though at present apt to show limitations with greater focus on extrinsic factors sometimes to the detriment of intrinsic and historical considerations. Africanists, for example, utilize functionalism and contextualism to concentrate on art and cultural phenomena, often focusing on a specific ethnic area wherein they give primary attention to ritual, audience and symbolism, and their collective significance. Historian/ art historian Jan Vansina criticizes the limitation of this conventional anthropological ahistorical approach and calls for the inscription of a historical (diachronic) approach to the study of African art (Vansina, 1984).

Marxist archeological and critical scholarship, which overlaps the Africanist, is also useful to a Black feminist critique though its emphasis on the economic base of social history and its insistence on the instrumental value of art to society are somewhat problematic. The Marxist and functionalist/ contextualist critiques of African art are especially relevant to those of cultural nationalists, particularly in regard to the latter's concern with the social value of Black aesthetics and the functions of art and artists in society; as the work and philosophy of the Afri-COBRA group demonstrate (Thorson, 1990: 26–31). An examination of selected social issues along with the examination of art objects contributes to understanding the dynamics of events and attitudes of historical periods in relation to the themes and styles of art objects, and the ideologies of artists. This means that investigations of art must include intrinsic and extrinsic analyses.

Feminist analyses in general are assumed to be fundamental to a Black feminist critique in that they raise questions of gender in formal, contextual, psychoanalytical or other critical approaches. Their interrogation of patriarchy, elitism and classism is especially useful; however, the assumed Europeanisms of British Marxist scholars that suppress or dismiss critical awareness of the art of people of African descent reveal their limitations.[21] Some American feminist critiques also fail on the issue of race,[22] others do ascribe to minimal inclusion with discussions of art by African-American women in the USA and/or the inclusion of essays by Black women art historians, critics, etc.[23]

What is especially important about the various voices of contextualism and functionalism is a fundamental rejection of the formalist paradigm of modernist criticism that Roger Fry, Clive Bell, Clement Greenberg, and other critics dogmatically utilized, convinced that appreciation of the art object must rest on its intrinsic values, i.e. its "significant form" alone.[24] Such rejection coalesces with the conventions of such African-Americanist scholars as philosopher Alain Locke and art historians artists James Porter, David Driskell, Samella Lewis, and Richard Powell, whose critical approaches synthesize formalism and contextualism from diverse perspectives to document and integrally interpret form, content, social and cultural meanings, audiences and reception among other factors.[25] African-Americanist approaches in the area of art history and criticism are most relevant to the proposed critique since their investigations engage material culture and social history that include the issue of race and more recently gender in the archeological recovery of the lives and works of Black women and men.

Contextualism and functionalism, as Africanist anthropologist Warren d'Azevedo explains, alert us to the importance of understanding both the art object's aesthetic qualities and the context in which it originates: "The significance of any object – its 'form' – can be ascertained only with reference to the esthetic values of the members of a given sociocultural system for whom it functions esthetically" (d'Azevedo, 1958: 702–14).

Black feminist art criticism must both utilize aspects of existing paradigms and introduce new ways of thinking about art as it inserts its distinctiveness in subjects and perspectives, to: (1) assert the visibility and production of Black women artists in the USA and in other areas of the African diaspora and Africa, uncovering and documenting their lives, works, and interventions in society; (2) reject any question of universal truth or beauty since its basic assumption is that art is interactive with the specific cultural values of the context in which it originates and to which it contributes; (3) recognize the importance of both the African continuum and the European continuum in the development of African-American art which, in fact, is American art; (4) reject the established hierarchy of materials extant in conventional art history, and alternatively recognize the diversity in the artistic production (fine art, crafts and popular) by academic and nonacademic artists and assume that each has to be evaluated in terms of its particular form, function and value to its audience/s; (5) examine representation, particularly in regard to the history and politics of race, gender, class, and sexuality; (6) speak across the boundaries of race, class, gender, sexuality, age and discipline, to be enriched by and to enrich existing knowledge; (7) remain open to utilizing aspects of conventional methods (style-iconography-iconology) and revised approaches (influenced by literary criticism, anthropology, sociology, psychology, and interrelated political movements) while exploring new ways to inscribe and critique a yet to be written critical history of art of Black women artists.

Given its anticipated performative function, a Black feminist critique would resist the basic assumptions in the canons of art history that identify artists as "great"/inspired "geniuses" and their art as "masterpieces", an idea highly influenced by Florentine culture and derived from the ideals of ancient Greek models (Vasari, 1987: vii). Its interrogation of the canon would recognize that the current exclusionary art world practices are based on judgments derived from Eurocentric art-historical knowledge, particularly that developed during the Italian Renaissance with artist/art historian

Giorgio Vasari's publication, *Le Vite de'più eccellenti Pittori, Scultori e Archi-tettori Italiani* [Lives of the most excellent Painters, Sculptors and Architects]; dated 1550 and expanded 1568. Because of its official standardization of the discipline of art history, Vasari's *Lives* has been identified as "perhaps the most important book on the history of art ever written" (Osborne, 1987: 1177). Art historian Hans Belting observes that Renaissance art historiography "erected a canon of values, and in particular a standard of ideal or classic beauty," a norm of historical progress toward "a universal classicism, against which all other epochs are to be measured" (Belting, 1987: 8). In her resistant reading art historian Nannette Solomon surmises, "Vasari introduced a structure or discursive form that, in its incessant repetition, produced and perpetuated the dominance of a particular gender, class, and race as the purveyors of an art and culture" (Solomon, 1992: 223). A Black feminist critique would reject the preeminence and persistence of that influence and its adverse impact on art history texts, university curricula and museums throughout the world, and especially in art world practices that enthrone art/artifacts of European cultures while devaluing those of people of color (see Lewis, 1982: 42).

Art historian John Tagg reminds us that any adequate critique of art history must critique not only its paradigm of art, but also its "repertoire of legitimate objects with which art histories have engaged," since art history "operates with and defends a given definition of its object of knowledge, while limiting the permissible methods for constructing and establishing such knowledge" (Tagg, 1992: 42–3). African-Americanists and Euro-feminists have already legitimated their own forms in their publications, museums, galleries, exhibitions and other networks, but Black women artists have minimally benefited from these developments. Ultimately, the concept "canon" has to be challenged with the question "Whose canon?" By recognizing canonicity within constructs of its particular culture, whether Italian Renaissance or Yoruba antiquities, the critical art historian must reject universalizing tendencies, and work toward constructing analyses based on informed judgments that are validated by cultural grounding.

Material cultural theory would be particularly useful here for it raises many questions beyond conventional approaches that would allow the incorporation of vernacular forms into art history. Jules D. Prown informs us that material culture refers to manmade artifacts as well as to the study of beliefs through artifacts, of "values, ideas, attitudes, and assumptions – of a particular community or society at a given time" (Prown, 1982: 1–18). The inclusion of vernacular forms by pioneer African-American James Porter set the precedent for considering crafts with fine arts. An understanding of vernacular forms is highly significant to the development of a critical art history of African-American art for pottery, basketry, quiltmaking and others provide primary evidence of historical, material and aesthetic links to the history of African-American fine arts in the USA, and links to the past/ African heritage; i.e. African art, aesthetics and cultural elements that entered the country with enslaved Africans during forced migration and slavery. Material culture as discussed by John Vlach, Robert Thompson and others offers some direction for the proposed critique; however, they fall short of gender analyses though women's material production is included. We must go beyond mere inclusion.

Given the precedent in African-American art history surveys to include both "fine art" and "folk art" and the interrelated qualities of the two, the proposed critical art history must carefully inscribe both and show how they contribute to the overall picture, but with greater depth. It would resist the problematic assumption of a hierarchy in materials, recognizing that the life and work of nineteenth-century Harriet Powers (1837–1911), an enslaved and later "freed" quilter of Athens, Georgia, are as important for investiga-tion as those of Edmonia Lewis (c. 1845–c. 1911), a "free" woman of color who produced marble sculpture in the neo-classical tradition during the same period. Both artists significantly participated in the shaping of the history of African-American art and both interacted within their various contexts to make an imprint that merits attention. Powers is often excluded and Lewis often included in Euro-feminist and African-American art-historical scholar-ship, though brief discussion of quilting and other craft traditions occurs; but Powers is included and Lewis excluded in the work of material culturalists. A Black feminist critique must carefully review the data of both, and of those who produce on either side of the "fine art"/"craft" boundary, in order to reconstruct the proposed critical art history.

The craft tradition is significant material evidence of woman's personal expression, aesthetic taste, productive labor, and intervention in her given social structure. Crafted forms constitute a functional body of work that was and remains interactive with fine arts in the larger scheme of development in African-American women's art history and often signify a Black woman's difference in artistic production, raising the debate of essentialism and con-structionism. Regardless of the stance there taken, a distinct expressiveness in quiltmaking forms by Black women has become well known through the scholarship of Maude Wahlman, John Vlach, Reginia Perry, Eli Leon, and others. Specific identifiable qualities in quiltmaking traditions[26] and other African-American folk art forms are derived from conventional aesthetic values within the communities wherein those works are produced and whose aesthetic and moral tastes they, in turn, influence. Vernacular values are diffused with the migration of African-Americans (including fine artists), for Black women took their traditional skills with them and generally passed them on to their daughters.[27]

But simply inscribing folk, fine art, and popular art by Black women artists is not enough to justify the uniqueness of a Black feminist critique. Here the multiplicative-simultaneity factor of race, gender, class, and sexuality requires specific attention, in regard to Black women's work, the works of others and many critical issues.

A brief contextual consideration of nineteenth-century artists Harriet Powers and Edmonia Lewis will exemplify the potential instrumental value of a Black feminist critique in the production of a critical art history.

Lewis was Northern, "free" (not enslaved), college-educated, "privileged" (access to limited economic and patriarchal power) and single (free of man and child); Powers was enslaved and later emancipated, "uneducated," without privilege (money and power), married and with children. Lewis was born possibly in New York, possibly in Greenhigh, Ohio; attended Oberlin College and later made her mark in art history, after expatriating to Rome in 1865; she is believed to have died there c. 1911. Powers, on the other hand, lived and died in Georgia. Little is known about her life or travel, except that she and her husband were landowners and that she was able to care for herself after his departure, perhaps through her farm animals and sewing abilities (Fry, 1990: 84–91). The works of both artists are preserved in major museum collections, though only two of Powers's are known; but Powers's works were powerful enough to launch her into posterity. Powers's quilts are, in fact, canonical works: they link African-American quilting traditions to African textile traditions (West and Central), though often compared specifically with the Fon appliqué of the Republic of Benin. One quilt consists of 15 rectangular and square motifs arranged in strip design, each framing human, animal, or astronomical silhouettes in high-contrast colors. The pictorial character that combines imagery from biblical, local history and social commentary is linked to the Fon appliqué in its structure, technique, and narrative function. Its formal rhythmical style, combining both structured organization and improvisational qualities, reveals a dynamically controlled horizontal composition with limited color scheme, dominated by warm tonalities, though dramatically activated by its high-contrast design. Art historian Gladys-Marie Fry notes that Powers's "fascination with biblical animals and characters probably stemmed from hearing vivid sermons in church on Sundays" and that the core of Powers's religious imagery invoked biblical figures who "struggled successfully against overwhelming odds" (Fry, 1990: 84–5). Could this work perhaps be seen as a composition that expressed the artist's personal view of life, a view related to her desire to intervene in her contexts to present aesthetic beauty that articulated her particular sociopolitical stance? Is it possible to interpret the selection of particular empowered imagery, consonant with prevailing African-American religious-political metaphors of her period, as a practice expressive of her own individuality and shared "cultural memory" and material conditions? Representation of religious genre and historical events suggests this possibility. The Bible quilt is of special interest in this regard. How might such imagery be interpreted in light of Powers's low economic status, strong religious beliefs, and her victimization by slavery, racism, and patriarchy? Such thoughts would be invoked and investigated in a Black feminist critique.

The question of subject-matter in Lewis's work is also important in addition to form and context. Hagar, for example, though different in materials and style from Powers's biblical imagery, faced tremendous odds as the Egyptian maidservant of Hebrew Sarah, wife of Abraham. Renita Weems calls attention to Hagar's symbolism; slave woman, powerless, reproductive/exploited/manipulated body, unprotected, cast out into the desert with her son/Abraham's son; a story of victimization. Yet Lewis, daughter of a Chippewa mother (who remained in her environment and maintained her lifestyle) and an African-American butler father, rendered Hagar in an ennobled dramatic gesture, subverting the oppressive imagery of Hagar and in a sense of oppressed people of color, as did other African-American women such as educator Anna Julia Cooper (1858–1964), who "authored the first Black feminist analysis of the condition of Blacks and women" (Guy-Sheftall, 1990: 25). Lewis's works intervened in public spaces in exhibitions to assert the dignified representation of Black, Native American and biblical figures, displaying a resonance that radically expanded conventions of her neo-classical style beyond Greek influence. Her sculpted marble forms, characteristically ennobling Black and Native American subjects in gesture and overall effect with a characteristic dramatic grandeur, were oppositional to prevailing degrading representations of Black people in the popular Euro-patriarchist media that proliferated during her period (Lemons, 1977: 102–16). They also differed from the hierarchically encoded and delimited representations of Black subjects by fine artists of European descent.[28] In referring to Hagar (1875), Lewis noted that the subject-matter was inspired by her "strong sympathy for all women who have struggled and suffered" (Hartigan, 1985: 94). The empowered presentment of the form immediately calls to mind the strong female biblical characters of African-American orators and educators who synthesized religious beliefs and political resistance. Though her work adheres to the European canon, some of her subject-matter and its iconography emerge from specific lived experience, social conditions and interpretations interactive with those experiences and conditions.

The form and meaning in the works of Powers and Lewis reveal that the artists intervened in their contexts with their own particular Black feminist or womanist voice and drew upon shared cultural and social attitudes not unrelated to their shared racial identities. Their materials are related to the class and opportunities available to each, while their esthetic effect is related to the qualities that most appealed to their individual sensitivities. Meaning and associative values in the two works substantiate the point that "low" craft and "high" fine art traditions in the history of African-American art interpenetrate each other and are both essential to the critical art history of Black women's art.

Unlike Powers, who apparently "stayed put" as wife and mother, and unlike Black women of the intelligentsia, Cooper and Maria Stewart, who grounded themselves in the ideals of the "Cult of True Womanhood" of the nineteenth century as they fought for the rights of Black women and men, Lewis chose to bypass such ideals and, independent of children, men and the "Cult", became a member of the "White, Marmorean Flock" of American women sculptors in Rome (Thorp, 1959), where she reportedly exhibited her "strong-mindedness" (Hartigan, 1985: 94) though tenuously regarded as an "exotic" other.

By reviewing the imprint of these important nineteenth-century figures, one can resist the canonical debate of high *v.* low art and begin to think with greater depth about the importance of fine art and craft to African-American life and history and to the construction of a critical art history that centers the lives and production of Black women artists.

The question that art historian Linda Nochlin asked in 1971, "Why Have there Been No Great Women Artists?"[29] assumes that greatness is defined by the ideology of the speaker and his/her constituency, and therefore remains problematic. A Black feminist critique would instead ask who were/are Black women artists; what styles, subject-matter, and meanings did they produce in their various forms; how did their specific circumstances contribute to or restrict their production; how did those works intervene in the society of which they were a part; what was their particular reception; where, by whom, and why? Questions pertaining to Black women's simultaneous production (art)/reproduction (children) roles and those addressing woman-identified-women must be integrally explored. Simultaneously it must debunk historical racialist theories that promoted "Negro" inferiority with articulations that declared the "Negro's inability to produce art though having a 'natural talent for music'" (Fredrickson, 1971: 105), theories fundamental to the current exclusionism extant in the art world today for they reinforce the stereotyped idea that while African-Americans might appear to appreciate the visual art, they were/are "manifestly unable to produce it" (Hartigan, 1985: 73). Such myths cannot be ignored though they cannot be the focus of discussion in a Black feminist critique.

As Black women artists speak and work throughout the country today, they reveal cultural and political commonalities that are coextensive with their shared histories and material conditions, though their differences are apparent in the individuality of their personalities and vision. Their different styles, media, themes, reputations and professional roles display a heterogeneous body of work that ranges from abstract formalized structures meant to invoke mere aesthetic contemplation, to evocative performance pieces which synthesize aesthetic and extra-aesthetic qualities that are intended to activate immediate political responses from the spectator. No monolithic quality defines their style, though there is often some reference to their identities, and beyond the work itself, a commonality in the race and gender of those identities; also class and sexuality though perhaps more variable. It is their identity, in fact, that situates them outside of dominant art history and at the periphery of the art establishment. Those locations and the artists' response to them are coextensive with their collective history, culture and ideologies that link them to each other and to other African-American women in the USA, past and present. To engage these various aspects of Black women artists' lives and works is the challenge of a Black feminist critique and the larger art-historical discourse. Until that particular discourse is constructed, Black women artists and their production will remain behind the veils of art history. But as we collectively activate our knowledge and power, we can inscribe new discourses on art wherein we can locate our histories and construct critiques that will appropriately inscribe our lives, production, and interventions in this world.

Notes

1 Art history is a discipline that regulates the scholarly investigation of selected works of art and the historical evidence pertaining to them. The discipline systematically focuses on the fine art and lives of men of European descent. It chronicles developments of works of art (primarily painting, sculpture, and architecture) by styles and periods, giving attention to form (structure), iconography (meaning), iconology (subject-matter, meaning, and cultural attitudes), biography and historical contexts among other concerns. Its conventional purpose is to provide knowledge about developments of "major works" "masterpieces" by "major figures" "geniuses" and ultimately to influence appreciation of them. Despite much debate over the past 20 years about its racial and gender biases, little has been done to alter the exclusion of people of color in the basic texts, professional journals, museum practices, etc. The art of African-Americans and various people of color (excepting forms of Africa often designated as "primitive") remain virtually excluded. The past decade, however, has seen an increasing number of exhibitions of the art of people of color, an influence perhaps of the rhetoric of multiculturalism, but group exhibitions are disproportionately male and the solo exhibition is invariably a "one man show". Criticism is integrally related to art history, though it produces evaluative responses to art objects. Such responses are

grounded in the art-historical knowledge and cultural values/biases/subjectivities of the critics who are, by and large, Eurocentric in their orientation.

2   The patriarchy of men of European descent that regulates the art world operates a hierarchical system that asserts Euro-male superiority and domination over everyone else and the value of Euro-male production over that of others. In referring to the networking powers of Euro-male dominance, Elizabeth Grosz identifies three terms in particular that she says are not mutually exclusive: (1) sexism – an empirical phenomenon wherein women are treated as unequal to men; (2) patriarchy – a structure that "systematically evalutes masculinity in positive and femininity in negative terms"; (3) phallo-centricism – two types, the first being modes of representation that reduce differences to a common denominator of masculinity, and the second a process of hierarchization wherein one sex is judged as better than its counterpart (Grosz, 1990: 152). See Royland and Klein, 1990: 277. The noted terms and definitions identify the character and operation of the dominant art world.

3   *Artwriting* is the term used by David Carrier (1991: introduction) to refer to texts by art historians and art critics.

4   The term *art world* generally refers to "universes of regularized responses" that "coalesce around the production, creation, distribution, and evalution of various" art works. See Vlach and Bronner, 1986: 1–10. The dominant art world (Euro-patriarchy) places emphasis on fine art, setting and regulating standards according to the particular interests of its controllers. Vlach and Bronner call attention to the networks of folk art and utilize the term *folk art worlds* to designate different aspects of the larger network that is yet another component of the overall multi-layered system of art. The term *art worlds* is appropriate since there are others beside the dominant one; i.e. African-American, Euro-feminist, Africanist, Chicano/a, etc. Each of the structures, developed because of specific interest, reclaims and promotes the art of specific heritage/s as they interpenetrate the dominant art world, while resisting devaluation and exclusion from museum and gallery spaces. I will use "art world" or "dominant art establishment" to refer to the ruling fine art world of the Euro-patriarchy.

5   See: Bontemps and Bontemps (1980); Driskell (1976); Jones (1990); Lewis, (1990); Sims (1990); Vlach (1990).

6   Many Black women artists have articulated the problems that they encounter in the "art world", concurring that those problems are often related to race, gender, and difference in aesthetic taste. See Piper, (1990b: 15–20).

7   Piper identifies specific comments made by Euro-American critics to illustrate Eurocentric biases, generalizations, and impositions on African-American artists (often masked by utterances citing undefined notions of quality): Rosalind Krauss "doubts that there is any unrecognized African-American art of quality because if it doesn't bring itself to her attention, it probably doesn't exist"; Roberta Smith notes "that the real problem with the art of African-Americans is that it just isn't any good, that it would be in the mainstream galleries if it were, that she's been up to The Studio Museum in Harlem a couple of times and hasn't seen anything worthwhile, that it's all too derivative"; Hilton Kramer protests "the current

interest in issues of race and gender that, he claims, leave quality by the wayside" (Piper, 1990b: 15–17). Such remarks are representative of the prevailing Euro-centric proclivities with which Black women, men, and all people of color must contend; one has to question and critically interrogate uniformed/uneducated judgments by individuals who merely observe isolated objects with no historical depth. They reinforce the ongoing devaluation of Afro-American art from the beginning of an art history which is grounded in the cultural hegemony of Europeanism. The noted statements of the postmodernist era are, in fact, no different from the negative Eurocentric critiques of modernism. We all remember Hilton Kramer from the 1960s with his hostilities toward Black art.

8   See: Flomenhaft (1990); Tesfagiorgis (1987a; reproduced in Garrard and Boude, 1992); Wallace (1984).

9   See Tesfagiorgis (1987a), for more in-depth discussion of Ringgold's work. On African-American art and culture, see Powell (1989) and Thompson (1983). For example, Thompson discusses the multiple meter in African-American music (derived from traditional African music) and the emphatic multistrip composition in African-American textiles (derived from textile traditions in various regions in Africa). Maultsby (1990) extends her discussion of the interplay of aesthetics and function in African-American and African music to include the visuality of performance and calls attention to the "array of colors and fashions seen in concert halls, Black churches, and other Black performance sites" as well as the dynamics of body language and other visual qualities that she links to African traditions.

10   See Tesfagiorgis (1989); an interview with Therese Mosoke, in Nairobi, Kenya where Mosoke lives.

11   Tesfagiorgis (1987b): an interview with Sokari Douglas Camp, in London, UK, where Camp lives. I had the opportunity to interview Sokari Douglas Camp in her London studio where I also viewed her work and acquired minimal understanding of her conceptualizations and processes. (This research trip was funded by the University of Wisconsin Graduate School.) Later I was able to interact with her works in a formal display at her one-woman exhibition at the National Museum of African Art, Smithsonian (November 11, 1988–January 29, 1989).

12   Douglas briefly studied woodcarving with the neo-traditionalist Lamidi Fakeye, defying gender boundaries since woodcarving in Nigeria and other African countries is conventionally a male profession. She also briefly studied a powerful Kalabari priestess, Amonia Horsfall. Such opportunities were related to her Kalabari, Nigeria identity, academic training and somewhat outsider status given that she has lived in London much of her life though also in her hometown periodically.

13   In discussing the freedom that she feels by recognizing her "outsider" relationship to the dominant art world, particularly to the "tastemakers," Ringgold indicates that such a position negates their influence because "she is not a member of those groups who would profit from being on the cutting edge." "I'm not a man and I'm not white. So I can do what I want and that has been my greatest gift. It's kind of a backhanded gift, but it sets me free," she insists. See Flomenhaft (1990: 15).

14 This concept expands sociologist Frances Beale's concept of "double jeopardy, double consciousness" that referred to the racism and sexism experienced by Black women. See King (1988).

15 Collins (1989). Not all Black women artists claim a Black feminist consciousness; in fact some disclaim it. The same is true of Black women in general. Other nomenclatures have been imposed to identify the assertive stance taken by Black women both to enact self-determination and to resist oppression; i.e. the term *womanist* was proposed by Alice Walker and Chikwenye Okonjo Ogunyemi, etc *Afrofemcentrism*, which I proposed as an either/or term for Black feminism, was rejected by theorist Molefi Asante (in discussions at the University of Wisconsin-Madison, December, 1991) because he viewed Afrocentrism as an ideology that encompassed the stance of men and women; though he did note that gender differences were being discussed at Temple University where he was chair of the Department of Afro-American Studies at the time. I will use *Black feminism*, the prevailing term used to identify the currents of Black women's critical social engagement at various levels, as I continue to rethink Afrofemcentrism. However, the various terms are not fixed, and regardless of what, if any, we settle on, what matters is that Black women are articulating their empowerment in oral and written form while actively asserting their thoughts and actions to transform society.

16 For greater discussion of criticism see: Pepper (1970); George Dickie, *Evaluating Art*, Philadelphia, PA: Temple University Press, 1988; Jim Cromen, *Criticism: History, Theory and Practice of Art Criticism in Art Education*, Reston, VA: National Art Education Association, 1990.

17 In an exhibition catalogue, King-Hammond and Sims (1989: Introduction) discuss the works of the 13 exhibited multi-media artists, 11 of them Black women and two Black men. The text's illuminating and insightful interpretations offer a minuscule view of the wealth of art by Black women and men that remains largely hidden in the gaps of Eurocentric art history, criticism, and the larger art world.

18 Pondro (1989). Pondro uses the term *critical art history* to signify artwriting that includes art history and art criticism.

19 Michele Wallace's work is particularly insightful in this regard, especially her film criticism. Wallace makes it clear, for example, that as Black male film-makers join the workforce of Hollywood, their production also joins the existing practice of exploiting the images of Black women. The shift of authority from White to Black male producer/speaker extends the tradition of locking Black women into negative imagery that reduces them to passive, sexualized objects of various types. See Wallace (1990).

20 Like Wallace, bell hooks is a significant cultural critic; see 1981, 1984 and especially 1990. See art historians/curators/artists: Lewis, (1984, 1990); Sims (1990), Jones, (1990); Wilson, (1988); Tesfagiorgis, (1990); Frieda High W. Tesfagiorgis, "Elizabeth Catlett," *Black Women in the United States: An Historical Encyclopedia*, Boston, MA: South End Press, 1993. Wallace and hooks are foremost among Black feminist theorists to discuss the visual arts. Their focus

tends, however, to be on popular and folk art, though Wallace does include fine art. Black women art historians, curators, and artists are significantly contributing to the recovery and reinscribing of the lives, works and interventions of Black women artists. Our task, however, has hardly begun.

21 See Pollock (1988) and Wolfe (1990).
22 Ann Sutherland Harris and Linda Nochlin (1976) definitely fail.
23 Chatwick (1990); Garrard and Boude (1992); Raven et al. (1988).
24 Greenberg (1965); Chipp (1975).
25 See: Locke (1925); Porter (1943); Driskell (1976); Lewis (1990); Powell (1989); Richard Powell, *Homecoming: The Art and Life of William H. Johnson*, Washington, DC: the National Museum of American Art, Smithsonian Institution (1991); Robinson and Greenhouse (1991); Wright and Reynolds (1989); Campbell (1985); Leon (1987). Other catalogue texts: Studio Museum in Harlem, *Harlem Renaissance: Art of Black America*, New York: Harry N. Abrams, 1987; the Abby Aldrich Rockefeller Folk Art Center, *Joshua Johnson: Freeman and Early American Portrait Painter*, Williamsburg, MD: the Abby Aldrich Rockefeller Folk Art Center and Maryland Historical Society, 1987; Philadelphia Museum of Art, *Henry Ossawa Tanner*, New York: Rizzoli, 1991; Studio Museum in Harlem, *Memory and Metaphor: The Art of Romare Bearden, 1940–1987*, New York: Oxford University Press, 1991. Fortunately, there is an increasing interest in African-American art; the focus on male subjects and marginalization of women, however, need to be corrected.
26 Vernacular principles and such elements as color scheme (generally warm and high contrast), polyrhythms, strip design, and others have been defined and linked to specific qualities in various locations of Africa. See: Vlach (1990) Thompson (1983); Ferris (1983); University Art Museum, University of Southwestern Louisiana, *Baking in the Sun: Visionary Images from the South*, Lafayette, LA, 1987; Wardlaw *et al.* (1989); Tesfagiorgis (1992): 28–37, 39.
27 Above texts reveal this pattern. Also see: Kunene-Pointer (1985).
28 See Boime (1990); Fredrickson (1971); McElroy et al. (1990).
29 This is a vital essay in feminist art history which was first published in 1971 and has been reprinted in Nochlin (1988).

Bibliography

Ackerman, J. (1963) "Western Art History," in his *Art and Archeology*, Englewood Cliffs, NJ: Prentice-Hall.

Belting, H. (1987) *End of Art History*, Chicago: University of Chicago Press.

Boime, A. (1990) *The Art of Exclusion: Representing Black in the Nineteenth Century*, Washington, DC: Smithsonian Press.

Bontemps, A. and Bontemps J. (1980) *Forever Free: Art by African-American Women 1962–1980* (exhibition catalogue), Alexandria, VA: Stephenson.

Braxton, J. M. and McLaughlin, A. N. (eds) (1990) *Wild Women in the Whirlwind: Afro-American Culture and the Contemporary Literary Renaissance*, New Brunswick, NJ: Rutgers University Press.

Bryson, N., Holly, M. A. and Moxey, K. (eds) (1991) "Semiology and Visual Interpretation," in *Visual Theory: Painting and Interpretation*, New York: HarperCollins.

Busia, A. P. A. (1988) "Words Whispered over Voids: A Context for Black Women's Rebellious Voices in the Novel of the African Diaspora," *Studies in Black American Literature*, Volume III, *Black Feminist Criticism and Critical Theory*, ed. Joe Weixlman and Houston A. Baker, Jr., Greenwood, FL: Penkevill.

Campbell, M. S. (1985) *Tradition and Conflict*, New York: Studio Museum in Harlem.

Carby, H. (1987) *Reconstructing Womanhood: The Emergence of the Afro-American Woman Novelist*, Oxford: Oxford University Press.

Carrier, D. (1991) *Principles of Art History Writing*, University Park, PA: Pennsylvania State University Press.

Chatwick, W. (1990) *Women, Art, and Society*, London: Thames and Hudson.

Chipp, H. (1975) *Theories of Modern Art: A Source Book by Artists and Critics*, Berkeley, CA: University of California Press.

Collins, P. H. (1989) "The Social Construction of Black Feminist Thought," *Signs: Journal of Women in Culture and Society* (4) (Summer): 745–73.

——(1991) "Learning from the Outsider Within: The Sociological Significance of Black Feminist Thought," in *(En) Gendering Knowledge: Feminists in Academe*, ed. Joan E. Hartman and Ellen Messer-Davidow, Knoxville, TN.: University of Tennessee Press.

Davies, C. B. and Graves, A. A. (eds) (1986) *Ngambika: Studies of Women in African Literature*, Trenton, NJ: Africa World Press.

Davis, A. (1981) *Women, Race and Class*, New York: Random House.

——(1989) *Women, Culture and Politics*, New York: Random House.

d'Azevedo, W. L. (1958) "A Structural Approach to Aesthetics: Toward a Definition of Art in Anthropology," *American Anthropologist* (5): 702–14.

Driskell, D. (1976) *Two Centuries of Black American Art* (exhibition catalogue), Los Angeles, CA: Los Angeles Country Museum.

——(1987) "Speakeasy", *New Art Examiner* 15 (September): 13–15.

Eagleton, T. (1989) *Literary Theory: An Introduction*, Minneapolis, MN: University of Minnesota Press.

——(1990) *The Significance of Theory*, Oxford: Basil Blackwell.

Failing, P. (1989) "Black Artists Today: A Case of Exclusion," *Art News* (March): 124–31.

Ferguson, R. (1990) "A Box of Tools: Theory and Practice", in *Discourses: Conversations in Postmodern Art and Culture*, ed. Russell Ferguson, William Olander, Marcia Tucker and Karen Fiss, Cambridge, MA: Massachusetts Institute of Technology.

Ferris, R. (ed.) (1983) *Afro-American Folk Art and Crafts*, Jackson, MS: University Press of Mississippi.

Flemming, P. (1991) "Pluralistic Approaches to Art Criticism," in *Pluralistic Approches to Art Criticism*, ed. Doug Blandy and Kristin G. Congdon, Bowling Green, OH: Bowling Green State University Press: pp. 60–5.

Flomenhaft, E. (1990) *Faith Ringgold: A 25 Year Survey*, Heightsend, LI: Fine Arts Museum of Long Island.

Foucault, M. (1980) *Knowledge/Power: Selected Interviews and Other Writings 1972–1977*, ed. Colin Gordon, New York: Pantheon Books.

Fowler, R. (1990) "Feminist Knowledge: Critique and Construct," in Sneja Gunew (ed.) *Feminist Knowledge: Critique and Construct*, London: Routledge: 13–35.

Fredrickson, G. M. (1971) *The Black Image in the White Mind: The Debate on Afro-American Destiny, 1817–1914*, New York: Harper and Row.

Fry, G.-M. (1990) "Harriet Powers: Portrait of an African-American Quilter," in *Stitched from the Soul: Slave Quilts from the Ante-Bellum South* (exhibition catalogue), New York: Dutton Studio Books in association with Museum of American Folk Art: 84–91.

Fuss, D. (1989) *Essentially Speaking: Feminism, Nature and Difference*, London: Routledge.

Gaither, E. (1989) "Heritage Reclaimed: An Historical Perspective and Chronology," in *Black Art: Ancestral Legacy: The African Impulse in African-American Art* (exhibition catalogue), Dallas, TX: Dallas Museum of Art: 11–54.

Garrard, M. D. and Boude, N. (1992) *The Expanding Discourse: Feminism and Art History*, New York: HarperCollins.

Gates, H. L., Jr (1992) *Loose Canons: Notes on the Culture Wars*, New York: Oxford University Press.

Greenberg, C. (1965) *Art and Culture: Critical Essays*, Boston, MA: Beacon Press.

Grosz, E. (1990) "Philosophy," in Sneja Gunew (ed.) *Feminist Knowledge: Critique and Construct*, London: Routledge: 59–120.

Guy-Sheftall, B. (1990) *Daughters of Sorrow: Attitudes Toward Black Women, 1880–1920*, Brooklyn, NY: Carlson.

Harris, A. S. and Nochlin, L. (1976) *Women Artists: 1550–1950*, Los Angeles, CA: County Museum of Art; distrib. New York: Random House.

Hartigan, L. R. (1985) *Sharing Traditions: Five Black Artists in Nineteenth-century America* (exhibition catalogue), Washington, DC: Smithsonian Institution Press.

hooks, b. (1981) *Ain't I a Woman: Black Women and Feminism*, Boston, MA: South End Press.

——(1984) *Feminist Theory: From Margin to Center*, Boston, MA: South End Press.

——(1989) *Talking Back: Thinking Feminist, Thinking Black*, Boston, MA: South End Press.

——(1990) *Yearning: Race, Gender, and Cultural Politics*, Boston, MA: South End Press.

Hull, G. T., Bell-Scott, P. and Smith, B. (eds) (1982) *All the Women are White, All the Blacks are Men, but Some of Us are Brave*, Old Westbury, NY: Feminist Press.

Johnson, B. E. (1989) *Afro-American Literary Study in the 1990s*, Chicago: University of Chicago Press.

Jones, K. (1990) "In their own Image," *Art Forum* 29 (November): 132–8.

King, D. (1988) "Multiple Jeopardy, Multiple Consciousness: The Context of a Black Feminist Ideology," *Signs: Journal of Women in Culture and Society* 14 (1) (August): 42–72.

King-Hammond, L. and Sims, L. S. (curators) (1989) *Art as a Verb* (exhibition catalogue, Baltimore, MD: Maryland Institute, College of Art.

Kunene-Pointer, L. (1985) "Continuities of African-American Quilting Traditions in Wisconsin" MA thesis, Department of Afro-American Studies, University of Wisconsin-Madison.

Lemons, S. (1977) "Black Stereotypes as Reflected in Popular Culture, 1880–1920," *American Quarterly* 29: 102–16.

Leon, E. (1987) *Who'd a Thought It: Improvisation in African-American Quiltmaking*, San Francisco: San Francisco Craft & Folk Art Museum.

Lewis, S. (1982) "Beyond Traditional Boundaries: Collecting for Black Art Museums," *Museum News* (3) (January–February).

—— (1984) *Elizabeth Catlett*, Claremont, CA: Handcraft Studios.

—— (ed.) (1990) *International Review of African-American Art (African-American Women Artists: Another Generation)* (2) (October).

—— (1990) *Art: African-American* reprint edn, Los Angeles, CA: Handcraft Studios.

Locke, A. (1925) "Ancestral Legacy," *The New Negro*, New York: Maxwell Macmillan: 254–67.

Lorde, A. (1984) *Sister Outsider, Essays and Speeches*, Freedom, CA: Crossing Press.

McDowall, D. (1980) "New Directions in Black Feminist Criticism," *Black Feminist Literary Forum* 14 (4) (Winter): 153–8.

McElroy, G. C. et al. (1990) *Facing History: The Black Image in American Art 1710–1940*, Washington, DC: Bedford Arts.

Maultsby, P. (1990) "Africanisms in African-American Music," *Africanisms in American Culture*, ed. Joseph E. Holloway, Bloomington, IN: Indiana University Press: 185–210.

Nochlin, L. (1988 [1971]) "Why Have There Been No Great Women Artists?" in *Women, Art, and Power and Other Essays*, New York: Harper and Row: 145–78.

Osborne, H. (1987) *The Oxford Companion to Art*, Oxford: Clarendon Press.

Parker, R. and Pollock, G. (eds) (1990) "Fifteen Years of Feminist Action: From Practical Strategies to Strategic Practices," in *Framing Feminism: Art and the Women's Movement 1970–1985*, London: Pandora Press (Routledge and Kegan Paul): 3–78.

Pepper, S. C. (1970) *The Basis of Criticism in the Arts*, Cambridge, MA: Harvard University Press.

Perry, R. (1982) "Black American Folk Art: Origins and Early Manifestations," in *Black Folk Art in America: 1930–1980* (exhibition catalogue), Jackson, MS: University Press of Mississippi.

Pindell, H. (1989) "Art World Racism: A Documentation," *New Art Examiner* 16 (7) (March).

Piper, A. (1990a) "The Joy of Marginality," *Art Papers* 14 (4) (July–August): 12–13.

—— (1990b) "The Triple Negation of Colored Women," *Next Generation: Southern Black Aesthetics* catalogue): Southeastern Center for Contemporary Art.

Pollock, G. (1988) *Vision and Difference: Feminity, Feminism and the Histories of Art*, New York: Routledge.

Pondro, M. (1989) *The Critical Historians of Art*, New Haven, CT: Yale University Press.

Porter, J. (1942) "Four Problems in the History of Negro Art," *Journal of Negro History* 27 (January)

—— (1943) *Modern Negro Art*, New York: Dryden Press.

Powell, R. J. (1989) *The Blues Aesthetic: Black Culture and Modernism* (exhibition catalogue), Washington, DC: Washington Project for the Arts.

Prown, J. D. (1982) "Mind in Matter: An Introduction to Material Culture Theory and Method," *Winterthur Portfolio* 17 (Spring): 1–18.

Raven, A., Langer, C. L. and Frueh, J. (eds) (1988) *Feminist Art Criticism: An Anthology*, Ann Arbor, MI: UMI Research Press.

Ringgold, F. (1984) *Faith Ringgold: Twenty Years of Painting, Sculpture and Performance (1963–1983)*, ed. Michele Wallace, New York: Studio Museum in Harlem.

—— (1990) "Interviewing Faith Ringgold/A Contemporary Heroine" (interview by curator Eleanor Flomenhaft), *Faith Ringgold: A 25 Year Survey*, Heightsend, LI: Fine Arts Museum of Long Island.

Robinson, J. T. and Greenhouse, W. (1991) *The Art of Archibald J. Motley, Jr.*, Chicago: Chicago Historical Society.

Royland, R. and Klein, R. D. (1990) "Radical Feminism: Critique and Construct," in Sneja Gunew (ed.) *Feminist Knowledge: Critique and Construct*, London: Routledge: pp. 271–300.

Sims, L. (1990) "The Mirror: The Other," *Art Forum* 28 (March): 111–15.

Smith, B. (1982) "Toward a Black Feminist Criticism," in Gloria T. Hull, Patricia Bell-Scott and Barbara Smith (eds) *All the Women are White, All the Blacks are Men, but Some of Us are Brave*, Old Westbury, NY: Feminist Press: pp. 157–75.

—— (ed.) (1983) *Home Girls: A Black Feminist Anthology*, New York: Kitchen Table, Women of Color Press.

Solomon, N. (1992) "The Art Historical Canon: Sins of Omission," in Joan E. Hartman and Ellen Messer-Davidow (eds) *(En)Gendering Knowledge: Feminists in Academe*, Knoxville, TN: University of Tennessee Press.

Steady, F. C. (ed.) (1981) *The Black Woman Cross-Culturally*, Cambridge, MA: Schenkman.

Tagg, J. (1992) *Grounds of Dispute: Art History, Cultural Politics and the Discursive Field*, Minneapolis, MN: University of Minnesota Press.

Terborg-Penn, R., Harley, S. and Rushing, A. B. (eds) (1989) *Women in Africa and the African Diaspora*, Washington, DC: Howard University Press.

Tesfagiorgis, F. H. W. (1987a) "Afrofemcentrism and its Fruition in the Art of Elizabeth Catlett and Faith Ringgold (A View of Women by Women)," *SAGE: A Scholarly Journal on Black Women* IV (1) (Spring): 25–32.

—— (1987b) "Interview with Sokari Douglas Camp" (taped field interview, August 26), London, UK.

Tesfagiorgis, F. H. W. (1989) "Interview with Therese Mosoke" (taped field interview, September), Nairobi, Kenya.
—— (1990) "African Artists" and "African-American Artists," *Women's Studies Encyclopedia Project: Literature, Arts and Learning* II (Fall).
—— (1992) *Black Art: Ancestral Legacy, African Arts* (catalogue review) XXV (2) (April).
Thompson, R. (1983) *Flash of the Spirit: African and Afro-American Art and Philosophy*, New York: Random House.
Thorp, M. F. (1959) "The White, Marmorean Flock," *New England Quarterly* 32 (2) (June).
Thorson, A. (1990) "AfriCobra – Then and Now: An Interview with Jeff Donaldson," *New Art Examiner* 17 (March): 26–31.
Vansina, J. (1984) *African Art and History*, New York: Longman.
Vasari, G. (1987) *Lives of the Artists*, trans. G. Bull, Vol. II, New York: Penguin.
Vlach, J. (1990) *The Afro-American Tradition in the Decorative Arts*, Athens, GA: University of Georgia Press.
Vlach, J. and Bronner, S. J. (eds) (1986) *Folk Art and Art Worlds*, Ann Arbor, MI: UMI Research Press.
Walker, A. (1983) *In Search of our Mothers' Gardens*, New York: Harcourt Brace Jovanovich.
Wall, C. (ed.) (1989) *Changing Our Own Words: Essays on Criticism, Theory and Writing by Black Women*, New Brunswick, NJ: Rutgers University Press.
Wallace, M. (ed.) (1984) *Faith Ringgold: Twenty Years of Painting, Sculpture and Performance (1963–1983)*, New York: Studio Museum in Harlem.
—— (1990) *Invisibility Blues: From Pop to Theory*, London: Verso.
Wardlaw, A. et al. (1989) *Black Art: Ancestral Legacy: The African Impulse in African-American Art*, Dallas, TX: Dallas Museum of Art.
Weems, R. J. (1988) *Just a Sister Away: A Womanist Vision of Women's Relationships in the Bible*, San Diego, CA: LuraMedia.
White, D. G. (1985) *Ar'n't I a Woman? Female Slaves in the Plantation South*, New York: W. W. Norton.
White, E. F. (1990) "Africa on my Mind: Gender, Contemporary Discourse and African-American Nationalism," *Journal of Women's History* II (1) (Spring).
Wilson, J. (1988) "Art," in *Black Arts Annual 1987/88*, ed. Donald Bogle, New York: Garland.
Wolfe, Janet (1990) *Feminine Sentences: Essays on Women and Culture*, Berkeley, CA: University of California Press.
Wreford, H. (1886) "A Negro Sculptress," *The Athenaeum*, no. 2001 (March 3): 177.
Wright, B. J., Reynolds, G. A. et al. (1989) *Against the Odds: African-American Artists and the Harmon Foundation*, Newark, NJ: Newark Museum.

10

In Their Own Image

Kellie Jones

Jones, Kellie. "In Their Own Image." *ArtForum*, 29 (November, 1990): 132–8.

Somewhere in the interstices between the much maligned mutability of "pluralism" and the marginalized trajectory of "difference" is the common ground where most artists work. It is baffling to consider that in most art-historical texts, a handful of practitioners represents the industry and ideas of 50 years, while hundreds go unaccounted for – until such time, of course, as they serve the purposes of the commercial or cultural power structure. History, after all, tends to be written by winners. As Lowery Stokes Sims has pointed out, the fictional "other" is little more than a cathartic symbol, and "difference" a detour sign deflecting us from issues of power and control of a narrowly defined, nonrepresentative (art) world.[1] If today there is a "reworking of existing cultural frames of reference,"[2] it is a movement occasioned by the need to redefine a skewed perspective that has somehow cast more than two-thirds of the world's people – and their culture – as "minority."

Taking a look at the recent history of photography and text art, it should not be surprising to find women of color who are involved with this medium, though most books, articles, and general documentation might lead you to believe that only white males have created anything of lasting value.[3] Indeed, it is with individually identifying these Black women practitioners rather than abstractly acknowledging their existence that problems arise, that the record has to be set straight. In exploring the work of the Americans Lorna Simpson, Clarissa Sligh, Pat Ward Williams, and Carrie Mae Weems, and the Britons Zarina Bhimji, Roshini Kempadoo, Ingrid Pollard, and Mitra Tabrizian, one recognizes not only constructive strategies familiar in contemporary photography, but also the international dialogue their works have with each other, and the extent to which they expand the parameters of photography and text. These are women whose work is, with a few exceptions, well known in Black and, to some extent, academic art-world circles, but whose recognition within the larger art community is still minimal although growing.[4]

The eight artists discussed here all began combining text with photography during the early to mid 1980s. Most had done documentary work and adopted the photography/text format as a method to both delimit and expand the implicit meanings in standard "straight" photography. On the one hand, joining words to the photograph could clarify the reception of the single image, grounding ideology and meaning and leaving less chance for misinterpretation. This approach, of course, also mirrors the way photographs usually circulate in the world: in magazines, newspapers, and advertising, and on television an image is always accompanied by a verbal cue. On the other hand, adding text can also expand the meaning of the single image. Furthermore, the addition of a textual element changes the traditional relationship between the photographer and the subject, forcing the practitioner in some way to explain her voyeurism. At the same time these works challenge the viewer's customary response. A "typical" family portrait layered with script is no longer seen as a regular family photograph but must be read in a different way, relative to a specific situation; an image of a woman sitting alone in a bucolic field, for example, becomes not a figure of meditation or contemplation but one signifying isolation and danger as directed by the caption below. Implication expands, creating layers and levels of intent; words do not have to allude to pictures nor pictures to words, but can signify ideas outside this framework. These photographers were also drawn to the intrinsic social, almost didactic, function of the format. Because the act of reading expands the time one actually spends with any given work, photography and text do more to engage the viewer as reader/participant.

Of course, shared language and concerns also connect the work of these British and American photographers to that of other women artists. There is an interest in making visible women's lives and in revealing the range of their experiences as a valid starting point for art-making. In some cases, the commodification and objectification of women may be addressed. In others, strident texts appropriate a "male" voice, critiquing the foundations of authority, much like the work of Barbara Kruger. The female image might be used as archetype – the visualization of an exemplar or transcendent idea – that becomes a vehicle for the investigation of many issues and an instrument not limited to/by discussions of gender. As with Jenny Holzer's multimedia incursions, the photography and text of these British and American women may be said to be "the realization of the 'new' female voice, speaking for women but not exclusively to women; it forces the issue, to be sure, of initiating a feminist practice within the male-dominated culture but not containing it within 'issues' that can be conveniently labeled (and thus dismissed) as feminist."[5]

Indeed, the work of these artists also speaks to issues of cultural or racial identity. As women of African, Asian, or Caribbean descent living or born in the United States and Britain, they draw on a variety of world views and ethoses. It is often a fragmented existence, described by W. E. B. DuBois at the turn of the century as one lived behind a veil, a life *in* but not entirely *of* the dominant/modern culture. Yet it is interesting that the postmodern condition of the decentered (Western) individual sans "master narrative" has much in common with the quandary in which people of color find themselves in the West. As Stuart Hall has noted, "Now that, in the post-modern age, you all feel so dispersed, I become centered. What I've thought of as dispersed and fragmented comes, paradoxically, to be *the* representative modern experience!"[6] The work of these artists thus extends and supplements our understanding of Western culture and cultural practices.

So while the techniques and formal methods used by the photographers here are recognizable, there is something – image, language, reference – by which they make them their own. Self-expression cannot be culled from a "limitless replication of existing models,"[7] à la Cindy Sherman, for few exist. And simply recontextualizing found images (as does Sherrie Levine or Richard Prince) will often not get through to an audience including people of color, who have a hard time getting past stereotypes and slurs that still sting from habitual (and current) use. As Angela Davis and Michele Wallace have both pointed out, exposing myth as fabrication does not dispel the myth; the "revelation" simply takes its place next to the fiction as another version of this fiction.[8]

All of these photographers are concerned with identity and its recreation to some extent, but Kempadoo, Tabrizian, and Simpson in particular confront this issue in both personal and larger cultural terms. Kempadoo speaks about it from a very intimate place. A group of four untitled pieces from 1989 alludes formally and contextually to the reality of the multiple self through the juxtaposition of older Black and white family snapshots with more recent color photographs she took herself. Kempadoo's "self" is composed of a mixture of races – she claims a mixed East Indian, West Indian, Amerindian, and European heritage, but also identifies herself as a Black woman – and is one that finds "home" – the site where identity is nurtured – in not one but a variety of places. The pieces are generally composed as triptychs, with two photographic images accompanied by a single panel of text. The words become the mediator between Caribbean and British locales, between the family universe and that of the world. Kempadoo explores ideas of fragmentation and dislocation, attempting through her photographs to build a new identity that might be wholly inclusive.

One piece from the series juxtaposes a photograph of a brown couple in an affectionate pose, who sit on the prow of a boat and overlook a beautiful tropical landscape, with a vintage picture of what appears to be the woman from the first shot, now laughing and seated on a very English heath. The work's text reads:

> I wonder if it is possible to position
> myself from both
> HERE and THERE?
> No one experience
> no one history
> but from this an identity
> in constant change

The work neither attempts to explain the images nor the photographer's definitive stance but plays with ambivalence and fluctuations in meaning. In a series of Black and white self-portraits from 1990, Kempadoo focuses on identity as masquerade. One untitled work presents, for instance, a triple exposure of the artist dressed in African, Western, and Asian garb, accompanied by the text "Who do they expect me to be today." In this and other photographs, the essential character or substance that identity is assumed to be is shown as fluid, easily interchanged from one situation – or picture – to the next. Identity becomes a disguise, the subtle changes one makes in different company, the various personae one adopts in different circumstances.

Tabrizian's photographs employ the language and structure of film. Using this familiar and popular visual form she deconstructs "standard" or "given" definitions of sexuality and race, calling into question the power relations that structure our identity and existence. In a Black and white series of works from 1985–6 entitled "Correct Distance," Tabrizian focuses on woman as enigma, re-presenting the femme fatale of forties and fifties *films noirs*. At once mysterious, charming, and seductive, the femme fatale was up to no good and spelled trouble for any man captured by her spell. Tabrizian twists this stereotypical reading of the ultrafeminine evil temptress and succeeds in offering an alternate and positive vision of these women who appropriate femininity as power.

"The Blues," 1986–7, a series of photographs Tabrizian made in collaboration with Andy Golding, uses the scale and poses of movie posters, as well as the inflammatory declarative style of their text. Spare interiors bathed in blue light call attention to the melodramatic action of their subjects. *Her Way*, a detail from one of three triptychs in the series, reveals a bathroom interior with a Black woman lying on the floor, dead; the words "See my blood is the same colour as yours" are scrawled on a mirror that also reflects the face of a white man; overlaid text on the lower right provides additional commentary: "He was a man who had all the answers until she started asking the questions." Such staged scenarios declare the "fabricated nature of the photographic image"[9] and the folly of cultural and social categorization. Installed in a gridlike formation, "The Blues" is also reminiscent of a movie storyboard, and recalls the disjunctive, nonchronological narrative found in John Baldessari's work, although Baldessari's interest in the banality of our lives is almost diametrically opposed to Tabrizian's controversial investigations of racial issues and difference. And race is engaged in this work in subtle and various ways. While the staging of each frame seems to be based on the conventions of contemporary espionage films, almost every image has an interracial cast of characters and a text that explores themes of assimilation, acculturation, and difference. The exploration of these constructs extends to Tabrizian's appropriation, as a unifying motif, of the African-American musical form of the blues. Her use of this musical metaphor is indeed significant, for as James H. Cone has noted, the blues can offer a "perspective on the incongruity of life and the attempt to achieve meaning in a situation fraught with contradictions."[10]

Inherent in Simpson's work is a critique of the formulas of "straight" photography, its prescribed voyeurism, and the patented responses to social disaster or beauty it expects from viewers. Simpson's pieces begin with gesture. They isolate a movement and analyze the sentiment or attitude that that motion or stance suggests. In the triptych *Necklines*, 1989, for example, alternate views of a Black woman's neck appear in panels up to 5 feet high, overwhelming us with their smooth and sensuous curves; but in small plastic plaques below the photographs, words implying the sexual (necking, neckline) are interspersed with those alluding to violence (neckless, breakneck) problematizing the reading of the images as simply beautiful.

In Simpson's fragmented photographic processions, her generic women are never presented as whole. Instead, the figures insist on their completeness through synecdoche – in which the part becomes a proxy for the total entity. On a formal level these works share similarities with both Eadweard Muybridge's and Vito Acconci's photo pieces recording isolated body movements. But whereas Muybridge's works are purely documents of motion, and Acconci's texts read as bland operational instructions, Simpson forcefully inserts the woman's – and particularly the Black woman's – voice and experience. In *Five Day Forecast*, 1988, a sequence of five torsos with folded arms is accompanied by two tiers of plastic plaques. The plaques positioned above the images designate the days of the work week (Monday, Tuesday, etc.), those below supply an alliterated variety of ways women are misinterpreted in the professional (with inferences to the larger) world. This lower level of text also puns on the honorific for an unmarried woman, "Miss," so that the five women pictured have alternate identities as "misconstrue" or "misinformation," and so on.

Simpson has a wonderful feel for language, and she finds inspiration everywhere, in children's rhymes and the sophisticated innuendo of the blues, as well as in the Conceptual art-language gymnastics of such artists as Joseph Kosuth and Lawrence Weiner. But her work also confronts us over and over again with the Black female body as beautiful in itself and worthy of contemplation.[11]

Weems is also interested in language, not so much in its properties of definition *per se* but as cultural signifier. Trained as a folklorist as well as as an artist, Weems has found the implications and subtlety of folklore more interesting than text used didactically; for her, it's an unmediated form of communication that has the ability to speak more directly to deeper issues. A series from the mid-eighties entitled "Ain't Jokin'" employs jokes as a way to explore how such humorous narratives are used to legitimate the negative treatment of designated groups in a society. There are sexual jokes that allow sexist comments to slip by "in the spirit of fun"; there are ethnic jokes whose protagonists may be easily substituted – Polish, African-American, Jewish – depending on the company you're in; and as the saying goes, "There is truth in jest." Weems seems effortlessly to combine the directorial mode of staged photographs with a more documentary/photojournalistic style in her various limited-edition books (produced over the last decade) and multipanel pieces. While earlier photographs focused on an explosive condemnation of race relations and were addressed to changing the minds of whites, newer pieces are concerned with communicating with a Black audience.

In her recent book *Then What? Photographs and Folklore* (Buffalo: CEPA Gallery, 1990), Weems looks at traditional beliefs to show the power and beauty of African-American culture and, offering new readings of old folk-tales, considers the function of folklore as a way African-Americans have learned to live life in America. For example, one belief has it that if a hat is placed on a bed someone will go to jail. But across Weems's photograph of this scenario runs the text: "Girl evidently the man plans on staying cause when I got home from work yesterday his hat was on my bed." On the page facing this image is a stanza from a blues song: "Some got six months, some got a solid year, but me and my buddy we got lifetime here." While in this case the blues verse might convey the original meaning of the hat/bed conjunction, it might just as well be a comment on the durability of personal relationships as raised by the phototext. Through the language of African-American folk wisdom, culture, and the blues, Weems attempts to locate her own voice, in a present-day extension and reinterpretation of tradition. Like Baldessari's "blasted allegories," her texts are " 'exploded,' pieces and bits of meaning floating in the air, their transient syntax providing new ideas."[12] By questioning what is remembered, the photographer changes contemporary understanding.

Kempadoo, Sligh, and Pollard have all incorporated family snapshots into their work; Kempadoo uses them to piece together a persona, Pollard to rectify history, and Sligh to weave narratives and fables of her/a family. Sligh's interest in recording her own reality (as distinct from that supplied by the media or by the white, male, megalomaniacal power structure of Wall Street, where she worked as a financial analyst for ten years) first led her from documentary work to her family photos. But in these as well she found only fictive poses that did not convey her history as she remembered it. By collaging and marking the images, wrapping them in her own incantations, she reinvents herself in her own image. Using cyanotype and kallitype processes, Sligh preserves the old look of her family photographs while her practice of *cliché-verre* and other forms of directorial manipulation insist on the works' contemporaneity. Handwritten repetition of words further integrates language into the image.

Most recently Sligh has moved into installation with the piece *Mississippi Is America*, 1990, dedicated to the civil-rights martyrs James Earl Chaney, Andrew Goodman, and Michael Henry Schwerner. Here the photographer used "rediscovered" FBI photos of the three culled from back issues of *Time*. Three 7-foot strips of these portraits hang from a billboard-scale panel bearing the work's title, which itself is hung from the ceiling. On the floor underneath is detritus from a car accident – a smashed fender and headlights – and torn fragments of a poem about the incidents surrounding the murder of these three activists that Sligh composed in the style of a civil-rights freedom song. For Sligh this piece is just as personal as her earlier photographs because she lived through and was very much affected by the civil-rights era. Through three-dimensional installation, the photographer feels she further clarifies her intentions for the viewer: to provide a larger and more powerful context within which to consider the murders as signals of America's persistent (under)current of racial hostility.

Combining personal photographs (family pictures and vacation shots) with traditional views of the English countryside, Pollard questions and reconstructs the concept of "Britishness." Hand-coloring emphasizes the lushness and seduction of the photographs and is applied equally to the landscape and the Black people who populate it, conflating ideas of so-called "natural beauty." In *Pastorale Interludes*, 1986, these images provide alternatives to representations of Black Britons as rioting ne'er-do-wells. But they also query the "metaphor of individual freedom and transcendence"[13] that the English countryside represents by alluding to the violence and isolation faced by people of color living there. "It's as if the Black experience is only lived within an urban environment," declares Pollard's text.

In later works the narrative voice is replaced by the language of tourism. "The Seaside Series," 1989, is modeled on the intimate format of the postcard; the photographs must be viewed quite closely to pick out the camouflaged Black figure. In this work Pollard questions the location of the "other" and contrasts actual physical similarity or material likeness with perceived or socially constructed difference. Through text Pollard further elaborates on this comparison, pointing up the fictive uniformity of travel brochures and postcards directed to a "British" – read white – audience with the reality of a Black British presence. *Oceans Apart*, 1989, is an attempt to see her contemporary image making through the eyes of history, particularly that of the slave trade and Britain's imperialist legacy. Unpopulated photos of crashing waves and craggy shores take on an ominous quality when paired with vintage shots of a Black family enjoying themselves at the beach. Ordinary messages from postcards echo with the pain of separation ("missing you," "wish you were here," "keep safe till I see you again") as we begin to consider them in the context of the dislocations of slavery. Also included in this sequential work are more contemporary (though somehow ageless) images of Black people enjoying the seaside, contrasting with the unpictured horrors of history. Framing the piece are two color lithographs that layer historical imagery: maps charting the Atlantic Triangle (the slave-trading route between Africa, the West Indies, and England), colonial family crests, old Scottish currency with portraits of slaves, colonial ships, and "happy-go-lucky" "immigrant" laborers.

Like Pollard, Bhimji and Ward Williams fuse personal and collective history. Through installation and other alternate photographic processes, they attempt to further direct the viewers' reading/experience of their work. For Bhimji the movement of her photography into space is a way to connect with the larger reality of life itself by including the viewer's presence as an element of the work's "performance." Large, at times grainy photographs hung from the ceiling position us as children in an adult world. Bhimji activates the floor with spices, rose petals, and delicate muslin cloth that has been violated by burning. Many of her texts are abstracted from diaries kept over the years, but the words connect with the broader issues of migration, displacement, and identity. (*TOUCHING YOU*) – *Discovering the history of my ancestors makes my blood purr*, 1989, takes the form of an unspoken conversation between mother and daughter, divided by generations and differing perceptions of "self" and "home." How does one locate the self as an Asian born in Uganda and living in England for decades? As writer and director Hanif Kureishi has said, " 'My Country' isn't a notion that comes easily. It is still difficult to answer the question, where do you come from?"[14] Graphs included in the piece detail patterns of migration for Asians since the 1940s. Vaguely defined objects connected with "Indianness" (e.g., a buddha's head, a doll clothed in traditional dress) float in and out of view. This piece, like many of Bhimji's, is, in the artist's words, "based on memory, dreams, conversations from East African Indian and English backgrounds. I wanted to use them as metaphors, since I am concerned with not imitating the world, but recreating it."[15]

How can we rely on memory with no extant documents to support our claim to existence? If, in the images given, we are pictured as exotic, violent, or victims, then what? Ward Williams sees herself not only as a recreator but as an active part of the chronicle. "I had to DIG for my history but in doing so gained the ability not only to redefine [it], but also to see my role as a participant."[16] Her three-dimensional pieces commemorating Philadephia's MOVE tragedy or Henry "Box" Brown might be seen as political because they don't conform to either "popular" images or to those of broad historical currency. But these, too, are stories, part of the individual tales that reveal the larger issues of a society. For Ward Williams, nonsilver and physically and conceptually constructed photographs better convey her ideative stance. Her installations further define meaning by creating an environment within which the photograph may be seen, thus communicating more of the photographer's intent – the difference between Ward Williams creating a piece on lynching using "found" imagery (*Accused/Blowtorch/Padlock*, 1986) and a member of the KKK finding the same image and tacking it up on his wall. The impetus for much of Ward Williams' text comes from "word-bites" – snatches of language culled from books and magazines, overheard or remembered from family sayings – that she expands on or bounces off.

Michele Wallace has pointed out that women of color fall outside the constructs of Western binary logic.[17] In a society predicated upon such oppositions as Black/white, male/female, and "universal"/"other," women of color remain excluded from the either/or formula in which the polarities to white male are occupied by Black (as in male) and female (as in white). In the schema of Western discourse, then, women of color inhabit a space of complete invisibility and negation that Wallace refers to as "the 'other' of the 'other.'"[18]

Much of the photography and text work discussed in this essay has to do with "making ourselves visible," redefining the image/position of the woman/person of color within the larger discourse. It engages aspects of what the Border Arts Workshop in San Diego has termed "reterritorialization," a way of locating oneself in the world.[19] Reterritorialization includes recapturing one's (combined and various) history, much of which has been dismissed as an insignificant footnote to the dominant culture. These objects then become texts of redemption and emancipation. Not simply adaptations of Western codes, they construct and (re)define the record of their makers' own existence, challenging as well meanings and definitions once thought to be fixed.

Notes

1 Lowery Strokes Sims, "The Mirror the Other: The Politics of Esthetics," *Art Forum* XXVIII (7) (March 1990), 111–15.

2 Gilane Táwadros, *LUMO '89: The Boundaries of Photography*, exhibition catalogue, Jyväskylä, Finland: Alvar Aalto Museo, 1989, n.p.

3 Throughout this essay I at times use the phrase "people/women of color" interchangeably with "black people/women." This is because in Britain "Black" has broader racial implications – encompassing peoples of African, Afro-Caribbean, and Asian descent – and is closer in significance to what we mean by "people of color" in the United States. Currently, however, there is much debate in Britain as to the essentialist (inherent, cultural) connotations of the use of the term versus its importance in signifying a shared political oppression. That discussion, however, falls outside the purview of this essay and will have to be taken up in a later article.

4 Lorna Simpson is certainly the most well-known of the eight in the United States, having had numerous solo shows over the last three years, most recently at the Museum of Modern Art in New York. She also appeared in this year's "*Aperto 90*" exhibition at the Venice Biennale.

5 William Olander, "Re-coding the Codes: Jenny Holzer/Barbara Kruger/Richard Prince," *Holzer Kruger Prince*, exhibition catalogue, Charlotte, NC: Knight Gallery, 1984, n.p.

6 Stuart Hall, "Minimal Selves," *ICA Document 6: Identity*, London, 1987, p. 44.

7 Lisa Phillips, "Art and Media Culture," *Image World: Art and Media Culture*, exhibition catalogue, New York: Whitney Museum of American Art, 1989, p. 67. The two basic acceptable personae for women of color in the West are the mammy/maid and the prostitute. Betye Saar and Carrie Mae Weems are among the artists who have successfully appropriated these debased models.

8 Angela Y. Davis, "Underexposed: Photography and Afro-American History," *Women, Culture and Politics* (London: Women's Press, 1990), pp. 224–5. Michele Wallace, "Variations on Negation and the Heresy of Black Feminist Creativity," *Heresies* 24 1989: 69–75.

9 Tawadros.

10 James H. Cone, *The Spirituals and the Blues: An Interpretation* (New York: Seabury Press, 1972), p. 116.

11 I would like to thank Lowery Stokes Sims for reemphasizing how Lorna Simpson's work connects with images of beauty, making a place for the recognition of Black beauty on its own terms. See Sims, p. 115.

12 John Baldessari, quoted in *John Baldessari*, exhibition catalogue, Eindhoven: Van Abbemuseum, 1981, p. 49.

13 Tawadros, "Other Britains, Other Britons," in *Aperture: British Photography: Towards a Bigger Picture*, no. 113, (Winter 1988), p. 41.

14 Hanif Kureishi, "The Rainbow Sign" (extract), in *Fabled Territories: New Asian Photography in Britain*, exhibition catalogue, Leeds: Leeds City Gallery, 1989, p. 9.

15 Zarina Bhimji, quoted in *Employing Image*, exhibition catalogue, Manchester: Corner House Gallery, 1987, n.p.

16 Pat Ward Williams, cited in Kellie Jones, "Towards a Visible/Visual History," exhibition catalogue, *Constructed Images: New Photography*, New York: New York Public Library Astor Lenox and Tilden Foundations/The Schomburg Center for Research in Black Culture, 1989, p. 9.

17 Wallace, p. 69.

18 Ibid.

19 Coco Fusco, "The Border Arts Workshop/Taller de Arte Fronterizo: Interview with Guillermo Gómez-Peña and Emily Hicks," *Third Text* 7, Summer 1989, p. 66.

11

The Freedom to Say what She Pleases:

A Conversation with Faith Ringgold

Melody Graulich and Mara Witzling

Graulich, Melody and Mara Witzling, "The Freedom to Say what She Pleases: A Conversation with Faith Ringgold," *NWSA Journal*, 6(1) (Spring, 1994): 1–27.

You asked me once why I wanted to become an artist. It is because it's the only way I know of feeling free. My art is my freedom to say what I please.
        – Willia Marie Simone, in The French Collection, Part I

In "Aesthetic Inheritances: History Worked by Hand," bell hooks looks for – and finds – a model of a woman who has defied the "further erasure of the aesthetic legacy and artistic contributions of black women":

> This writing was inspired by the work of artist Faith Ringgold, who has always cherished and celebrated the artistic work of unknown and unheralded black women. Evoking this legacy in her work, she calls us to remember, to celebrate, to give praise. (*Yearning*: 115)

Ringgold's innovative work, which combines visual imagery and stories, has become increasingly known and celebrated in recent years. Her latest series of story quilts, *The French Collection, Part I*, is her most ambitious work to date. She is currently at work completing a related series of quilts, *The French Collection, Part II*. Because they represent her most recent work, we were particularly interested in discussing many aspects of *The French Collection* with Ringgold, especially the topic she defines as a central theme in one of the quilts, "The Picnic at Giverny": "the role of women [and especially African-American women] in art." Throughout the following interview, Ringgold looks from many angles at the role of women in art and the diverse influences on African-American women artists. She discusses the "great masters" of the French modernist tradition and African-American artists and writers, her family's storytelling tradition, feminist interpretations of the past, unheralded artists who worked in fabric and other media, the importance of recreating the lives and voices of historical African Americans, the production of her art, the writing of children's books and her understanding of children as an audience, and current issues in art history concerning female sexuality and the male gaze.

Ringgold has been an important figure in a course we team-teach at the University of New Hampshire on American women artists and writers because her work addresses our mutual interests as a literary critic and an art historian; although she was trained as a visual artist, the written word has been an essential aspect of Ringgold's work for the past decade. Throughout the interview, held in Ringgold's studio in Manhattan's garment district in July 1992, we had a rare opportunity to contemplate the second quilt of *The French Collection, Part II.* "Dinner at Gertrude Stein's," recently completed, shows a fictional gathering of literary and artistic greats, starring Zora Neale Hurston. The guests in Stein's art-filled salon are prominently painted in the large central area of the quilt. As in most of Ringgold's story quilts, the painted pictorial area is bounded by several levels of fabric frames.[1] A thin single band of fabric surrounds the image; then a horizontal, light-colored band, on which the story's text is written, is placed above and below the image; and finally, a broad, brightly colored patched border frames the entire quilt. Thus, the pictorial image and its accompanying narrative are literally pieced together and held within the same frame. In "Café des Artistes," a work in progress, we were lucky to get a closer look at Ringgold's working method. Although Ringgold said that she usually completed her paintings before they were placed in their quilted border, the painting in this work was incomplete, although it was already set in its quilted frame. Ringgold said she had "only painted on it about twice." Indeed, the figures were barely blocked in, and rough sketches in magic marker were taped to the walls. We stood directly in front of this quilt when we discussed it late in the interview, taking turns reading aloud from the narrative bands which had already been inscribed and quilted.

Faith Ringgold is one of the most outstanding artists alive today. Born in 1930 in the Harlem neighborhood where she still spends half the year, Ringgold came from a close family, whose love of storytelling was an important early influence. By her senior year in high school, she had decided she wanted to become an artist. She enrolled in New York's City College in 1948 and graduated in 1955 with a BS in art education – having married, divorced, and had two daughters within a year of each other. In 1955 she began teaching art in the New York City public schools, where she stayed until

1973. In 1984 she became a professor of art at the University of California, San Diego, where she teaches two quarters a year.

Ringgold's self-definition as an artist began in earnest in the early 1960s, after she received her Master's of Fine Arts degree and her children no longer required constant care. She took her mother and her two daughters to Europe to see the art that she had been studying. When she returned, she claimed her former dining room as her studio, an important gesture establishing art making as a major priority in her life. She began to try to find a way to create images of Black people, technically by finding a way to render Black skin tones, and thematically by producing portraits of members of her community, of "real" Black people, whose images had been absent in her formal art education. "Instead of looking to Greece, I looked to Africa," she said.

Ringgold's first mature style, formulated by the late sixties, is characterized by such paintings as "The Flag is Bleeding," with its bold, flat colors, abstracted form, and political message, which distinguishes it from the then current pop art, which it superficially resembles. Inspired by African masks and Tibetan tankas and influenced by her mother, Willi Posey, a dress designer, Ringgold began during the seventies to work with fabric to frame her paintings and to create a series called *The Family of Women*, fierce, haunting, mixed-media masks, with their mouths open, allowing them to speak. Her collaboration with her mother lasted until Posey's death in 1981. By the mid-1970s, Ringgold was animating the characters she made, first by stuffing their bodies to give them greater dimension, and then by creating environmental performances with the figures she had made, as in "The Wake and Resurrection of the Bicentennial Negro."

In the early 1980s, Ringgold achieved a breakthrough when she conceived the story quilt. For Charlotte Robinson's "The Artist and the Quilt" project, a collection of quilts made by contemporary women who usually worked in high art media, she collaborated with her mother on her first quilt, "Echoes of Harlem," portraying the painted faces of people she had known while growing up (Robinson: 103–5). When she could not find a publisher for her autobiography, *Being My Own Woman*, she realized editors and publishers controlled what Black women could write about their lives, and she began to embed narratives in her quilts, at first in single works such as "Who's Afraid of Aunt Jemima?" (1983) and then in multiple-quilt series such as *The Bitter Nest* (1988), an intricately plotted story about some of Ringgold's major themes: marriage, sexuality, family, mother–daughter relations, African-American social history, and female self-expression. All the narrators of Ringgold's quilts are African-American women who speak with authority in their own voices. Some are young girls who speak with the spunk and assertiveness of Toni Cade Bambara's narrators; others ponder their sexuality and their relations to men and to their mothers, like Hurston's Janie Crawford or Alice Walker's Celie; others tell stories about their communities, like Gloria Naylor's narrators. Many of Ringgold's stories – "Slave Rape Story Quilt" (1985), for example – reflect the interest in piecing together and retelling historical fragments we see in works by Toni Morrison or Sherley Anne Williams. Long acclaimed as an important visual artist, Ringgold deserves more attention as a writer, and *Being My Own Woman* certainly should be published.

With eight quilts in Part I and four in Part II, *The French Collection* is her most complex work to date, a *Künstlerroman* in quilts in which Ringgold inserts an African-American presence into the tradition of Parisian modernism in which she was trained. Her protagonist is a young African-American woman, Willia Marie Simone, who goes to Paris to study art in the 1920s; her story Ringgold describes as a "fantasy," "a surreal meditation on things we've never done but would have liked to have done" ("An Introduction to *The French Collection*" 11). Willia probably takes her name from Willi Posey, for Ringgold says that the series is a "tribute" to her mother, but that Willia can also "best be described" as her own "alter ego."

Each quilt presents a fictional gathering of a cast of characters interpolated with at least one "masterpiece" of the Eurocentric tradition. As in "Dinner at Gertrude Stein's" (p. 1), in each quilt a large painted image is bordered by a textual narrative from which the quotations below are taken.[2] In the first quilt of the series, the three daughters of Willia's friend Marcia go "Dancing at the Louvre" (p. 6), in front of the Mona Lisa and other works by Leonardo. In "The Picnic at Giverny," Willia is painting a group of contemporary feminists who sit, clothed, in Monet's famous garden, while a naked little Pablo Picasso sits in the corner, a reversal of Manet's *Déjeuner sur l'herbe*, in which two clothed men picnic with a nude woman. In the story, Willia speculates about a woman's freedom to "paint like a woman," to find her own subjects, to "inspire – Liberate" (21, 20).

Ringgold creates interesting counterpoints between images and texts. In "The Sunflowers Quilting Bee at Arles," (cover) the National Sunflower Quilters Society of America, whose membership includes activists such as Sojourner Truth, Harriet Tubman, and Mary McLeod Bethune, meet in a sunflower field at Arles, where they encounter a "tormented little man," Vincent van Gogh, whose presence is disturbing because he reminds them of Dutch slavers. The dead members of Ringgold's family are shown gathered in "Matisse's Chapel at Vence" discussing slavery. Grandma Betsy tells one of her mother's stories about the mother's uncompromising encounter with the grandson of a "slaver" and concludes that "white man got to live his own story and we got to live ours." The story emphasizes the importance of sharing stories of the past generations; Great-Grandma Susie, "looking strong at 110, just sat there being real proud of Grandma Betsy, her story-teller daughter" (30).

The series also explores themes related to being a woman artist, especially of African-American heritage, in the bastion of male artistic hegemony. Through Willia, Ringgold asserts that, rather than being models and muses, women can be the speaking subjects of their lives. While posing in "Picasso's Studio" (p. 8), Willia is told by the African masks in his "Les demoiselles d'Avignon", "You go ahead, girl, and try this art thing.... We just want to let you know you don't have to give up nothing" (33). Willia's Aunt Melissa says, "The only thing you have to do is create art of importance to YOU. Show us a new way to look at life" (33). The quilts are a strong affirmation of the creative authority of African-American women and its redemptive potential. The National Sunflower Quilters say, "Now we can do our real quilting, our real art – making this world piece up right" (24). They remind Willia that "one of the ways we know our true history and culture [is] from the art," and she vows: "Some day I will make you women proud of me too" (24).

The affirmative vision of *The French Collection* characterizes all of Ring-gold's work. Discussing a quilt from her "Woman on a Bridge" series, "The Winners," which shows a woman running across a bridge to win the New York City Marathon, she said, "If it hasn't happened, I just make it up. Much of it has to do with believing you can do something"; "drive and determina-tion," she said, go a lot further than talent in becoming a successful artist.[3] Spunk, faith and confidence also characterize Cassie Louise Lightfoot, the narrator of Ringgold's first children's book, *Tar Beach*, a Caldecott honor book, and the winner of both the Coretta Scott King Award for illustration and a *Parent's Choice* Gold award. Based on Ringgold's story quilt, "Tar Beach," now owned by the Solomon R. Guggenheim Museum, and echoing African folk stories about people who fly, *Tar Beach* presents Cassie flying over the George Washington Bridge and concludes "anyone can fly." Ring-gold's second children's book, *Aunt Harriet's Underground Railroad in the Sky* (her first book written especially for children), was published in 1992, and she is currently working on another children's book, *Dinner at Aunt Connie's House*, a revision of another story quilt, "The Dinner Quilt." Soon Ringgold will expand her vision into yet another medium with her recently commissioned mosaic for the 125th Street IRT subway station. She plans to execute two murals, each 30 feet wide, showing people flying. During the fall of 1992 she traveled to Morocco to research the mosaic process.

Ringgold's daughter, Michele Wallace, a noted cultural critic, has said of her family that "our fascination with language, storytelling, and naming is our legacy" ("Baby Faith", 154). Now let's listen to Faith Ringgold claim her "freedom to say what she pleases."

MW   As you know, both Melody and I heard your talk last spring at the University of New Hampshire, where you showed slides from *The French Collection*, so we're so glad to have this opportunity to talk with you about the series. What is the allure of France?

FR   I was trained, very early, to copy French artists – Degas, Utrillo, Cézanne. Actually not so much Picasso and Matisse as the earlier ones. They were the masters that we were made to emulate. Those artists were in me, and I had to get that out. That can be very deadly, you know, that probably finished off a lot of people, not being able to get those artists out of their heads.

MW   Your aim in *The French Collection* was to come to grips with the influence of those modern masters?

FR   Obviously I've been influenced by them, but they're not bothering me. They were at one time. That's why I can now go back to France, because now I can just enjoy it. I found my own way, and I can use them or not use them. I consider influences they have had on me positive, and I accept them. That early training gave me a certain respect, let's say, and taught me the art of copying and so every now and then I have to go back and do that. Even before I went to school I used to copy from my brother's and sister's history books. They had these great etchings of the Niña, the Pinta, and the Santa Maria, and then they would have all the presidents. I would copy them just to see if I could draw Abraham Lincoln looking just like Abraham Lincoln.

MG   There probably weren't many African Americans in those history books. The novelist Paule Marshall has described going to the library as a little girl and the importance of her discovery of the African-American poet Paul Lawrence Dunbar to her belief that she might become a writer.

FR   In my church school we saw some of the accomplishments of African Americans, but in public school, no way, uh-uh. But later I found those people on my own.

MG   Was that the reason you began writing children's books?

FR   Oh, yes, that's a nice idea. But other people are also doing it now. But I didn't have any children's books like that when I was a kid. Neither did my daughters, but my grandchildren do. You have a tendency to forget, but it's true, if I think back, my kids didn't have that but my grandchildren, they're getting it all. It's wonderful.

MW   Do you read your children's books to your grandchildren?

FR   Oh, they've heard it. When I had the book up on the wall, little Faith danced around and read each one out loud and little Teddy and the little baby pretended she could read.

MW   Do they ever say, "Oh, come on, Grandma, I don't like this," and then you change it?

FR Sure. They'll say, "Wait a minute, I don't understand that." And I'll say, "I haven't worked on that yet. I didn't get that down yet. I'm working on that. Do you think that needs work?" "Yeah, I do." It's great. They're very savvy.

MW One of the things that intrigued me about *Tar Beach* was how you developed sequences of paintings in the book from the panoramic view of the quilt.

FR Some people try to figure out how I did the whole book from just that one picture. I had to think up those other pictures just by looking at the story. My stories are always visually vivid, anyway, because I'm an artist. So it's easy to make a picture out of what I write because that's the way I think. Each section engages you, holds you, makes you read the next one. And anywhere you start reading is okay. You don't have to start at the beginning. You can start anywhere and you should start seeing things. When they see one of my story quilts a lot of people go away with all different kinds of ideas about what the picture is because they're seeing things they've read sometimes, not things that are there.

MW How did you coordinate the images and the text?

FR We made the dummy book first and then added the words. You get your story and then you put it on the pages. I know how many pages I want text on before I start the story. And that's the same thing I do with the quilts. I know exactly how many frames I have to write: it's six at the top and six at the bottom. I know it's six frames, I know how deep the frames are – six 12-inch-by-3-inch blocks – then I find out how many words I can fit in there. It's very technical. The woman who does the writing for me always complains, "You're putting too many words here, I can't get them in." And if she makes a mistake, we're dead, so everything has to be very carefully calculated.

MW So someone else actually prints the text.

FR Yes, somebody else physically writes the text. I have to keep my mind on what I'm doing in the paintings, not be thinking about anything else, be very tunnel-visioned. She's very good. She also lays out my books. Her name is Lisa Yi, and she's a wonderful quilt maker and painter.[4]

MW Are you working on other books?

FR I just finished *Aunt Harriet's Underground Railroad in the Sky*. This is the first text I've written for children. *Tar Beach* was not written for children, it's just written for people, but it turns out to be great for children too. It was written to help recall childhood, to help you think back on your childhood.

MW Well, I once flew as a child. You're also working on a children's book based on "The Dinner Quilt"?

FR   Yes. That story is finished, and I hope to put the book illustrations up on the wall this weekend. I like to put my books on the wall, line 'em up so I can see each page break and the whole thing. But I have not done the drawings for the book yet. It's called *Dinner at Aunt Connie's House.*

MG   Aunt Connie is the character who embroiders placemats, which always reminds me of Judy Chicago.

FR   Well, the story's changed, because although "The Dinner Quilt" is about childhood, it is really a very adult story.

MG   With lots of sexuality. The little girl narrator, Melody, "plays doctor" with her cousin.

FR   Yes. There are a lot of nudes in my paintings, and I never thought about it. I've always had sexuality in my art because I think it's normal, it's a part of life. So when it comes to relating to children, I don't want to be caught in a trap and made to do asexual things. But I don't want to expose them to things they don't understand. I mean I don't want to lead a sexual revolution for children. So I would consider "The Dinner Quilt" not for children. It's about the kind of thing that children do, all of them [expose themselves to each other], but I don't need to point it out to them now. It's more interesting when you become an adult and you look back on what you did as a child. A child probably wouldn't understand it in the way it should be understood, so I rewrote it. Now, rather than placemats, there are painted portraits of women who come alive. Rosa Parks invites them into the attic and she tells the children that Aunt Connie made them, created us to speak to you, to tell you who we are and about our struggle.[5]

MG   And it sounds like Aunt Connie is an avatar of Faith Ringgold because, isn't that part of your goal, to tell kids about historical figures and about their African-American heritage?

FR   Sure. Kids are such a wonderful audience. For them learning is fun, it's wonderful, because every day is full of new things to try and they're not ready yet to be blasé about it. So it's nice to teach kids.

MW   Does this relate to your years as a teacher?

FR   Oh, yeah, you never get away from teaching, do you? That's in you, and I come from a long line of teachers, so there you go. My mother's stories were like lessons.

MG   Do you retell her stories at all in your work? Alice Walker says in "In Search of our Mothers' Gardens": Is the story I tell really my mother's story? Do you see yourself doing that?

FR   No, I don't think I retell her story, but I tell stories for the same reason she did. There's something similar about it. She told stories to show you the continuity and to emphasize her moral code, her culture. She was giving you all the reasons why you should x, y, and z through stories, and they were always about real people and real events and real things. You know I never heard any of those myths.

MG   No stories about little girls flying?

FR   No. I heard stories about real people doing real things that would be similar to actually taking wing and flying – people making great achievements from very humble beginnings.[6] She wanted you to know who everybody else was too and so she would illustrate everything with a story. So that's really what I'm coming from. I guess I did that with my kids too. They hated it. They were very bored. Well, I couldn't roll my eyes at my mother. I had to sit there and listen. And she would tell stories to our friends, and I would say, "Oh mother, please," but they would say, no, we want to hear this.

MG   Unlike your mother's stories, yours don't have clear morals; they are so nonjudgmental and often end ambiguously. Some people have pointed out that they're like the West African dilemma stories in that sense: they don't resolve an issue or come to a conclusion.[7]

FR   My mother's stories did, though. That also makes us really different. My mother knew exactly what everything should be and why, and her stories illustrated that.

MG   Do you think your daughters will feel that way about you?

FR   Sure, absolutely, that's right, we just continue that process. My mother was outlandish, and my daughters think I am. You know, I wanted her to just calm down and be natural and normal like other people and she never would, and they would like me to do that, and I never will.

MG   Did the relationship of Celia Prince to her mother in *The Bitter Nest* Quilt reflect your relationship with your mother?[8]

FR   That's all of us – that's me and my daughter, that's me and my mother. Yes, because my mother was like that, my mother was very much the center of anyplace she was. If she was there, everybody knew it. I never heard her say she was nervous or felt shy. And I never saw her looking as if she were shy, feeling shy or nervous. She would sing out in church and she had a terrible voice; she sang off key but that didn't bother her one bit. She would have sung for the whole group if they had asked her.

MW   Celia also resented her mother CeeCee for making herself the center of attention, but CeeCee was deaf and mute.

FR   Well, CeeCee's a lot like my mother but then she's a lot not like her. Her muteness was the way to get past her husband, the doctor, and all of what he was in a time when women weren't important, and social standards were very important. So she had a very difficult time. I'm saying that maybe she was never deaf, maybe she just pretended to be deaf to get the attention, in order not to kill herself. A lot of women become drunks in a situation like that, they become quiet alcoholics, they go into themselves and they go into hospitals, a lot of people go crazy. She found a way to live her life which is what everybody's trying to do anyway. That was her way, and she had the courage to do it.

MG   She emerges after her husband's death and gets her voice back. Finding one's voice is such a recurring theme in your work. Was *The Bitter Nest* series inspired by *The Color Purple* and the trouble some families have?

FR   Yeah, I was writing it in 1985, the same year I read *The Color Purple*, and I was really fascinated, thinking, "Boy, family, you know, what does that mean, why do families have to stay together, why can't they just break up and go their way? Somebody's going to be bad like that, to hell with it. Let him go. Why did she feel like they had to stay together – that's interesting."

MG   Family, marriage, and sexuality are often very positive themes in your work.

FR   Yes, I don't have people doing really bad things to each other.

MG   The husband in *The Bitter Nest* series is oppressive because he's a patriarch, the "head of the family" rather than an abusive husband like those in *The Color Purple*. I was struck at UNH when you said, "We are deeply limited in the kinds of lives we can claim as our own." You went onto talk about how publishers want to publish stories about African-American women that deal with incest or rape or all sorts of terrible victimizing experiences.

FR   And if they're not there they want you to put them there. I always have to look for their insertions, or their translations of something I say, or what they think the African-American woman's experience is. And they want to hear that again and again and again and again. It's a huge problem for African-American women and other people of color: other people decide what their experience is and they want to hear that and nothing else. Artists don't see themselves that way. They don't see themselves in this limited framework as always being a Black family that is centered on a specific kind of adversity or pressure which is like a formula – the strong Black mother and the father who's not there and the kid who's bad and can't read. It's not the way it is all the time. It's like that sometimes, but it would be nice to be able to have the different levels and shades of being that white men allow themselves to have. They can be anything. And they present themselves on television, movies, everywhere, as anything, every level of anything. That's what we're all trying to do, show, give our lives the broad context and not limit ourselves to somebody else's picture of who we are. Native Americans and Asians face the same problem.

MW   So were you told that "nothing happened" in your autobiography, *Being my own Woman*?

FR   Yeah, right, nothing happened. You didn't get thrown out the window. You didn't get beat up. Nothing happened. And I don't know when that's going to change. I did publish some pieces of *Being my own Woman*, like the one where my kids go to Mexico.[9] And there are some other ones.

MG   The two published pieces I've seen both concern mothering – one about your mother and one about your struggles as a mother.

FR   But in my book there are also stories about my father.

MW   I'd love to hear a story about your father.

FR   Let me see if I can think of one about him. Well, my father used to take me to the bar. I sat on the bar and I was given milk to drink, which I was actually allergic to, and then I would entertain his drinking buddies by reading the different signs in the bar. My mother was very upset but there was nothing she could do because my mother was a housewife. My mother, like all women in the thirties, couldn't get jobs. In the forties women started going to work because of the war, so my mother started working in 1942 and divorced my father. Took back her maiden name and divorced him. But before that she had to be a housewife. She had to be taken care of by him, and so the courts said you gotta let this man take his daughter out on his day off. My father worked for the sanitation department, he drove their truck, he had one day off during the week, and he was our support. Once, my father disappeared with me. He came to the courthouse, where my mother would pick up support money from his paycheck, and he grabbed me and ran down the street with me and we got on the train. I remember him asking me where did I want to go and what did I want to do – he wanted to make sure I had some fun before he took me home. My mother went back into the courthouse and she said, "My husband just ran off with my little girl." And they said, "Oh, don't worry about that, he'll be back before nightfall. He has to go to work tonight, so he'll have her back before sundown." And I was, but that was very scary to my mother. But my father was a very unthreatening person; he never hit us. No, my father was a lot better than I gave him credit for when he was alive. I should have appreciated him more because his life was hard, unfulfilled. My mother fulfilled her life; she went out and did. They started out together, you know on the rooftop, in the twenties, playing their violins, going to church and with their dreams. And then they got married, they had three kids and my father got stuck in a dead-end job. I think that he knew that and she knew that he wasn't going to be able to grow. He had a family to take care of.

MG   Like your quilt, "Who's Afraid of Aunt Jemima?" that story is such a challenge to stereotyping of African-American men, who supposedly always walked away from their families.

FR   If it had been true, we wouldn't have survived, because there were no jobs for women.

MG   Did you develop the idea of story quilts because you wanted to tell your own stories, the ones the publishers wouldn't accept in *Being my own Woman*?

FR   Yeah, I think that's what artists do, generally speaking: they have a vision to communicate and feel their story is not being told. I wanted to do it for women. I wanted to show what that life was for an African-American woman.

MW   You once said that your quilts are not autobiographical.

FR   No, but they are based on what I know from growing up. They're stories that come from the period that I knew and the people that I knew, not necessarily me. Take *Tar Beach*. Unlike the father in the story, my father was not a construction worker on a bridge, and he *was* in the union, in the Teamster's Union. But I don't think he liked his job. I think he would have aspired to do more. My father is the kind of person who would have made a great teacher. He was very famous for what we call "chastising," which was a long, long story. Oh, a super-duper story about all the reasons why you should never do what it was you did. Which didn't seem bad at all before he started but we would just end up crying and he would be crying. And we would all be crying and it was worse than any spanking ever could be. He was a wonderful public speaker. He could really retain your attention. He was extremely entertaining and good with groups of people. So was my mother. He didn't have choices and that's what that book was about – it's about not having choices.

MW   But your quilts often present characters with *lots* of choices, with possibilities.

FR   I have choices, but that's me. That's not everybody. I had some things that a lot of people that I grew up with didn't have. I mean there weren't a lot of African-American people going to college when I went. I never realized that until later. I realized there were none in my class, but I didn't really realize how unusual that was, to be my age with degrees. I don't feel personally limited. I feel there were limitations placed on me, but I don't feel any personal limitation.

MG   One of the things I really like about your work in that respect is that you simultaneously show the limitations that African-American women face and then you also show the creative possibility, the richness of Afro-American culture and the ways to transcend those limitations or to make choices. Seems like you're sometimes doing two things at once.

FR   Yeah, and that's easy to do because in order to do any of this you have to get rid of all the limitations at least in your head.

MG   One of the things that really struck me in *The French Collection* was when Willia said, "Should I paint some of the great and tragic issues of our world, a Black man with his chin to the ground toting a heavy load, a Black woman nursing the world's population of children or the two of them together as slaves? No, I want to paint something to inspire, to liberate. I want to do some of this women's art." I thought that was just great. It really reminded me of the whole conflict between Richard Wright and Zora Neale Hurston. Does one paint the tragic reality of life or do you inspire and liberate the imagination?

FR You do what you want to do. One of the good things about writing children's books is that I don't get a lot of attention from the African-American literary community because they don't think children's books are important. My daughter said to me, "Are there children's bookstores that just sell children's books?" I said, "Michele, what's wrong with you? You've been in them." But what she was really saying was, "You mean to say these children's books merit a whole bookstore." I haven't attracted their attention in any big way so they're not trying to tell me how to explain the race.

MG I'm reminded of your quilt on Bill Cosby, "Camille Cosby's Husband's Quilt," and all the flack he took from African Americans about his show, about how unrealistic it is when in fact it mirrors his life.

FR Right, his life and a number of other African Americans who live that way. I'm an artist, which is also not at the center of African-American culture as far as the literati is concerned. They don't think visual art is important. I do. Because visual art, visual artists, are seen as these struggling poor people who spend their whole lives being anonymous, making things that nobody wants. And nobody understands why they want to do that. They say, "I certainly don't want *my* kids to go to college to be any kind of artist. Be a doctor, be a lawyer, be something. Don't do this art stuff." These people have been totally cut off from their experience as artists. In Africa you see a whole different thing. They want their kids to go to school to be doctors and lawyers and stuff, but they also love their art and they use it. And they can't conceive of life without it. There are groups of people who have been creating art for centuries. We don't have that here. The art here comes from our Black middle class, essentially. So it's always with a great deal of struggle that any Black person becomes an artist because they don't have the support of their community. But it's good in another way, because they're not watching you, they're not trying to tell you what to do because they're really not paying any attention and by the time they do pay attention, you're so well formed, it doesn't matter what they think. It's too late for them to have any real effect on your production, on your life. Whereas that's not true with writing.

MW You were talking about African-American community not thinking much about visual artists, but you yourself have written about some earlier

African-American artists. When did you become aware of the work of Lois Mailou Jones, for example?[10]

FR She had a show in New York in nineteen sixty something. And I went running down there. That's what would happen – I'd read in the paper that someone was having a show. Romare Bearden had his show in '64 and Jones had her show.[11] It was hard to find these things out. There weren't all that many opportunities to discover these people. And so it was nice to go and see if you could meet them. So I've actually known her since then. Romie Bearden I never did get to know.

MG Meta Warwick Fuller appears in some of your quilts. Has she influenced your work?[12]

FR Her work is so wonderful. I love her work.

MG When we first started, you were talking about needing to get out of your head some of the classic painting tradition. But do you ever have that kind of a reaction to people like Meta Warwick Fuller or Jones? Are they people that you're trying hard to get into your head, rather than having to get rid of, as influences?

FR I see them as pre-women's identity. I don't emulate their work. I emulate them. I think that their spirit is wonderful, that they were able to do what they did was wonderful, but I'm much more inspired by the younger women today who are doing art out of being a woman.

MW and MG Like who, for instance?

FR Well, Clarissa Sligh. Emma Amos.[13]

MW Do you know Barbara Chase-Riboud's work? She wrote that article in *Essence* about the exhilaration of being an African-American woman artist living in Paris.[14]

FR Yes, she loves it. She's been there forever. She's part of the scene.

MW Do you think that she's in some way acting out that French Parisian *artiste* role? Like Willia, she couldn't be an artist in America?

FR Because of the racism. See, that's what I was trying to deal with with Willia. She went to Paris in the 1920s when she's 16. She's gotta figure out all these things. Who am I? That's constantly coming up, and I know that a lot of the Americans that are over there now, when I'm over in Paris – there's this constant thing where they're saying, "Oh, don't do that. The French don't like that." I don't care what the French like. African Americans and white Americans, too, feel put up against the wall when they go to Europe because we don't have this strong, recognizable cultural base. But that's why everybody emulates us, for our persistent vulgarity.

MG The Sunflower Quilters (cover) really express an issue that I think is central to the rest of your work when they say to Willia, "We are all artists. Piecing is our art. We brought it straight from Africa." And by sending all those women who "are our freedom" and who sit around the quilt, Aunt

Melissa makes Willia realize that "we know our true history and culture from the art" (*The French Collection, Part I*, 24). You were talking about the lack of a cultural base but you repeatedly point to a really strong cultural base, passed through women.

FR Yes, but that's why they don't want to recognize it, because of those last few words that you said – "passed through women." It didn't make any money so it's not important. But you have to decide what's important and not allow those other people to do it. And that's the way we've always managed to change things. That's why we need to have everything vulgarized, because if art is not vulgarized, then the rest of us can't participate. We gotta knock it down and vulgarize it or a whole lot of us can't get in there.

MG Do you agree that we are all artists?

FR Yeah. Art is free. That's why you don't make any money at it. Because it doesn't cost anything to make it. You don't have to really go anywhere to do it. You can make your dolls. You can make your quilts, you can make them out of rags, you can use old clothes, you can use your friends, you can sit around and commune with your friends and have some dinner. You can make a social event; the slaves did it. After working in the fields all day, they would have a quilting bee, and it was like a party. And they could actually make something that they could give to somebody: they could pass something on. They couldn't enjoy the luxury of an object. They were cut off from the drum, they were cut off from the mask. But they weren't cut off from those skills of sewing and appliquéing and piecing things together. And when they were sitting there they were talking and respecting each other because the best way to learn to respect another person is to work with them. And to let them show you their skills and then you see theirs and together you make something and there is a bond that grows there. Now, that hasn't been talked about a lot, but it should be. The visual art tradition of Black people has been seriously cut off, which affected us during the sixties as we tried to find ourselves and to discover who we were as artists. Because if we look back to the 1800s with Bannister and Joshua Johnston and those artists who did the landscapes, they had no connection with Black people.[15] They painted portraits of white people, they did landscapes that were just like anybody else's landscapes, and they had no vision of anything that had their image. Black people did not define themselves until the twenties. And that's why I love Meta Warwick Fuller and Sargent Johnson and William Johnson.[16] I love his work. He's been a strong influence on me. So William Johnson and Palmer Hayden and Aaron Douglas came up with those Black figures which must have been very controversial and very upsetting, but they were the first ones who did.[17] That was the Harlem Renaissance.

MW   And that was the first time that there was an African-American visual aesthetic...

FR   Image of ourselves.

MW   But you must know Harriet Powers and her famous "Bible Quilt."[18] Do you think she was the only...

FR   Harriet Powers was a quilt maker, and the quilt makers were ahead of everybody. It's not until the 1900s, early 1900s, that abstract art became prevalent. The quilters were doing it before that, but nobody thought it was art so it didn't matter. Powers certainly did it; they all did. We need to take the everyday and make it the high. And we can take that high and we can make it the everyday.

MG   In a way the art becomes a comment on the everyday or a way of exploring the significance of the everyday in our lives. We both read an article about you and Elizabeth Catlett, who also writes about art being of the people.[19] Was she an important figure for you? She's a little older than you.

FR   She is an absolutely wonderful artist. I came to know about her rather late because she's a woman, and she was not thrust at me with the same vigor that the men were when I did finally find out about them. I know a lot about her now, but she was not one of those who could influence me because when I was in that formative period I didn't know about her. It was the men and it was the tradition that the quilt makers come from which is the traditional African crafts – fabrics and all of that stuff – that is really embedded in all of my work.

MG   We're looking at the wonderful Gertrude Stein quilt where you're trying on Stein's voice. Could you talk a little bit about voices that might have influenced you?

FR   Each time I write a story I have to try to find the voice. Until I get the voice I can't get very far. I have to figure out who's talking and why? So, with this one I knew I wanted to have them there [the figures on the quilt include "two white women," Stein and Toklas; "two Black women," Willia and Zora Neale Huston; "three Black men," James Baldwin, Richard Wright, and Langston Hughes; and "three white men," Pablo Picasso, Ernest Hemingway, and Leo Stein]. I knew that there would be some strange feelings for everybody in the room, you know. And that it would be a very intellectual evening that some people might vulgarize...

MG   Like Zora, for instance, the only one laughing.

FR   Of course. And I didn't want Gertrude to speak, but how are you going to have her there without having her speak? So then I used her voice, to speak – to let other people speak. So that was the way I worked that out. And I got an idea for doing that from reading a book she wrote that's about three African-American women. [Ringgold probably has in mind

Melanctha.] And that was a very revolutionary idea for a story. But I found I couldn't get a story out of that story. But I really like the way she writes. It feels a lot to me like the blues. You keep repeating it: "Woke up this mornin and I was blue as I could be. Oh lord I woke up this mornin..." You just keep saying it over and over. So Stein is wonderful, yeah. And then I wanted to put Zora in there because I knew she would be outlandish and wild, and so I let her speak. I couldn't let James Baldwin speak at all because, though he is so very eloquent on so many subjects, he didn't know what to say where women were concerned. Well, you can't do everything. But Baldwin is the one who calls Richard Wright a "Mississippi Pickaninny." And of course they all were just absolutely thrown by that. So this is part of my humor, I guess. My playing around with these intellectuals, the literati. And that's what Hurston did; they hated her for that; they made her pay. They ousted her, they covered her up, they got rid of her. They totally got rid of her until the seventies when Alice Walker uncovered her.

MG   Is that when you read her, in the seventies, or did you come across her before?

FR   No. I didn't. Nobody did. Zora Neale Hurston, who's she? So they can do that; they can really cover you up. They got her good and covered up. She appears in a lot of my work. She will be in *Dinner at Aunt Connie's* [Ringgold's latest children's book, mentioned earlier].

MG   You've said you'd like to try on Hurston's voice. Are you trying it on there?

FR   She doesn't necessarily speak in her voice. There are 12 women, and they're not able to speak that much. I use historical African-American women a lot; they just keep coming back to me. They tell what they came through and who they were, which is enough for kids to comprehend. Because the kids won't know any of these people. That they exist at all and did such remarkable things is going to be an amazement. In "The Dinner Quilt," Aunt Connie gives a lecture on the women she's embroidered on each placemat, but in *Dinner at Aunt Connie's*, Aunt Connie's voice fades into the background, and the portraits of the women get off the wall and get in the chairs. And then they start talking to the children. The adults don't know about this, only the children. And so I selected three women to speak, because economy is it. But that's the magic of storytelling anyway; you don't tell everything. So when the pictures go sit in the chairs and talk, I have to figure out, who should speak? And what do I want them to say? So I figured that Sojourner Truth should speak. And she does a very short "And Ain't I a Woman?" She talks about having 13 children and most all of them were sold into slavery. And then Harriet Tubman gives her famous statement about "If I couldn't be free."[20] And then the last speaker is Maria W. Stewart. She is the first American-born woman to speak in public. She was a lecturer, and she was criticized for speaking. And I don't know where I'm going to find a picture of her. Maybe there are no pictures of her.[21]

MG Earlier you talked about having to edit certain things out from children's books, especially sexuality, and about Zora Neale Hurston, whose treatment of female sexuality emphasizes both its richness and its costs. You seem to share her ambiguous treatment of relations between women and men. Your work simultaneously shows the strong sexual connection between men and women and the sometimes problematic consequences. You raise the issue of how men look at women in several places, in the "Matisse's Model" quilt in *The French Collection* and elsewhere, where you have said, "It is time that we women comment on our men. They have always done it to us" (quoted in Gouma-Peterson, 13).

FR Oh, yeah, they comment on us. I don't have the same fear about commenting on them that some younger women have. I feel that I can do what I want.

MW You're really giving men the female gaze in *The French Collection*, in quilts like "A Picnic at Giverny," where Picasso is sitting in his birthday suit surrounded by clothed women, an obvious comment on Manet's *Déjeuner sur l'herbe*. Was that a deliberate comment on the whole problem of women being presented in the male gaze?

FR Oh sure, and women do, sure we look at them all the time. That's why they wear those suits, a heavy-duty symbol of power and male identity, that suit.

MG In *The French Collection*, you also present daughters gazing at their mothers, so to speak. In your preface you imply that Willia's story is a fantasy retelling of your mother's life that merged into your own life. Thinking of a comment you made at UNH, "As much as possible I think artists ought to be writers. When you just leave it to other people to say who you are you might turn out to be anybody at all," I wonder how you would feel about your daughter, the writer, telling your life.

FR Oh, I would be horrified, because I don't think she knows and/or understands my life in the way that I understand my life. I don't think that she's able to comprehend it. She doesn't really know my work either. I know we had a really big discussion one day about women working, and I was saying that when I was growing up women didn't work. It didn't matter what color they were, they didn't work. They worked in the home and tried to find something they could do in the home. If they worked outside the home, they were domestics or teachers. If they were teachers and they were Black, they could not teach in New York, so when they came

North they lost their jobs. They could teach in the South. My mother's mother was a teacher and when she came to New York, she had to stop teaching and be a dressmaker; all the women in my family sewed.

MG   Because it was something they could do in the home, like the soft sculptures you did when your children were young?

FR   Right. I was back in there sewing in the house with ironing board up and everything, ironing . . . So I said you have to understand that men had to support their wives. But Michele just didn't want to talk about it; to her that was not important; it was not significant; it was almost antifeminist. But that's the way it was, if you want to understand the development of a group of people's culture from that to this. Michele has a tendency not to want to see that, and I don't think she's different from other young women, not to want to understand some of the humdrum kinds of everyday, nitty-gritty things that used to be, that are very important to understand so that you can not get stuck in a lot of stereotypes. I also seriously resent the feminist attitude of the seventies that said "our mothers had no voices; they can't speak, so we must speak for our mothers." I mean, what is that? Who made that one up, you know?

MG   You have to look for different ways of speaking. Alice Walker believes her mother spoke with her garden. Instead of focusing on muteness and tragic victimhood, you need to look for the possibilities for self-expression that were really there.

FR   You really have to let people do what they can do and they want to do and don't try to change them. I think in a lot of ways, daughters in the early seventies saw feminism as an opportunity for them to be their mother's mother. To have something to say about who their mothers were. But you see that's what I was trying to have Michele see, because I think she thought her grandmother, my mother, was always out of the house working, but when I was a child she was right there in the house. I'd wake up in the morning she would have already been up and she would be washing clothes in the tub. And I would hear her, no washing machines, there would be this scrubbing of the clothes on the washboard and it would be uh-uhm, uh-uhm, uh-uhm, and she would be talking. My mother was a big talker to herself. She used to talk to herself out loud, hold lengthy conversations with herself, and the conversation would be her plans for the day. Instead of sitting down and writing it out, while she was washing she'd say, "Yes, God spare me today." It was always, "God spare me today. I'm going to take Andrew to get his eyeglasses and then I got to get that dress for Barbara that is on sale at Klein's for half price. Then I've got to take Faith to the doctor, she's gotta get her shot," and she'd go through her whole day. She was very organized. And from listening to that I knew just what was going to happen with everybody in the family that whole day. She would be in there washing and telling herself what it was going to be.

MG   *The French Collection* raises so many questions about mothering, which I wanted to ask you about in terms of your own life. When Willia says, "I wanted to make art, not babies," she faces that age-old dilemma of the woman artist: can I be an artist *and* a mother? And she sends the kids back to Aunt Melissa to raise. How do you feel about that dilemma? Do you think that being a mother kept you from being an artist?

FR   It kept me from being an artist until 1964. And I was 33 going on 34. And I had my kids young and that was the reason I could do it because they had gotten up to some size where they could give me a few minutes. I could actually get them over there and I could be over here, and without saying, "Get out of here." I don't see how young women do it who have children.

MG   Would you give up the opportunity to have kids then if...?

FR   Oh I don't know about having them today; I don't want you to ask me that question. Once I had them ... because I didn't know about having children, I love children, but with both of my boyfriends – my husband that I first married and the second one – we always had a lot of kids around us. But I never said, "I'm gonna get married and have kids," and when I saw myself married, when I was fantasizing about me and my husband, I didn't see any kids: it was just the two of us. He was a famous musician and I was a famous artist and there were just us two: no kids, no kids.

MW   So is that one of the ways in which Willia is an alter ego for you, as you have said: she has kids but she doesn't have to care for them or give up her career for them?

FR   Yeah, right, and guess what? They love her. She doesn't even have to pay the price, which is why most women wouldn't dare give up their kids. I could have rather easily given up my kids and walked away because I had that kind of mother, the kind who could take care of everything. But I didn't want to have to explain that. I don't want to live any part of my life and then have to live it over again, trying to fix it. My mother didn't walk away from me, so why would I want to walk away from my children? They were great kids. But I could understand somebody who was very career-conscious.

MG   Do you think your art has been enriched by your having not only been a mother, but having been a caregiver to children?

FR   Well, I don't think there is any way you can substitute that experience. And having made those kinds of sacrifices is something you can't substitute either. And I don't think it was detrimental. I think my art would be different. And many of my friends have said to me, "I don't have kids and I couldn't do what you've done, so what the hell are you talking about?"

But I think it made me want to grow, to make up for all those years when I couldn't.... I sent them to baby camp, and I remember the first year when I came back home alone, I didn't know what to do with myself. I couldn't believe that I didn't have anything to do because they weren't home.

MG   What are you working on now?

FR   I am going to Morocco to look at the mosaics and to do "The Moroccan Holiday" quilt for *The French Collection, Part II*. And right now I'm finishing the café quilt for that series, the one on the wall, the "Café des Artistes," which is about Willia and the café. She's getting very sophisticated, and she makes proclamations. That's what they used to do in those cafés. Guys would get up and proclaim this and make a manifesto about that: "From here on all artists should..." And they would argue about it. And so she makes up a manifesto and proclaims that artists have to pay attention to the contributions of African-American women. And of course they have to listen to her, it's her café. Come on over here and let me show you who's sitting up there when she makes this manifesto. [We all walk to quilt.] She's got all the Black artists over here. Yes, this is Tanner and Jake Lawrence and this is Sargent Johnson, this is Romie Bearden, and this is Ray Saunders, my friend in Paris.[22] And this is William Johnson. I don't care whether they were actually there or not, I put them there. And this is my friend who is in Paris, Ed Clark.[23] Now, here are Toulouse-Lautrec, Utrillo, and van Gogh and Gauguin. And here's Elizabeth Catlett, and this will be Augusta Savage and Lois Mailou Jones and Meta Warwick Fuller and Edmonia Lewis.[24] Hell of a crowd, right? And so they're just all there listening to Willia talk all this stuff. Her café is on the Boulevard St.-Germain in Paris. That's my favorite section of Paris with the church right across the street. And you know she shows her art in her café – she's actually quite successful. She makes a lot of money selling her work. But she has to map it out in her own way.

MG   This is great [reading]: "I have a proclamation to make for which I beg your indulgence. This is the colored women's manifesto of art and politics."

MW   And then these are the voices of the people in the café who are listening?

FR   Yeah, they keep yelling out stuff at her.

MG   "Go home," they yell.

MW   "You should go home. Silence. Shut up."

FR   "I am an international woman," she says. "My African ancestry dates back to the beginnings of human origins, a million years ago in Ethiopia. The art and culture of Africa have been stolen by Western Europeans and white people have the power, enslaved and forgotten."

MG   "We wear the mask that has a new use in cubist art." I love the little references like that in your work [to Paul Laurence Dunbar's poem "We Wear the Mask"].

MW   Can I ask about your technique in executing these quilts? Is the image in your mind before the story or is the story in your mind?

FR   I really have to know what the story is. That's why I can't do "Moroccan Holiday" yet. I know that Willia goes to Morocco to meet her daughter, and the idea is that she's going to have this talk with her to explain to her why she didn't raise her. And when they're there, they meet with Martin Luther King, Malcolm X, Marcus Garvey, Paul Robeson, people like that. And she is explaining to her daughter how difficult it is for a woman to have a voice, especially in the presence of these kinds of men, and how you have to learn to hear what they say, appreciate what they say, and learn to translate it into terms that you can understand and use.

MG   Which is what you've been doing in the whole *French Collection*. That whole story reminds me of the contributions of Aunt Melissa. I mean, she couldn't have done that without Aunt Melissa. And there are always those women who keep the everyday life going, who sustain the life of the artist going to Paris.

FR   And I didn't want them to be raised by Willia's mother because you have a different kind of relationship with your mother. So I wanted it to be the auntie who would give her the money and say, "Go ahead girl, do it. You can do it." So, in "The Moroccan Holiday," the daughter is actually a filmmaker, and she's on her way to South Africa to do a film. And her mother thinks that she's giving her political savvy, opening her eyes to what's going on in the world and fantasizing that she's a part of that. But in reality this kid is going to South Africa; she's going to make a film. She's saying, "What are you talking about?" She's doing it without her mother.

MG   Perhaps the greatest fantasy in *The French Collection* is Willia's husband dying and leaving her enough money to support her art. Can you be an artist and still have children or have a heterosexual relationship with a man?

FR   You can have a heterosexual relationship with a man; it doesn't have to be positive. That, I think, is a very difficult issue because I don't think that men like their wives being artists. I really don't think they like that. It seems that it's not like having a job, it's having too much of a voice, it attracts too much attention. And when I say artists I mean any kind of work where you're making statements. Where you're really doing work that has nothing to do with getting paid, actually. I mean you get paid for it but you would do it anyway. You'll never take a day off unless you want to. And kids don't like that and men don't like that. So, it's very hard. But

I've been married 30 years. It took me a long time to figure out what I was supposed to be doing. I do what I want to do. I do exactly as I please, for the first time in my life.

Notes

1   In her first quilts, such as "Who's Afraid of Aunt Jemima?" Ringgold painted each block separately, but soon she settled on the procedure of using the entire central area as a field for her imagery.

2   Ringgold has reprinted the stories and Black-and-white reproductions of the quilts from *The French Collection, Part I* in a book of the same name. Page numbers refer to that book.

3   This comment and a number of others within the interview come from a talk Ringgold gave at the University of New Hampshire in March 1992.

4   Lisa K. Yi received her MFA from Columbia in 1987. She makes her own quilts now and collaborated with Ringgold on a story quilt, "My Best Friend."

5   The women are Sojourner Truth, Harriet Tubman, Maria Stewart, Augusta Savage, Dorothy Dandridge, Bessie Smith, Billie Holiday, Madame Walker, Mary McLeod Bethune, Marion Anderson, Fannie Lou Hamer, and Rosa Parks.

6   Ringgold discusses flying as an African-American folk tradition in the afterword to *Tar Beach*.

7   See, for instance, Thalia Gouma-Peterson, "Faith Ringgold's Narrative Quilts."

8   "The Bitter Nest," a story in five quilts about Dr. Celia Markham Prince and her "eccentric, artistic mother," Cee Cee, also highlights "the romantic period of the Harlem Renaissance." The first two "chapters" are excerpted in Witzling, *Voicing Our Visions*.

9   In this excerpt, Ringgold explores her daughters' teenage rebellions and her response to them. See "from *Being my own Woman*" in Baraka and Baraka, *Confirmation: An Anthology of African-American Women*. Along with other pieces of Ringgold's writing, portions of *Being my own Woman* are reprinted in Witzling, *Voicing our Visions: Writings by Women Artists*.

10   Lois Mailou Jones (b. 1905, Boston, MA), a painter, is currently Professor Emerita at Howard University. She participated in the Harlem Renaissance, studied at the Académie Julian in Paris, and has made several trips to Africa. She was the teacher of many leading Black artists. For more information, see Charlotte Rubinstein, *American Women Artists*. Ringgold has also written a short piece, "Lois Mailou Jones."

11   Romare Bearden (1914–88), one of the most noted contemporary African-American artists, worked with mixed media and collages; he applied cubist formal means to Black experience.

12   Meta Vaux Warwick Fuller (1877–1968), a realist-impressionist sculptor, studied in Paris, where her style was influenced by that of Auguste Rodin. She was ahead of her time in using African-American subjects in her work. See Rubinstein for further information.

13 Clarissa Sligh is a narrative photographer who also makes artist's books. Her first solo show was in 1984. Emma Amos attended Antioch College, studied art in London, and was an original member of the Spiral Group in the 1960s. She makes mixed-media works from paint, kente cloth, and her own weaving. She appears in Ringgold's "The Picnic at Giverny." For further information see Lucy Lippard, *Mixed Blessings*.

14 Barbara Chase-Riboud (b. 1936), a sculptor and writer who has lived in Paris since 1961, received her BFA from the Tyler School of Art in Philadelphia. In "Why Paris?" she discusses the long-standing "love affair" between Paris and Black Americans who were able to experience acceptance without racism there.

15 Edward M. Bannister (1828–1901) was born in Canada and lived in Providence, RI; he was a landscape painter. Joshua Johnston (1790–1824) was the first professional Black portrait painter in the United States.

16 Sargent Johnson (1888–1967) was a sculptor, painter, and ceramist. William Johnson (1901–70) was born in South Carolina, then went to New York and eventually abroad to study art. He painted African Americans involved in a variety of cultural activities, in a broad, flat style and in bright colors. In a recent children's book which resembles Ringgold's books, *Li'l Sis and Uncle Willie*, Gwen Everett uses Johnson's paintings from the National Museum of American Art to tell the story.

17 Palmer Hayden (1890–1973) painted rural and urban aspects of the Black experience and worked for the WPA. Aaron Douglas (1899–1979) was a muralist with works in the New York Public Library and Fisk University Library.

18 Harriet Powers (1837–1900?), an ex-slave living in Georgia, made two known "Bible Quilts," distinguished by their use of appliqué to depict biblical narratives and astronomical events. The first, owned by the Smithsonian, was purchased in 1890 by a white schoolteacher, Jennie Smith, who recorded Powers's description of the panels. The second is owned by the Boston Museum of Fine Arts. Powers's "Bible Quilt" is probably the one Alice Walker writes about as made by an "anonymous Black woman" in "In Search of our Mothers' Gardens."

19 Elizabeth Catlett (b. 1919), an American-born sculptor and printmaker who has lived in Mexico since 1947. She studied with Lois Mailou Jones at Howard University and received her MFA from the University of Iowa. She says that she "works from dual necessities – social as well as aesthetic" and that "uneducated people have the same cultural needs that we fortunate university people do... Since the earliest times people have had this compulsive need to express themselves" (quoted in Witzling 340–1). The article comparing Ringgold and Catlett is Freida High Tesfagiorgis, "Afrofemcentrism and its Fruition in the Art of Elizabeth Catlett and Faith Ringgold."

20 The full statement is, "There was one of two things I had a *right* to, liberty, or death; if I could not have one, I would have the other; for no man should take me alive; I should fight for my liberty as long as my strength lasted, and when the time came for me to go, the Lord would let them take me" (Bradford; 65).

21 Maria Stewart's dates are 1803–79. She reprinted her speeches and writings
    from the 1830s in *Meditations from the Pen of Mrs. Maria W. Stewart* in 1879.
22 Henry O. Tanner (1859–1937), a painter of religious subjects, studied with
    Thomas Eakins and was an expatriate in France. Jacob Lawrence (b. 1917)
    worked for the WPA, did paintings about Harlem and about civil rights, and
    taught at the University of Washington in Seattle.
23 Ed Clark (b. 1926) is a painter.
24 Augusta Savage (1900–62), who studied in Paris, was a sculptor and teacher. She
    has been described as the "moving spirit" behind the Harlem Art Center of the
    Federal Art Project. Her sculpture commissioned for the 1939 World's Fair,
    "Lift Every Voice and Sing," a tribute to Black American music, was destroyed
    after the fair.
    (Mary) Edmonia Lewis (1843?–1909?), a sculptor, was the daughter of a Black
    father and a Chippewa Indian mother, raised by her mother's tribe after her
    father's death. She attended Oberlin College, studied in Boston, and lived in
    Rome after 1867, where she was associated with a group of American women
    sculptors condescendingly dubbed "the white Marmorean flock" by Henry
    James.
    For more information on both women, see Rubinstein.

Works Cited

Baraka, Amiri, and Amina Baraka, eds, *Confirmation: An Anthology of African-
American Women* (New York: Quill, 1983).

Bradford, Sarah, *Harriet Tubman, the Moses of Her People.* Excerpted in Gerda Lerner,
Black Women in White America (New York: Vintage, 1973): 63–5.

Chase-Riboud, Barbara, "Why Paris?" *Essence* 18 (October 1987): 65–6.

Everett, Gwen, *Li'l Sis and Uncle Willie* (New York: Rizzoli, 1991).

Gouma-Peterson, Thalia, "Faith Ringgold's Narrative Quilts." *Faith Ringgold,
Change: Painted Story Quilts* (New York: Bernice Steinbaum Gallery, 1987): 9–16.

hooks, bell, *Yearning: Race, Gender, and Cultural Politics* (Boston: South End Press,
1991).

Lippard, Lucy R., *Mixed Blessings: New Art in Multi-cultural America* (New York:
Pantheon, 1990).

Ringgold, Faith, *Aunt Harriet's Underground Railroad in the Sky* (New York:
Crown, 1992).

—— *Dinner at Aunt Connie's House* (New York: Crown, 1993).

—— *The French Collection, Part I* (New York: Being my own Woman Press, 1992).
For copies, write directly to Faith Ringgold, PO Box 141, New York, NY 10031.

—— "An Introduction to *The French Collection*," The French Collection, Part I
(New York: Being my own Woman Press, 1992).

—— "Lois Mailou Jones," *Women's Caucus for Art Conference Honor Awards, 1986*
(Philadelphia: Moore College of Art, 1986): 7–8.

—— *Tar Beach* (New York: Crown, 1991).

Ringgold, Faith, and Lisa K. Yi, "My Best Friend." *Heresies: A Feminist Publication on Art and Politics* 6.4, Issue 24 (1989).

Robinson, Charlotte, *The Artist and the Quilt* (New York: Knopf, 1983).

Rubinstein, Charlotte, *American Women Artists* (New York: Avon, 1982).

Stewart, Maria W., *Meditations from the Pen of Mrs. Maria W. Stewart, Negro* (Washington, DC: n.p., 1879.

Tesfagiorgis, Freida High, "Afrofemcentrism and its Fruition in the Art of Elizabeth Catlett and Faith Ringgold," *SAGE* 4.1 (Spring 1987): 25–32.

Wallace, Michele, "Baby Faith," *Ms.* (July/August 1987): 154–6.

Witzling, Mara, ed. *Voicing our Visions: Writings by Women Artists* (New York: Universe, 1991).

Supplementary Readings and Media Resources

Supplementary Readings

Benjamin, Tritobia H., *The Life and Art of Lois Mailou Jones* (San Francisco, CA: Pomegranate Artbooks, 1994).

Fonvielle-Bontemps, Jacqueline, *Forever Free: Art by African-American Women, 1862–1980*. (Normal, Ill: Illinois State University, 1980).

Henkes, Robert, *The Art of Black American Women: Works of Twenty-four Artists of the Twentieth Century* (Jefferson, NC: McFarland & Co., Inc., 1993).

King-Hammond, Leslie and Lowery Stokes Sims, eds. *Art as a Verb: The Evolving Continuum, Installations, Performances and Videos by 13 African-American Artists* (Baltimore, MD: Maryland Institute, College of Art, 1989).

Lewis, Samella S., *African American Art and Artists*, 2nd ed. (Berkeley, CA: University of California Press, 1994).

Moore, Sylvia, ed. *Gumbo Ya Ya: Anthology of Contemporary African-American Women Artists* (New York: Midmarch Arts Press, 1995).

Moutoussamy-Ashe, Jeanne, *Viewfinders: Black Women Photographers* (New York: Dodd, Mead & Co., 1986).

Zeidler, Jeanne, ed. *Elizabeth Catlett, Works on Paper, 1944–1992* (Hampton, VA: Hampton University Museum, 1993).

Media Resources

Blue, Carroll Parrott, *Smithsonian World*: "Nigerian Art: Kindred Spirits." 60 minutes, video, color, 1990. (PBS Video.)

Edwards, Amber, *Against the Odds: The Artists of the Harlem Renaissance*. 60 minutes, video, color, 1993. (PBS Video.)

Freeman, Monica, *Valerie: A Woman, an Artist, a Philosophy of Life*. 15 minutes, 16mm, color, 1975. (Phoenix Films.)

Irving, David, *Faith Ringgold: The Last Story Quilt*. 30 minutes, video, color, 1991. (L & S Video Enterprises.)

Mora, Juan, *The Work of Elizabeth Catlett*. 28 minutes, color, video, 1976. (Third World Newsreel.)

Part IV

Music and Spoken Word

Overview: Music and Spoken Word

The subversive uses of language, or "the word," are explored in the four articles that make up Part IV. Importance is placed on coding, multiple meanings, and precise constructions connoting particular significance to various audiences. In chapter 12, "Black Women and Music: A Historical Legacy of Struggle," political activist and cultural scholar Angela Y. Davis lays a foundation for the historical development of Black women's social consciousness. Davis confirms that music in Black life has both shaped and expressed a collective awareness of social and political conditions. Gertrude "Ma" Rainey is especially significant because she was the first Black professional entertainer who grounded poor Black people in the Southern tradition of unity and struggle.

Davis maintains that Ma Rainey initiated the "Classic Blues" era, incorporating both personal and group social experiences in song. Furthermore, asserts Davis, Ma Rainey's blues metaphors signified a spectrum of economic, social, and psychological circumstances and gave dimension to Black women's experiences during the first decades of the twentieth century. Ma Rainey's musical contributions exhorted the women to develop their personal resources to attain individual and social independence. Her song lyrics and performances were instrumental in prompting a stronger understanding of women's personal attributes, a clearer perspective on male–female relationships, and the importance of female-centered bonds in Black women's lives.

Provocative cultural representations of Black females have been ubiquitous throughout history. Sustained resistance and opposition to these images by Black women has been continual, yet new and different manifestations persist. In the contemporary era, much debate and criticism revolves around the derogation of Black females in rap lyrics and music videos produced by Black male rappers. Cultural historian Tricia Rose, in "Never Trust a Big Butt and a Smile," provides clarification of the role of female rap artists in the current cultural maelstrom. Rose submits that the women are contesting predominant representations of Black females in both male lyrics and in mainstream criticism of rap. Through interviews with the women – specifically rap artists M.C. Lyte, Salt-N-Pepa, and Queen Latifah – and explication of their lyrics and music videos, Rose explains the influence of these artists.

Female rap artists occupy a public space that gives voice to diverse communities within Black life. They engage in a dialogue with audiences and male rappers about significant issues within these communities: sexual promiscuity, emotional commitment, infidelity, the drug trade, racial politics, and Black cultural history. The popularity of Black female rappers, indicated by record sales, broadcasts of music videos, and sold-out performances, demonstrates that the women are attuned to their audiences' concerns. Their lyrics and public personae challenge dominant assumptions about identity and sexuality, heterosexual courtship, and aesthetic constructions of the body.

Cultural critic Evelyn McDonnell, in "Divas Declare a Spoken-Word Revolution," presents the medium of spoken word, a combination of poetry, performance and/or music, as politically grounded rather than just a response to male artists, as is the case with female rap artists. McDonnell states that women are dominating the domain of spoken word more so than in hip-hop. The writing by the women has antecedents in the political thrust of the 1960s and the 1970s, resonating with the social commentary of poets such as Gwendolyn Brooks, Nikki Giovanni, Sonia Sanchez, and the pathbreaking writing and performances of Ntozake Shange. Spoken word evolved from a poetry form known as "the slam," that originated in Chicago in the mid-1980s. New York nightspots, Nuyorican Poets' Café and Fez, later became established as a forum for Black female poets in the early 1990s. Combining the authority of literature with the impact of performance, spoken word brought the concerns of Black females to wider public discussion.

McDonnell notes the critical distinction between performance poetry and spoken word: in performance poetry the main focus is on the act; with spoken word, the central element is the text, whether written, memorized, and/or improvised. The words, the writing, the political and social reconstitution of Black women's images, are crucial components of spoken word. Pioneer poets discussed in McDonnell's article include Wanda Coleman, Sapphire, Jayne Cortez, Dana Bryant, hattie gossett, Tracie Morris, Patricia Smith, and Ntozake Shange.

The trauma of urban life, the travails and triumphs of Black women living there are examined further in Carolyn Mitchell's "'A Laying on of Hands': Transcending the City in Ntozake Shange's *for colored girls who have considered suicide/when the rainbow is enuf*." A poet, playwright, and novelist, Shange has inspired Black feminist artists throughout several decades. Her innovative use of language, writing, performance, and theatrical form has influenced present-day music, poetry, literature, and drama. For Shange, language, images, and form are malleable in the service of arousing audiences' passion and comprehension of the lives of those severely damaged by oppression, injustice, and societal trauma.

Shange originated the choreopoem – a combination of poetry, prose, song, dance, movement, and music – with *for colored girls who have considered suicide/when the rainbow is enuf* (1976). The work, a portrayal of the lives of seven Black women, has been performed in community theaters, off-Broadway, at Joseph Papp's New York Shakespeare Festival, on Broadway at the Booth Theatre, internationally, and was adapted for Public Television Service broadcast in 1982.

The media selected for Part IV further illuminate Black women's participation in music, poetry, and other forms of performance art. The political and social contributions of a renowned a cappella musical group are documented by independent filmmaker Michelle Parkerson in *Gotta Make this Journey: Sweet Honey in the Rock* (1983). Formed by music historian and social activist Bernice Johnson Reagon in 1973, Sweet Honey has performed in a multitude of political arenas, providing the vocal inspiration for numerous social justice activities.

The video *The United States of Poetry* (1996) contains footage of many of the spoken-word artists discussed in chapter 14, by Evelyn McDonnell. Shown performing their works are Tracie Morris, Wanda Coleman, Dana Bryant, and Patricia Smith. Independent video artist Cyrille Phipps examines the depiction of Black women in music videos created by Black male rappers in *Respect is Due* (1992). Discussions involve Black youth, art critics, and rappers such as "Sista Souljah" concerning sexism and gender roles, and Black women's portrayal in rap lyrics and music videos are presented.

The world of early Black female comics is shown in Debra J. Robinson's documentary *I Be Done Been Was Is* (1984). Insightful observations and scenes of the women performing in nightclubs and on stage spotlight an aspect of feminist commentary that has rarely been examined. Comics profiled include Alice Arthur, Rhonda Hansome, June Galvin-Lewis, and Marsha Warfield, who later starred in the television series *Night Court*.

12

Black Women and Music: A Historical Legacy of Struggle

Angela Y. Davis

Davis, Angela Y. "Black Women and Music: A Historical Legacy of Struggle." In Joanne M. Braxton and Andrée Nicola McLaughlin, eds. *Wild Women in the Whirlwind: Afra-American Culture and the Contemporary Literary Renaissance* (New Brunswick, NJ: Rutgers University Press, 1990), pp. 3–21.

Throughout the history of the African presence in America, song and dance have informed the collective consciousness of the Black community in vital and enduring ways. Music has long permeated the daily life of most African-Americans; it has played a central role in the normal socialization process; and during moments characterized by intense movements for social change, it has helped to shape the necessary political consciousness. Any attempt, therefore, to understand in depth the evolution of women's consciousness within the Black community requires a serious examination of the music which has influenced them – particularly that which they themselves have created.

Social consciousness does not occur spontaneously. As Marx and Engels pointed out, it arises on the basis of concrete conditions of human life in society. "It is not the consciousness of men [and women! – AYD] that determines their being, but, on the contrary, their social being that determines their consciousness."[1] If it is true that music in general reflects social consciousness and that African-American music is an especially formative element of Black people's consciousness in America, the roots of the music in our concrete historical conditions must be acknowledged. For Black women in particular, music has simultaneously expressed and shaped our collective consciousness.

African-American women who have had the most enduring impact on popular culture have been deeply rooted in the ethnic musical traditions of our community, traditions forged originally on the continent of Africa, then reshaped and honed by the conditions of slavery, the Reconstruction years, and the two world wars. And indeed, precisely because Black music resides on a cultural continuum which has remained closest to the ethnic and socio-historical heritage of African-Americans, it has been our central aesthetic expression, influencing all the remaining arts. Black music, writes James Cone,

> unites the joy and the sorrow, the love and the hate and the despair of Black people and it moves the people toward the direction of total liberation. It shapes and defines Black being and creates cultural structures for Black expression. Black music is unifying because it confronts the individual with the truth of Black existence and affirms that Black being is possible only in a communal context.[2]

In this essay I will first examine some of the critical moments in the history of Black music before the "Classic Blues" era, initiated by Gertrude "Ma" Rainey, emerged. My emphasis will be on the roles women played in shaping that history. I then will explore the musical contributions of Rainey, a seminal female figure in the Black music tradition, while analyzing and evaluating her catalytic role in awakening collective social consciousness about the African-American predicament. This analysis will attempt to single out some of the specific ways her music gave expression to the emotional dimensions of Black women's lives during the first decades of this century – their consciousness of self, their grasp of the dynamics of male–female bonds as well as female-centered relationships, and the link between these processes and the objective factors conditioning Black women's lives.

W. E. B. Du Bois wrote that Black music is "the most beautiful expression of human experience born this side of the seas.... It remains as the singular spiritual heritage of the nation and the greatest gift of the Negro people."[3] During the period of slavery, music alone escaped the devastating cultural genocide wrought by the slaveocracy on the lives of Africans who were involuntarily and forcibly transported from their homeland to the shores of North America. While Black people were denied the right to speak in their native tongues, to engage in their traditional religious practices, to build their traditional families and communities, they were able to sing as they toiled in the fields and as they practiced their newfound Christian religion. Through the vehicle of song, they were able to preserve their ethnic heritage, even as they were generations removed from their original homeland and perhaps even unaware that their songs bore witness to and affirmed their African cultural roots. If they were permitted to sing, it was only because the slaveocracy's ethnocentric naiveté prevented them from comprehending the social function of African music, or indeed of music in general. Interpreting the slave songs as amusement or, at best, as a phenomenon facilitating work or the Christian religious indoctrination they hoped would result in the collective internalization of social inferiority on the part of the slaves, the slaveholders either acquiesced in or actively encouraged the slaves to sing their work songs and their spirituals.

Traditional West African music was never merely amusement or entertainment; it was always functional and was a central ingredient of every facet of community life. Always inextricably linked to economic activity, communal interrelationships, and spiritual pursuits, all of which were themselves interrelated, music as an aesthetic abstraction from the activities of daily life was unknown to the African ancestors of slaves in the United States. Ernest Borneman has enumerated eight different kinds of song which functioned in a basic way to regulate the community's cultural patterns. Among these are the songs associated with young men whose purpose was to influence young women: "songs of courtship, songs of challenge, songs of scorn."[4] One can't help but speculate that the author's failure to acknowledge the possibility that young women also sang songs to influence the men is an omission that must be attributed to the influence of sexism on his scholarship, for the societies to which he makes reference had distinct female courtship customs. Borneman further enumerates mothers' educational and calming songs: play songs, game songs, and lullabies. Again he discusses the songs older men used in the preparation of boys for manhood, but fails to recognize the corresponding songs used for the passage from girlhood to womanhood. Among the remaining types of songs he acknowledges are those "used by workers to make their tasks easier: work songs to stress the rhythm of labor, group songs to synchronize collectively executed work, team songs sung by one team to challenge and satirize the other."[5] West African music was functional in the deeper sense that it was more than an external tool, utilized to facilitate a given human activity. Rather, it was always considered to be a part of the activity itself. Thus music was not employed as an aesthetic instrumentality, external to work but facilitating its execution; rather, work songs were inseparable from the very activity of work itself. Janheinz Jahn has referred to the West African philosophical concept of *Nommo* – "the magic power of the word" – as being the very basis of music. According to the world-view of West African culture – if such a generalization is permitted – the life force is actualized by the power of the word. "According to African philosophy man has, by the force of his word, dominion over 'things.' He can change them, make them work for him and command them."[6]

Song is the practice of *Nommo*. As an African proverb affirms, "the spirit cannot descend without song." This song is not rigorously differentiated from everyday speech as came to be the case with European music, for most West African languages incorporate several of the basic structural elements of music: pitch, timbre, and timing.[7] A word uttered at a certain pitch may have a different meaning from the same word spoken at another pitch. The same dynamic applies to timbre and timing.

A further factor differentiating African from European music is the structural emphasis on rhythm as opposed to the emphasis on melody and harmony in European music. Rhythm's central role derives from its part in the process of *naming*, of imbuing things with the life force, in short, of humanizing the environment. There is a striking parallel to be drawn between the West African notion of *Nommo* and Karl Marx's definition of labor as "the living, shaping fire."[8] It can be argued, in fact, that the process of "naming" is something of a spiritual transmutation of the labor process – an ideological expression of what human labor can accomplish in society.

Throughout the history of Black music in the United States, *Nommo* was destined to remain the very essence of Black music making. African-American women musicians would rely on the power of *Nommo*, which would permit them to incorporate in their music and to impart to others by means of their music a collective consciousness and a very specific communal yearning for freedom. *Nommo* would moreover assist them in shaping through song an expression of the special meaning of Black womanhood, its realities, its limitations, its socio-historical legacy, and its collective potential with respect to the forging of a new society, based on economic, racial, and sexual equality.

Once Africans were forcibly planted in North America, they began to practice music-making in conjunction with the economic activity imposed on them by the conditions of slavery. The work songs they sang were "more than simply a means to ease hard physical labor."[9] They provided opportunities for commentary on the oppressiveness of slave work.

> Well, captain, captain, you mus' be blin'
> Look at you watch! See ain't it quittin' time?
> Well captain, captain, how can it be?
> Whistles keep a-blowin' you keep a-working me.[10]

The slaves sang in the old African tradition, but injected a new content into their music, a content that quite specifically reflected the conditions of their oppression and their desire to transform their collective predicament. But there were often references to the African past.

> The Negro work song became another example of the Negro's attempt to make the agonies of slavery bearable by integrating them with the images of his African past. There was no getting away from the miseries of plantation labor, so the work was infused with the songs of better days and soon the songs were to influence the music of the slaves and their descendants.[11]

Aside from lullabies sung by slave women to white babies (and indeed those sung to their own as well) and possibly other songs related to specifically female domestic tasks, one discovers few gender distinctions in the great body of work songs of the slaves. This is not surprising, since there was a distinct lack of a sexual division of labor in the chattel slave system. Economically, the women were called upon to perform the same tasks as the men and while sexual abuse and the violation of women's reproductive rights, for example, constituted a special form of oppression for women, the overall predicament was not qualitatively differentiated from that of their brothers, fathers, sons, and husbands. Like the work songs, the spirituals place little or no emphasis on the specificity of women's experiences within their commentary on the collective experience of oppression. The historical and spiritual transcendance of the religious slave songs did not, however, establish a male supremacist vision of the slave experience. On the contrary, the aesthetic community forged by means of the spiritual was one which was based in the concrete participation of the individual slaves, men and women alike.

> The spirituals are historical songs which speak about the rupture of Black lives; they tell us about a people in the land of bondage and what they did to hold themselves together and to fight back. We are told that the people of Israel could not sing the Lord's song in a strange land. But, for Blacks, their *being* depended upon a song. Through song they built new structures for existence in an alien land. The spirituals enabled Blacks to retain a measure of African identity, while living in the midst of African slavery, providing both the substance and the rhythm to cope with human servitude.[12]

The incorporation of concrete historical conditions related to the slaves' desire to live free, human lives, into religious songs which, on their face, transcended concrete historical realities, can be clearly illustrated by the songs employed by the woman who became the most prominent conductor on the Underground Railroad – Harriet Tubman. In his 1942 article entitled "General Tubman, Composer of Spirituals," Earl Conrad argued that Harriet Tubman made abundant use of spirituals to facilitate the process of leading masses of people to their freedom. Although "Old Chariot" may have had an obvious eschatological meaning, its worldly dimension involved a public proclamation of the preparations under way for the trek northwards. Harriet herself, in fact, was also known as "Old Chariot" – a name that rhymed with her own.[13]

> When the old chariot comes,
> I'm going to leave you.
> I'm bound for the promised land.
> I'm going to leave you.

Conrad gives an account of one of Harriet Tubman's trips during which she was compelled to leave a party of fugitive slaves in order to find food for them:

> She dared not go back to them til night, for fear of being watched....They listen eagerly for the words she sings, for by them they are to be warned of danger or informed of safety. Nearer and nearer comes the unseen singer, and the words are wafted to their ears.
>
> Hail, oh hail, ye happy spirits,
> Death no more shall make you fear,
> Grief nor sorrow, pain nor anguish
> Shall no more distress you there.
>
> Around him are ten thousand angels,
> Around him are ten thousand angels.
> They are always hovering around you
> Till you reach the heavenly land.
>
> Jesus, Jesus will go with you;
> He will led you to his throne;
> He who died has gone before you
> Trod the winepress all alone.
>
> He whose thunders shake creation;
> He who bids the planets roll;
> He who rides upon the tempest
> And his sceptre sways the whole.
>
> Dark and thorny is the desert
> Where the pilgrim makes his ways.
> Yet beyond this vale of sorrow
> Lies the field of endless days.

This spiritual served as a sign that the slaves should listen for a further song-signal. If she sang this one a second time, they knew that they could leave their hiding places, but if she sang a verse of "Go Down Moses," this was an indication that there was danger and they should remain hidden.[14] Other verses of "Go Down Moses" were used to summon together those who would be accompanying Harriet Tubman on the long journey to freedom, and "Wade in the Water" warned the fugitive slaves that bloodhounds were on their track and if they walked in the shallow waters of rivers and streams, the dogs would lose their scent.[15]

Tubman's spirituals were functional not only in the sense that they provided concrete information about the struggle for liberation, they also were functional in the sense that they assisted in the forging of a collective social consciousness – indeed of both an aesthetic and a socio-historical community of individuals who had a very basic need to be free. Collective consciousness of freedom does not automatically accompany oppression. That consciousness must be actively created. For Black people in the United States during the era of slavery, the spiritual played a fundamental role in communicating the ingredients of that collective consciousness to masses of slaves. Freedom was named – literally and metaphorically – in accordance with the West African tradition of *Nommo*.

> Oh Freedom, oh Freedom!
> Oh Freedom, I love thee!
> And before I'll be a slave,
> I'll be buried in my grave,
> And go home to my Lord and be free.

Another outstanding Black woman of the slave era also used song to make her point about freedom. Sojourner Truth used religious hymns to convey her message of freedom and she even composed her own verses, such as the following ones, which were sung at an abolitionist meeting.

> I am pleading for my people,
> A poor downtrodden race,
> Who dwell in freedom's boasted land,
> With no abiding place.
>
> I am pleading that my people,
> May have their rights restored;
> For they have long been toiling,
> And yet have no reward.
>
> They are forced the crops to culture,
> But not for them they yield,
> Although both late and early
> They labor in the field.
>
> Whilst I bear upon my body
> The scars of many a gash,
> I am pleading for my people
> Who groan beneath the lash.[16]

W.E.B. Du Bois described the coming of freedom for Black slaves in the South as the rising of a new song:

> There was joy in the South. It rose like perfume – like a prayer. Men stood quivering. Slim dark girls, wild and beautiful with wrinkled hair, wept silently;

young women, Black, tawny, white and golden, lifted shivering hands and old
and broken mothers, Black and gray, raised great voices and shouted to God
across the fields, and up the rocks and the mountains.

A great song arose, the loveliest thing born this side the seas. It was a new
song. It did not come from Africa, though the dark throb and beat of that
Ancient of Days was in it and through it. It did not come from white America –
never from so pale and hard and thin a thing, however deep these vulgar tones
had driven. Not the Indies nor the hot South, the cold East or heavy West
made that music. It was a new song and its deep and plaintive beauty, its great
cadences and wild appeal wailed, throbbed and thundered on the world's ears
with a message seldom voiced by man. It swelled and blossomed like incense,
improvised and born anew out of an age long past, and weaving into its texture
the old and new melodies in word and thought.[17]

However, the new-found freedom was to present a whole host of new
problems for the former slaves, indeed, entirely new modes of oppression
emanating from a transitional socio-economic system which had left slavery
behind and would rapidly move in the direction of industrial capitalism. A
new song was indeed eventually consolidated, but it was not the song of
freedom, corresponding to the goal so passionately sought in the spirituals
of slavery times. It was a song called the blues, which enumerated, again in
the West African tradition of *Nommo*, the new troubles Black people faced
in a world that still refused to accept them as equals, a society that thrived on
the systematic exploitation and discrimination meted out to the former
slaves. The blues also incorporated a new consciousness about private love
relationships, which had been denied to Black people, except in a rudiment-
ary way, as long as they were slaves. In many ways, in fact, interpersonal
relationships functioned as metaphors for the freedom they sought: trouble
in the relationship was trouble in the overall social universe. The happiness
they sought in their relationships indicated by the expression of a need for "a
good woman" or for "a man who won't treat me mean" symbolized their
search for a life which would be free of the countless brutal realities encountered in post-slavery America. If there was a hidden meaning behind the
religious language of the spirituals, there was also a hidden meaning behind
the sexual language of the blues. As the spirituals consolidated a collective
social consciousness of the need to fight for freedom under slavery, the blues
also forged a communal consciousness, one that was based on the communication and sharing of African-Americans' individual suffering and the
expression of the possibility of prevailing over the most intransigent
problems.

Gertrude "Ma" Rainey was called the "Mother of the Blues" because she
was the first widely known Black entertainer who used blues as the basis
of her repertoire. The first blues singers, who were predominantly male, were

not formal entertainers, but rather individuals who engaged in the same economic activity as their peers, but who were most capable of incorporating the group's personal as well as social experiences into song. Ma Rainey, on the other hand, performed in circuses, tent shows, minstrel and medicine shows, singing all the same about the Black predicament and establishing the basis in song for the sharing of experiences and the forging of a community capable of persevering through private tribulations and even of articulating new hopes and aspirations. Ma Rainey's most essential social accomplishment was to keep poor Black people grounded in the Southern tradition of unity and struggle, even when they had migrated to the North and Midwest in search of economic security. As Sandra Lieb has pointed out,

> For her audience, whether listening to her records in a small Mississippi town or watching her perform in Chicago, she was a reminder, a witness, an affirmation of Southern Black culture as positive, resilient, and life-affirming, even as great numbers of people were being uprooted and displaced from that culture by migration to the North.[18]

The most vivid account of Ma Rainey's impact on her audience is contained in a poem by Sterling Brown. He describes the audience as consisting of people who had come from all around on mules and on trains, from the river settlements, from lumber camps and from "Blackbottom cornrows." He continues, in the third and fourth verses:

> Ma Rainey,
> Sing yo' song:
> Now you's back
> Whah you belong.
> Git way inside us,
> Keep us strong . . .
> Sing us 'bout de hard luck
> "Roun" our do";
> Sing us 'bout de lonesome road
> We mus' go . . .
>
> I talked to a fellow, an' the fellow say,
> "She jes' catch hold of us, somekindaway.
> She sang 'Backwater Blues' one day . . .
> An' de folks, dey natchally bowed dey heads an' cried,
> Bowed dey heavy heads, shet dey moufs up tight an' cried,
> An' Ma lef' de stage, an' followed some de folks outside,"
> Dere wasn't much more de fellow say;
> She jes' gets hold of us dataway.[19]

The vast majority of Ma Rainey's blues revolve around problems emanating from personal relationships. However, the meaning of sexual love for the former slaves and their descendants was far more central than it might have been if their lives had offered more options for creative expression. Because of the objective limitations imposed by the economic circumstances surrounding them – Black people in the South during that period were by and large sharecroppers or tenant farmers and those in the North who found work were miserably exploited and always risked being the first fired – their only immediate hopes for happiness resided in the possibility of establishing a love relationship that would provide them with personal fulfillment. Moreover, the language of sexual love in Ma Rainey's blues metaphorically reveals and expresses a range of economic, social, and psychological difficulties which Black people suffered during the post-Civil War era. And the desire to find a good man symbolizes the desperate desire to create a life free of poverty, discrimination, and all the other material causes of the blues. It is most often the case that Ma Rainey's songs do not explicitly point to the causes of Black people's misery; they are generally referred to simply as the "blues." And indeed, in the West African tradition of *Nommo*, she often simply names the blues. Consider the text of "Blues Oh Blues":

> Oh blues, oh blues, oh blues, oh blues, blues, oh blues.
> I'm so blue, so blue, I don't know what to do.
> Oh blues, oh blues, oh blues.
>
> I'm going away, I'm going to stay; I'm going away, I'm going to stay
> I'm going away, oh mama's going to stay.
> I'm going to find the man I love some sweeet day.
>
> Oh blues, oh blues, oh blues, oh blues, blues, oh blues.
> I'm so blue, so blue, oh mama don't know what to do.
> Oh blues, I'm blue, oh blues.[20]

In this song, Rainey calls the name of the blues over 20 times, thus conjuring up all the various causes of her miserable predicament and at the same time using the power of the word to magically assert control over circumstances otherwise far beyond her reach. This magical, aesthetic assertion of control over the blues is an implicit expression of the real need to transform the objective conditions that are at the root of these blues: a camouflaged dream of a new social order. This is the powerful utopian function of the blues. The language in which this dream is expressed is the language of sexual love, thus "I'm going to find the man I love some sweet day." If Ma Rainey's audience was as deeply moved as Sterling Brown's poem indicates, they must have sensed the deeper meaning of her words.

A characteristic dynamic of Ma Rainey's music is the public communication of private troubles. This dynamic contains an implicit recognition of the social nature of Black people's individual situations and at the same time it allows for the development of a collective social consciousness within the Black population. The consciousness of the social character of Black people's suffering is the precondition for the creation of a political protest movement – and, indeed, by the 1920s, such movements had begun to crystallize.

"Bad Luck Blues" begins by alerting the audience of the singer's intention to publicize her own situation: "Hey, people, listen while I spread my news (*Repeat*)/I want to tell you people all about my bad luck blues." She continues by asking the audience to acknowledge the commonality of her problem and theirs, for implied in the question of the second stanza is that they have certainly experienced something similar to the episode which has caused her to be afflicted with the blues.

> Did you ever wake up just at the break of day,
> Did you ever break up just at the wake of day,
> With your arm around the pillow just where your daddy used to lay?

While her words refer to a concrete situation – the loss of a love partner – the deeper meaning of this language has to do with need or desire in general. Certainly every Black person who listened to Ma Rainey sing was in need of something critically important in her or his life. Sharing and communicating need was a central feature of the blues, and the process of developing an awareness of the collective nature of the experience of need was very much related to the ability of the African-American people to survive when all odds were against them.

During the historical era leading up to the 1920s, the Jim Crow system of segregation was consolidated, Black people were systematically disfranchised, and the Ku Klux Klan and other terrorist groups were responsible for untold thousands of lynchings. The economic predicament of Black people in the South caused many to travel northwards in search of jobs, and there they discovered that racism was often just as devastating as in the South. During the summer months of 1919, there were so many bloody riots directed against African-American people, that this season came to be known as the Red Summer of 1919. Certainly Ma Rainey's fans perceived the deeper meaning of songs like "Bad Luck Blues." A few of Ma Rainey's songs directly attacked the issue of Black people's economic misery, and some of them, such as "Ma and Pa's Poorhouse Blues," use humor to soften the cutting edge of oppression. This blues was recorded together with "Papa" Charlie Jackson and is introduced by a dialogue between them about the hard times they are both experiencing. The dialogue concludes:

MA   Charlie, you know I'm broke?
CHARLIE   Ma, don't you know I'm broke too? What we gonna do?
MA   Let's both go to the poorhouse together.
CHARLIE   All right, let's go together.

At the end of this blues, they both sing: "We better go to the poorhouse, try to live anyhow." The comic dimension of this particular song, unambiguously conveyed by the duo's performance, reveals and simultaneously encourages the African-American community's resilience and its powers of perseverance. Its message is clear: unity is the community's saving grace.

In other songs, Ma Rainey calls upon Black people who have traveled North to look back to their Southern homeland for consolation and inspiration. "South Bound Blues" specifically evokes the situation of a woman who has accompanied her man to the North, only to have him leave her in that alien world:

> Yes I'm mad, my heart's sad,
> The man I love treated me so bad;
> He brought me out of my home town,
> Took me to New York and threw me down.

> Without a cent to pay my rent,
> I'm left alone, without a home;
> I told him I would leave him and my time ain't long.
> My folks done sent the money, and I'm Dixie bound.

Her decision to return home gives her the strength to consider the eventuality of challenging the man who is responsible for her troubles: "I told him I'd see him, honey, some of these days, / And I'm going to tell him 'bout his low down dirty ways." The last verse is celebratory and optimistic:

> Done bought my ticket, Lord, and my trunk is packed,
> Going back to Georgia, folks, I sure ain't coming back.
> My train is in the station, I done sent my folks the news,
> You can tell the world I've got those Southbound blues.

The message of this song clearly indicates that African-American culture rooted in the Southern experience is the source of Black people's creative energy and of their ability to survive as a people. As in most of Ma Rainey's songs, the focal point is an interpersonal relationship, and the man in the relationship is evoked in an accusatory fashion. However, the adversities attributed to male behavior within a love relationship can also be interpreted as the material hindrances of racism. What is needed to survive these difficulties is the inspiration that comes from knowing that Black people in the South have survived the Middle Passage from Africa and at least two centuries of slavery, as well as the horrendous racism in the aftermath of slavery. The actual return by train to Georgia described in "South Bound Blues" is also a spiritual identification with the Black ethos of the South. That ethos incorporates the cumulative struggles Black people have collectively waged over the centuries, struggles that alone have insured our survival.

"South Bound Blues" also evokes the special problems encountered by Black women – since its protagonist is a woman who finds herself betrayed and mistreated by a man whom she has accompanied to an alien and hostile world. The spiritual identification encouraged with the Black culture of the South is with a culture that necessarily produced a standard of womanhood based on self-reliance and independence. In other words, "South Bound Blues" also appeals to women to summon up within themselves the courage and independence of their foremothers.

Several of Ma Rainey's songs are direct exhortations to Black women to develop a spirit of self-reliance that directly contradicts the ideological notion of womanhood prevalent in the larger society. "Trust No Man" advises women not to depend absolutely on their men if they do not wish to be deceived.

> I want all you women to listen to me,
> Don't trust no man no further than your eyes can see;
> I trusted mine with my best friend,
> But that was the bad part in the end.
>
> Trust no man, trust no man, no further than your eyes can see.
> I said, trust no man, no further than your eyes can see.
>
> He'll tell you that he loves you and swear it's true,
> The very next minute, he's going to trifle on you;
> Ah – trust no man, no further than your eyes can see.

While on its face, this song might appear to be utterly, though perhaps only temporarily, antimale, its deeper meaning might have less to do with the proclamation of Black men's negative traits than with the need for Black women to develop economic and psychological independence. W. E. B. Du Bois's essay, "The Damnation of Women" describes the development of economic independence among Black women during the post slavery era and argues that African-American women's experiences demonstrated to the larger society that women could not be imprisoned in the home and that they could not be required "on pain of death to be nurses and house-keepers."[21] "Trust No Man" implies that women should not be compelled to be appendages to men, blindly following their lead, but rather should carry forth the historical legacy of independence forged throughout the history of Black women's presence in North America.

Another song that directly addresses women, "Prove It on Me Blues" has most frequently been interpreted simply as a bold affirmation of lesbianism. Of course Ma Rainey's emotional and sexual ties with women have been documented and it has been speculated that she and Bessie Smith engaged at one time in relations with each other. On the surface, "Prove It on Me Blues" is a flaunting song about women-identified emotional and sexual relations, but it is also about the affirmative emotional links between Black women, whatever their sexual identification might be.

> I went out last night with a crowd of my friends,
> They must have been women, 'cause I don't like no men.
> Wear my clothes just like a fan,
> Talk to the gals just like any old man;
> 'Cause they say I do it, ain't nobody caught me,
> Sure got to prove it on me.

Certainly close emotional relationships between Black women – as family members, as workers, or as political activists – have been an important source of female independence. These relationships have so often been denied by those who would portray Black women as chronically competitive personalities, especially where men are concerned.

Gertrude "Ma" Rainey made an inestimable contribution both to the musical culture of the Black community and to the development of a collective social consciousness related to the specificity of the African-American predicament. Until very recently, her cultural value had been virtually ignored. Derrick Stewart-Baxter's *Ma Rainey and the Classic Blues Singers* was the only book-length study devoted to the blueswomen of Ma Rainey's era, and only a few pages in that short book were actually dedicated to Ma Rainey herself. In 1981, Sandra Lieb published her pioneering book, *Mother of the Blues: A Study of Ma Rainey.* Her book is an extremely valuable scholarly contribution, although it does not explore the entire spectrum of meaning in Ma Rainey's songs. A further study should evaluate the texts of Ma Rainey's blues, relating them to the general socio-historical context in which they were created and performed, which includes not only the objective conditions of her time, but also the music's cultural continuum, a continuum that reaches back to Harriet Tubman's spirituals, to slave women's work songs, and indeed to the original West African musical tradition of *Nommo.* Only then will we be in a position to accurately evaluate the part played by Ma Rainey's music in the forging of Black social consciousness and ultimately in the creation of a vital mass movement for Black equality.

Bessie Smith's music, much of it recorded simultaneously with Ma Rainey's –
and, indeed, some of it prior to her elder's first recordings – was created in
the same tradition as that of the "Mother of the Blues." The women's blues
tradition also directly influenced the work of Billie Holiday. While it is not
possible here to examine the body of these two women's work, an appropriate conclusion of this essay might be the texts of the most revealing
political songs of these two artists. For Bessie Smith, it is "Poor Man's
Blues":

Mr. rich man, rich man, open up your heart and mind (*Repeat*)
Give the poor man a chance, help stop these hard, hard times.

While you're living in your mansion, you don't know what hard times mean (*Repeat*)
Poor working man's wife is starving, your wife is living like a queen.

Please listen to my pleadin', 'cause I can't stand these hard times long (*Repeat*)
They'll make an honest man do things that you know is wrong.

Now the war is over; poor man must live the same as you (*Repeat*)
If it wasn't for the poor man, mister rich man, what would you do?

For Billie Holiday, it is, of course, "Strange Fruit":

> Southern trees bear a strange fruit
> Blood on the leaves, blood on the root
> Black bodies swinging in the Southern breeze
> Strange fruit hanging from the poplar trees
> Pastoral scene of the gallant South
> The bulging eyes and the twisted mouth
> Scent of magnolia sweet and fresh
> Then the sudden smell of burning flesh
> Here is a fruit for the crows to pluck
> For the rain to gather, for the wind to suck
> For the sun to rot, for the tree to drop
> Here is a strange and bitter crop.

Notes

1 Karl Marx and Frederick Engels, *Marx and Engels on Literature and Art* (Mos-
   cow: Progress Publishers, 1976), p. 41.
2 James Cone, *The Spirituals and the Blues* (New York: The Seabury Press, 1972),
   p. 5.
3 W. E. B. Du Bois, *The Souls of Black Folk* (New York: New American Library,
   1969), p. 265.

4   Ernest Borneman, "The Roots of Jazz," in *Jazz*, ed. Nat Hentoff and Albert J. McCarthy (New York: Da Capo Press, 1975), p. 3.
5   Ibid., p. 4.
6   Janheinz Jahn, *Muntu, The New African Culture* (New York: Grove Press, 1961), p. 135.
7   Borneman, "Roots," p. 6.
8   Karl Marx, *Grundrisse der Kritik der Politischen Oekonomie* (Berlin: Dietz Verlag, 1953), p. 266.
9   Giles Oakley, *The Devil's Music: A History of the Blues* (New York: Harcourt Brace Jovanovich, 1976), p. 39.
10 Ibid., p. 39.
11 Borneman, "Roots," p. 14.
12 Cone, *Spirituals and the Blues*, pp. 32–3.
13 Earl Conrad, "General Tubman, Composer of Spirituals: An Amazing Figure in American Folk Music," *The Etude* (May 1942): p. 305.
14 Ibid.
15 John Lovell, Jr., *Black Song: The Forge and the Flame* (New York: The Macmillan Company, 1972), p. 196.
16 Jacqueline Bernard, *Journey toward Freedom, The Story of Sojourner Truth* (New York: W. W. Norton and Company, 1967), pp. 149–50.
17 W. E. B. Du Bois, *Black Reconstruction in America* (New York: Meridian Books, 1964), p. 124.
18 Sandra Lieb, *Mother of the Blues: A Study of Ma Rainey* (Amherst: University of Massachusetts Press, 1981), p. 79.
19 Ibid., pp. 14–15.
20 This text and the remaining texts of Ma Rainey's, Bessie Smith's, and Billie Holiday's songs are based on my own transcriptions.
21 W. E. B. Du Bois, *Darkwater: Voices from within the Veil* (New York: Harcourt, Brace and Howe, 1920), p. 18.

13

Never Trust a Big Butt and a Smile

Tricia Rose

"Never Trust a Big Butt and a Smile." *Camera Obscura: A Journal of Feminism and Film Theory*, 23 (May, 1990): 108–31

If you were to construct an image of rap music via accounts of rap in the established press, you would (besides betraying limited critical instincts about popular culture) probably perceive rap to reflect the violent, brutally sexist reality of a pack of wilding "little Willie Hortons."[1] Consequently, you would wonder what a group of young Black women rappers were doing fraternizing with these male rappers and why they seemed to be having such a good time. If I were to suggest that their participation in rap music produced some of the most important contemporary Black feminist cultural criticism, you would surely bemoan the death of sexual equality. As Public Enemy's Chuck D has warned regarding the mainstream press, "Don't believe the hype." Sexism in rap has been gravely exaggerated by the mainstream press. Rap is a rich, complex multi-faceted African-American popular form whose male practitioners' style and subject matter includes the obsessive sexism of a 2 Live Crew, the wacky parody of Biz Markie, the "edutainment" of Boogie Down Productions, the gangster-style storytelling of Ice Cube, the gritty and intelligent speed rapping of Kool Moe Dee, and the explicit Black nationalism of X-Clan. Women rappers are vocal and respected members of the Hip Hop community, and they have quite a handle on what they are doing.

Fortunately or unfortunately (I'm not sure which), most academics concerned with contemporary popular culture and music have avoided sustained critical analysis of rap. A few literary scholars and theorists have explained the historical and cultural heritage of rap as an African-American form, while others have made passing reference to it as an important site of postmodernist impulses or as the prophetic voice of an angry disenfranchised group of young African-Americans.[2] The work on women rappers (while making claims that women rappers are pro-women artists) has been published in popular monthly periodicals and consequently has been limited to short but provocative inquiries.[3]

While any positive, critical attention to rap comes as a welcome relief, almost all of these accounts observe rap music outside of its socio-historical framework, as texts suspended in time. Such distanced readings, especially of a musical form to which it is difficult to gain direct and sustained access, leave open the possibility of grave misreadings regarding meanings and context. Women rappers are especially vulnerable to such misreadings precisely because their presence in rap has been consistently ignored or marginalized, even by those social critics who have published some of the most insightful analyses of rap. This essay, which is part of an extended project on rap music, will try to correct some of these misunderstandings, or as Chuck D states, "give you something that I knew you lacked. So consider me a new jack."[4] Better yet, here's Queen Latifah:

> Some think that we can't flow (can't flow)
> Stereotypes they got to go (got to go)
> I'm gonna mess around and flip the scene into reverse
> With what?
> With a little touch of ladies first.[5]

The summer of 1989 marked the tenth anniversary of rap music's explosive debut in the recording industry. In honor of its unexpected longevity, Nelson George, a pro-Hip Hop music critic and *Village Voice* columnist, published a sentimental rap retrospective in which he mourned rap's movement from a street subculture into the cold, sterile world of commercial record production. George points out that, until recently, music industry powers have maintained a studied indifference to rap music, but now that rap's "commercial viability has been proven" many major recording companies are signing any half way decent act they can find. What worries George, and rightly so, is that corporate influence on Black music has led, in the past, to the dissolution of vibrant Black cultural forms and that rap may become the latest victim. The problem is complex, real and requires analysis. However, Nelson George, like media critics generally, imbeds his descriptions of "authentic rap" and fears of recent corporate influence on it in gender-coded language that mischaracterizes rap and silences women rappers and consumers. In his tenth anniversary piece, George traces major shifts in rap, naming titles, artists and producers. He weaves over 20 rap groups into his piece and names not a single female rapper. His retrospective is chock-full of prideful, urban Black youth (read men), whose contributions to rap reflect "the thoughts of city kids more deeply than the likes of Michael Jackson,

Oprah Winfrey et al." His concluding remarks make apparent his underlying perception of rap:

> To proclaim the death of rap, is to be sure, premature. But the farther the control of rap gets from its street corner constituency and the more corporations grasp it – record conglomerates, Burger King, Minute Maid, Yo! MTV Raps, etc. – the more vulnerable it becomes to cultural emasculation.

For George, corporate meddling not only dilutes cultural forms, it also reduces strapping testosterone-packed men into women! Could we imagine anything worse? Nelson George's analysis is not unusual; his is merely the latest example of media critics' consistent coding of rap music as male in the face of a significant and sustained female presence.

Many social critics who have neglected to make separate mention of women rappers would probably claim that these women are in many ways just "one of the boys." Since they are as tough as male rappers, women rappers fit into George's mind-boggling yet emblematic definition of rap as an "ultra-urban, unromantic, hyperrealistic, neo-nationalist, antiassimilationist, aggressive Afrocentric impulse." For George, and for media critics generally, it is far easier to re-gender women rappers than to revise their own gender-coded analysis of rap music.[6]

Since the summer of 1989, there has been a marked increase in media attention to women rappers. Most of the articles have been written by women and have tried to shed some light on female rappers and offer a feminist analysis of their contributions. I would like to extend some of the themes presented in these pieces by showing how women rappers participate in a dialogue with male rappers and by revising some of the commonly held assumptions about what constitutes "feminist" expression.

As Nancy Guevara notes, the "exclusion and/or trivialization of women's role in Hip Hop" is no mere oversight.[7] The marginalization, deletion and mischaracterization of women's role in Black cultural production is routine practice. Angela Davis extends this criticism by stating that this is "an omission that must be attributed to the influence of sexism." In her article, "Black Women and Music: An Historical Legacy of Struggle," Davis makes three related arguments that are of particular importance here. First, she contests the marginal representation of Black women in the documentation of African-American cultural developments and suggests that these representations do not adequately reflect women's participation. Second, she suggests that music (song and dance) are especially productive sites for examining the collective consciousness of Black Americans. And third, she calls for a close reexamination of Black women's musical legacy as a way to understand Black women's consciousness. She writes:

> Music has long permeated the daily life of most African-Americans; it has
> played a central role in the normal socialization process; and during moments
> characterized by intense movements for social change, it has helped to shape
> the necessary political consciousness. Any attempt, therefore, to understand in
> depth the evolution of women's consciousness within the Black community
> requires a serious examination of the music which has influenced them –
> particularly that which they themselves have created.[8]

She continues by offering a close reading of Gertrude "Ma" Rainey's music
as a step toward redressing such absences. Dealing with similar issues, Hazel
Carby charges that white dominated feminist discourse has marginalized
(and I would add often ignored) non-white women and questions of Black
sexuality. She further argues that representations of Black women's sexuality
in African-American literature differs significantly from representations of
sexuality in Black women's blues.[9]

Carby and Davis, while concerning themselves specifically with women's
blues, are calling for a multi-faceted analysis of Black women's identity and
sexuality as represented by their musical production. Stating that "different
cultural forms negotiate and resolve different sets of social contradictions,"
Carby suggests that Black women writers have been encouraged to speak on
behalf of a large group of Black women whose daily lives and material
conditions may not be adequately reflected in Black women's fiction. For
example, the consumption patterns and social context of popular music differ
significantly from those of fiction. The dialogic capacity of popular music,
especially that of rap music, engages many of the social contradictions and
ambiguities that pertain specifically to contemporary urban, working-class
Black life.

George Lipsitz, applying Mikhail Bakhtin's concept of "dialogic" criticism
to popular music, argues that:

> Popular music is nothing if not dialogic, the product of an ongoing historical
> conversation in which no one has the first or last word. The traces of the past
> that pervade the popular music of the present amount to more than mere
> chance: they are not simply juxtapositions of incompatible realities. They reflect
> a dialogic process, one embedded in collective history and nurtured by the
> ingenuity of artists interested in fashioning icons of opposition.

Lipsitz's interpretation of popular music as a social and historical dialogue is
an extremely important break from traditional, formalist interpretations of
music. By grounding cultural production historically and avoiding the application of a fixed inventory of core structures, dialogic criticism as employed
by Lipsitz is concerned with how popular music "arbitrates tensions between
opposition and co-optation at any given historical moment."[10]

This notion of dialogism is especially productive in the context of African-American music. The history of African-American music and culture has been defined in large measure by a history of the art of signifying, recontextualization, collective memory and resistance. "Fashioning icons of opposition" that speak to diverse communities is part of a rich Black American musical tradition to which rappers make a significant contribution. Negotiating multiple boundaries, Black women rappers are in dialogue with each other, male rappers, other popular musicians (through sampling and other revisionary practices), and with Hip Hop fans.

Black women rappers are integral and resistant voices in Hip Hop and in popular music generally. They sustain an ongoing dialogue with their audiences and male rappers about sexual promiscuity, emotional commitment, infidelity, the drug trade, racial politics and Black cultural history. Rappers interpret and articulate the fears, pleasures and promises of young Black women and men whose voices have been relegated to the silent margins of public discourse. By paying close attention to rap music, we can gain some insight into how young African-Americans provide for themselves a relatively safe free-play zone where they creatively address questions of sexual power, the reality of truncated economic opportunity, the pain of racism and sexism and, through physical expressions of freedom, relieve the anxieties of day-to-day oppression.

If you have been following the commercial success of rap music, it is difficult to ignore the massive increase in record deals for women rappers following Salt-N-Pepa's double platinum (two million) 1986 debut album *Hot, Cool and Vicious*. Such album sales, even for a rap album by a male artist, were virtually unprecedented in 1986. Since then, several female rappers, many of whom have been rapping for years (some since the mid-1970s), have finally been recorded and promoted.[11] Says female rapper Ms. Melodie:

> It wasn't that the male started rap, the male was just the first to be put on wax. Females were always into rap, and females always had their little crews and were always known for rockin' house parties and streets or whatever, school yards, the corner, the park, whatever it was.[12]

In the early stages, women's participation in rap was hindered by gender considerations. M.C. Lady "D" notes that because she didn't put a female crew together for regular performances, she "didn't have to worry about getting [her] equipment ripped off, coming up with the cash to get it in the first place, or hauling it around on the subways to gigs – problems that kept a lot of other women out of rap in the early days."[13] For a number of reasons (including increased institutional support and more demand for both male and female rappers), such stumbling blocks have been reduced.

MC Lyte's 1988 release, "Paper Thin," sold over 125,000 copies in the first six months with virtually no radio play. Lady B, who became the first recorded female rapper in 1978, was Philadelphia's top-rated DJ on WUSL and is founder and Editor-in-Chief of *Word Up!*, a tabloid devoted to Hip Hop.[14] Salt-N-Pepa's first single, "Expressions," from their latest album release *Black's Magic*, went gold in the first week and stayed in the number one position on *Billboard*'s Rap Chart for over two months.

But these industry success-markers are not the primary focus here. I intend to show that the subject matter and perspectives presented in many women's rap lyrics challenge dominant notions of sexuality, heterosexual courtship, and aesthetic constructions of the body. In addition, music videos and live performances display exuberant communities of women occupying public space while exhibiting sexual freedom, independence and, occasionally, explicit domination over men. Women's raps grow more and more complex each year and, with audience support, many rappers have taken risks (regarding imagery and subject matter) that a few years ago would have been unthinkable. Through their lyrics and video images, Black women rappers – especially Queen Latifah, MC Lyte and Salt-N-Pepa – form a dialogue with working-class Black women and men, offering young Black women a small but potent culturally reflexive public space.

In order to understand the oppositional nature of these women rappers, it is important to have at least a sketch of some of the politics behind rap's battle of the sexes. Popular raps by both men and women have covered many issues and social situations that pertain to the lives of young, Black working-class teens in urban America. Racism, drugs, police brutality, sex, crime, poverty, education and prison have been popular themes in rap for a number of years. But raps about celebration, dance, styling, boasting and just "gittin' funky" (in Kid-N-Play's words) have been equally popular. Raps about style and prestige sometimes involve the possession of women as evidence of male power. Predictably, these raps define women as commodities, objects and ornaments. Others are defensive and aggressive raps that describe women solely as objects of male pleasure. In rap music, as in other popular genres, women are divided into at least two categories – the "kind to take home to mother" and the "kind you meet at three o'clock in the morning." In Hip Hop discourse, the former is honest and loyal – but extremely rare (decidedly not the girl next door). The latter is not simply an unpaid prostitute, but a woman who only wants you for your money, cars and cash, will trap you (via pregnancy or other forms of manipulation), and move on to another man (probably your best friend). It would be an understatement to suggest that there is little in the way of traditional notions of romance in rap. Sexist raps articulate the profound fear of female sexuality felt by these young rappers and by many young men.

In a recent *Village Voice* interview with ex-NWA member Ice Cube, notorious not only for harsh sexist raps but for brilliant chilling stories of ghetto life, Greg Tate (one of the best Hip Hop social critics) tries to get "some understanding" about the hostility toward women expressed in Ice Cube's raps:

TATE   Do you think rap is hostile toward women?
ICE CUBE   The whole damn world is hostile toward women.
TATE   What do you mean by that?
ICE CUBE   I mean the power of sex is more powerful than the motherfuckers in Saudi Arabia. A girl that you want to get with can make you do damn near anything. If she knows how to do her shit right, she can make you buy cigarettes you never wanted to buy in life. . . . Look at all my boys out here on this video shoot, all these motherfuckers sitting out here trying to look fly, hot as a motherfucker, ready to go home. But there's too many women here for them to just get up and leave. They out here since eight o'clock in the morning and ain't getting paid. They came for the girls.[15]

Ice Cube's answer may appear to be a non sequitur, but his remarks address what I believe is the subtext in rap's symbolic male domination over women. Ice Cube suggests that many men are hostile toward women because the fulfillment of male heterosexual desire is significantly checked by women's capacity for sexual rejection and/or manipulation of men. Ice Cube acknowledges the reckless boundaries of his desire as well as the power women can exercise in this sexual struggle. In "The Bomb," Ice Cube warns men to "especially watch the ones with the big derriers" because the greater your desire, the more likely you are to be blinded by it, and consequently the more vulnerable you are likely to be to female domination. From the perspective of a young man, such female power is probably more palpable than any woman realizes. Obviously, Ice Cube is not addressing the institutional manifestations of patriarchy and its effects on the social construction of desire. However, he and many Black male rappers speak to men's fears and the realities of the struggle for power in teenage heterosexual courtship in a sexist society.

During the summer of 1990, Bell Biv Divoe, a popular R & B/Rap crossover group, raced up the charts with "Poison," a song about women, whose chorus warns men not to "trust a big butt and a smile." The song cautions men about giving in to their sexual weaknesses and then being taken advantage of by a sexy woman whose motives might be equally insincere. The degree of anxiety expressed is striking. "Poison" explains both their intense desire for and profound distrust of women. The capacity of a woman to use her sexuality to manipulate *his* desire for *her* purposes is an important facet of the sexual politics of male raps about women. Bell Biv Divoe are telling men: "You may not know what a big butt and a smile really means. It might not mean pleasure; it might mean danger – poison."

All of this probably seems gravely sexist – so much so that any good feminist would reject it out of hand. However, I would like to suggest that women rappers effectively engage with male rappers on this level. By expressing their sexuality openly and in their own language, yet distinguishing themselves from poisonous and insincere women, Black women rappers challenge men to take women more seriously. Black women rappers might respond by saying: "That's right, don't automatically trust a big butt and a smile. We've got plenty of sexual power and integrity, but don't mess with us." I am not suggesting that women have untapped power that once accessed will lead the way to the dismantling of patriarchy. Ice Cube and Bell Biv Devoe's expressions of fear must be understood in the context of their status as men and the inherent social power such a gender assignment affords. But, understanding the fear of female sexuality helps explain the consistent sexual domination men attempt to sustain over women. Without such fears, their efforts would be unnecessary.

Women's raps and my interviews with female rappers display similar fears of manipulation, loss of control, and betrayal at the hands of men. What is especially interesting about women rappers is the way in which they shift the focus of the debate. Male rappers focus on sexually promiscuous women who "want their money" (in rap lingo they are called skeezers) and almost never offer a depiction of a sincere woman. Female rappers focus on dishonest men who seek sex from women (much like the women who seek money from men), and they represent themselves as seasoned women with sexual confidence and financial independence.

During my interview with Salt (one half of the female rap duo Salt-N-Pepa), I pressed her about how she could envision a committed relationship without some degree of emotional dependence. She replied:

> I just want to depend on myself. I feel like a relationship shouldn't be emotional dependence. I, myself, am more comfortable when I do not depend on hugs and kisses from somebody that I possibly won't get. If I don't get them then I'll be disappointed. So if I get them, I'll appreciate them.[16]

Salt's lyrics reflect much of how she feels personally: "You know I don't want to for your money"; "I'm independent, I make my own money, so don't tell me how to spend it"; "You can't disguise the lies in your eyes, you're not a heartbreaker"; "You need me and I don't need you."[17]

Women rappers employ many of the aesthetic and culturally specific elements present in male rap lyrics while offering an alternative vision of similar social conditions. Raps written by women which specifically concern male/female relationships almost always confront the tension between trust and savvy, between vulnerability and control. Women rappers celebrate their sisters for "getting over" on men. Some raps by women such as Icey Jaye's "It's a Girl Thang" mock the men who fall for their tricks. But for the most part, women rappers promote self-reliance and challenge the depictions of women in male raps, addressing the fears about male dishonesty and infidelity that most women share.

Raps written and performed by women regarding male/female relationships can be divided into at least three categories: (1) raps that challenge male dominance over women within the sexual arena, (2) raps, that by virtue of their authoritative stance, challenge men as representatives of Hip Hop, and (3) raps that explicitly discuss women's identity and celebrate women's physical and sexual power. Across these three categories, several popular female rappers and their music videos can serve as illuminating examples.[18]

MC Lyte and Salt-N-Pepa have reputations for biting raps that criticize men who manipulate and abuse women. Their lyrics tell the story of men taking advantage of women, cheating on them, abusing them, taking their money and then leaving them for other unsuspecting female victims. These raps are not mournful ballads about the trials and tribulations of being a woman. Similar to women's blues, they are caustic, witty and aggressive warnings directed at men and at other women who might be seduced by men in the future. By offering a woman's interpretation of the terms of heterosexual courtship, these raps cast a new light on male/female sexual power relations and depict women as resistant, aggressive participants.

Salt-N-Pepa's 1986 single, "Tramp," speaks specifically to Black women, warning us that "Tramp" is not a "simple rhyme," but a parable about relationships between men and women:

> Homegirls attention you must pay to what I say
> Don't take this as a simple rhyme
> 'Cause this type of thing happens all the time
> Now what would you do if a stranger said "Hi"
> Would you dis him or would you reply?
> If you'd answer, there is a chance
> That you'd become a victim of circumstance
> Am I right fellas? Tell the truth
> Or else I'll have to show and prove
> You are what you are I am what I am
> It just so happens that most men are TRAMPS.

In the absence of any response to "Am I right fellas?" Salt-N-Pepa "show and prove" the trampings of several men who "undress you with their eyeballs," "think you're a dummy" and "on the first date, had the nerve to tell me he loves me." Salt-N-Pepa's parable, by defining promiscuous *men* as tramps, inverts the social construction of male sexual promiscuity as a status symbol. This reversal undermines the degrading "woman as tramp" image by stigmatizing male promiscuity. Salt-N-Pepa suggest that women who respond to sexual advances are victims of circumstance. It is the predatory, disingenuous men who are the tramps.

The music video for "Tramp" is a comic rendering of a series of social club scenes that highlight tramps on the make, mouth freshener in hand, testing their lines on the nearest woman. Dressed in Hip Hop street gear, Salt-N-Pepa perform the song on television, on a monitor perched above the bar. Since they appear on the television screen, they seem to be surveying and critiquing the club action, but the club members cannot see them. There are people dancing and talking together (including likeable men who are coded as "non-tramps"), who seem unaware of the television monitor. Salt-N-Pepa are also shown in the club, dressed in very stylish, sexy outfits. They act as decoys, talking and flirting with the tramps to flesh out the dramatization of tramps on the prowl, and they make several knowing gestures at the camera to reassure the viewer that they are unswayed by the tramps' efforts.

The club scenes have no dialogue. The tramps and their victims interact only with body language. Along with the music for "Tramp," we hear Salt-N-Pepa's lyrics, which serve respectively as the club's dance music and the video's voice-over narration. Viewing much of the club action from Salt-N-Pepa's authoritative position through the television monitor, we can safely observe the playful but cautionary dramatization of heterosexual courtship. Rapping to a woman, one tramp postures and struts, appearing to ask the stock pick-up line, "What is your zodiac sign, baby?" When she shows disgust and leaves her seat, he repeats the same body motions on the next woman who happens to sit down. Near the end of the video a frustrated "wife" enters the club and drags one of the tramps home, smacking him in the head with her pocketbook. Salt-N-Pepa stand next to the wife's tramp in the club, shaking their heads as if to say "what a shame." Simultaneously, they point and laugh at him from the television monitor. At the end of the video, a still frame of each man is stamped "tramp," while Salt-N-Pepa revel in having identified and exposed them. They leave the club together without men, seemingly enjoying their skill at exposing the real intentions of these tramps.

Salt-N-Pepa are clearly "schooling" women about the sexual politics of the club scene. They are engaged in and critiquing the drama of heterosexual courtship. The privileged viewer is a woman who is directly addressed in the lyrics and can fully empathize with the visual depiction and interpretation of the scenes. The video's resolution is a warning to both men and women.

Women: Don't fall for these men either by talking to them in the clubs or believing the lies they'll tell you when they come home. Men: You will get caught eventually and you'll be embarrassed. The "Tramp" video also tells women that they can go to these clubs and successfully play along with the game as long as the power of female sexuality and the terms of male desire are understood.

In her video, MC Lyte has a far less playful response to her boyfriend Sam, whom she catches in the act of flirting with another woman. MC Lyte's underground hit, "Paper Thin," is one of the most scathing raps about male dishonesty/infidelity and the tensions between trust and vulnerability. Lyte has been burned by Sam, but she has turned her experience into a Black woman's anthem that sustains an uncomfortable balance between brutal cynicism and honest vulnerability:

> When you say you love me it doesn't matter
> It goes into my head as just chit chatter
> You may think it's egotistical or just very free
> But what you say, I take none of it seriously.
>
> I'm not the kind of girl to try to play a man out
> They take the money and then they break the hell out
> No that's not my strategy, not the game I play
> I admit I play a game, but it's not done that way
> Truly when I get involved I give it my heart
> I mean my mind, my soul, my body I mean every part
> But if it doesn't work out – yo, it just doesn't
> It wasn't meant to be, you know it just wasn't
> So, I treat all of you like I treat all of them
> What you say to me is just paper thin.

Lyte's public acknowledgment that Sam's expressions of love were paper thin is not a source of embarrassment for her, but a means of empowerment. She plays a brutal game of the dozens on Sam while wearing her past commitment to him as a badge of honor and sign of character. Lyte presents commitment, vulnerability and sensitivity as assets, not indicators of female weakness. In "Paper Thin," emotional and sexual commitment are not romantic Victorian concepts tied to honorable but dependent women; they are a part of her strategy, part of the game she plays in heterosexual court-ship.

The high energy video for "Paper Thin" contains many elements present in Hip Hop. The video opens with Lyte (dressed in a sweatsuit and sneakers) abandoning her new Jetta because she wants to take the subway. A few members of her male posse follow along behind her, down the steps to the subway tracks. Once in the subway car, her D.J. K-Rock, doubling as the conductor, announces that the train will be held in the station due to crossed signals. While they wait, Milk Boy (her body guard) spots Sam at the other end of the car, rapping heavily to two stylish women. Lyte, momentarily surprised, begins her rhyme as she stalks toward Sam. Sam's attempts to escape fail; he is left to face MC Lyte's wrath. Eventually, she throws him off the train to the tune of Ray Charles's R & B classic, "Hit the Road Jack," and locks Sam out of the subway station, symbolically jailing him. The subway car is filled with young Black teenagers, typical working New Yorkers and street people, many of whom join Lyte in signifying on Sam while they groove on K-Rock's music. MC Lyte's powerful voice and no-nonsense image dominate Sam. The tense, driving music – which is punctuated by sampled guitar and drum sections as well as an Earth Wind and Fire horn section – complement Lyte's hard, expressive rapping style.

It is important that "Paper Thin" is set in public and on the subway, the quintessential mode of urban transportation. Lyte is drawn to the subway and obviously feels comfortable there. She is also comfortable with the subway riders in her video; they are her community. By setting her confrontation with Sam in the subway, in front of their peers, Lyte moves a private problem between lovers into the public arena and effectively dominates both spaces.

When her D.J., the musical and mechanical conductor, announces that crossed signals are holding the train in the station, he frames the video in a moment of communication crisis. The notion of crossed signals represents the inability of Sam and Lyte to communicate with one another, an inability that is primarily the function of the fact that they communicate on different frequencies. Sam thinks he can read Lyte's mind to see what she is thinking and then feed her all the right lines. But what he says carries no weight, no meaning. His words are light, they're paper thin. Lyte, who understands courtship as a game, confesses to being a player, yet expresses how she feels honestly and in simple language. What she says has integrity, weight and substance.

After throwing Sam from the train, she nods her head toward a young man standing against the subway door, and he follows her off the train. She will not allow her experiences with Sam to paralyze her, but she does have a new perspective on dating. As she and her new male friend walk down the street, she raps the final stanza for "Paper Thin," which sets down the ground rules:

So, now I take precautions when choosing my mate
I do not touch until the third or fourth date
Then maybe we'll kiss on the fifth or sixth time that we meet
'Cause a date without a kiss is so incomplete
And then maybe, I'll let you play with my feet

> You can suck the big toe and play with the middle
> It's so simple unlike a riddle....

MC Lyte and Salt-N-Pepa are not alone in their critique of men's treatment of women. Neneh Cherry's "Buffalo Stance" tells men: "You better watch, don't mess with me / No money man can buy my love / It's sweetness that I'm thinkin' of"; Oaktown 3-5-7's "Say That Then" lashes out at "Finger poppin', hip hoppin', wanna be bed rockin' " men; Ice Cream Tee's "All Wrong" chastises women who allow men to abuse them; and MC Lyte's "I Cram to Understand U," "Please Understand" and "I'm Not Havin' It" are companion pieces to "Paper Thin."

Women rappers also challenge the popular conception that male rappers are the only M.C.s who can "move the crowd," a skill that ultimately determines your status as a successful rapper. Black women rappers compete head-to-head with male rappers for status as the preeminent M.C. Consequently, rhymes that boast, signify and toast are an important part of women's repertoire. Antoinette's "Who's the Boss," Ice Cream Tee's "Let's Work," MC Lyte's "Lyte as a Rock," Salt-N- Pepa's "Everybody Get Up," and Queen Latifah's "Dance for Me" and "Come into My House" establish Black women rappers as Hip Hop M.C.s who can move the crowd, a talent that is as important as writing "dope" rhymes. Latifah's "Come into My House" features Latifah as the dance master, the hostess of physical release and pleasure:

> Welcome into my Queendom
> Come one, come all
> 'Cause when it comes to lyrics I bring them
> In Spring I sing, in Fall I call
> Out to those who had a hard day
> I've prepared a place on my dance floor
> The time is now for you to party....
> I'm on fire the flames too high to douse
> The pool is open
> Come Into My House.[19]

As rap's territory expands, so does the material of female rappers. Subjects ranging from racism, Black politics, Afrocentrism and nationalism to homelessness, physical abuse of women and children, drug addiction, AIDS and teen pregnancy can all be found in female rappers' repertoire. "Ladies First," Queen Latifah's second release from her debut album, *All Hail the Queen*, is a landmark example of such expansions. Taken together, the video and lyrics for "Ladies First" is a statement for Black female unity, independence and power, as well as an anti-colonial statement concerning Africa's southern region. The rap recognizes the importance of Black female political activists, offering hope for the development of a pro-female, pro-Black, diasporatic political consciousness. A rapid-fire and powerful rap duet between Queen Latifah and her "European sister" Monie Love, "Ladies First" is thus a recital on the significance and diversity of Black women. Latifah's assertive, measured voice in the opening rhyme sets the tone:

> The ladies will kick it, the rhyme it is wicked
> Those who don't know how to be pros get evicted
> A woman can bear you, break you, take you
> Now it's time to rhyme, can you relate to
> A sister dope enough to make you holler and scream?

In her almost double-time verse, Monie Love responds:

> Eh, Yo! Let me take it from here Queen
> Excuse me but I think I am about due
> To get into precisely what I am about to do
> I'm conversatin' to the folks who have no whatsoever clue
> So, listen very carefully as I break it down to you
> Merrily merrily, hyper happy overjoyed
> Pleased with all the beats and rhymes my sisters have employed
> Slick and smooth – throwing down the sound totally, a yes
> Let me state the position: Ladies First, Yes?

Latifah responds, "YES!"

Without attacking Black men, "Ladies First" is a wonderful rewriting of the contributions of Black women into the history of Black struggles. Opening with slides of Black female political activists Sojourner Truth, Angela Davis and Winnie Mandela, the video's predominant theme features Latifah as Third World military strategist. She stalks an illuminated, conference table-size map of Southern Africa and, with a long pointer, shoves large chess-like pieces of briefcase carrying white men off white dominated countries, replacing them with large Black power style fists. In between these scenes, Latifah and Monie Love rap in front of and between more photos of politically prominent Black women and footage of Black struggles that shows protests and acts of military violence against protestors. Latifah positions herself as part of a rich legacy of Black women's activism, racial commitment and cultural pride.

Given the fact that protest footage rap videos (which have become quite popular over the last few years) have all but excluded scenes of Black women leaders or foot soldiers, the centrality of Black women's political protest in "Ladies First" is refreshing. Scenes of dozens of rural African women running with sticks raised above their heads toward armed oppressors, holding their ground alongside men in equal numbers and dying in struggle, are rare media images. As Latifah explains:

> I wanted to show the strength of Black women in history. Strong Black women. Those were good examples. I wanted to show what we've done. We've done a lot; it's just that people don't know it. Sisters have been in the midst of these things for a long time, but we just don't get to see it that much.[20]

After placing a Black power fist on each country in Southern Africa, Latifah surveys the map, nodding contentedly. The video ends with a still frame of the region's new political order.

Latifah's self-possession and independence is an important facet of the new cultural nationalism in rap. The powerful, level-headed and Black feminist character of her lyrics calls into question the historically cozy relationship between nationalism and patriarchy. The legendary Malcolm X phrase, "There are going to be some changes made here," is strategically sampled throughout "Ladies First." When Malcolm's voice is introduced, the camera pans the faces of some of the more prominent female rappers and D.Js including Ms. Melodie, Ice Cream Tee and Shelley Thunder. The next sample of Malcolm's memorable line is dubbed over South African protest footage. Latifah evokes Malcolm as part of a collective African-American historical memory and recontextualizes him not only as a leader who supports contemporary struggles in South Africa, but also as someone who encourages the imminent changes regarding the degraded status of Black women and specifically Black women rappers. Latifah's use of the dialogic processes of naming, claiming and recontextualizing is not random; nor is it simply a "juxtaposition of incompatible realities." "Ladies First" is a cumulative product that, as Lipsitz would say, "enters a dialogue already in progress." It affirms and revises African-American traditions at the same time that it stakes out new territory.

Black women rappers' public displays of physical and sexual freedom challenge male notions of female sexuality and pleasure. Salt-N-Pepa's rap duet, "Shake Your Thang," which they perform with the prominent go-go band E.U., is a wonderful verbal and visual display of Black women's sexual resistance. The rap lyrics and video are about Salt-N-Pepa's sexual dancing and others' responses to them. The first stanza sets them in a club "shakin' [their] thang to a funky beat with a go-go swing" and captures the shock on the faces of other patrons. With attitude to spare, Salt-N-Pepa chant: "It's my thang and I'll swing it the way that I feel, with a little seduction and some sex appeal." The chorus, sung by the male lead in E.U., chants: "Shake your thang, do what you want to do, I can't tell you how to catch a groove. It's your thang, do what you wanna do, I won't tell you how to catch a groove."[21]

The video is framed by Salt-N-Pepa's interrogation after they have been arrested for lewd dancing. New York police cars pull up in front of the studio where there music video is being shot, and mock policemen (played by Kid-N-Play and their producer Herbie Luv Bug) cart the women away in handcuffs. When their mug shots are being taken, Salt-N-Pepa blow kisses to the camera-man as each holds up her arrest placard. Once in the interrogation room, Kid-N-Play and Herbie ask authoritatively, "What we gonna do about this dirty dancing?" Pepa reaches across the table, grabs Herbie by the tie and growls, "We gonna do what we wanna do." Outdone by her confidence, Herbie looks into the camera with an expression of shock.

The mildly slapstick interrogation scenes bind a number of other subplots. Scenes in which Salt-N-Pepa are part of groups of women dancing and playing are interspersed with separate scenes of male dancers, co-ed dance segments with Kid-N-Play, E.U.'s lead singer acting as a spokesman for a "free Salt-N-Pepa" movement, and picketers in front of the police station calling for Salt-N-Pepa's release. When he is not gathering signatures for his petition, E.U. chants the chorus from a press conference podium. The camera angles for the dance segments give the effect of a series of park or block parties. Salt-N-Pepa shake their butts for the cameras and for each other while rapping, "My jeans fit nice, they show off my butt" and "I Like Hip Hop mixed with a go-go baby, it's my thang and I'll shake it crazy. Don't tell me how to party, it's my dance, yep, and it's my body."

A primary source of the video's power is Salt-N-Pepa's irreverence toward the morally-based sexual constrictions placed on them as women. They mock moral claims about the proper modes of women's expression and enjoy every minute of it. Their defiance of the moral, sexual restrictions on women is to be distinguished from challenges to the seemingly gender-neutral laws against public nudity. Salt-N-Pepa are eventually released because their dancing isn't against the law (as they say, "We could get loose, but we can't get naked"). But their "dirty dancing" also teases the male viewer who would misinterpret their sexual freedom as an open sexual invitation. The rappers make it clear that their expression is no such thing: "A guy touch my body? I just put him in check." Salt-N-Pepa thus force a wedge between overt female sexual expression and the presumption that such expressions are intended to attract men. "Shaking your thang" can create a stir, but that should not prevent women from doing it when and how they choose.

At the video's close, we return to the interrogation scene a final time. Herbie receives a call, after which he announces that they have to release the women. The charges will not stick. Prancing out of the police station,

Salt-N-Pepa laughingly say, "I told you so." The police raid and arrests make explicit the real, informal yet institutionally-based policing of female sexual expression. The video speaks to Black women, calls for open, public displays of female expression, assumes a community-based support for their freedom, and focuses directly on the sexual desirability and beauty of Black women's bodies. Salt-N-Pepa's recent video for "Expression" covers similar ground but focuses more on fostering individuality in young women.

Salt-N-Pepa's physical freedom, exemplified by focusing on their butts, is no coincidence. The distinctly Black, physical and sexual pride that these women (and other Black female rappers) exude serves as a rejection of the aesthetic hierarchy in American culture that marginalizes Black women. There is a long Black folk history of dances and songs that celebrate big behinds for men and women (e.g., the Bump, the Dookey Butt, and most recently E.U. and Spike Lee's Black chart topper, "Da Butt"). Such explicit focus on the behind counters mainstream definitions of what constitutes a sexually attractive female body. American culture, in defining its female sex symbols, places a high premium on long thin legs, narrow hips and relatively small behinds. The vast majority of white female television and film actresses, musicians and even the occasional Black model fits this description. The aesthetic hierarchy of the female body in mainstream American culture, with particular reference to the behind and hips, positions many Black women somewhere near the bottom. When viewed in this context, Salt-N-Pepa's rap and video become an inversion of the aesthetic hierarchy that renders Black women's bodies sexually unattractive.

Obviously, the common practice of objectifying all women's bodies complicates the way some might interpret Salt-N-Pepa shaking their collective thangs. For some, Salt-N-Pepa's sexual freedom could be considered dangerously close to self-inflicted exploitation. Such misunderstanding of the racial and sexual significance of Black women's sexual expression may explain the surprisingly cautious responses I have received from some white feminists regarding the importance of female rappers. However, as Hortense Spillers and other prominent Black feminists have argued, a history of silence has surrounded African-American women's sexuality.[22] Spillers argues that this silence has at least two faces; either Black women are creatures of male sexual possession, or else they are reified into the status of non-being. Room for self-defined sexual identity exists in neither alternative. The resistant nature of Black women's participation in rap is better understood when we take the historical silence, sexual and otherwise, of Black women into consideration. Salt-N-Pepa are carving out a female-dominated space in which Black women's sexuality is openly expressed. Black women rappers sport Hip Hop clothing and jewelry as well as distinctively Black hairstyles. They affirm a Black, female, working-class cultural aesthetic that is rarely depicted in American popular culture. Black women rappers resist patterns of sexual objectification and cultural invisibility, and they also resist academic reification and mainstream, hegemonic, white feminist discourse.

Given the identities these women rappers have fashioned for themselves, it is not surprising that they want to avoid being labeled feminists. During my conversations with Salt, MC Lyte and Queen Latifah, it became clear that these women saw feminism as a signifier for a movement that related specifically to white women. They also thought feminism involved adopting an anti-male position, and they did not want to be considered or want their work to be interpreted as anti-Black male.

In MC Lyte's case, she remarked that she was often labeled a feminist even though she did not think of herself as one. Yet, after she asked for my working definition of feminist, she wholeheartedly agreed with my description, which was as follows:

> I would say that a feminist believed that there was sexism in society, wanted to change and worked toward change. [She] either wrote, spoke or behaved in a way that was pro-woman, in that she supported situations [organizations] that were trying to better the lives of women. A feminist feels that women are more disadvantaged than men in many situations and would want to stop that kind of inequality.

MC Lyte responded, "Under your definition, I would say I am." We talked further about what she imagined a feminist to be, and it became clear that once feminism was understood as a mode of analysis rather than as a lable for a group of women associated with a particular social movement, MC Lyte was much more comfortable discussing the importance of Black women's independence: "Yes, I am very independent and I feel that women should be independent, but so should men. Both of us need each other and we're just coming to a realization that we do."[23] For MC Lyte, feminists were equivalent to devoutly anti-male, white middle-class members of the National Organization of Women.

Queen Latifah was sympathetic to the issues associated with feminism, but preferred to be considered pro-woman. She was unable to articulate why she was uncomfortable with the term "feminist" and preferred instead to talk about her admiration for Faye Wattleton, the Black president of Planned Parenthood, and the need to support the pro-choice movement. As she told me:

> Faye Wattleton, I like her, I look up to her. I'm pro-choice, but I love God. But I think [abortion] is a woman's decision. In a world like we live in today you can't use [God] as an excuse all the time. They want to make abortion illegal, but they don't want to educate you in school.[24]

Salt was the least resistant to the term *feminism* yet made explicit her limits:

> I guess you could say that [I'm a feminist] in a way. Not in a strong sense where
> I'd want to go to war or anything like that [*laughter*]. . . . But I preach a lot
> about women depending on men for everything, for their mental stability, for
> their financial status, for their happiness. Women have brains, and I hate to see
> them walking in the shadow of a man.[25]

For these women rappers, and many other Black women, feminism is the label for members of a white woman's social movement, which has no concrete link to Black women or the Black community. Feminism signifies allegiance to historically specific movements whose histories have long been the source of frustration for women of color. Similar criticisms of women's social movements have been made vociferously by many Black feminists who have argued that race and gender are inextricably linked for Black women – and I would add, this is the case for both Black and white women.[26] However, in the case of Black women, the realities of racism link Black women to Black men in a way that challenges cross-racial sisterhood. If a cross-racial sisterhood is to be forged, serious attention must be paid to issues of racial difference, racism within the movement, and the racial blind spots that inform coalition building. In the meantime, the desire for sisterhood among and between Black and white women cannot be achieved at the expense of Black women's racial identity.

If feminist scholars want to contribute to the development of a women's movement that has relevance to the lives of women of color (which also means working-class and poor women), then we must be concerned with young women's reluctance to be associated with feminism. We should be less concerned with producing theoretically referential feminist theories and more concerned with linking these theories to practices, thereby creating new concrete ways to interpret feminist activity. This will involve broadening the scope of investigations in our search for Black women's voices. This will involve attending to the day-to-day conflicts and pressures that young, Black working-class women face and focusing more of our attention on the cultural practices that are most important to their lives. Academic work that links feminist theory to feminist practice should be wholeheartedly encouraged, and an emphasis on making such findings widely available should be made. For feminist theorists, this will not simply entail "letting the other speak," but will also involve a systematic reevaluation of how feminism is conceptualized and how ethnicity, class and race seriously fracture gender as a conceptual category. Until this kind of analysis takes place a great deal more often than it does, what any of us say to MC Lyte will remain paper thin.

One of the remarkable talents Black women rappers have is their capacity to attract a large male following and consistently perform their explicitly pro-woman material. They are able to sustain dialogue with and consequently encourage dialogue between young men and women that supports Black women and challenges some sexist male behavior. For these women rappers, feminism is a movement that does not speak to men; while on the other hand, they are engaged in constant communication with Black male audiences and rappers, and they simultaneously support and offer advice to their young, Black female audiences. As MC Lyte explains, "When I do a show, the women are like, 'Go ahead Lyte, tell em!' And the guys are like, 'Oh, shit. She's right.'"[27] Obviously, such instances may not lead directly to a widespread Black feminist male/female alliance. However, the dialogues facilitated by these female rappers may well contribute to its groundwork.

In a world of worst possibilities, where no such movements can be imagined, these Black female rappers provide young Black women with a small, culturally-reflexive public space. Rap can no longer be imagined without women rappers' contributions. They have expanded rap's territory and have effectively changed the interpretive framework regarding the work of male rappers. As women who challenge the sexist discourse expressed by male rappers yet sustain dialogue with them, who reject the racially-coded aesthetic hierarchies in American popular culture, who support Black women and Black culture, Black female rappers constitute an important voice in Hip Hop and contemporary Black women's cultural production generally. As Salt says:

> The women look up to us. They take us dead seriously. It's not a fan type of thing; it's more like a movement. When we shout, "The year 1989 is for the ladies," they go crazy. It's the highlight of the show. It makes you realize that you have a voice as far as women go.[28]

Notes

I would especially like to thank MC Lyte, Queen Latifah and Salt for their generosity and for their incredible talents. I would also like to thank Stuart Clarke for his thoughtful comments and criticism on earlier versions of this article and its title.

1 For a particularly malicious misreading of rap music, see David Gates, "The Rap Attitude," *Newsweek Magazine* (19 March 1990): 56–63. While "The Rap Attitude" is an outrageous example, the assumptions made about the use and intent of rap are quite common. Exceptions to misreadings of this nature include Michael Dyson, "The Culture of Hip Hop," *Zeta Magazine* (June 1989): 45–50,

and the works of Greg Tate, a *Village Voice* staff writer, who has been covering rap music for almost a decade.

2 See Henry Louis Gates, Jr., "Two Live Crew De-Coded," *New York Times* (19 June 1990): 31; Bruce Tucker, "Tell Tchaikovsky the New: Postmodernism, Popular Culture and the Emergence of Rock n Roll," *Black Music Research Journal* (Fall, 1989): 271–95; Anders Stephanson, "Interview with Cornel West," *Universal Abandon?: The Politics of Postmodernism*, ed. Andrew Ross (Minneapolis: University of Minnesota Press, 1989); 269–86.

3 See the special issue entitled "The Women of Rap!" *Rappin Magazine* (July 1990); Dominique Di Prima and Lisa Kennedy, "Beat the Rap," *Mother Jones* (Sep./Oct. 1990): 32–5; Jill Pearlman, "Rap's Gender Gap," *Option* (Fall 1988): 32–6; Marisa Fox, "From the Belly of the Blues to the Cradle of Rap," *Details* (July 1989): 118–24.

4 Public Enemy, "Don't Believe the Hype," *It Takes a Nation of Millions to Hold Us Back*, Def Jam Records, 1988.

5 Queen Latifah, "Ladies First," *All Hail the Queen*, Tommy Boy Records, 1989.

6 Nelson George, "Rap's Tenth Birthday," *Village Voice* (24 October, 1989): 40.

7 Nancy Guevara, "Women, Writin', Rappin', Breakin'," *The Year Left* 2, ed. Mike Davis et al. (New York: Verso, 1987): 160–75.

8 Angela Davis, "Black Women and Music: A Historical Legacy of Struggle," *Wild Women in the Whirlwind: Afro-American Culture and the Contemporary Literary Renaissance*, ed. Joanne M. Braxton and Andrée Nicola McLaughin (Brunswick, NJ: Rutgers University Press, 1990): 3.

9 Hazel V. Carby, "It Jus Be's Dat Way Sometime: The Sexual Politics of Women's Blues," *Radical America* 20(4) (1986): 9–22.

10 George Lipsitz, *Time Passages: Collective Memory and American Popular Culture* (Minneapolis: University of Minnesota of Press, 1990): 99.

11 Roxanne Shante was the first commercial breakthrough female artist. Her basement-produced single was "Roxanne's Revenge" (1985).

12 Pearlman: 34.

13 Di Prima and Kennedy: 34.

14 Pearlman: 34.

15 Greg Tate, "Manchild at Large: One on One with Ice Cube, Hip Hop's Most Wanted," *Village Voice* (11 September, 1990): 78.

16 Salt (Cheryl James from Salt-N-Pepa), personal interview (17 August, 1990).

17 Salt-N-Pepa, *Black's Magic*, Next Plateau Records, 1990.

18 Salt-N-Pepa, "Tramp," *Cool, Hot and Vicious*, Next Plateau Records, 1986; Salt-N-Pepa, "Shake Your Thang," *A Salt With a Deadly Pepa*, Next Plateau Records, 1988; Queen Latifah, "Ladies First," *All Hail the Queen*, Tommy Boy Records, 1989. As you will see, none of my analysis will involve the music itself. The music is a very important aspect of rap's power and aesthetics, but given my space limitations here and the focus of my argument, I have decided to leave it out rather than throw in "samples" of my own. For an extended cultural analysis of rap's music, see Tricia Rose, "Orality and Technology: Rap Music and

Afro-American Cultural Theory and Practice," *Popular Music and Society* 13(4) (1989): 35–44.

19   Queen Latifah, "Come into My House," *All Hail the Queen*, Tommy Boy Records, 1989.

20   Queen Latifah (Dana Owens), personal interview, 6 February, 1990.

21   The melody and rhythm section for "Shake Your Thang" is taken from the Iseley Brothers single "It's Your Thang," which was on *Billboard*'s Top Forty charts in the Winter of 1969.

22   Hortense Spillers, "Interstices: A Small Drama of Words," *Pleasure and Danger: Exploring Female Sexuality*, ed. Carol Vance (Boston: Routledge and Kegan Paul, 1984): 73–100.

23   MC Lyte, personal interview, 7 September, 1990.

24   Queen Latifah, personal interview.

25   Salt, personal interview.

26   See Carby, Davis and Spillers cited above. Also see bell hooks, *Ain't I a Woman: Black Women and Feminism* (Boston: South End Press, 1982) and *Feminist Theory: From Margins to Center* (Boston: South End Press, 1984); Barbara Smith, ed., *Home Girls: A Black Feminist Anthology* (New York: Kitchen Table, 1983); Cheryl A. Wall, ed., *Changing Our Own Words: Essays on Criticism, Theory and Writing by Black Women* (Brunswick, NJ: Rutgers University Press, 1989).

27   MC Lyte, personal interview.

28   Salt, personal interview.

14

Divas Declare a Spoken-Word Revolution

Evelyn McDonnell

McDonnell, Evelyn. "Divas Declare a Spoken-Word Revolution." *Ms.* (January–February, 1996): 74–9.

It's one thing to be a diva, but the diva who writes her own script . . . " Dana Bryant's eyebrows rise as her words drop off. The onetime lounge singer is describing the night she dropped a performance poem into her set of jazz standards. "I was getting tired of listening to glasses clanking and people talking right in front of me, so I decided to do something that fed my soul," says the six-foot-one Warner Brothers recording artist. "I performed this poem by Ntozake Shange and had a friend of mine play upright bass. And the whole room went quiet."

That night five years ago, Bryant discovered the power of a millennia-old art form currently enjoying a renaissance – the spoken word. Poetry, that medium once considered by many to be as square as opera, is suddenly as hip as rap. And African American women are dominating the world of spoken word in ways that they never have in the seemingly misogynist world of rap and hip-hop. In verse declared in cafés, scatted to the accompaniment of jazz bands, rapped at clubs, captured on CDs, even read at presidential inaugurations, a growing number of African American women are mixing the authority of literature with the impact of performance.

When New York poet hattie gossett spins stories about the "temp" work, maid's chores, and welfare that are the daily realities underlying her self-mythologized role as the "modern incarnation of wildwoman diva sister no blues," she's marrying two strong cultural traditions. On the page, her poetry illuminates the lives of Black women with the same vibrant energy as do the writings of Zora Neale Hurston, Toni Morrison, and Alice Walker; onstage, she cuts a figure as powerful and expressive as Bessie, Billie, Aretha, and Chaka. And, as Los Angeles writer Wanda Coleman says: "I've done a lot of things, but poetry is my only freedom. It's the only place I have absolute freedom to say what I want to say the way I want to say it."

So, amidst the intense debate about Black males, these poets bring the concerns of Black females to the public discussion, celebrating identity while turning stereotype after sterotype on its ass.

The device that has really brought poetry out of the closet is the slam – a contest where poets read off against each other before judges, and the poem with the highest score wins (sort of like diving competitions). The slam was birthed at Chicago's Green Mill Jazz Club in the mid-eighties. The first slam star was Patricia Smith, who went on to win national slams in 1990, 1991, 1993, and 1995. She now lives in Boston, where she has launched a new slam scene.

But it is New York City that is home to many of the best new poets. There, rap has had an enormous influence on young writers who quickly discerned within its rhymes and rhythms a form of poetry. "I'm a baby of hip-hop: the style, the discipline, everything comes from that," says 99, a 23-year-old poet, born Dietra Moses, who has worked with Prince and has an album coming out later this year on the Beastie Boys' Grand Royal label.

The center of the New York scene is the influential Nuyorican Poets Café. Located in an old tenement on the Lower East Side, the Nuyorican is a reincarnation of a poets' haunt from the seventies that bore the same name (the term refers to Puerto Ricans who live in New York). The café's famed Friday night slam has introduced such formidable talents as Dana Bryant, Tracie Morris, Dael Orlandersmith, and Samantha Coerbell to the poetry community.

But it was at a trendy nightspot named Fez that it became clear that spoken word could be a forum for Black women otherwise silenced in hip-hop. For irregular monthly intervals in 1992–3, "The Ayatollah's Granola: Rapp Meets Poetry" appeared at Fez. It was a raucous showcase of writers and microphone commandos that quickly developed an audience filled with industry insiders. The strong presence of female poets at Fez was in stark contrast to shows in other hip-hop arenas, and women weekly brought the house down.

What was fresh about these new poets? "Women in poetry don't use males as the basis for their rhymes," says M.C. (she prefers the term to poet) Shä-Key, whose debut album. *A Headnaddas Journey to Adidi-Skizm*, was released last year. "They get to go off and do what they want to do. But the women in hip-hop are like, 'I've got to act like a man, I've got to grab something I don't have, I have to be accepted by men before I'm accepted, period.'"

One infamous night, male rapper Essence Donn tried to deliver rhymes with the commonplace hip-hop message that when women dress like prostitutes, they should be treated like "hos." But "The Ayatollah's" was no typical hip-hop venue. Boos gradually drowned Donn out, and poet Bahiyyah Watson stood up and shouted at him until he left the stage.

The "Ayatollah's Granola" greatly heightened the visibility of the spoken-word scene: the producers of MTV's *Spoken Word Unplugged* scouted talent there, and record-biz reps were always in the house. The flip side of such exposure is that it signaled the end of the poetry scene as a self-contained community and opened it up to commercialism. "Fez was business, you actually went there for business," 99 says. In one poem, Tracie Morris described the scene as a snakepit. "It was a critique of how the entertainment industry changes people, how you're dealing with these pressures whether you're aware of it or not," says the writer, who has been expanding her work into theater and music. "The point I was trying to explore is to not let that compromise your aesthetic, to at least know what the dynamics are so you're not in a position of weakness. We talk about how this happens to other Black art forms: the death of rhythm and blues, what happened to rock 'n' roll. But [spoken word] is something that I'm actually in as it's exploding."

Reading poetry aloud is, of course, neither new nor a specifically Black or feminine medium. The oral tradition predates the written; the ancient Greeks as well as griots used memorized verse, often recited with music, to preserve and pass on cultural legends and history. Oral forms thrived in African American culture as the sole medium connecting slaves to their African past, and many Black writers have pointedly maintained a connection to the word as spoken or sung – perhaps out of social and political need to connect their work with a community rather than see it merely reside on library shelves. Langston Hughes, for example, wrote blues verse, and in 1958 was one of the first poets to record poetry recited over jazz.

"In our community there was always somebody jumping up reciting something with music," says Jayne Cortez, who has been performing poetry with jazz musicians since 1964. "We're connected back to Africa, where this was the tradition, this was the way that you read. The *kora* [West African stringed instrument] players are all griots, they can all recite histories and play music."

Cortez is a pioneer of the modern version of poetry combined with music, a combination that gave rise to rap (in her declamatory style one can hear the antecedent of Public Enemy's Chuck D.) and informs the current spoken-word scene. Cortez's collaborations with such jazz players as Ornette Coleman and Edward Blackwell, and with her own band, Firespitters, reverberate in the work of Dana Bryant and Tracie Morris.

Spoken word's more recent antecedents can be found in the sixties and seventies. In the wake of the Black arts movement of the 1960s, and the growing political awareness of oral literature's role as an African form, a number of artists began focusing on live and recorded performances of their poems. In this trend were Gwendolyn Brooks, Maya Angelou, Nikki Giovanni, and Sonia Sanchez, who presented poetry as something that flows in and out of a human community, rather than something locked away in an ivory tower.

Ntozake Shange's influential 1975 play, *for colored girls who have considered suicide/when the rainbow is enuf*, brought poetry to a new, multimedia level and the larger forum of the Broadway stage. The verse-portraits of the "choreopoem" introduced a type of performance art that expresses and incorporates women's and African American cultures. *For colored girls* also presented a call to arms for poets:

> somebody/anybody
> sing a Black girl's song
> bring her out
> to know herself
> to know you

In the late seventies, poets like Sapphire, Aida Mansuer, and Irare Sabasu heeded Shange's call and formed NAPS, a Black lesbian performing group; Sapphire has gone on to become one of the most riverting poets in the country. Robbie McCauley and Laurie Carlos met doing the original *for colored girls* in San Francisco and formed Thought Music, a collaborative, experimental group. Their performances paved the way for many of the spoken-word artists who emerged from the New York scene in the nineties.

Many poets were originally actors. Spoken-word pioneer Wanda Coleman first learned to perform at workshops in the Watts section of LA in the sixties. Her experience helped determine the performance style that characterizes the spoken word of the nineties. "When I started doing readings I brought that acting baggage with me and adapted it to the poetry-reading style," she says. And yet, although the distinction is subtle, there's a difference between what's called performance poetry and what's known as spoken word: in spoken word, the text itself (written, memorized, or even improvised) controls the performance; in performance poetry, the act is central. "The oral thing is like a side dish for me," says Coleman. "My main focus is the writing."

African American women taking over the mikes signals not just a poetic resurgence, but a mass interest in women's stories. Many of the new poets come from oppressed communities where issues of identity are forced upon them every day; where they are not allowed to forget that they're Black, Latina, poor, female, gay, whatever. For female poets, this demands confronting sexuality and challenging taboos that are forms of repression. And these poets respond with great passion – Bryant's body heaves as she recalls sweat trickling down worshipers' bosoms at a southern sermon; and with a sense of humor – Morris unveils foot fetishes in a rollicking blues number.

Following in the protest tradition of Cortez, much of the current poetry is topical. Lillian Allen, an originator of the reggae-based "dub" style of verse, writes about the displaced and dispossessed in pieces like "There's No Place like Home" and "Social Worker." Tracie Morris' "The Old Days" talks about the backward slide of justice, from Thurgood Marshall to Clarence Thomas: "Folks ain't even faking like/we free." On "Love...Never That," a track on her self-titled debut EP, Jazz Lee Alston speaks from the viewpoint of a cousin who was murdered, allegedly by her estranged husband:

> My man loved me so fucking much
> Christmas night he blew my head
>   wide open
> All over the living room floor.

Pieces like these constitute political acts by documenting women's real stories: the tragedies, trials, and triumphs of being African American and female in the US. Dael Orlandersmith (who last year starred in an Off-Broadway adaptation of her writings) and Sapphire write chillingly about incest. Coleman describes her encounters with racism in the film industry. Many poets write frankly about their sex lives: 99 repeatedly brought the house down at Fez with a poem about the struggle to get a man to wear a condom. In "The Romanticization," Samantha Coerbell compares the rose-colored version of loss of virginity with her own experience of date rape.

In "Canis Rufus," an ode to mythically wild funk singer Chaka Khan, Bryant rhapsodizes about the howl that unleashed the best minds of her generation:

> I say
> SCREAM SISTA
> your ward 8
> sensibility
> speaks for me.

Bryant knows, however, that there's danger in glamorizing Khan. "There's nothing wrong with being a wild woman, but we've been blud-geoned by that image," she says. "It's important that [the image] be harnessed by women and redefined for what it truly is. My poem isn't necessarily about Chaka. It has more to do with the feeling that sound makes happen in me, the possibilities that it opens, to break free of the fetters of self-censorship. It's important for me as a Black woman because

I've always shrunk away from my sexuality, because it's been wielded as a blunt instrument against me."

But as word divas become more successful, navigating the hot-button issues of race and sex becomes trickier. Once-brave declarations of identity, sexuality, and race are now exploited to win a slam, or as hot topics at readings held by collectives with names like the Pussy Poets. Poets like 99 are rebelling against the trend: "I think that we've made enough of an impact in the poetry scene that we don't have to label ourselves after our body parts. We don't have to disrespect our womanhood just to sell."

The allure of the mass media threatens the autonomy nourishing these women's work. But now, after years of women being dummied-up in pop and R&B and shut up in hip-hop and rock, poetry offers an alternative entrée into pop culture.

Bryant, 99, and Shä-Key believe they can maintain their freedom and complexity from inside the record biz. Morris is more skeptical. "I don't want people to pressure me to compromise my aesthetic just to get over," she says. "They like the sassy Black woman vibe, and that's just one aspect of my personality. I don't want to be stereotyped, but I do want to challenge people's perceptions of women as passive victims, as weak and silly."

"I write, arrange, and play all the instruments," says Maverick recording artist Me'Shell NdegéOcello, whose music mixes spoken word into funk and rock. "I'm not into so many of these new artists, because lyrically it's like, would a woman ever think that? Hell, a guy wrote this song – it just doesn't float."

On NdegéOcello's 1993 debut, *Plantation Lullabies*, she sings about love, but it is an intense, political, Black-on-Black love that goes way beyond the usual pop platitudes. In "Step into the Projects," she raps about the struggle to attain "peace from within" when you're urban and poor:

> straight from the womb
> right smack dab in the middle of...
> poverty
> insecurity
> no one to save me.

The mainstream success of NdegéOcello – a short, Black, shaven-headed, bass-slapping, out bisexual single mother – shows it's possible for an artist who doesn't fit the traditional stereotypes to infiltrate the pop world. Her second album, along with debuts from Bryant and 99, all due early this year, may further push the envelope. None of these artists are alike: NdegéOcello plays poetic permutations of the go-go music she was weaned on in Washington, DC, Bryant primarily works with acid jazz musicians and producers, Allen dubs over reggae, while 99's album is hip-hop. And that's the point.

"The community I'm from is constantly being denigrated or mystified or diminished or dismissed," Morris says. "Because the mainstream culture is so hostile to these contributions, we only get to hear one voice. And we don't even realize that that one voice is an assimilation of so many other voices. And when you hear the range of thought, the range of aesthetic, that's out there, it's mind-boggling."

15

"A Laying on of Hands":
Transcending the City in
Ntozake Shange's *for colored girls who have considered suicide/when the rainbow is enuf*

Carolyn Mitchell

Mitchell, Carolyn. " 'A Laying on of Hands': Transcending the City in Ntozake Shange's *for colored girls who have considered suicide/when the rainbow is enuf.*" In Susan Merrill Squier, ed. *Women Writers and the City: Essays in Feminist Literary Criticism* (Knoxville, TN: University of Tennessee Press, 1984), pp. 230–48.

Ntozake Shange's choreopoem, *for colored girls who have considered suicide/ when the rainbow is enuf*, presents the paradox of the modern American city as a place where Black women experience the trauma of urban life, yet find the strength to transcend the pain.[1] The women depicted by Shange become physically and spiritually whole, thus free, through the psychic/psychological healing power that resides in the ancient, fundamentally religious act called "the laying on of hands." The believer "knows" that touch can heal if the one who touches is empowered by God; thus, touching stabilizes a person physically while freeing the troubled soul to soar spiritually.

Shange uses the physically and morally desolate cityscape as a backdrop before which to reveal her spiritual vision of female strength and survival. In this respect, therefore, *colored girls* differs from the legion of literary works that depict the lives of urban Afro-Americans.[2] She neither denies nor romanticizes urban Black experiences: the choreopoem graphically describes the complex ways in which the rape victim is further victimized by the "authorities"; it reveals the loneliness and guilt of the woman who decides to have an abortion; it details the betrayal women continue to experience in their relationships with men.[3]

While none of these problems is uniquely urban, they are exacerbated by the human estrangements that characterize city life. But Ntozake Shange does have a larger vision. One might think of this vision in terms of two concentric circles, with the outer circle temporarily more powerful than the other. The geographical and psychological "settings" represent one circle; the other is a fragile circle promising transcendence. The external circle is clearly discernible from the beginning; the internal is revealed slowly, growing in strength and intensity until *it* is the dominant one at the end. The second circle, at first a figurative one, becomes a visible, magic enclosure of women who, in joining hands, bless and heal one another while naming their own empowering female god.

Though the presence of the women in the cities cited by Shange may be a matter of exigency, the question of how to find and maintain hope in the face of despair is a crucial one. In spite of the dichotomies established between country and city and though much is made of the romance of country life, humankind has relentlessly gravitated to biblical, literary, and historical cities, the problems and pitfalls notwithstanding. To substitute the word "metropolis" for "city" sheds some light on what seems to be the primal search of all people for a centered, balanced existence. This partial explanation is valid because cities are geographically contained or "centered" entities, as opposed to the random "layout" of the country. Thus, two important ideas surface immediately from the notion of the city as a "contained entity." Paul Tillich, the theologian, offers both: the city as a "centralizing and inclusive place" and the city as a place that accepts both the "strange and the familiar."[4]

First, Tillich, in discussing the "centralizing and inclusive" nature of the city which, he says "influences the character of *man's* (emphasis mine) spiritual creativity," suggests that

> we may take our point of departure from the Greek word *metropolis*, signifying the mother or central city. Everything that exists has the power to be only insofar as it is centered. This is especially true of human personalities and social groups. The power of being, often called vitality, increases in proportion to the degree of diversity which is united at a center. Therefore, man has more power of being than any animal, and a spiritual man has greater vitality than a man with an underdeveloped spirituality....
>
> In applying this ontology of the metropolis to the spiritual life of man, we find that the big city has two functions. It serves in a centralizing capacity and also in an including capacity, and each is dependent upon the other.[5]

According to Tillich, a "metropolis...is a center city. It is likewise an including city. It includes everything of which it is the center, and encompasses diversity and freedom of individual creativity and competition."[6]

Tillich uses the word "mother" to identify the genesis of the city, but the
city he describes, paradoxically, is masculine.[7] It is an idealized, romanticized,
theoretical place where men interact, where ideas flow, where creativity
flourishes, and where competition works for the good of all. This vision of
the city is one which supports equality of aspiration, mobility of action, and
freedom of community that women, in fact, have never known. Tillich and
Shange are diametrically opposed to one another in their interpretations of
the city; I shall discuss later the ways in which Tillich's idealized city is
transformed by Ntozake Shange into a more realistic image. Her poem, "i
usedta live in the world," is the psychological turning point in the play and is
most indicative of her different view.[8]

"i usedta live in the world" is set in Harlem, the Black city within New
York City, which figures in Afro-American literature as "Mecca," "the City
of Refuge," and in current vernacular as the "Big Apple."[9] However, Harlem has not lived up to its promise; thus it is no surprise that one of the most
powerful poems in *for colored girls* is located there.

The woman in blue compares the vastness of her former life in the
"world" to life in Harlem where her "universe is now six blocks."

> i usedta live in the world
> then i moved to HARLEM
> & my universe is now six blocks
>
> when i walked in the pacific
> i imagined waters ancient from accra/ tunis
> cleansin me/ feedin me
> now my ankles are coated in grey filth
> from the puddle neath the hydrant
>
> my oceans were life
> what waters i have here sit stagnant
> circlin ol men's bodies
> shit & broken lil whiskey bottles
> left to make me bleed. (28)

She juxtaposes the memory of wading in the Pacific and being washed and
nurtured to the filthy water running in the city gutter. The "oceans" were
life to her, which suggests the religious reading of the ocean as "Source" or
God.[10] In contrast, the city water, instead of cleansing, holds suspended
whiskey bottles whose jagged edges threaten her life. The stagnant water also
symbolically holds suspended the bodies of old men – the winos, the "flot-
sam and jetsam" of city humanity. These men and the water circling them
form part of the gross external circle mentioned above. They are the reasons
why the spiritual self/circle is such a fragile entity, for it is impossible at this

point to deal with this self in the face of the threat to basic survival; the broken bottles in the hands of these men are potential murder weapons.

The poem continues, revealing "a tunnel with a train//i can ride anywhere// remaining a stranger" (29). The image of the tunnel/train simultaneously suggests two meanings: the momentary enclosure necessary to arrive at a "larger" destiny/destination and the ultimate enclosure of estrangement which is the life of the stranger in the city. The city subways do reach destinations and one can "ride" them "anywhere," but, in fact, the lady in blue "rides" the subway and finds herself trapped by a 12-year-old boy who makes sexual advances. She responds,

NO MAN YA CANT GO WIT ME/ I DONT EVEN
KNOW YOU/ NO/ I DONT WANNA KISS YOU/
YOU AINT BUT 12 YRS OLD/ NO MAN/ PLEASE
PLEASE PLEASE LEAVE ME ALONE/ TOMORROW/ YEAH/ (29)

Her hysterical response and the extorted promise of a meeting tomorrow capture the fear women in the city have for their lives. Granted that the boy may not be a fully grown sexual being, but he most likely possesses a gun or a knife, clearly approved extensions of male sexuality and power. The ambiguous words, "NO/PLEASE/I CAN'T USE IT," suggest that this neophyte of a man, having been temporarily stalled, attempts to give or sell some trinket to the woman. This offer further belittles and objectifies the woman, who mourns the loss of her freedom metaphorically rendered in her "imagined waters." Commenting on her current life, she says, "i come in at dusk// stay close to the curb," clearly common-sense tactics for survival in the city.

The 12-year-old on the subway becomes an urban "everyman" whose violence is contained by the "tunnel" image now suggested in the "straight up brick walls" of the city tenements. The "young man fulla his power" emerges in relief against the limp, powerless "women hangin outta windows//like ol silk stockings." The lady in blue continues:[11]

wdnt be good
not good at all
to meet a tall short Black brown young man fulla his power
in the dark
in my universe of six blocks
straight up brick walls
women hangin outta windows
like ol silk stockings. (29)

The helter-skelter, impersonally violent life in Harlem is compared to a more gentle existence when:

I usedta live in the world
really be in the world
free & sweet talkin
good morning & thank-you & nice day. (30)

The poem concludes, and the woman, no longer trusting, courteous, out-going, reveals that her six-block universe is a cruel, hopeless, inhuman dead end, a closed tunnel ending the promise of freedom in the city. Life in Harlem is a cruel hoax:

i cant be nice to nobody
nice is such a rip-off
reglar beauty & a smile in the street
is just a set-up

i usedta be in the world
a woman in the world
i hadda right to the world
then i moved to harlem
for the set-up
a universe
six blocks of cruelty
piled up on itself
a tunnel
closin (30–1)

The city described by Shange offers none of the characteristics idealized by Tillich. Rather than encompass diversity, it reflects the fear of racial and sexual diversity. "Individual creativity" is perverted into desperate schemes for survival. "Competition" becomes the "dog-eat-dog" syndrome, rather than the mythologized earn-and-share, secular spirituality of the market-place. Few can discover a spiritual center in this environment. For Shange, the city must be demystified and demythologized so that the price of human survival there can be truly estimated. The paradox is that the women embody the essence of the *metropolis*, even though they (as Black women) are doubly absent from the "defining" language.

Paul Tillich's second point is that the metropolis supports both the strange and the familiar:

The anti-provincial experience furnished by the metropolis is typified by encounters with that which is strange. Meeting the strange can have two consequences. It can produce hate against the strange, and usually against the stranger, because its existence threatens the self-certainty of the familiar. Or it can afford the courage to question the familiar. In the metropolis, it is impossible to remove the strange and the stranger, because every neighbor is mostly a stranger. Thus the second alternative of questioning the familiar ordinarily prevails . . . .

Since the strange leads to questions and undermines familiar tradition, it serves to elevate reason to ultimate significance. If all traditions are question-able, nothing but reason is left as the way to new spiritual content. There lies the connection between the metropolis and critical rationality – between the metropolis and the intelligentsia as a social group. The importance of the encounter with the strange for all forms of the spiritual life cannot be over-estimated.[12]

For Tillich, the "strange" and the "familiar" are separate forces that collide with one another, providing the change necessary for a dynamic spiritual life. For Ntozake Shange, the strange and the familiar are the double face of a single entity colliding with itself and with its societal counterpart. The strange/stranger is housed within the individual self *and* in the neighbor next door; the "familiar" has an unrecognizable "face." The orderly process by which "the strange leads to questions and undermines familiar tradition" and finally elevates "reason to ultimate significance" is absent, for, as Shange shows, the path to spiritual transcendence for the urban dispossessed is a decidedly irrational one.

The family is the traditional, familiar entity which provides the sanctuary from which the strange is questioned. Contrary to form, Shange's "family" revealed in "a nite with beau willie brown," shows how the strange and the familiar coexist as one. For example, violence is at once "strange" and "famil-iar," as are the ignorance, poverty, and promiscuity that preclude any poss-ibility of Willie and his "wife," Crystal, belonging to Tillich's "intelligentsia." Willie and Crystal are the "underside," the "sewer" side of the metropolis.

"a nite with beau willie brown" is set geographically in the prototypical ghetto (Harlem is suggested to me) and psychologically in Vietnam, whereas "i usedta live in the world" is split between the geographical Harlem and a psychological place on the Pacific Ocean. The mounting tension in the play as a whole climaxes in "beau willie" because there are no pleasant mythic memories (as in the "imagined waters" of the Pacific); there are only the nightmare memories of Vietnam. Vietnam, in this context, clearly embodies the strange and the familiar simultaneously: a strange place and people, but familiar violence. The madness at the core of America is reflected in the Vietnam experience and in the fact that Beau Willie is "shell-shocked" long before he reaches Vietnam. He is a young version of the old men in "i usedta live in the world." They are static, trapped in stagnant water, and Willie is like Fred Daniels in Richard Wright's short story, "The Man Who Lived Under-ground," who is almost swept away by the torrent of sewer water into which he has dropped while running from the police.[13] One knows instinctively that

Willie will not live long enough to grow static, for the aftermath of Vietnam finds him speeding to destruction. Beau Willie is the perennial stranger in American life for whom the familiar only provides additional trauma.

Tillich's familiar seems obvious in the family structure represented by Willie, Crystal, and their children Naomi Kenya and Kwame Beau Willie Brown. But Shange creates a monster in Beau Willie. He is hardly the comfortable image of the next-door-neighbor-as-stranger. Willie is ruined by the war experience, which is clearly the last in a series of psychological events that have crippled him. He is the dominant figure in the poem, but he is bound to his woman Crystal. He is a dope addict; he is paranoid. The lady in red speaks for him:

> there was no air/ the sheets made ripples under his
> body like crumpled paper napkins in a summer park/ & lil
> specks of somethin from tween his toes or the biscuits
> from the day before ran in the sweat that tucked the sheet
> into his limbs like he was an ol frozen bundle of chicken/
> & he'd get up to make coffee, drink wine, drink water/ he
> wished one of his friends who knew where he waz wd come by
> with some blow or some shit/ anythin/ there was no air/
> he'd see the spotlights in the alleyways downstairs movin
> in the air/ cross his wall over his face/ & get under the
> covers & wait for an all clear or till he cd hear traffic
> again/ (43–4)

The words "there was no air" suggest that Willie's external and internal environment are closing in on him. Both are hostile elements because he is shell-shocked from his war experience and reacts to his urban world as if he were still under fire, as he clearly is. He is obsessed with Crystal who has been

> his girl since she waz thirteen/ when he caught her on the stairway/
>
> he came home crazy as hell/ he tried to get veterans benefits
> to go to school & they kept right on puttin him in
> remedial classes/ he cdnt read wortha damn/ so beau
> cused the teachers of holdin him back & got himself
> a gypsy cab to drive/ but his cab kept breakin
> down/ & the cops was always messin with him/ plus not
> getting much bread/
> & crystal went & got pregnant again/ beau most beat
> her to death when she tol him/ (44)

Like Richard Wright's Fred Daniels, Willie is harassed by the police. His attempt to make a living driving a cab backfires. He has no money. As I mentioned above, he is the perennial stranger; his city is the cruel, demeaning world of social ignorance, illiteracy, promiscuity, and unemployment.

Beau Willie's madness increases as the poem progresses. His "war" is complicated and Crystal is the object of his anger and hostility because her ambivalence about marrying him calls his manhood into question. For Beau, Crystal is clearly crazy because

> ... he just wanted
> to marry her/ that's what/ he wanted to marry her/ &
> have a family/ but the bitch was crazy/ beau willie
> waz sittin in this hotel in his drawers drinkin
> coffee & wine in the heat of the day spillin shit all
> over hisself/ laughin/ bout how he was gonna get crystal
> to take him back/ & let him be a man in the house/ & she
> wdnt even have to go to work no more/ he got dressed
> all up in his ivory shirt & checkered pants to go see
> crystal & get this mess all cleared up/
> he knocked on the door to crystal's rooms/ & she
> didn't answer/ he beat on the door & crystal & naomi
> started cryin/ beau gotta shoutin again how he wanted
> to marry her/ & waz she always gonna be a whore/ or
> did she wanna a husband/ (46)

The poem comes to a monstrous end as Beau breaks down the door and pleads with Crystal for another chance, coaxing her to let him hold the children. Using them as hostages and holding them out of the fifth story window, Beau extorts the promise of marriage from Crystal. He urges her to "say to alla the neighbors// you gonna marry me/" (48), but she is too stunned to speak above a whisper:[14]

> i stood by beau in the window/ with naomi reachin
> for me/ kwame screaming mommy mommy from the fifth
> story/ but i cd only whisper/ & he dropped em (48)

Though Willie is the focus of the poem, the story is, in fact, Crystal's story. Shange uses the portrait of male violence to comment on the ways in which women are robbed of life. Willie's monstrous act strips Crystal of her identity as a woman and a mother. Just as Willie is an extension of the 12-year-old boy, she is truly the sister of the woman who tells her story in "i usedta live in the world." She is also the symbolic sister of all the women who speak in and identify with the play. The extremity of her life mirrors the worst that can happen to a woman's dreams and aspirations. Through Crystal's story Shange reveals the inner circle mentioned above. Having broken down the city and its female inhabitants to their most elemental level, and, having redefined the conventional interpretations of the strange and the familiar offered by Tillich, Shange re-creates a picture more faithful to the irrational forces that have traditionally shaped female lives and female spirituality.

The name Crystal is interesting, for Willie is truly addicted to her as if she were indeed heroin. He cannot live with or without her and what should be the sanctuary of a love relationship instead "inspires" him to brutality. On the other hand, Crystal's name suggests the clarity and purity of the vision of the city of God:

> Then he showed me the river of the water of life, sparkling like crystal, flowing from the throne of God and of the Lamb down the middle of the city's streets.[15]

To understand the dual role that Crystal plays is to understand the quantum leap from "a nite with beau willie brown" to the last poem, "a layin on of hands," for her reality is grounded both in the gross world of Willie and the ghetto and in the spiritual vision of the women she represents. Her tragedy insures the transcendence of the women for her tears are like the waters of the biblical river.

The fragile inner circle that represents the spiritual is first apparent in the title and is alluded to throughout the choreopoem. The promise of transition from despair to hope is revealed in the words of lady in brown, "& this is for colored girls who have considered suicide// but moved to the ends of their own rainbows" (3). The first "community" mentioned in the play is one composed of "colored girls who have considered suicide." Suicide, whether physical, psychological, or spiritual, is a dominant factor in modern life; therefore, it is significant that this is the point around which the "new" community is rebuilt, for gathering together to deny suicide is a life-affirming, spiritual act. Shange says, "One day I was driving home after a class, and I saw a huge rainbow over Oakland. I realized that women could survive if we decide that we have as much right and as much purpose for being here as the air and mountains do."[16] Preparation for the "layin on of hands" and the discovery of God at the end of the play begins here. Women should have the freedom to live and must claim it. The rainbow suggests the mythic covenant between God and Noah, symbolizing hope and life; it foreshadows the end when the declaration, "i found god in myself," explains why the "rainbow is enuf."

To claim the right "to be" is to confront antilife forces. This self-affirmation is the first step toward spiritual affirmation. The rainbow represents the promise of a whole life, and Shange reveals her unique vision, for she draws a new covenant when she alters the gender of God, finding "her" in self, and declaring love for "her." This "mother" god will certainly heal her battered daughters. For this reason, too, Crystal's loss of her children is significant; the rules of patriarchy which allow mother and children to be held hostage must be rewritten.[17]

The sisterhood revealed at the conclusion of the play is foreshadowed in several poems about stunted male/female relationships. The poem, "pyramid," discusses the competitiveness of dating in which women are pitted against one another – primarily because men are in short supply. The man in "pyramid" "plays the field," thereby compromising the friendships of three women, but the poem ends on a positive note as the women console one another:

> she held her head on her lap
> the laps of her sisters soakin up tears
> each understandin how much love stood between them
> how much love between them
> love between them
> love like sisters (33)

Here the women affirm the power of touch ("she held her head on her lap") and the power of sisterly love. The ambiguous use of the pronoun "her" in the first line addresses the merger of the individual woman into collective "woman," whose psyche cannot be divided by competition.

The lady in orange turns her love song into a "requiem" for her old self because she can no longer avoid her own face; she needs to "die" to be "reborn" into spiritual life and to claim her own identity:

> so this is a requium for myself/ cuz i
> have died in a real way/not wid aqua coffins & du-wop cadillacs/
> i used to joke abt when i waz messin round/ but a real dead
> lovin is here for you now/ cuz i dont know anymore/ how
> to avoid my own face wet with my tears/ cuz i had convinced
> myself colored girls had no right to sorrow/ & i lived
> & loved that way & kept sorrow on the curb/ allegedly
> for you/ but i did it for myself/
> i cdnt stand it
> i cdnt stand being sorry & colored at the same time
> it's so redundant in the modern world (34)

In "no more love poems #3," the lady in blue deals with the accusation that Black women are too emotional:

> we deal wit emotion too much
> so why dont we go on ahead & be white then/
>
> .   .   .   .   .
>
>   i'll find a way to make myself
> come witout you/ no fingers or other objects just thot
> which isnt spiritual evolution cuz its empty & godliness
> is plenty ripe & fertile/ (35)

The definition of godliness as "plenty ripe & fertile" is a crucial turning point in female consciousness. Shange here addresses the central contradiction in Tillich's identification of the *metropolis* as "mother or central city," but defining its primary function as the repository of reason, when reason is the one attribute women are accused of lacking. The fecundity of women's emotions with their life-giving and life-sustaining properties is juxtaposed to "thot [thought]// which isn't spiritual evolution cuz its empty." The words "plenty ripe & fertile" echo at the end of the play, for the bonding of the women suggests the female fertility cults of old.

In "no more love poems #4," the lady in yellow makes the essential link between wordly and spiritual love:

> but bein alive & bein a woman & bein colored is a metaphysical
> dilemma/ i havent conquered yet/ do you see the point
> my spirit is too ancient to understand the separation of
> soul & gender/ my love is too delicate to have thrown
> back on my face (36)

At the end of these poems, the ladies celebrate the beauty and energy of their love, lifting it above romantic trivialization. To disavow the "separation of// soul & gender" prefigures the female god, both as human woman claiming her place and as "god the mother." Of the many lines the women sing to describe the significance of their love, the most telling is chanted by the lady in purple: "my love is too sanctified to have thrown back on my face" (36), which places absolute value on human love and prefigures the sanctified holy love implicit in the laying on of hands.

Crystal, then, is the woman whose specific tragedy is an adumbration of all female tragedy. She is the victim who is overwhelmed, at least momentarily, by the fury of the madman. Through Crystal, each woman discovers the hope in herself, with "all the gods comin into me// laying me open to myself" (49). Each woman now understands what the lady in red means when she says "i waz missin somethin" (49). The lady in blue declares that what is missing is "not a man" (50). And the lady in purple is clear that it is neither her mother, nor motherhood that is missing:

not my mama/ holdin me tight/ sayin
i'm always gonna be her girl
not a layin on of bosom & womb
a layin on of hands
the holiness of myself released (50)

The lady in red considers suicide:

I sat up one night walkin a boardin house
screaming/ cryin/ the ghost of another woman
who waz missin what i was missin
i wanted to jump outta my bones
& be done wit myself
leave me alone
& go on in the wind
it was too much (50)

She is split into two beings, but this confrontation with self (strange and the familiar) is the point at which healing and renewal begins:

i fell into a numbness
til the only tree i cd see
took me up in her branches
held me in the breeze
made me dawn dew
that chill at daybreak
the sun wrapped me up swingin rose light everywhere
the sky laid over me like a million men
i waz cold/ i waz burnin up/ a child
& endlessly weavin garments for the moon
wit my tears (50)

The concrete landscape of the city with its occasional tree – unremarkable, lone, bare, struggling for survival in an environment indifferent or hostile to it – unfolds here. The lady in red "fell into a numbness" that, paradoxically, is relieved through the life-giving properties of the tree. Adrienne Rich suggests that the tree "is a female symbol," and is scared.[18] Shange's tree is the sacred "mother," and her branches loving, cradling arms. The tree connects symbolically with Crystal as the final arbiter for the women, an idea that is enhanced by these words from Revelations, "On either side of the river stood a tree of life . . ., the leaves of the tree[s] serve for the healing of nations" (22:2).

The sun embraces the lady in red and "the sky laid over [her] like a million men." Shange alludes to the classical notion of the sky as male principle and the break with "earthly" men makes realignment with nature's balance possible. Through the images of hot and cold, she re-creates the fever associated with childhood, and prepares the way for rebirth. Female affinity and empathy with the moon are suggested in the image of one "endlessly weavin garments for the moon// with my tears." All the cosmic forces come together here as a unifying and healing whole.

The lines from the end of "no more love poems #4" provide a context for the discovery of God. The lady in yellow says:

> do you see the point
> my spirit is too ancient to understand the separation of
> soul & gender/ (36)

These lines suggest that body (gender) and soul cannot be separated; thus the woman knows wholeness. The final words of the lady in red contain the triumph of all the women, for she is finally and fully centered as she says, "i found god in myself/ & i loved her fiercely." The identification of God as female is one of the most problematic points in the play, for it redefines the image of God. But Shange truly understands what it means to be created in the image of God, for discovery of self is discovery of God. This is a declaration of freedom from a patriarchial god who supports the men from whom the women have split.

The poem, "a layin on of hands," suggests a specially formed community which has grown from the brokenness of life in the city. Crystal reminds me of Revelations, but the connection between her transcendence and that found in *colored girls* is that Shange's triumphant city is not the product of an apocalyptic vision, but is the result of new sight, for the physical metropolis remains unchanged. As Denise Levertov in her poem, "City Psalm," says,

> Nothing was changed, all was revealed otherwise;
> not that horror was not, not that the killings did not continue,
> not that I thought there was to be no more despair,
> but that as if transparent all disclosed
> an otherness that was blesséd, that was bliss.
> *I saw Paradise in the dust of the street.*[19]

Levertov's image of the "transparent all" echoes the moment of crystal purity, which is the moment of revelation that "disclosed / an otherness." It is "in the dust of the street" that Shange's women suffer and grow in knowledge of the "strangeness of the familiar." It is their immersion in this paradoxical reality which forces them to confront themselves and which prepares them to have a dynamic spiritual vision. The women simply could not have been reborn had they not been cleansed and bound together by these unique experiences. They are not ghouls, children of horror, the joke, animals, or crazy people. They no longer need "somebody/anybody" to sing their song. They are no longer scattered half-notes.[20] But they differ radically from the idealized city beings hypothesized by Tillich. Through the life-enhancing hope of the rainbow, they form a covenant with a woman-God. They are "new" and now sing their own "righteous gospel." The laying on of hands is validated in the "holiness of myself released" (50). The women enter into a tightly wrought circle, symbolic of their spiritual vision and their earthly solidarity. This is the second, "inner" circle mentioned above, which is in tension throughout the play with the external circle. Here, the power and meaning of the inner circle are fully revealed. And the lady in brown dedicates the moment:

> this is for colored girls who have considered
> suicide/ but are movin to the ends of their own
> rainbows (51)

Notes

1   Ntozake Shange, *for colored girls who have considered suicide/when the rainbow is enuf* (New York: Macmillan, 1977). All citations are from this edition and are given in the text parenthetically. Shange does not use punctuation in a conventional way. Thus, the double slash (//) is used in my text to indicate the end of line of poetry since Shange uses the single (/) throughout the choreopoem as a poetic device.

  The term "choreopoem" is used in my text as a synonym for the word "play." This is Shange's word and is found on the title page of her book. It reflects Shange's intent that the play be understood as a choral recitation of poems upon which limited dramatic form has been imposed.

2   The cities have been repositories of promise for Blacks migrating from rural to urban America. They have sought economic and political freedom, psychological and cultural autonomy. During the first two decades of the twentieth century Southern Black people, seeking to escape white violence and economic disaster, migrated to the North. The traditional myth of opportunity in the North was enhanced by national preparations for World War I and the hope for employment in the emerging defense industries. The promise of safety and a better economic life is usually seized upon by analysts as the sole interest of the emigrating Black masses, but Alain Locke, editor of the anthology *The New Negro* (New York: Atheneum, 1970), 6, suggests in the title essay that the Black peasant was inspired by a newly emerging and more complex vision:

> The tide of Negro migration, northward and cityward, is not to be fully explained as a blind flood started by the demands of war industry coupled with the shutting off foreign migration, or by the pressure of poor crops

coupled with increased social terrorism in certain sections of the South and Southwest. Neither labor demand, the boll-weevil nor the Ku Klux Klan is a basic factor, however contributory any or all of them may have been. The wash and rush of this human tide on the beach line of the northern city centers is to be explained primarily in terms of a new vision of opportunity, of social and economic freedom, of a spirit to seize, even in the face of an extortionate and heavy toll, a chance for the improvement of conditions. With each successive wave of it, the movement of the Negro becomes more and more a mass movement toward the larger and more democratic chance – in the Negro's case a deliberate flight not only from countryside to city, but from medieval America to modern.

These migration patterns continued until the 1970s, when many Black people, inspired by the gains of the Civil Rights Movement, retraced the steps of their ancestors back to the South. However, since the original migrations were to the North, life in Northern cities is the focus of many twentieth-century Afro-American writers. Authors such as James Weldon Johnson, Rudolph Fisher, Wallace Thurman, Jessie Fauset, to name a few early writers of the decade, and more modern, perhaps better-known writers such as Langston Hughes, Richard Wright, James Baldwin, Ann Petry, Ralph Ellison, Gwendolyn Brooks depict the Afro-American urban experience.

3 The first two poems mentioned here are "latent rapists" [*sic*] (12–16), "abortion cycle #1" (16–17). Most of the poems in *for colored girls* deal in some way with betrayal, but this is the specific theme of "no assistance" (10), and "somebody almost walked off wid alla my stuff" (39–41).

4 Paul J. Tillich, "The Metropolis: Centralizing and Inclusive," and "The Strange and the Familiar in the Metropolis," in *The Metropolis in Modern Life*, ed. Robert Moore Fisher (New York: Doubleday, 1955), 346–7. Shange identifies the "familiar" cities, but establishes the women as "strangers." For example, the characters in the play do not have "proper names," except in poems where she creates a story within a story; the women are "named" by the colors they wear, suggesting anonymity. They are placed *outside* the cities: the lady in red, "i'm outside baltimore"; the lady in blue, "i'm outside manhattan," etc.

5 Ibid., 346.

6 Ibid., 346–7.

7 Tillich's language is exclusively masculine. His central image is power; his primary example of power is the pope and the Roman Catholic Church.

8 The preceding poems interweave fascinating pictures of city landscape with the emerging consciousness of the women as they grow from late adolescence in, for example, "graduation nite" (4–7), to adult complexity in the poem entitled "one" (24–8), in which a lonely urban woman takes a stranger home to bed, but must finally face the fact that the chance encounter is not satisfying and that she is lonelier than ever at its conclusion.

9   A mentor to many of the young Black artists flocking to Harlem in the twenties, described it as "one of the most beautiful and healthful sections of the city." He ended his commentary on Harlem with the following words:

> I believe that the Negro's advantages and opportunities are greater in Harlem than in any other place in the country, and that Harlem will become the intellectual, the cultural, and the financial center for Negroes of the United States, and will exert a vital influence upon all Negro people.

James Weldon Johnson, "Harlem: The Culture Capital," in *The New Negro*, ed. Alain Locke (New York: Atheneum, 1970), 311. Johnson's words proved not to be prophetic. The promise of Harlem in the 1920s as a place where the urban dream of American Blacks would come true failed and Harlem's prominence has eroded in the last two decades. It is interesting that Johnson's ideas are a secular echo of Tillich's and ironic that the diversity of the city described by Tillich is not fully realized as whites flee from areas into which Black people move thereby compromising the vitality of place and creating ghettoes. Johnson's dream, therefore, cannot be realized because "the intellectual, the cultural, and the financial" are defined and controlled by white people, who remove these elements when they leave.

10 I am thinking, here, of the connection made by Jonathan Edwards, in his meditation number 77 on "Rivers" from *Images or Shadows of Divine Things*, "There is a wonderful analogy between what is seen in rivers, their gathering from innumerable small branches beginning at a great distance one from another in different regions . . . yet all gathering more and more together the nearer they come to their common end and ultimate issue, and all at length discharging themselves at one mouth into the same ocean. Here is livelily represented how all things tend to one, even to God, the boundless ocean" (*The Norton Anthology of American Literature*, I, ed. Gottesman, Holland, Kalstone, et al., [New York: Norton, 1979], 261).

11 In the stage directions, the other women silently enter here; their presence is a symbolic commentary on the universality of the problem.

12 Tillich, 347.

13 Richard Wright, "The Man Who Lived Underground," in *Black Voices*, ed. Abraham Chapman (New York: New American Library, 1968), 114–60. Shange's image of old men suspended in stagnant water is reminiscent of Wright's character who finds – literally and figuratively – all of life's potential amenities rotted or dead floating by in the sewer water. Just as I suggested that Willie and Crystal are the "sewer" side of the metropolis, so Fred Daniel's world is that of the sewer, a metaphorical commentary on the quality of Afro-American life in the city.

14 The starkness of Beau Willie's infanticide has led critics to accuse Ntozake Shange of hating men. It is my opinion that she graphically, but compassionately, depicts the inhumanity of a system that in its racist, biased indifference to life, stunts a man's aspirations, makes him a murderer, and reduces him to insanity. His time in Vietnam is the most important factor to consider in his treatment of

Crystal and the children. This point is endorsed by one of the most powerful dramatic productions of the postwar Vietnam veteran's life. This play is Emily Mann's *Still Life*, in which Mark, the veteran, in talking of his projection of violence, identifies his wife, Cheryl, as the war casualty.

15 Revelations 22:1, *New English Bible* (New York: Cambridge University Press, 1971). Crystal's name also suggests the paradox of experience for the Afro-American mother that is captured in Langston Hughes's poem, "Mother to Son," in *Black Writers of America: A Comprehensive Anthology*, ed. Kinnamon and Barksdale (New York: Macmillan, 1972), 518.

Well, son, I'll tell you:
Life for me ain't been no crystal stair.
It's had tacks in it,
And splinters,
And boards torn up,
And places with no carpet on the floor –
Bare.
But all the time
I'se been a-climbin' on,
And reachin' landin's,
And turnin' corners,
And sometimes goin' in the dark
Where there ain't been no light.
So boy, don't you turn back.
Don't you set down on the steps
'Cause you finds it's kinder hard.
Don't you fall now –
For I'se still goin', honey,
I'se still climbin',
And life for me ain't been no crystal stair.

16 Carol P. Christ, *Diving Deep and Surfacing: Women Writers on Spiritual Quest* (Boston: Beacon, 1980), 99, as quoted from Ntozake Shange, *For Colored Girls Who Have Considered Suicide/When the Rainbow Is Enuf* (original Broadway cast recording) (New York: Buddha Records, 1976), jacket notes. One of the most sensitive, cogent, and pertinent discussions of the choreopoem appears in Carol Christ's essay, " 'i found god in myself . . . & i loved her fiercely': Ntozake Shange." Christ's analysis of *for colored girls* stresses the processes of self-discovery, self-healing, and spiritual transcendence. In Christ's interpretation, the truth of the "colored girls" growth into personhood and faith overshadows the bitter commentary and misinterpretation that characterize most criticism, which is that the play "trashes" Black men, and reveals things about Black people that would be better left unsaid or certainly not said in public. Christ, however, does not deal with the significance of the city in the play.

17 The basis for my thoughts on patriarchy comes from Adrienne Rich, "The Kingdom of the Fathers," in *Of Women Born: Motherhood as Experience and Institution* (New York: Norton, 1976), 56–83.
18 Ibid., 100.
19 Denise Levertov, "City Psalm," *The Sorrow Dance* (New York: New Directions, 1966), 72.

The killings continue, each second
pain and misfortune extend themselves
in the genetic chain, injustice is done knowingly, and the air
bears the dust of decayed hopes,
yet breathing those fumes, walking the thronged
pavements among crippled lives, jackhammers
raging, a parking lot painfully agleam
in the May sun, I have seen
not behind but within, within the
dull grief, blown grit, hideous
concrete facades, another grief, a gleam
as of dew, an abode of mercy,
have heard not behind but within noise
a humming that drifted into a quiet smile.
Nothing was changed, all was revealed otherwise;
not that horror was not, not that the killings did not continue,
not that I thought there was to be no more despair,
but that as if transparent all disclosed
an otherness that was blessèd, that was bliss.
I saw Paradise in the dust of the street.

20 The images in these three sentences are taken from the first poem in *for colored girls* entitled, "dark phases" (1–2).

Supplementary Readings and Media Resources

Supplementary Readings

Davis, Angela Y., *Blues Legacies and Black Feminisms: Gertrude "Ma" Rainey, Bessie Smith, and Billie Holiday* (New York: Pantheon, 1998).

Magistrale, Tony, "Doing Battle with the Wolf: A Critical Introduction to Wanda Coleman's Poetry," *Black American Literature Forum* 23:3 (Fall 1989): 539–57.

Reagon, Bernice Johnson, *We Who Believe in Freedom: Sweet Honey in the Rock ... Still on the Journey* (New York: Anchor Books, 1993).

Roberts, Robin, " 'Ladies First': Queen Latifah's Afrocentric Feminist Music Video," *African American Review* 28:2 (Summer 1994): 245–57.

Rose, Tricia, *Black Noise: Rap Music and Black Culture in Contemporary America* (Hanover, NH: Wesleyan University Press, 1994).

Selinger, Eric Murphy, "Trash, Art and Performance Poetry," *Parnassus: Poetry in Review* 23: 1–2 (Spring–Summer 1998): 356–81.

Media Resources

Parkerson, Michelle, *Gotta Make this Journey: Sweet Honey in the Rock*. 58 minutes, video, color, 1983. (Women Make Movies.)

Pellington, Mark, *The United States of Poetry*. 120 minutes, video, color, 1996. (PBS Video.)

Phipps, Cyrille, *Respect is Due*. 10 minutes, video, color, 1992. (Third World Newsreel.)

Robinson, Debra, *I Be Done Been Was Is*. 60 minutes, video, color, 1984. (Women Make Movies.)

Part V

Material Culture

Overview: Material Culture

In the midst of oppressive circumstances the possibilities exist for personal transformation that can lead to profound changes in society. The four chapters in Part V on "Material Culture" examine the means by which Black women have been able to survive and challenge adverse forces. The first chapter, "The Uses of the Erotic: The Erotic as Power," is written by Audre Lorde, well-respected social and cultural activist. Lorde's conception of "the erotic" provides an overarching paradigm to comprehend Black women's creative achievements in the face of overwhelming obstacles. The erotic is a crucial aspect of women's agency: the capacity to recognize that change is possible. It involves personal awareness of inner resources and consciousness that injustices, however manifested, can be stopped. The erotic is creative power merged with the spiritual and political. Encompassing "moral passion" fundamental to activism, Lorde explains that once it has been experienced, women refuse any oppression imposed on them. Lorde identifies the erotic as a "resource within each of us that lies in a deeply female and spiritual plane." The erotic personifies creative power and harmony, offering "a well of replenishing and provocative force."

The creative spirit and artistic undertakings sustaining Black women during centuries of enslavement are evident in a range of cultural forms. Quilts are tangible manifestations linking Black women's cultural traditions with a heritage of resistance. Quilt historian and scholar Cuesta Benberry, in "African American Quilts: Paradigms of Black Diversity," verifies that Black quilters have constructed quilts "since the earliest days of the Republic." Benberry counters early quilt historians' omission of Black women from quilt history and their later assertions that Black women made only one kind of quilt, the strip quilt. The strip quilt is connected in mainstream scholarly writings exclusively with West African textiles, thus their emphasis on a narrow aspect of Black quilters' involvement in quilt design and construction. By focusing on only one kind of quilt, researchers overlook the great contribution of Black quilters to quiltmaking developments.

Benberry's research proves that Black quilters were an integral part of American quiltmaking traditions, experts in all quiltmaking techniques, and originators of specific quilt designs. Moreover, enslaved women's skills in quilt construction were paralleled by their expertise in needlework, sewing, weaving, textiles, fiber construction, and dye-making. Although these were skills essential for their survival they were also means of aesthetic expression, accomplishments are all the more remarkable, notes Benberry, because of the hardship conditions under which enslaved women achieved them.

Quilt researcher Gladys-Marie Fry, in "Harriet Powers: Portrait of an African-American Quilter," documents the life of a legendary figure in quilt history. Harriet Powers (1837–1911), born into enslavement in Georgia, produced two exemplary quilts that have been preserved in museums. *The Bible Quilt*, created in 1886, is in the National Museum of Natural History, Smithsonian Institution; *The Creation of Animals*, made in 1896, is housed in the Museum of Fine Arts, Boston, Massachusetts. Fry declares that Power's Bible quilts are "visual masterpieces, jewels of creative imagination and artistic expression."

The two known surviving quilts by Powers are narrative quilts depicting Biblical stories. Fry traces the appliqué technique used by Powers to historic Eastern and Middle Eastern civilizations, noting its discernible roots in African culture. The figures and stories illustrated in the quilts are notably similar to the tapestries traditionally made by people of West Africa. These African retentions form a significant link of cultural continuity, establishing a powerful legacy for contemporary artists.

The historical forces impelling Black women's resistance by way of their imaginative constructions, is analyzed in "Empathy, Energy, and Eating: Politics and Power in *The Black Family Dinner Quilt Cookbook*," by Sally Bishop Shigley. The cookbook was designed as a fundraiser for the National Council of Negro Women and their National Center for African American Women. Additionally, it is a tribute to the Council's president, Dr. Dorothy I. Height, protégée of Mary McLeod Bethune, formerly enslaved, later founder of the organization. Dr. Bethune was a civil rights leader and Cabinet member during the presidency of Franklin Delano Roosevelt.

The cookbook is an encomium to the diverse communities of Black women who have held families together and have forged lives of possibilities and hope. Essential to both these endeavors are traditions and ceremonies referred to in the title, *The Black Family Dinner Quilt Cook-*

book. Communal activities surrounding quiltmaking and food preparation are critical areas of socialization and preservation of cultural continuities. Especially significant are the rituals involved in the preparation
and consumption of heritage foods, such as pigs' feet, hog jowls and
intestines, evocative of a history of principled survival despite inhumane
conditions. These customs and traditions perpetuate the symbolic values
of social groups. Joining the two in the cookbook links the transformative
capacity of enduring rituals with Black women's cultural history.

The videos selected to accompany these articles present images of Black
women in significant historical periods. Julie Dash's *Four Women* (1975) is
a seven-minute experimental film illustrating Black women's reaction to
their treatment in American society. Using a dancer moving to the words
and rhythms of Nina Simone's song "Four Women," Dash renders various
aspects of Black women's resistance and struggle against the oppressive
forces in their lives, including the tortuous journey through the Middle
Passage, enslavement, and the flight to freedom.

Independent filmmaker Zeinabu irene Davis created *Mother of the
River* (1995) to visualize the history of enslavement through the eyes of
a young Black girl. The film is based on a story with familiar themes
recurring throughout Africa and the African Diaspora. *Mother of the
River* depicts the experiences of a young, independent enslaved girl who
wanders into the woods and encounters a mysterious and magical woman
named Mother of the River. The narrative relies on the power of folktales
and riddles to dramatize a story of friendship between a young girl and a
woman of magic.

A Litany for Survival: The Life and Work of Audre Lorde (1995) documents the political, social, and cultural activism of this celebrated and
influential person. Produced and directed by independent filmmakers
Ada Gay Griffin and Michelle Parkerson, the film utilizes Lorde's poetry,
archival footage, music, and interviews to commemorate the vision of
Lorde. Audre Lorde linked three critical social justice movements: civil
rights, feminism, and the struggle for lesbian and gay rights. The film
contains interviews with Lorde in various settings, conversations with
family members and friends, and statements from artists and activists.
Among those appearing in the film are Barbara Smith, Sonia Sanchez,
Sapphire, Adrienne Rich, and Essex Hemphill.

16

Uses of the Erotic:
The Erotic as Power

Audre Lorde

Lorde, Audre, "Uses of the Erotic: The Erotic as Power." In Audre Lorde. *Sister Outsider* (Freedom, CA: The Crossing Press, 1984), pp. 53–9.

There are many kinds of power, used and unused, acknowledged or otherwise. The erotic is a resource within each of us that lies in a deeply female and spiritual plane, firmly rooted in the power of our unexpressed or unrecognized feeling. In order to perpetuate itself, every oppression must corrupt or distort those various sources of power within the culture of the oppressed that can provide energy for change. For women, this has meant a suppression of the erotic as a considered source of power and information within our lives.

We have been taught to suspect this resource, vilified, abused, and devalued within western society. On the one hand, the superficially erotic has been encouraged as a sign of female inferiority; on the other hand, women have been made to suffer and to feel both contemptible and suspect by virtue of its existence.

It is a short step from there to the false belief that only by the suppression of the erotic within our lives and consciousness can women be truly strong. But that strength is illusory, for it is fashioned within the context of male models of power.

As women, we have come to distrust that power which rises from our deepest and nonrational knowledge. We have been warned against it all our lives by the male world, which values this depth of feeling enough to keep women around in order to exercise it in the service of men, but which fears this same depth too much to examine the possibilities of it within themselves. So women are maintained at a distant/inferior position to be psychically milked, much the same way ants maintain colonies of aphids to provide a life-giving substance for their masters.

But the erotic offers a well of replenishing and provocative force to the woman who does not fear its revelation, nor succumb to the belief that sensation is enough.

The erotic has often been misnamed by men and used against women. It has been made into the confused, the trivial, the psychotic, the plasticized sensation. For this reason, we have often turned away from the exploration and consideration of the erotic as a source of power and information, confusing it with its opposite, the pornographic. But pornography is a direct denial of the power of the erotic, for it represents the suppression of true feeling. Pornography emphasizes sensation without feeling.

The erotic is a measure between the beginnings of our sense of self and the chaos of our strongest feelings. It is an internal sense of satisfaction to which, once we have experienced it, we know we can aspire. For having experienced the fullness of this depth of feeling and recognizing its power, in honor and self-respect we can require no less of ourselves.

It is never easy to demand the most from ourselves, from our lives, from our work. To encourage excellence is to go beyond the encouraged mediocrity of our society. But giving in to the fear of feeling and working to capacity is a luxury only the unintentional can afford, and the unintentional are those who do not wish to guide their own destinies.

This internal requirement toward excellence which we learn from the erotic must not be misconstrued as demanding the impossible from ourselves nor from others. Such a demand incapacitates everyone in the process. For the erotic is not a question only of what we do; it is a question of how acutely and fully we can feel in the doing. Once we know the extent to which we are capable of feeling that sense of satisfaction and completion, we can then observe which of our various life endeavors bring us closest to that fullness.

The aim of each thing which we do is to make our lives and the lives of our children richer and more possible. Within the celebration of the erotic in all our endeavors, my work becomes a conscious decision – a longed-for bed which I enter gratefully and from which I rise up empowered.

Of course, women so empowered are dangerous. So we are taught to separate the erotic demand from most vital areas of our lives other than sex. And the lack of concern for the erotic root and satisfactions of our work is felt in our disaffection from so much of what we do. For instance, how often do we truly love our work even at its most difficult?

The principal horror of any system which defines the good in terms of profit rather than in terms of human need, or which defines human need to the exclusion of the psychic and emotional components of that need – the principal horror of such a system is that it robs our work of its erotic value, its erotic power and life appeal and fulfillment. Such a system reduces work to a travesty of necessities, a duty by which we earn bread or oblivion for ourselves and those we love. But this is tantamount to blinding a painter and then telling her to improve her work, and to enjoy the act of painting. It is not only next to impossible, it is also profoundly cruel.

As women, we need to examine the ways in which our world can be truly different. I am speaking here of the necessity for reassessing the quality of all the aspects of our lives and of our work, and of how we move toward and through them.

The very word *erotic* comes from the Greek word *eros*, the personification of love in all its aspects – born of Chaos, and personifying creative power and harmony. When I speak of the erotic, then, I speak of it as an assertion of the lifeforce of women; of that creative energy empowered, the knowledge and use of which we are now reclaiming in our language, our history, our dancing, our loving, our work, our lives.

There are frequent attempts to equate pornography and eroticism, two diametrically opposed uses of the sexual. Because of these attempts, it has become fashionable to separate the spiritual (psychic and emotional) from the political, to see them as contradictory or antithetical. "What do you mean, a poetic revolutionary, a meditting gunrunner?" In the same way, we have attempted to separate the spiritual and the erotic, thereby reducing the spiritual to a world of flattened affect, a world of the ascetic who aspires to feel nothing. But nothing is farther from the truth. For the ascetic position is one of the highest fear, the gravest immobility. The severe abstinence of the ascetic becomes the ruling obsession. And it is one not of self-discipline but of self-abnegation.

The dichotomy between the spiritual and the political is also false, resulting from an incomplete attention to our erotic knowledge. For the bridge which connects them is formed by the erotic – the sensual – those physical, emotional, and psychic expressions of what is deepest and strongest and richest within each of us, being shared: the passions of love, in its deepest meanings.

Beyond the superficial, the considered phrase, "It feels right to me," acknowledges the strength of the erotic into a true knowledge, for what that means is the first and most powerful guiding light toward any understanding. And understanding is a handmaiden which can only wait upon, or clarify, that knowledge, deeply born. The erotic is the nurturer or nursemaid of all our deepest knowledge.

The erotic functions for me in several ways, and the first is in providing the power which comes from sharing deeply any pursuit with another person.

The sharing of joy, whether physical, emotional, psychic, or intellectual, forms a bridge between the sharers which can be the basis for understanding much of what is not shared between them, and lessens the threat of their difference.

Another important way in which the erotic connection functions is the open and fearless underlining of my capacity for joy. In the way my body stretches to music and opens into response, hearkening to its deepest rhythms, so every level upon which I sense also opens to the erotically satisfying experience, whether it is dancing, building a bookcase, writing a poem, examining an idea.

That self-connection shared is a measure of the joy which I know myself to be capable of feeling, a reminder of my capacity for feeling. And that deep and irreplaceable knowledge of my capacity for joy comes to demand from all of my life that it be lived within the knowledge that such satisfaction is possible, and does not have to be called *marriage*, nor *god*, nor *an afterlife*.

This is one reason why the erotic is so feared, and so often relegated to the bedroom alone, when it is recognized at all. For once we begin to feel deeply all the aspects of our lives, we begin to demand from ourselves and from our life-pursuits that they feel in accordance with that joy which we know ourselves to be capable of. Our erotic knowledge empowers us, becomes a lens through which we scrutinize all aspects of our existence, forcing us to evaluate those aspects honestly in terms of their relative meaning within our lives. And this is a grave responsibility, projected from within each of us, not to settle for the convenient, the shoddy, the conventionally expected, nor the merely safe.

During World War II, we bought sealed plastic packets of white, uncolored margarine, with a tiny, intense pellet of yellow coloring perched like a topaz just inside the clear skin of the bag. We would leave the margarine out for a while to soften, and then we would pinch the little pellet to break it inside the bag, releasing the rich yellowness into the soft pale mass of margarine. Then taking it carefully between, our fingers, we would knead it gently back and forth, over and over, until the color had spread throughout the whole pound bag of margarine, thoroughly coloring it.

I find the erotic such a kernel within myself. When released from its intense and constrained pellet, it flows through and colors my life with a kind of energy that heightens and sensitizes and strengthens all my experience.

We have been raised to fear the *yes* within ourselves, our deepest cravings. But, once recognized, those which do not enhance our future lose their power and can be altered. The fear of our desires keeps them suspect and indiscriminately powerful, for to suppress any truth is to give it strength beyond endurance. The fear that we cannot grow beyond whatever distortions we may find within ourselves keeps us docile and loyal and obedient, externally defined, and leads us to accept many facets of our oppression as women.

When we live outside ourselves, and by that I mean on external directives only rather than from our internal knowledge and needs, when we live away from those erotic guides from within ourselves, then our lives are limited by external and alien forms, and we conform to the needs of a structure that is not based on human need, let alone an individual's. But when we begin to live from within outward, in touch with the power of the erotic within ourselves, and allowing that power to inform and illuminate our actions upon the world around us, then we begin to be responsible to ourselves in the deepest sense. For as we begin to recognize our deepest feelings, we begin to give up, of necessity, being satisfied with suffering and self-negation, and with the numbness which so often seems like their only alternative in our society. Our acts against oppression become integral with self, motivated and empowered from within.

In touch with the erotic, I become less willing to accept powerlessness, or those other supplied states of being which are not native to me, such as resignation, despair, self-effacement, depression, self-denial.

And yes, there is a hierarchy. There is a difference between painting a back fence and writing a poem, but only one of quantity. And there is, for me, no difference between writing a good poem and moving into sunlight against the body of a woman I love.

This brings me to the last consideration of the erotic. To share the power of each other's feelings is different from using another's feelings as we would use a kleenex. When we look the other way from our experience, erotic or otherwise, we use rather than share the feelings of those others who participate in the experience with us. And use without consent of the used is abuse.

In order to be utilized, our erotic feelings must be recognized. The need for sharing deep feeling is a human need. But within the european-american tradition, this need is satisfied by certain proscribed erotic comings-together. These occasions are almost always characterized by a simultaneous looking away, a pretense of calling them something else, whether a religion, a fit, mob violence, or even playing doctor. And this misnaming of the need and the deed give rise to that distortion which results in pornography and obscenity – the abuse of feeling.

When we look away from the importance of the erotic in the development and sustenance of our power, or when we look away from ourselves as we satisfy our erotic needs in concert with others, we use each other as objects of satisfaction rather than share our joy in the satisfying, rather than make connection with our similarities and our differences. To refuse to be conscious of what we are feeling at any time, however comfortable that might seem, is to deny a large part of the experience, and to allow ourselves to be reduced to the pornographic, the abused, and the absurd.

The erotic cannot be felt secondhand. As a Black lesbian feminist, I have a particular feeling, knowledge, and understanding for those sisters with whom I have danced hard, played, or even fought. This deep participation has often been the forerunner for joint concerted actions not possible before.

But this erotic charge is not easily shared by women who continue to operate under an exclusively european-american male tradition. I know it was not available to me when I was trying to adapt my consciousness to this mode of living and sensation.

Only now, I find more and more women-identified women brave enough to risk sharing the erotic's electrical charge without having to look away, and without distorting the enormously powerful and creative nature of that exchange. Recognizing the power of the erotic within our lives can give us the energy to pursue genuine change within our world, rather than merely settling for a shift of characters in the same weary drama.

For not only do we touch our most profoundly creative source, but we do that which is female and self-affirming in the face of a racist, patriarchal, and anti-erotic society.

17

African American Quilts:
Paradigms of Black Diversity

Cuesta Benberry

Benberry, Cuesta. "African American Quilts: Paradigms of Black Diversity." *International Review of African-American Art*, 12(3) (Summer, 1995): 30–7

African Americans have made quilts for approximately two centuries yet the phenomenon was conspicuously absent in the annuals of American quilt history until the publication of a few ground-breaking studies in the 1970s. Interest in the topic grew steadily, and today individuals working in a number of fields – quilt historians, art historians, folklorists, anthropologists, literature professors, feminist authors and independent scholars – are producing articles, essays, treatises, monographs, comparative studies, dissertations and exhibition catalogue texts on this subject. Their writings explore topics such as the origins of African American quilts; aesthetics, design characteristics and symbolic meanings; regional variations, the chronological development of African American quilts, and have provoked debates about what the various research findings actually reveal.

Three events (two in 1976 and one in 1977) were seminal efforts to promote the appreciation of African American quilts: Regenia Perry's inclusion of the Harriet Powers' *Bible Quilt* in her exhibition *Selections of Nineteenth century Afro-American Art at the Metropolitan Museum of Art*; Gladys-Marie Fry's landmark essay "Harriet Powers: Portrait of a Black Quilter" in *Missing Pieces: Georgia Folk Art, 1770–1776*; and Roland Freeman's exhibition of quilts from the Mississippi Heartland, *More than Just Something to Keep you Warm*. It was, however, when the scope of the scholars' examinations moved from a specific theme (Harriet Powers Bible quilts or Mississippi Black-made quilts) to a general theme (an all-encompassing study of African American quilts) that the public became aware of the diverse nature of African American quilting.

A major thrust of my work has been to demonstrate that there is no such thing as a "typical" African American quilt.

Other indicators of the escalating enthusiasm for African American quilts have been the presentation of local and nationally-traveled quilt exhibitions[1] and the formation of quilters' circles and organizations. For example, many Black quiltmakers, who formerly worked in isolation and were unaware of each other's works, became united when Carolyn Mazloomi organized an international association, the Women of Color Quilters' Network.[2] The Network also became a vehicle for promoting the works of modern African American quilters.

One significant area of inquiry concerns the various means by which African American quilts can be differentiated from quilts made by white Americans. Researchers in this area include Robert Farris Thompson, Mary Arnold Twining, John Michael Vlach, Maude Wahlman, Gladys-Marie Fry and Eli Leon. Citing Black quiltmakers' repeated use of the strip construction technique, these researchers established a school of thought which identifies a "typical" African American quilt – a strip quilt that is linked to West African textiles (woven on narrow looms in narrow strips and then sewn edge-to-edge). This school proposes that despite African Americans' long residence in America, their retention of unconscious cultural memories strongly influences them to make strip quilts. Because of a lack of knowledge of quilt history, however, this school was unaware that strip quilts are not a quilt technique unique to African Americans. In the North of England and in Wales, strip quilts have been a favored form since the late eighteenth century; and in Southern, rural, impoverished white American communities, strip quilts were frequently made as utilitarian bedcovers.

After locating a small group of Black-made quilts that visually differ profoundly from the accepted aesthetic of traditional American patchwork quilts, proponents of the "typical" school examined the quilts closely for stylistic variances, construction techniques, fabric color choices and symbolic motifs and developed visual criteria for recognizing African American quilts: strips forming and organizing the design space; large-scale designs; strong, highly contrasting colors; offbeat patterns; multiple rhythms.[3] When this brief and convenient checklist of characteristics was proposed and accepted as fact, some absurd uses of the inventory were made. Armed with a catechism of African American quilt visual and construction "absolutes," persons inexperienced in quilt construction and completely untutored in quilt history, could with self-confidence, label even the most anonymous quilt as an "African American quiltwork."

Karl Kusserow's essay "Attributing an Anonymous Quilt to an African American Maker"[4] is a prototypal example of the phrase "a little knowledge can be a dangerous thing." Kusserow attempted to prove an anonymous quilt's African American origins by applying Maude Wahlman's six criteria for identifying an African American quilt. Handicapped by an obvious lack of understanding of even elementary quilt construction methods, Kusserow's analyses were seriously skewed. When he stated, "Similarly, African American quiltmakers frequently fashion their quilts from numerous discrete blocks that are sewn together in strips[;] [t]hese, in turn, are joined in the creation of the larger complete quilt top,"[5] Kusserow was apparently unaware that he had described a universal, basic block construction process of quiltmaking, and not a procedure exclusive to Black quilters.

Kusserow further asserted, "The second feature typifying African American quilts is their frequent use of large design elements," and, in an astoundingly contrived way, he applied that description to the anonymous quilt. There is not one large-scale design element on the anonymous quilt! Not only did he display a very superficial knowledge of quilt construction, he appeared, moreover, not to fully comprehend the substance of Wahlman's criteria on which he based his thesis. When Kusserow cited Maude Wahlman's criterion of "the use of bright colors," he referred to two quilt blocks out of 42 blocks on the anonymous quilt as containing vivid hues. Wahlman's actual interpretation is quite different. Discussing African American quilts' bright colors within the context of the quilts' *overall visual impact*, she characterizes the colors as large, brilliantly hued fabrications – not as one or two small blocks among many. She points out that "bright colors and large designs are more important, since they can be seen from a distance."[6] The anonymous quilt's most noticeable feature is the intricate piecing of tiny strips – not strong, bright colors and large design elements.[7] While it is hoped that the handsome, nonconformist, anonymous quilt will eventually be proven to have an African American origin, Kusserow's gravely flawed treatise does not supply that confirmation.

Nineteenth-century African American Quilts

A study of nineteenth-century African American quilts and quiltmakers runs counter to some of the popular myths currently being circulated about Black-made quiltworks. Findings from research conducted on the works of both enslaved and free Blacks of the antebelum period and emancipated Black quilters demonstrate the enormous diversity of African American quilters. Extant quilts from the 100-year span are testaments to the versatility of African American quilters who employed every known quiltmaking technique. These quilts, consisting of both quickly made, utilitarian bedcovers and meticulously crafted works, exhibit a number of techniques, including fine piecing, appliqué, whole cloth quilting, thread embroidery, broderie perse (cutout chintz) – singularly or in various combinations, and in skill level, range from pedestrian to extraordinarily accomplished. Based on a group of quilts made by African Americans living in the South during the mid to late twentieth century, the "typical" school inaccurately represents these quilts as being Black people's sole, original contribution to quiltmaking in America.

Surveying the historical record for glimpses of African American textile creation, one gleans an important insight: Black seamstresses achieved remarkable skill despite often having to work and live under degrading, abject conditions. Influenced by romantic novels, charming but unrealistic paintings and nostalgic films of life in the Old South, the notion persists that, compared with field slaves, slave seamstresses enjoyed a superior, rather idyllic existence because they often lived in their masters' homes. However, slaves' living conditions varied, depending upon the character and temperament of their masters. Angelina Grimké, a noted member of Female Anti-Slavery Society, testified:

> I have also known instances where seamstresses were kept in cold entries to work by staircase lamps for one or two hours, every evening in winter – they could not see without standing up all the time, though the work was often too large and heavy for them to sew it in that position without great inconvenience, and yet were expected to do their work well with cold fingers, and standing up, as if they had been sitting by a comfortable fire and provided with the necessary light.[8]

Eliza Jane Cason, a slave on a Missouri plantation, pieced a green and yellow tulip quilt that she took to Iowa upon receiving her emancipation. Memories of her life during slavery were so agonizing, she never wanted to speak of those times with her family. Years later Eliza Jane Cason's daughter donated the quilt to the State Historical Society of Iowa.[9]

In her book *Behind the Scenes: Thirty Years a Slave and Four Years in the White House*, Elizabeth Keckley, a consummate seamstress, describes how she was severely beaten by her slave master.[10]

In recent years, a mystifying dichotomy about the works of enslaved seamstresses has developed. Some slave seamstresses fashioned the most exquisite, deftly sewn, delicately embellished garments for their mistresses – articles which are praised and viewed with awe by scholars. Quilts of slave seamstresses showing a comparable level of skill, however, do not receive a comparable acclaim from these scholars. Quilts by Black makers that display high level technical skill and sophistication of design are not considered legitimate or "true African American" quilts. Rather than to see the exceptional quilts of the enslaved needleworkers as evidence of the diversity achieved by African Americans – Black people have made every kind of quilt known! – the slave quilts are demoted to mere mechanical reflections of the white slave mistresses' ideas and instructions. The quilt scholars do not take into account the numerous slave quiltmakers, who were self-taught seamstresses or who had received instructions from other Black women, usually relatives or friends.

Elizabeth Keckley is an outstanding example of a needle worker who was trained within the slave community. Taught to sew by her slave mother, Elizabeth Keckley grew to be an excellent seamstress. (Keckley sewed for two white women who could not sew at all, initially for her slave mistress, Mrs. Garland.) After buying her freedom and that of her son, Keckley worked in the White House as dressmaker for Mary Todd Lincoln, President Abraham Lincoln's wife. In her memoir, Keckley notes that she never saw Mrs. Lincoln with a needle in her hand.[11] Around 1870, Keckley made a pieced and embroidered silk quilt from scraps of Mary Lincoln's gowns. At its center, an embroidered word blazed with personal meaning for the maker. LIBERTY.[12] The Keckley quilt is now in the collection of Ross Trump.

A dazzling, original appliqué and pieced quilt was designed and created around 1850 by a young slave girl who lived on a plantation in McCracken County in the Jackson Purchase area, a Confederate stronghold of Kentucky. Each large block in this composition (now known as the *Reed Estate Quilt*) has a feathered circular motif in the center, surrounded by four red, green and yellow pieced and appliquéed fan-shaped pieces, also feathered. Interspersed between the fan motifs are single flowers, possibly tulips, and the overall quilting is exceptionally executed. The *Reed Estate Quilt* is in the collection of Averil Mathis.[13]

Although the census of 1860 recorded the presence of 1,000,000 free Blacks in the North, and another 488,000 free Blacks in the South, few quilts made by free Black seamstresses during the antebellum era have been located. Free Blacks – persons who were born free, manumitted, or were fugitives from slavery – lived in less concentrated, much broader geographic areas than did the enslaved population. Demographic details for the frequently fluctuating population of free Blacks are difficult to obtain in the many areas of the South where records were not carefully kept. Despite being located in a slave state, Baltimore, however, was an exception. Its early city directories contain a separate section for the free Black population, listing them by name, occupation and address[14] – data which have supplied important leads for my research.

Two broderie perse quilts, one from Baltimore, now in a private collection and another from the Avery Research Center collection in Charleston, South Carolina, were made with the utmost finesse. In trying to determine how these free Black quiltmakers acquired such virtuosity, I uncovered surprising information: there were schools, called academies, for free Black girls in antebellum Baltimore! In one academy, the girls were taught to sew by their Black principal, an Episcopal priest. In the Maryland Historical

Society's collection, there is a well-done sampler, dated 1830, executed by one of the free Black girls who attended the academy. Jennifer Goldsborough, chief curator of the Maryland Historical Society, has described this little known but important African American institution as a "fine academy for Black girls in a slave state at a time when hardly any girl of color or persuasion went to school, headed by a Black male priest who did and taught fine needlework at a time when both education and religion were technically illegal for African Americans, under the auspices of a wealthy white landowner."[15]

The antebellum lives and work of free Black needleworkers require continued research and promises to lead us to fascinating byways. My investigations have already revealed how freed Blacks, who were repatriated to Sierre Leone and Liberia, transported American quiltmaking styles to these areas of West Africa where the craft/ art flourishes today.[16] Because a number of the African American quiltmakers were emancipated slaves, it was possible for a seamstress to have one of her quilts designated as "slave-made" and another, identified as "made by a former slave." There is, however, a common practice to describe all quilts constructed by a person who was once enslaved as "slave made" regardless of creator's status at the time of the quilt's production. This practice exemplifies the easy generalizations and slipshod analyses that are often applied to African American quiltmaking.

Two of the nation's most famous quilts were made in the 1880s and 1890s by a former slave, Harriet Powers, of Athens, Georgia. Housed, one each, at the National Museum of American History, Smithsonian Institution and at the Museum of Fine Arts, Boston, Harriet Powers' Bible quilts have transcended mere popularity and are cherished to the extent that they have become virtual American icons. Analyzed extensively for continuities of West African design traditions, the quilts have been the subject of research studies, newspaper and magazine articles, scholarly essays, books and films.[17] While the Powers' quilts are acknowledged as the foremost examples of the Bible quilt genre, recent investigations find that the making of such quilts was not uncommon in Southern African American communities. Bible quilts provided the means through which Black people's fervent religious ardor and vigorous narrative tradition took dramatic visual form – a medium particularly appealing to African American needleworkers.

The *Bible Scenes* quilt made in the Drake family, Thomaston, Georgia, at the turn of the century, consists of four large pictorial blocks of the Garden of Eden and the Crucifixion.[18] On each of the two Garden of Eden blocks is a red and blue picket fence surrounding the Garden of Eden. Art historian Rosalind Jeffries interprets the Garden of Eden blocks as an "aerial view of a picket fence strongly suggest[ing] railroad tracks." She notes that the quilt "was made at a time when the Underground Railroad was remembered…"[19] In my youth, I remember seeing my Southern rural relatives and farm friends frequently enclosing their flower gardens in fences because their flower gardens were their special places of beauty. That the Southern rural Georgia creator of the *Bible Scenes* quilt would fence in her Garden of Eden, a special place of pristine beauty to a religious person, does not seem to be far-fetched idea. The *Bible Scenes* quilt is owned by Shelly Zegart.

Emancipation did generate a mass exodus of slaves from Southern farms and plantations, yet some persons chose to continue to live with their former slave masters. They included women who remained in those homes to become paid housekeepers and nursemaids and others who were not paid money but who elected to stay on, nevertheless. Hannah Morrow's life on a plantation near Lexington, Kentucky, was not changed by the Emancipation Proclamation but her personal status was. A highly proficient needleworker, Morrow became a professional seamstress in the area – paid a small salary by her former owners and obtaining considerable outside work for which she was also paid. After living on the plantation for many years, she married and moved away. With her earnings, she evidently purchased new fabrics for her quilts because her *Robbing Peter to Pay Paul* quilt is color-coordinated – white dot on red fabric alternating with red dot on white fabric blocks; there are no scrap fabrics in the quilt. Some of Hannah Morrow's quilts were handed down to her descendants.

Toward the end of the nineteenth century, African American needle-women were permitted to enter their works in a major event, the Chicago world's fair. Although confined to a racially segregated section, their quilts were among the various needlework items exhibited at the 1893 World Columbian Exposition. Elizabeth Keckley, who was at this time a home economics teacher at Wilberforce University in Ohio, took samples of her students' work and entered them in the fair. The Black women's handiwork was outstanding and received a laudatory review in the *New York Times* under the heading "Work of the Colored Women."[20]

The quilt of a former Virginia slave repatriated to Liberia was also entered at the 1893 fair but not in the segregated American colored women's section. Martha Ann Rick's *Coffee Tree* quilt arrived in Her Majesty, Queen Victoria's British Needlework contingent to the venue.[21] Ricks had given the quilt to Queen Victoria during a special audience with the Queen at Windsor Castle.

Since the earliest days of the Republic, countless thousands of African Americans, mostly women, have – despite bondage, hardships and oft-times cruel treatment – utilized every known quiltmaking technique, made every type of quilt, participated in the evolutionary development of what is now called the "traditional American patchwork quilt" and contributed original concepts to American quiltmaking.

When scholars discovered a unique group of quilts made by African Americans during the mid to late twentieth century, the news was received

with joy; Black-made quilts had been ignored far too long. As the claims of
the researchers regarding their discovery of the "true" African American
quilt stridently mounted, an effect was that the thousands of "other" Black-
made quilts were considered of no moment. A kind of segregation was
imposed on the African American quilt world. There should be a clear
indication that the researchers were investigating one type of African American quilt in the vast panorama of quilts made by African Americans. To do
less is to relegate quilts that do not conform to the scholars' absolutist
"Black" criteria to a place of inconsequence, again, as in slavery and Jim
Crow separation – a fate African American quiltmakers do not deserve.

Notes

1 *Nationally Traveled African American Quilt Exhibitions: The Afro-American
   Tradition in the Decorative Arts* (partially quilts) (1978), curated by John Michael
   Vlach. *Ten Afro-American Quilters* (1983), curated by Maude Wahlman. *Who'd A
   Thought It: Improvisation in African American Quiltmaking* (1987), curated by
   Eli Leon. *Stitching Memories: African American Story Quilts* (1990), curated by
   Eva Ungar Grudin, Williams College. *Stitched from the Soul: Slave Quilts from the
   Antebellum South* (1990), curated by Gladys-Marie Fry. *Always There: The African
   American Presence in American Quilts* (1992) curated by Cuesta Benberry. *More
   than Just Something to Keep you Warm: Tradition and Change in African Amer-
   ican Quiltmaking* (1992), curated by Roland Freeman. *Signs and Symbols: Amer-
   ican Images in African American Quilts* (1993), curated by Maude Wahlman.
   Spirit of the Cloth: The Women of Color Quilter's Network (1993), curated by
   Edjohnetta Miller.
2 Sandra German, "Surfacing: The Inevitable Rise of the Women of Color Quilters'
   Network," *Uncoverings*, 1993, ed., Laurel Horton, pp. 137–67.
3 Maude Wahlman and John Scully, "Aesthetic Principles in Afro-American
   Quilts," *Afro-American Folk Art and Crafts* (Boston: G. K. Hall, 1983), p. 86.
4 Karl Kusserow, "Attributing an Anonymous Quilt to an African-American
   Maker," *Folk Art* (Spring 1994), pp. 46–9.
5 Ibid., p. 46.
6 Maude S. Wahlman. *Signs and Symbols: American Images in African-American
   Quilts* (New York: Studio Books in association with Museum of American Folk
   Art, 1993), p. 35.
7 I saw and closely examined this quilt in 1986 before it ever went to Nashville, TN,
   to the Kramer's "Heart of the Country Antique Show" where it was sold to the
   New York dealers Kelter and Malce, who subsequently donated the quilt to the
   Museum of American Folk Art. Kusserow's research reveals no more factual
   information about the anonymous quilt than what was known in 1986. The
   colors in the quilt are not vivid, but the intricate piecing makes the cover a *tour
   de force*.

8 Gerda Lerner, *Black Women in White America: A Documentary History* (New York: Vintage Books, 1972), p. 21.

9 Patricia Cooney, "A Quilt's Journey: Up from Slavery," *The Des Moines Register* (June 26, 1977), p. 4E.

10 Elizabeth Keckley, *Behind the Scenes: Thirty Years a Slave and Four Years in the White House* (New York: G. W. Carleton, 1868; reprint New York: Arno Press, 1968), pp. 36–7.

11 Ibid., p. 225.

12 Jennifer Lane. "The Quilt that Mrs. Keckley Made," *Ohio Antiques Review* (February 1981), p. 23.

13 Averil Mathis, "On Display," *The American Quilter* (Summer 1986); Deborah Peterson, "Common Threads," *St. Louis Post Dispatch* (November 8, 1992), p. 1S.

14 Jennifer Goldsborough, chief curator, Maryland Historical Society, Baltimore, letter to author August 11, 1994.

15 Ibid.

16 Cuesta Benberry, *Always There: The African American Presence in American Quilts* (Louisville, KY: The Kentucky Quilt Project, Inc. 1992), pp. 35–9.

17 Gladys-Marie Fry, "Harriet Powers: Portrait of a Black Quilter," in *Missing Pieces; Georgia Folk Art, 1770–1976* (Atlanta, GA: Georgia Council for the Humanities, 1976), pp. 16–23.
   ——, *Stitched from the Soul: Slave Quilts from the Antebellum South* (New York: Museum of American Folk Art and Dutton Studio Books, 1990). Regenia A. Perry, *Harriet Powers' Bible Quilts* (New York: Rizzoli International Pub. 1994). Mary E. Lyons, *Stitching Stars: The Story Quilts of Harriet Powers* (New York: Charles Scribner's Sons, 1993).

18 Benberry, pp. 43–5.

19 Rosalind Jeffries, "African Retentions in African American Quilts and Artifacts," *International Review of African American Art*, Vol. 11, No. 2, 1994, pp. 32–3.

20 "Work of the Colored Women," *New York Times*, June 10, 1893.

21 Cuesta Benberry, "A Quilt for Queen Victoria," *Quilter's Newsletter Magazine* (February 1987), pp. 24–5.

18

Harriet Powers:
Portrait of an African-American Quilter

Gladys-Marie Fry

Fry, Gladys-Marie. "Harriet Powers: Portrait of an African-American Quilter." In
Gladys-Marie Fry *Stitched from the Soul: Slave Quilts from the Ante-Bellum South*, (New
York: Dutton Books, 1990), pp. 84–91. (Originally published in the Catalog *Missing Pieces:
Georgia Folk Art 1770–1976*) (Atlanta, GA: Georgia Council for the Humanities, 1976),
pp. 16–23.

Until recently very little was known about the life of Harriet Powers. Her
name, her state of residence, and the existence of her two quilts, both in
major museums, constituted her total legacy to the world. Yet it is precisely
this powerful legacy that makes her worth knowing. Her quilts are visual
masterpieces, jewels of creative imagination and artistic expression.

Harriet Powers was an African-American woman, originally a slave. Her
entire communication with the world was visual and oral, which she
expressed in narrative quilts using themes from her own experience and
techniques from the age-old crafts of African Americans.

Fascinated with stories from oral tradition, Mrs. Powers used three types:
local legends, biblical stories, and accounts of astronomical occurrences. Two
local legends are included on her quilts: those of an independent hog named
Betts, who ran from Georgia to Virginia (this is a traditional motif that
became fastened to Georgia); and a man frozen at his jug of liquor. Each
has the ring of a local incident, but is actually a traditional narrative known in
several versions.

The core of her religious material dealt with legends about biblical heroes,
usually those who had struggled successfully against overwhelming odds –
Noah, Moses, Jonah, and Job. Some of her material can be considered "the
Bible of the folk," in that she depicted traditional stories that extend biblical
narratives. The serpent is portrayed in the Garden of Eden with feet, before
he suffered God's curse. Adam's rib, from which Eve was made, is

prominently featured. The miracle of creation itself provides the subject matter for several blocks.

In addition to biblical folk materials, Harriet Powers seemed especially interested in astronomical phenomena. Legendary accounts of actual events – eclipses, meteors, and comets – were infused with traditional motifs. As these legends circulated in oral tradition, they became formularized.

In Harriet Powers's quilt lies an almost intriguing classic tale of the South: the skilled work of the slave craftsman embedded in the creator's African heritage and preserved by the patron.

Although narrative quilts are distinctly an American art form, they use an appliqué technique traceable to historic Eastern and Middle Eastern civilizations, but having discernible roots in African culture. Harriet Powers's quilt forms a direct link to the tapestries traditionally made by the Fon people of Abomey, the ancient capital of Dahomey, West Africa.

Slaves brought to the South this knowledge of appliqué, a technique in which design elements are cut from cloth and sewn onto background fabric after first being narrowly turned under to form a hemmed edge. Men made the appliqué in Dahomey, but the craft was part of the culture; in America, slave women perpetuated this kind of needlework.

Harriet Powers was born a slave in Georgia on October 29, 1837, during the period (1775–1875) when appliqué flourished in the South. The two quilts Mrs. Powers is known to have made follow the narrative tradition of depicting stories circulating orally, in different versions, and believed to be true, including biblical stories, and in her second quilt, local legends and astronomical phenomena.

Mrs. Powers's quilts can be compared with Dahomean tapestries in terms of design, construction technique, and the retention of stories associated with pictorial representations. The design process has been handed down for hundreds of years. Various figures are cut and appliquéed against a background cloth of black or gold. Humans are depicted in red or black. Animals are represented in colors not necessarily true to life, including purple, blue, green, and white. Patterns or templates of each design element are cut out of stiff paper and passed down from generation to generation in the Dahomean culture.

The construction technique may be derived from the bas-reliefs that decorated the wall of the palace in Abomey. Once cut, the cloth figures are basted onto the background cloth to ensure smoothness. Traditionally, the cloth is laid flat so that a running back or chain stitch can be directed away from the body to further ensure smoothness. In recent years, and such is the case with Mrs. Powers's quilts, the appliquéed cloth has been machine-made.

Often referred to as "living history books," these pictorial tapestries vary in subject from designer to designer. Tradition determines style and composition, but the individual designer decides which stories to relate, choosing from a common repertory. Stories from oral tradition and oral history are associated with each of the symbols. The Dahomeans most frequently reproduced symbols of the eleven kings who ruled Dahomey, connecting proverbs and sayings with the emblems of each king. Mrs. Powers's themes draw from well-known biblical stories, using symbols such as stars and figures of people and animals.

Just as biblical animals figure prominently in the stories illustrated by Harriet Powers, so many of the Dahomean tapestries contain animals as the central figures of proverbs or as symbols representing kings. Many of the kings are identified by totem animals, particularly the buffalo, pig, fish, bird, rooster, and lion. Stylistically, the animals on the Powers quilt and on the Dahomean tapestries are very similar. In both cases, the progression indicates the developing action through symbols.

Harriet Powers's fascination with biblical animals and characters probably stemmed from hearing vivid sermons in church on Sundays. According to Jennie Smith, the white woman who bought her first quilt, Mrs. Powers committed these sermons to memory and translated her impressions onto her quilts. Miss Smith observed that as evidence of her fondness for animals, Harriet expressed a desire to attend the Barnum and Bailey Circus when it came to Athens, Georgia, about 1890, because she wanted to see "all the Bible animals." But one compelling consideration that kept her away was the belief that it was a sin to go into a circus arena. (She may also have lacked the price of admission.) Her religion appeared to be fundamentalist, so that she believed in the literal word of the Bible.

Harriet Powers might have remained unknown outside of Athens had it not been for Jennie Smith, a Southern white woman of upper-middle-class connections. Miss Smith was responsible for bringing Mrs. Powers's first known quilt to the attention of the general public in Athens and Atlanta in the late nineteenth and early twentieth centuries.

Jennie Smith was born Oneita Virginia Smith in Athens in 1862. An artist of considerable local reputation, she received extensive training at the Lucy Cobb School in Athens and later in Baltimore, New York, and Paris. After living in the North and abroad, Jennie Smith returned to Athens and became head of the Art Department at Lucy Cobb for over 50 years. She was known affectionately by her many friends and pupils as "Miss Jennie." She died a spinster at the age of 84 in Athens in 1946.

Jennie Smith purchased Harriet Powers's first known quilt about 1890. Following her death, her estate was liquidated by Hal Heckman, head of the accounting department at the University of Georgia from 1921 to 1966. The quilt became part of the odds and ends of the estate that had not been specifically provided for in Miss Jennie's will. Mr. Heckman kept the quilt, eventually giving it to the Smithsonian, where it is now displayed.

Preserved along with the quilt was an 18-page handwritten narrative of about 1891, in which Miss Smith describes the series of events that led to her purchase of the 1886 quilt. The narrative is written in an extemporaneous prose style characteristic of the nineteenth century. She uses firm, vivid English, enlivened with humor and wit. She writes a little self-consciously, as if instinctively aware that her comments would be read by outsiders. Sprinkled throughout the narrative are references to pictorial symbols used by people in various cultures. These comments help to set Harriet Powers's quilt in its proper artistic and historic perspective.

This narrative is a major document because Jennie Smith is the only person to have left an eyewitness account of the remarkable Harriet Powers. It seems that Miss Smith viewed her as an exception within the general nineteenth-century idea of African-American inferiority. Although the narrative contains the stereotypical description of African Americans as musical but not artistic, religious but still liars and thieves, Miss Smith saw Harriet as a deeply religious woman of modesty and piety.

A Cotton Fair of 1886 first put the two women in touch with each other. The fair, according to Jennie Smith's narrative, had more attractions than the annual county fair; it included a Wild West show, two cotton weddings, and a circus.

Apparently the fair had a craft exhibit, where Jennie Smith saw Mrs. Powers's quilt hanging in a corner. Immediately fascinated by the originality of the design, she tracked down the maker. Miss Smith wrote: "I found the owner, a negro woman, who lived in the country on a little farm whereon she and her husband made a respectable living. She is about sixty-five years old, of a clear ginger cake color, and is a very clean and interesting woman who loves to talk of her 'old miss' and her life 'befo de wah.'" In fact, Harriet Powers was only 49 at the time of their first meeting. A life of hard work must have made her look considerably older.

Jennie Smith offered to buy the quilt after the 1886 fair, but Harriet refused to sell it then for any price. About 1890, Harriet, experiencing financial difficulty, sent word to Miss Smith that the quilt was now for sale. Jennie Smith was unable to purchase it in 1890, but apparently kept in contact with Mrs. Powers. In 1891 Jennie reopened negotiations. Her own words are very interesting:

> Last year I sent her word that I would buy it if she still wanted to dispose of it. She arrived one afternoon in front of my door in an ox-cart with the precious burden in her lap encased in a clean flour sack, which was still enveloped in a crocus sack.
>
> She offered it for ten dollars, but I told her I only had five to give. After going out consulting with her husband she returned and said "Owin to de

hardness of de times, my ole man lows I'd better tech hit." Not being a new woman she obeyed.

After giving me a full description of each scene with great earnestness, she departed but has been back several times to visit the darling offspring of her brain.

She was only in a measure consoled for its loss when I promised to save her all my scraps.

It is one of the ironies of history that, heartbreaking as it was for Harriet to part with her quilt, its sale to Jennie Smith preserved it for posterity.

"It is my intention," wrote Jennie Smith, "to exhibit this quilt in the Colored Building at the Cotton States Exposition in Atlanta, and I hope all who are interested in art or religion in their primitive state will take the time to go to see it."

The 1895 Cotton States and International Exposition in Atlanta drew the participation of 11 Southern states, including Georgia, and several foreign countries. One of the outstanding features of this exhibition was a so-called Negro Building, constructed for ten thousand dollars from funds raised in the African-American community. Each participating state had an allocated exhibition area. The exhibits included products of various trades, such as carpentry, furniture making, brickwork, carriage and wagon building, wheel-wrighting, harness making, and tinwork; agricultural products raised by African Americans on their own farms; mechanical goods assembled and built by African Americans, such as engines and boilers; photographs and models of African-American-owned businesses; paintings; and needle-work.

Unfortunately, the official list of individual exhibitors no longer exists. It seems almost certain, however, that Jennie Smith did send the quilt to the Atlanta Exposition, where it was seen by the faculty ladies of Atlanta University. These women commissioned a second narrative quilt to be made by Harriet Powers as a gift in 1898 to the Reverend Charles Cuthbert Hall, president of the Union Theological Seminary and for many years chairman of the board of trustees of Atlanta University. Hall's son, the Reverend Basil Douglas Hall, inherited the quilt from his father and sold it to the Russian-American folk art collector Maxim Karolik, who gave it to the Museum of Fine Arts in Boston in 1964.

Though both her quilts have been preserved, little besides her birthdate is known about Harriet Powers. No information is available from orally trans-mitted family histories or reminiscences, because Mrs. Powers apparently has no known living descendants. Nor could dozens of elderly residents inter-viewed in Clarke and the surrounding counties in Georgia provide any clues about her life.

It is only from official records that we can glimpse bits and pieces of Harriet Powers's family history. Unfortunately, there are large gaps in the total picture because information about births, marriages, deaths, and wills was not recorded as completely for the African-American community as it was for whites in the nineteenth century. Valuable but limited information concerning the Powers family is contained in the census data, tax rolls, and records of deeds for Clarke County.

The census of 1870 for the state of Georgia firmly establishes the family in Clarke County, listing the names of Harriet Powers, her husband, and their three children. Armstead Powers, her husband and head of the household, was 38 at the time the census was taken. Four years older than Harriet, he gave his occupation as farmhand. Harriet, 34 at the time, listed her occupation as "keeping house." The family owned no property in 1870, but estimated their personal estate to be worth three hundred dollars. Georgia was listed as the place of birth for the entire family. Census records indicate that neither Harriet nor Armstead could read or write. Two of the Powers children were apparently born in slavery: a daughter, Armanda, born in 1855, and a son, LeonJoe, born in 1860. Nancy, their youngest child, was born in 1866. All three children were living at home in 1870.

An examination of county tax records for a 60-year period provides a few additional clues concerning the family's living circumstances. The name Armstead Powers, listed as "Arms," appeared for the first time in the 1870 Clarke County Tax Digest. In that year Powers paid one dollar in poll taxes, and no area of residence was indicated. The next entry appeared in 1873. Armstead Powers again paid one dollar in poll taxes. The family resided in that year in the Buck Branch, Winterville district of Clarke County. Records indicate that the family alternated between the Buck Branch and Sandy Creek districts of Clarke County from 1870 to 1911. At least 12 years were spent in Buck Branch. The remaining 24 years, for which there are records, were spent in Sandy Creek.

The Powerses appeared to be a successful farm family. They gradually acquired a stock of animals, including horses, mules, cattle, and oxen. They owned plantation and mechanical tools. Their personal property, such as household furniture, clothing, and personal effects, increased yearly. And most important, the family managed to buy 4 acres of land, in 2-acre allotments. Records in the Office of the Clerk of the County Court do not indicate exactly when the Powers family purchased the 4 acres of land that the Tax Digest indicated they owned. It can be presumed that this occurred sometime in the 1880s, since the census records do not indicate land ownership in the 1870s, and part of the land had been sold off by the early 1890s.

In spite of two decades of moderate prosperity, the family's fortunes had begun to decline by 1891. In that year Armstead Powers sold 2 acres of land to John R. Crawford of Clarke County for $177.[1] Three years later, in 1894, Armstead defaulted on his taxes. Harriet's and Armstead's names appeared jointly for the first time in the 1894 Tax Digest. Thereafter, only Harriet's name appeared on the annual tax rolls. Apparently Armstead left the family and the farm. He was definitely alive during this period, for he appeared at the Clarke County courthouse on February 13, 1901, to sell his remaining 2 acres of land for $359 to the same John R. Crawford who had purchased property from the couple in 1891.[2] It was a joint transaction. Both Harriet and Armstead Powers affixed their marks to the warranty deed. This transfer of property is the last official record of the Powers family.

From 1894 to 1910 Harriet maintained herself quite independently on farmland in Sandy Creek. She paid her yearly taxes, she borrowed money, and she mortgaged property.

As an example of her business acumen, in 1897 at the age of 60, Harriet Powers decided to buy a buggy from a C. W. Cooper from Clarke County. A promissory note in the amount of $16.89 was drawn up in the Office of the Clerk of the County Court of Athens. Harriet agreed to pay the amount specified in a three-month period – August to November – with interest at the rate of 8 percent per year. The wording of the contract is interesting: "It is hereby agreed that the ownership of title to said buggy shall remain to said C. W. Cooper until this note is fully paid, and it is distinctly understood that I take all the risk of said dying."[3]

To ensure payment of the debt properly, Mrs. Powers mortgaged "one lot of land in Clarke County adjoining M. J. Kendricks on South side, joins McGuity of West and North and joins Armstead Powers on East, also M. J. Kendricks on East." On August 18, 1897, Harriet Powers made an *x* to indicate her signature to this agreement. Her name was written in by the county clerk.

It would appear that Mrs. Powers lived her remaining years alone. She did not remarry. Her children were grown when their parents separated. There is a strong possibility that they may have left Clarke County since their names do not appear on the tax rolls. Harriet may have maintained herself by sewing for people in the community. She either owned or had access to a sewing machine, as indicated by the machine stitching on her quilts.

Harriet Powers's standard of living became extremely low in her old age. Half of her household articles and farm animals were sold to meet expenses. Her total possessions – furnishings, farm tools, animals, and personal effects – amounted to $82 in 1901, and only $70 by 1911. In that year she died on a farm in Buck Branch. The word *dead* was penciled in beside her name in the 1911 Tax Digest. Her odyssey from Buck Branch to Sandy Creek to Buck Branch had come full circle. She was 74 years old.

The official records tell nothing, of course, of the contribution to American folk art for which Harriet Powers is remembered. With no idea of the value of her work, this woman who could neither read nor write nevertheless felt an obligation to record the meanings of the pictorial representations on her quilts. She dictated these to Jennie Smith, who contributed some amplifications; but the essential meaning and language are Harriet's own. The oral history behind four of the depictions has been identified. Explanations follow each depiction:

> The dark day of May 19, 1780. The seven stars were seen 12.N. in the day. The cattle all went to bed, chickens to roost and the trumpet was blown. The sun went off to a small spot and then to darkness.

Dark days have been observed for centuries by meteorologists. As the atmosphere becomes polluted with smoke from forest fires, day is turned into night. In the period from 1706 to 1910, 18 dark days were recorded. The most famous was May 19, 1780. Though popularly known as Black Friday, this day was characterized by an odor and gradually increasing yellowness. "During the dark day of 1780 ashes of burnt leaves, soot and cinders fell in some sections from forest fires in New York and Canada."[4] Scientists say this was confined to New England, but oral tradition concerning the dark day circulated throughout the country. Harriet Powers heard about it in Georgia. She was so deeply impressed by this spectacular occurrence, which had convinced observers that the end of the world was at hand, that she recorded it on her quilt.

Phineas Sprague of Melrose, Massachusetts, recorded in his diary an account of this extraordinary day:

> Friday, May the 19th 1780. – This day was the most Remarkable day that ever my eyes beheld. . . . About ten o'clock it began to Rain and grew vere dark and at 12 it was almost as dark as the Nite so that wee was obliged to lite our candels and Eate our dinner by candel lite at noon day. But between 1 and 2 o'clock it grew lite again but in the Evening the cloud caim over us again. The moon was about the full (but) it was the darkest nite that ever was seen by us in the world.[5]

Also:

> Candles were lighted up in the houses; the birds having sung their evening songs, disappeared and became silent; the fowls retired to their roosts. The cocks were crowing all around as at break of day; objects could not be distinguished but at a very slight distance, and everything bore the gloom and appearance of night.[6]

John Greenleaf Whittier immortalized May 19, 1780, in a poem titled "Abraham Davenport." The poem concerns Colonel Davenport, a member of the governor's council in Connecticut, who objected to a motion to adjourn the council because of darkness and urged that candles be brought so that work could continue.

> The falling of the stars on November 13, 1833. The people were frighten and thought that the end of time had come. God's hand staid the stars. The varmints rushed out of their beds.

Eyewitnesses to the extraordinary events of November 12–14, 1833, believed that "it was snowing fire," "the end of the world has come," "the sky is on fire," and "Judgement Day is here." What in fact took place was the famous Leonid meteor storm of 1833, which produced a dramatic display of shooting stars seen in greatest brilliance in North America. This meteor storm is significant because such events occur only three or four times a century, usually lasting no more than an hour. The Leonid storm of 1833, which was observed for eight hours, marks the beginning of scientific interest in meteors.

Scientific observers described the meteors as varying in size from the smallest visible points to fireballs equaling the moon in diameter. An unusual number of shooting stars was first seen as early as 10 p.m. on November 12. Their frequency increased until, between 2 and 6 a.m., it was impossible to calculate their number.[7] Estimates vary from 8,660 to 10,000 an hour. No sound whatever accompanied the display.

An eyewitness near Augusta, Georgia, gave the following account:

> At about nine p.m. the shooting stars first arrested our attention, increasing in both number and brilliancy until 30 minutes past 2 a.m., when one of the most splendid sights perhaps that mortal eyes have ever beheld, was opened to our astonished gaze. From the last mentioned hour until daylight the appearance of the heavens was awfully sublime. It would seem as if worlds upon worlds from the infinity of space were rushing like a whirlwind to our globe.... "[A]nd the stars descended like a snow fall to the earth...." Occasionally one would dart forward leaving a brilliant train which...would remain visible, some of them for nearly fifteen minutes.[8]

As interesting as this event was in scientific circles, it is important to note that common people attached great significance to it. Eyewitness accounts were handed down, becoming the topic of comment and speculation for many generations. It became a time-fixing device by means of which important events, such as births and deaths, were determined by the general population, including former slaves.

At least a half-dozen scientific sources repeated the following account by a white planter in South Carolina:

> I was suddenly awakened by the most distressing cries that ever fell on my ears. Shrieks of horror and cries of mercy I could hear from most of the negroes of the three plantations, amounting in all to about 600 to 800. While earnestly listening for the cause I heard a faint voice near the door, calling my name. I arose, and taking my sword, stood at the door. At this moment I heard the same voice still beseeching me to arise, and saying, "O my God, the world is on fire!" I then opened the door, and it is difficult to say which excited me the most – the awfulness of the scene, or the distressed cries of the negroes. Upwards of a hundred lay prostrate on the ground – some speechless, and some with the bitterest cries, but with their hands raised, imploring God to save the world and them. The scene was truly awful; for never did rain fall much thicker than the meteors fell towards the earth; east, west, north, and south, it was the same.[9]

This account corroborates Harriet Powers's statement that "the people were frighten and thought that the end of time had come."

> Cold Thursday, 10. of February, 1895. A woman frozen while at prayer. A woman frozen at a gateway. A man with a sack of meal frozen. Isicles formed from the breath of a mule. All blue birds killed. A man frozen at his jug of liquor.

According to *Climatological Data* for the state of Georgia (1895–8), the entire month of February 1895 was unseasonably cold, over 6 degrees below normal, with heavy snowfalls. On the morning of the eighth, the state experienced an unusually severe cold wave, which brought the temperature down to minus 1 degree in the Athens area. A second period of extreme cold, but not as severe, occurred several days later. In fact, February 10, which Mrs. Powers specifically mentioned, fell within the second cold snap. On that day the weather station in Athens registered the temperature as being 20 degrees in the early morning hours and 30 degrees at night. Sleet occurred at scattered points throughout the state. It should be noted that February 10, 1985, fell on a Sunday, rather than a Thursday.

Friday the eighth, then, was an extremely cold day for the southeastern United States, with a low temperature recorded at minus 1 degree. This two-day period, February 8–10, is probably the occasion of the frozen deaths suffered by humans and animals that Mrs. Powers recorded.

> The red light night of 1846. A man tolling the bell to notify the people of the wonder. Women, children, and fowls frightened but Gods merciful hand caused no harm to them.

This information, though of considerable interest, is insufficient to determine the exact nature of the phenomenon. Fireballs or meteors are the only relevant occurrences recorded in scientific literature for the year 1846. *The American Journal of Science and Arts* (vol. 3, May 1847, pp. 125–6) states that meteoric showers were visible on the evenings of August 10 and 11, 1846. They could be seen from the northeast, southeast, southwest, and northwest. A cloudy sky and the presence of the moon hindered observations on the tenth, but a clear sky on the evening of the eleventh revealed 23 shooting stars from a southeasterly direction. Even more stars were visible from other directions.

Meteors falling thickly together, as they descended low in the air, appeared large and fiery, and the sky and air seemed to be in flames, even the earth appearing ready to take fire. It is this vision of August 10 and 11, 1846, that may have inspired Mrs. Powers's red light night.

Probably the real significance of Harriet Powers's explanations of her quilt blocks is that oral history turns out to be startlingly accurate. This former slave depicted stories that she had only heard, never read, and they paralleled scientific records. But times were changing in Harriet's day, and she knew intuitively that the quilts she had so carefully and lovingly created should be explained, in written form, for those who would examine them in later years. This she did, with the help of someone who could write. Thus she recorded those stories that had impressed her, just as in the quilt itself Harriet Powers expressed both her life experiences and her African heritage.

Notes

1 Deed Record K.K., Clarke County, Office Clerk of County Court, Athens, Georgia, 1891.
2 Deed Record K.K., Clarke County, 1891.
3 Record of Mortgages Z, Clarke County, Georgia, Office of Clerk of County Court, Athens, Georgia, 1897.
4 Helen Sawyer Hogg, *Out of Old Books* (Toronto: David Dunlap Observatory, University of Toronto Press, 1974), 186–7.
5 Joseph Ashbrook, "Darkness at Noon," *Sky and Telescope* (April 1964), p. 219.
6 Ibid., Ashbrook, p. 219.
7 Daniel Kirkwood, *Comets and Meteors* (Philadelphia: J. B. Lippincott, 1873), p. 69.
8 Charles P. Oliver, *Meteors* (Baltimore: Williams and Wilkens, 1925), p. 25.
9 Mary Proctor, *The Romance of Comets* (New York: Harper and Brothers, 1926), p. 171.

Empathy, Energy, and Eating:
Politics and Power in *The Black Family Dinner Quilt Cookbook*

Sally Bishop Shigley

Shigley, Sally Bishop. "Empathy, Energy, and Eating: Politics and Power in *The Black Family Dinner Quilt Cookbook*." In Anne L. Bower, ed. *Recipes for Reading: Community Cookbooks, Stories, Histories* (Amherst, MA: University of Massachusetts Press, 1997), pp. 118–31, 252–3.

When freshman composition papers become too much for me, I read cookbooks. Instead of flinging marginal barbs that are more a product of my own impatience than a student's ineptitude, I put down my pencil and retreat to my chaise longue with a collection of culinary wisdom. My tastes are eclectic: when I want to be seriously distracted, I open *Joy of Cooking* and wade into the exhaustive, often wickedly witty instructions. For duck: "unless you choke your duck, pluck the down on its breast immediately afterward and cook it within 24 hours, you cannot lay claim to having produced an authentic Rouen duck.... If, as is likely, duck strangling would bring you into local disrepute, you may waive the sturdy peasant preliminaries and serve a modified version, garnished with quotation marks."[1] When in a page-turning mode, I scan the quaint illustrations of the *Moosewood Cookbook* or the rapid-fire presentation of *365 Ways to Cook Pasta*. When the thermal inversions of a Utah January leave me longing for the sun, I dream of sunlit verandas and *melanzane filanti con mozzarella* (egg-plant and mozzarella fritters from Luigi Carnacina's tomelike *Great Italian Cooking*), or of the beaches of Ixtapa and tart *cebiche* from Diana Kennedy's *The Cuisines of Mexico*. Margaret Atwood confesses a similar passion. She says: "I'm one of those people who read cookbooks the way other people read travel writing: I may not ever make the recipe, but it's fun to read about it, and to speculate on what kind of people would. One man's cookbook is another woman's soft porn; there's a certain sybaritic voyeurism involved, an indulgence by proxy.... Any cookbook, read in its entirety, creates its own imagined view of the world."[2]

Atwood's equation of cookbooks with a reality outside the realm of mere instructions is essential and is nowhere more evident than in a cookbook I have read with keen interest: the National Council of Negro Women's *The Black Family Dinner Quilt Cookbook* (1993).[3] Like any good book, this one takes the reader to different times and places: recipes for pinto bean pie and hoe cakes look back to the struggles of slavery, while strawberry tea cake and salmon lasagna remind us of happier, more comfortable times. Like any good cookbook, it contains detailed, well-organized instructions and, like a timely 1990s cookbook, it includes nutritional and caloric information for each recipe – yet the tone and the focus of this book/cookbook are different from those of its contemporaries.

This difference can best be explained if we start with the literal beginnings of the book: the title and the introductory material. The full title reads *The Black Family Dinner Quilt Cookbook: Health Conscious Recipes and Food Memories*. The purpose of this volume is twofold: to raise funds for the National Council of Negro Women's National Center for African American Women, and to pay tribute to Dr. Dorothy I. Height, civil rights leader and president of the NCNW. Anyone who regularly browses in bookstores has seen an ethnic cookbook, a family cookbook, a health-conscious cookbook, or a cookbook in memory of some great cook. This book combines them all and adds quilting to the mix as well. The metaphor of quilting holds the text together in a narrative that pieces together the history of the NCNW, food traditions, and shared meals. The NCNW as an organization is a kind of patchwork since it was formed initially to "harness" diverse Black women's clubs and groups into one, more efficient whole. This book illustrates with wit and humor how these empowered, interesting women from a variety of backgrounds conduct important business across a dinner table as effectively as they do over a conference table. More importantly, through its narratives, its "food memories," and its connecting of domestic and public worlds, it offers hope and a sense of continuity to a wide spectrum of women.

Each word of this book's title forms a mini-patchwork: the varied histories and ancestral nationalities of African Americans combine with the panoplies of family and the dizzying variation that is dinner. In addition, the book itself is part of a very small patchwork. Preceding this volume, the NCNW sponsored *The Black Family Reunion Cookbook* (1991) and dedicated it to Mary McLeod Bethune, a former slave who later became both a cabinet member in the Roosevelt administration and the founder of the NCNW.[4] This book contained recipes, food memories, and section dividers made from photocopies of batiks, kentes, dashiki prints, and other African fabrics. The more recent volume differs from its predecessor not in subject and focus but in its intricacy and organization. *The Black Family Dinner Quilt Cookbook* takes the ideas of textiles, cooking, nutrition and health, and the reality of women's lives and creates a richer, different kind of patchwork.

Appropriately, this book about cooking appears initially as a kind of metaphorical sandwich, as both the front and back covers show pictures of the quilts promised in the title. On the front cover, we see a quilt called "Mealtime Dialogue" by artist Faith Ringgold; it depicts Mrs. Bethune and Dr. Height in their Sunday clothes having tea together. In the background, other NCNW members create quilts. Near the edge of the quilt, the words of Bethune, her legacy, charge the viewer with hope, harmony, and the responsibility for future generations. The quilt on the back cover depicts Harriet Tubman, famous "conductor" in the Underground Railroad. This tapestry quilt was made by the History Quilt Clubs of Sausalito and Marin City, California, and was designed by architect Ben Irvin. It depicts Tubman standing against a midnight blue background and flanked by both an owl, symbolizing her wisdom and unerring night vision, and the North Star, which she used to navigate on her treacherous journeys. These two images of quilts serve as a distilled version of the narrative of this book. The modern women on the front join with the women of history to model the power of perseverance and hope despite difficult and dangerous odds. The woman opening this book holds in her hands a literal representation of what women could and can do.

Once opened, the book continues this message of optimism. "Women," a poem by Alice Walker, begins the dedication as we see

> They were women then
> My mama's generation
> Husky of voice – Stout of
> Step
> With fists as well as
> Hands.[5]

These women and others like them, the dedication tells us, showed Dorothy Height and the women who followed her how to survive and succeed in a world where gender and color are the first elements by which people are evaluated.[6] It is to women who still struggle with these prejudices, as well as Dr. Height, that this book most directly sends its messages. Part of the power of this book, however, is that it speaks to me, a middle-class, white, academic woman as well. The weaving of hope and despair, oppression and opportunity form a text that can transcend racial, ethnic, and class boundaries.

These ideas are conveyed through language, through pictures, and through recipes for both modern foods and traditional, "heritage" foods that were cooked during the bondage of slavery. The book is divided into six recipe sections (soups, salads, main dishes, side dishes, baked goods, desserts) with a facsimile of a quilt by or depicting African American women, in shades of black, white, and gray, introducing each section. On the reverse of each photocopied quilt is a history of how the quilt came into being and what inspired its subject. "Grandma's Porch," a quilt by Michael Cummings, depicts his grandmother standing on her porch and waving goodbye to him. The fabric clothing the figure in the quilt is the actual fabric he took from one of his grandmother's housedresses. "Reprise," by Marie Wilson, presents a patchwork of influential women, while "The Oldham Family Quilt," by Carolyn Mazloomi, represents the life and work of the family of Bettye Torrey Oldham.[7] Not all of the quilted images represent positive memories, however, as "Meredith" by Sandra German was conceived in the emergency room of a hospital where the child of the title was taken after being cruelly assaulted by an acquaintance; "I'll Fly Away," also by Michael Cummings, shows the early American icon of "an African American woman caught in the forced labor system of slavery."[8]

Nestled between each of these quilts are the recipes, complete with nutritional information on calories, sodium content, number of grams of fat, percentage of calories from fat, and cholesterol and protein amounts. On the literal margins of these recipes lie memories of food and history and leadership from famous political and social leaders and ordinary women. An irony too pointed to be accidental places the comments of these brave, insightful women and men in the margins, the edges, the outside. Yet as the reader opens the book, these margins face each other over nutritious and nurturing recipes – just like the women of the NCNW faced each other over the dinner table to work out the problems and opportunities in being "marginal." And when the book is closed, these margins come together to form sheet after shaded sheet of wisdom and solidarity. An anonymous woman relates how Dr. Height was forced to eat fried chicken and boiled eggs from a shoe box on a civil rights mission to the South because she could not be served in the restaurants.[9] Beverly Coleman describes with delight how Dr. Height met with Malcolm X, Lorraine Hansberry, and other Black leaders to try to form a united front among Black groups. Ms. Coleman's favorite part of the story, however, is how Dr. Height was taken to the meeting by Sidney Poitier in his brand new sports car.[10] Jason Crump tells of how an impressive young man was invited to dinner with Dr. Height. This delightful young man made a lasting impression on the older woman – his name was Martin Luther King, Jr.[11] On the leadership qualities of Dr. Height, whom she refers to as "the Godmother," the Honorable Eleanor Holmes Norton, member of the House of Representatives, comments: "Just as no man would submerge any vital part of his identity, his blackness or his maleness, Dorothy has taught us that integrity lies in being whole. She has taught us to be proud African-American women. The Godmother continues to watch over us. We know that we are safe."[12]

The integrated wholeness that Congresswoman Norton speaks of is composed of the parts that make up all women, and in the final "memory," Dr. Height includes all women in her call for women to speak their valuable voices and refuse, no matter what their position, to remain in silence.[13] The words of these exceptional people nourish the soul of the reader in a way that even the "soul food" recipes cannot. This book stands as a model of how Dr. Height and women like her have used their entire selves to succeed. The same hearts and hands and heads that quilt and cook can forge civil rights legislation and provide safe havens for women in danger. In this nexus of recipes and quilts and memories and nutrition sits a reminder that possibility and hope and power lie within the patchwork of mind, body, heart, and head that makes up all women.

As I have described this book, I have mentally stumbled trying to decide what to call it: it is filled with recipes, so is it a cookbook? It possesses a narrative, so is it a story? It has a persuasive intent to raise money, so is it rhetoric? The question becomes complicated because a hierarchy exists in our culture, especially academic culture, that divides "serious" books from all other kinds of written texts between covers. "Real" books, be they artistic or informative texts, possess automatic authority: the writer is an expert about something or an inspired creator, and the result is something that is approached reverently, read in a linear fashion, studied. Cookbooks, and especially community cookbooks, are not seen in this way. One may approach Julia Child's *The Way to Cook* with deference, but that is hardly the mood in which we traditionally approach a work such as *Let's Eat!* a fund-raising effort for the senior citizen's center of Brigham City, Utah. Most people scan commercial and fund-raising cookbooks for ideas when they are stumped about what to cook for dinner, or they go to them when they are faced with an unfamiliar or difficult culinary situation: the zucchini have come on and need disguising, or an intrepid shopper discovers couscous on sale and doesn't know what to do with it. Most cooks don't approach cookbooks for stories or support or feelings of solidarity. In fact, I doubt if many people consider what they do with these books to be *reading*.

Susan J. Leonardi tries to dismantle this hierarchy between books and cookbooks when she notes that "a cookbook which consisted of nothing but rules for various dishes would be an unpopular cookbook indeed. A recipe needs a recommendation, a context, a point, a reason-to-be." She adds that, through asides and evaluations at the beginning of recipes, the author becomes "an identifiable persona with whom the reader not only can agree or argue but is encouraged to agree or argue . . . each recipe thus comments on every other recipe in the section."[14] Leonardi sees cookbooks as implicit dialogues between individual recipe texts and between women, not as "how to" manuals. She notes that even in communities of women of different class or race or age, the sharing of recipes can go on. She calls it an "almost prototypical female activity."[15] As I write this statement, I can immediately think of several women who don't cook and who would find this remark sexist. I don't think that it was meant in this spirit, nor that it needs to be. Leonardi and other feminists, including myself, do not explore "traditional" activities in order to reify stereotypes or prove that women are limited. On the contrary, examination of cookbooks or quilts or other "female" domains illustrates how women have used the discourses available to them to make profound and effective statements.

In fact, it is just such a hierarchical disjunction between "domestic" and "professional" women, or between public and private spheres, that *The Black Family Dinner Quilt Cookbook* tries to undo. Laura Esquivel illustrates the dangers of this potentially oppressive binary division in her cookbook/novel *Like Water for Chocolate:* "the joy of living was wrapped up in the delights of food. It wasn't easy for a person whose knowledge of life was based on the kitchen to comprehend the outside world. That world was an endless expanse that began at the door between the kitchen and the rest of the house, whereas everything on the kitchen side of that door, on through the door leading to the patio and the kitchen and her gardens was completely hers."[16] The danger of all that lies outside the kitchen does not materialize in its feared form as the novel progresses. In fact, the protagonist's influence reaches far beyond the kitchen as her cooking influences the lives and loves and fates of everyone who eats it – and that is precisely the point that the NCNW wants to make with their book. The four women and one man who put together this book are not editors or compilers or co-chairs or any of the other designations that one usually sees at the beginning of community or fund-raising cookbooks. These people are talented professionals who find nothing remotely disjunctive in their interest in cooking and quilting and "domestic" art. Faith Ringgold is an artist. Brenda Rhodes Cooper is a novelist. Carolyn L. Mazloomi is a fiber artist and historian. Lonnie Robinson is a graphic designer. Lauren Swann is a nutritionist. The people writing the "marginal" food memories include members of congress and judges, community leaders, college professors, and clergypeople.

Foodways scholar Charles Camp supports this "intersection of food and culture" as an important part of community mythmaking. He argues that "ordinary people understand and employ the symbolic and cultural dimensions of food in their everyday affairs," adding that "what most people learn at home is a mix of information, skill, judgement, and meaning that recapitulates family, ethnic, religious, and social values." In Camp's mind, and in the judgment of sociologist Jack Goody, the so-called lines between the domestic and the professional, the private and the philosophic, are rather blurred.[17]

It seems no small coincidence then that, aside from the cover, everything that is not written "text" in this book exists in shades of gray. The quilts take their hues from the charcoals and lead tones of photocopying, and the marginal memories are highlighted in gray bands on the edge of each page. Black and white dichotomies of all kinds lose their centrality in this work as the focus shifts significantly to the gray and to the margins. This is not to suggest, however, that this book is in any way "color blind"; it is a work inspired by exceptional Black women to raise funds for less fortunate Black women, but it invites all women to accept the empowering message that it offers.

This cookbook avoids the worst pitfalls of the genre. Ethnic foodway scholars Linda Keller Brown and Kay Mussell note that in many instances "cookbooks and restaurants convey relatively static concepts of a subculture and reinforce stereotypical assumptions that are further diluted by the imperative of the marketplace."[18] The rich spices and traditions of the Mexican mole sauce, through a strange commercial metamorphosis, become the bland tomato sauce and hamburger concoctions at the local fast food taco stand. Americans can, in a sense, have their tortillas and their familiar tastes, too. The authors of *The Black Family Dinner Quilt Cookbook* have avoided this potential error by mixing recipes for the traditional food of African American culture with recipes that contemporary African Americans are cooking. The soul food or heritage recipes are not homogenized and made mainstream but are complemented with more updated dishes: both are essential components in the "canon" of African American cooking. The power of this text lies both in its refusal to accept the divisive power of cultural or racial binaries and in the individual, the distinctive, the potentially unfamiliar: in the memories that line each page, the shared meals, and the sense of community that knits the women of the NCNW together. Their power and spirit rests in the very diversity of background and experience that each woman brings to the organization. The difference, the blending, the "grayness" is key.

The importance of the gray marginalia deepens if we consider the history of cookbooks in general with reference to the idea of hierarchies. Food historian Reay Tannahill notes that as early as the "self-assured days of Pericles," food has been used as a marker of social and economic standing or class."[19] Tannahill names the ancient Greek writer "Archestratus...[as] the first in that long line of gastronomic pedants who have guided the world

ever since. The style remains familiar today. While most Athenians who liked
tuna had to make do with the dried or salted variety from the Black Sea,
Archestratus laid down that none but the fresh kind from Byzantium would
suffice, and that it should be eaten only in autumn."[20] Every cook, experienced or novice, recognizes this tone, usually accompanied by a disgusted
sniff of some kind, that suggests that anything less than an impossible to find
and obscenely expensive ingredient is not worth considering, let alone eating. Barbarians, these recipes suggest, and others who don't keep kilos of
saffron and pounds of paté in their pantries need not even attempt to cook.

   The Black Family Dinner Quilt Cookbook rejects such culinary ultimatums.
It not only illustrates the "domestic" activities of "professional" women,
and encourages "cooks" and others to expand their horizons, but achieves
this blending of skill and possibility in a genre that has traditionally been used
to establish hierarchies, not to dismantle them. This book refuses to be the
kind of work in which the sheer number of imported dried mushrooms,
hard-to-get spices, and incomprehensible cooking terms marginalizes all but
the most courageous chef. But that does not mean that it is unimaginative.
Cheesy Tomato and Beef Casserole and Wilma's Skillet Hash offer quick,
nutritious alternatives to the after work cook, while Pizza Garden Style offers
a low fat alternative of home-made dough, herb sauce, and fresca toppings so
appetizing that you'll never miss the artery-clogging pepperoni. Festive
occasions merit the Chicken Jerusalem with sherry and artichokes followed
by Saucy Vanilla Rum Bread Pudding. Eschewing culinary snobbery in favor
of exuberant eclecticism, this work invites all women – and men too – to
partake of both its recipes and its implicit model of hope and possibility.

   Scholars writing about African American quilters make a similar point as
they speak of the "creolization" of this form. Maude Southwell Wahlman
notes that "Afro-American quilts mirror the diverse influences that shape the
lives of Black women in the United States," and she adds that "Afro-
American artists maintaining this creolized aesthetic demonstrate the
power and vision of African cultural traditions in contemporary American
society."[21] The blend of recipes and diverse women's voices in the NCNW's
work achieves much the same end.

   The creolized gray margins of the book graphically mimic the goals of the
NCNW: to include all women in their quest for equality. The Black and white
print of the recipes exists in "community" with the grayness of the margins.
This point is made both within the cookbook and by another quilt and craft
scholar, William Ferris. He notes that "quilts are a salvage art in which quilt
makers recycle scraps of cloth into new shapes and color combinations. They
select colors and pattern designs which are easily distinguished from white
traditions in Amish and Appalachian communities."[22] The dedication of this
book invites all women to explore the possibilities within the pages: women

of color, "skin in shades of the rural Pennsylvania autumns [the authors] knew as a child"; "immigrant women, new to this country...women who made their own chewy breads, their own spicy sausages"; even "patrician" women, who helped the careers of women such as Dr. Height.[23] In this creolized ideal the roots of difference in Black women's struggles cannot be forgotten. Lauren Swann, the book's nutritional, consultant, provides both a "History of Soul Food," detailing the legacy of the "heritage" foods included in the book, and a section on nutritional, satisfying menu planning. In her history she notes that soul food "evolved from the rich heritage of African customs, was shaped by Southern cookery practices, expanded by the similarly tribal habits of Native Americans, and [was] regionally influenced by West Indian, Caribbean, and French cooking."[24] Swann adds that "as slaves, African Americans were not permitted to learn how to read or write, so they cooked not from recipes but by 'knowing,' giving strong credence to the essence of 'soul food.' Slaves had virtually no control or choice in life. So cooking became a way to express feeling, share love, and nurture family and friends. Meals were time for sharing common feelings of happiness and sorrow. Food was comfort while in bondage, and because they could control cooking, it was one of their few real pleasures, a way to feel free."[25] Cooking equals freedom in this book. Cooking also serves as a model for the dismantling of hierarchies both external and internal. *The Black Family Dinner Quilt Cookbook* allows all women to see how other women have overcome personal and political obstacles and achieved the freedom to move and act – that is, cook – as they chose. The same Dorothy Height that ate chicken out of a shoe box, this narrative implies, ate and eats with presidents.

Twenty-five years before *The Black Family Dinner Quilt Cookbook* emerged, Ruth Gaskins published a small cookbook entitled *Every Good Negro Cook Starts with Two Basic Ingredients: A Good Heart and a Light Hand* (1968).[26] Gaskins says she wrote this book because there was not one like it available, and she felt that it was important that these recipes be recorded. Both this work and the more recent one contain a history of soul food, traditional and modern recipes, and commentary on the lives of African Americans; yet Gaskins's book is very much a product of its time. Like Swann, Gaskins sees food in the lives of slaves as a metaphor for control; and like the contemporary authors, she discusses the importance of food in ceremonies and community events. The important difference lies in the audience addressed and the use of pronouns. When Swann discusses the nutritional choices of modern African Americans, she uses just that term: "Homecooked meals begin with food selection, and African-Americans have come a long way from having no choice but to accept pig parts and corn meal."[27] Gaskins, on the other hand, seems to be writing to an audience outside her cultural and ethnic group. When referring to the recipes and habits of African American cooks, she consistently uses the pronoun "we": "we cook for the friend who might drop by. They are our family, and we consider our family numberless," or "we rarely serve separate courses at our meals. Having it all on the table makes us feel good."[28] In the context of the painful and violent racial turmoil of the sixties, this unifying rhetorical gesture is understandable. Swann and the other authors chose the third person not to somehow ignore difference and suggest a resolved conflict, but to recognize diversity and invite dialogue. Brenda Rhodes Cooper writes: "The lives of Mary McLeod Bethune, Eleanor Roosevelt, Dorothy Height, and all the people who have come in contact with Dr. Height form a marvelous fabric that is not seamless, but is quilted together by threads of shared experiences. The quilt, made up of these lives, is varied and colorful. Pieced together out of scraps...moments of conversation during meals eaten in places high and low push open a door to the past."[29]

These scraps also provide keys to the doors of the present and future for all the various textures and patterns of women who make up the feminine patchwork. Ann Romines explains how this works when she argues that housekeeping and, we can assume, cooking, should be seen as more than a domestic, mundane activity: "If housekeeping can be inscribed, if the home plot can appear on the page, then it is acknowledged as continuing fact, problem, and resource of our common life. Such writing may postulate a life in which boundaries between public and private spheres and between male and female spheres become elastic, permeable, or perhaps even nonexistent."[30] By working through what Tannahill has defined as a potentially hierarchical and limiting genre, the writers of this cookbook have made a move to dissolve these binaries by illustrating that there is nothing anachronistic or compromising in the image of a professional woman in the kitchen, nor need anything prevent the so-called "domestic" woman from venturing outside that realm. Literary theorists Patricia Yeager and Andrea Nye make similar points. Yeager suggests that the possibility of only two poles or two extremes of women's discourse is overly limiting. She argues that we must find a mean between strictly women's writing and the marginalized silence that comes from trying to write against or within a patriarchal structure.[31] Nye expands on this idea as she adds that women must create a balance between claiming and honoring that which is inherently female and recognizing that they must utilize linear, "patriarchal" language in at least a limited way to interrogate that language.[32]

In writing their cookbook/narrative, the authors of *The Black Family Dinner Quilt Cookbook* have done just that. They have, in the words of Hélène Cixous, found the "two, as well as both, the ensemble of the one and the other."[33] They have presented the lives of these women as they are –

very complex – instead of dividing their worlds artificially between their professional lives and the rest of their lives. Within this full depiction of women's lives, food is as important as philosophy – perhaps more important. Mary Anne Schofield eloquently argues that "food cooked, eaten, and thought about provides a metaphoric matrix, a language that allows us a way to get at the uncertainty, the ineffable qualities of life . . . to write about food is to deal with the most important and the most basic human needs and desires."[34] In real women's worlds, food and life exist simultaneously, and, as this book has shown, in complement to one another.

Discussing the history of recipes, Susan Leonardi tells us that " 'rule' used to be a synonym for recipe – a kind of archetypal and model rule, which allows for infinite variations while still maintaining almost complete repro-ductability and literality."[35] Instead of standing above their audience and lecturing to them about life or roles or recipes, the editors and contributors who created *The Black Family Dinner Quilt Cookbook* offer models that inspire hope but encourage as many variations as there are women. Without moralizing or telling women to "have it all," this book shows how many women have dissolved the hierarchies in their own lives and minds and integrated all of the facets of themselves. Their stories list essential ingredients and do-able, if not "easy-to-follow" instructions for the women inspired to follow them.

Notes

1 Irma S. Rombauer and Marion Rombauer Becker, *Joy of Cooking*, vol. 1 (New York: Signet, 1964), pp. 587–8.

2 Margaret Atwood, "Introducing *The CanLit Foodbook*," in *Literary Gastronomy*, ed. David Bevan (Amsterdam: Rodope, 1988), p. 51.

3 Dorothy I. Height and the National Council of Negro Women, Inc., *The Black Family Dinner Quilt Cookbook: Health Conscious Recipes and Food Memories* (Memphis, TN: Wimmer Companies, 1993).

4 National Council of Negro Women, Inc., *Black Family Reunion Cookbook* (Memphis, TN: Wimmer Companies, 1991).

5 *Black Family Dinner Quilt Cookbook*, p. 5.

6 Ibid., pp. 5–6.

7 Ibid., pp. 12, 40, 114.

8 Ibid., pp. 22, 198.

9 Ibid., pp. 18–19.

10 Ibid., pp. 42–3.

11 Ibid., p. 157.

12 Ibid., pp. 158–9.

13 Ibid., pp. 192–3.

14   Susan J. Leonardi, "Recipes for Reading: Pasta Salad, Lobster à la Riseholme, and Key Lime Pie," in *Cooking by the Book: Food in Literature and Culture*, ed. Mary Anne Schofield (Bowling Green, OH: Bowling Green State University Popular Press, 1989), p. 129.
15   Leonardi, "Recipes for Reading," p. 131.
16   Laura Esquivel, *Like Water for Chocolate: A Novel in Monthly Installments with Recipes, Romances, and Home Remedies*, trans. Carol Christensen and Thomas Christensen (New York: Doubleday, 1992), p. 7.
17   Charles Camp, *American Foodways: When, Why, and How We Eat in America* (Little Rock, AR: August House, 1989), pp. 24, 29, 51; Jack Goody, *Cooking, Cuisine, and Class: A Study in Comparative Sociology* (Cambridge: Cambridge University Press, 1982), p. 13.
18   Linda Keller Brown and Kay Mussell, eds., *Ethnic and Regional Foodways in the United States: The Performance of Group Identity* (Knoxville, TN: University of Tennessee Press, 1984), p. 4.
19   Reay Tannahill, *Food in History*, new, fully rev. and updated, ed. (New York: Crown Publishers, 1988), p. 68.
20   Ibid., p. 69.
21   Maude Southwell Wahlman, "African Symbolism in Afro-American Quilts," *African Arts* 20 (1986): 70, 76.
22   William Ferris, ed., *Afro-American Folk Art and Crafts* (Boston: G. K. Hall & Co., 1983), p. 65.
23   *Black Family Dinner Quilt Cookbook*, pp. 5–6.
24   Ibid., p. 200.
25   Ibid.
26   Ruth L. Gaskins, *Every Good Negro Cook Starts with Two Basic Ingredients: A Good Heart and a Light Hand* (New York: Simon & Schuster, 1968).
27   *Black Family Dinner Quilt Cookbook*, p. 213.
28   Gaskins, *Every Good Negro Cook*, pp. vii, 2.
29   *Black Family Dinner Quilt Cookbook*, p. 9.
30   Anne Romines, *The Home Plot: Women, Writing and Domestic Ritual* (Amherst, MA: University of Massachusetts Press, 1992), p. 294.
31   Patricia Yaeger, *Honey-mad Women: Emancipation Strategies in Women's Writing* (New York: Columbia University Press, 1988), p. 3.
32   Andrea Nye, *Feminist Theory and the Philosophies of Man* (New York: Routledge, 1988), p. 148.
33   Hélène Cixous, "The Laugh of the Medusa," in *Women's Voices: Visions and Perspectives*, ed. Pat C. Hoy II, Esther H. Schor, and Robert Di Yanni (New York: McGraw-Hill, 1990), p. 487.
34   Mary Anne Schofield, ed., *Cooking by the Book: Food in Literature and Culture* (Bowling Green, CH: Bowling Green State University Popular Press, 1989), p. 1.
35   Leonardi, "Recipes for Reading," p. 134.

Supplementary Readings and Media Resources

Supplementary Readings

Benberry, Cuesta, Always There: The African-American Presence in American Quilts (Louisville, KY: The Kentucky Quilt Project, Inc., 1992).

Brown, Elsa Barkley, "African-American Women's Quilting: A Framework for Conceptualizing and Teaching African-American Women's History," Signs: A Journal of Women in Culture and Society 14:4 (Summer 1989): 921–9.

Fry, Gladys-Marie, Stitched from the Soul: Slave Quilts from the Ante-Bellum South (New York: Dutton Studio Books, 1990).

Grosvenor, Vertamae Smart, Vibration Cooking, or the Travel Notes of a Geechee Girl (New York: Doubleday, 1970); 2nd edn, New York: Ballantine, 1986; 3rd edn, New York: One-World Ballantine, 1992.

Media Resources

Dash, Julie, Four Women. 7 minutes, video, b/w, 1975. (Third World Newsreel.)

Davis, Zeinabu irene. Mother of the River. 30 minutes, video, color, 1995. (Women Make Movies.)

Griffin, Ada Gay and Michelle Parkerson, A Litany for Survival: The Life and Work of Audre Lorde. 88 minutes, 16 mm and video, color, 1995. (Third World Newsreel.)

Media Resources Directory of Distributors

California Newsreel
149 Ninth Street #420
San Francisco, CA 94103
  (415) 621–6196

Films for the Humanities
P.O. Box 2053
Princeton, NJ 08543–2053
  1–800–257–5126
  Fax 609 275 3767

Kino International Corporation
333 West 39th Street
New York, NY 10018
  1–800–562–3330

L & S Video Enterprises, Inc.
45 Stornowaye
Chappaqua, NY 10514
  (914) 238–9366

PBS Video

1320 Braddock Place
Alexandria, VA 22314–1698
  1–800–344–3337

Phoenix Films
468 Park Avenue South, 10th Floor
New York, NY 10016
  1–800–221–1274

Third World Newsreel
335 West 38th Street, 5th Floor
New York, NY 10018
  (212) 947–9277

Women Make Movies
462 Broadway, 5th Floor
New York, NY 10013
  (212) 925–0606 x360
  Fax 212 926 2052
  e-mail Orders@wmm.com
  www.wmm.com

Bibliography

Algarín, Miguel and Bob Holman, eds. *Aloud: Voices from the Nuyorican Poets Café* (New York: Henry Holt & Co., 1994).

Anderlini, Serena. " 'colored girls': A Reaction to Black Machismo, or Hues of Erotic Tension in New Feminist Solidarity?" *Journal of American Drama and Theatre*, 2 (Spring, 1990): 33–54.

Anglesey, Zöe, ed. *Listen Up!: Spoken Word Poetry* (New York: One World, 1999).

Bell, Roseann P., Bettye J. Parker and Beverly Guy-Sheftall, eds. *Sturdy Black Bridges: Visions of Black Women in Literature* (New York: Anchor Books, 1979).

Blum, Joshua, Bob Holman and Mark Pellington, eds. *The United States of Poetry* (New York: Harry N. Abrams, 1996).

Cade [Bambara], Toni, ed. *The Black Woman: An Anthology* (New York: New American Library, 1970).

Caldwell, Paulette M. "A Hair Piece: Perspectives on the Intersection of Race and Gender." *Duke Law Journal*, 1991(2): 365–96.

Christian, Barbara. "Camouflaging Race and Gender." *Representations*, 55 (Summer, 1996): 120–8.

Crawford, Vicki L., Jacqueline Anne Rouse and Barbara Woods, eds. *Women in the Civil Rights Movement: Trailblazers and Torchbearers 1941–1965* (Bloomington, IN: Indiana University Press, 1993). (Originally published New York: Carlson Publishers, 1990.)

Davis, Angela Y. *Women, Culture and Politics* (New York: Random House, 1988).

duCille, Ann. *Skin Trade* (Cambridge, MA: Harvard University Press, 1996).

Edwards. Audrey. "From Aunt Jemima to Anita Hill: Media's Split Image of Black Women." *Media Studies Journal*, 7 (1–2) (Winter–Spring, 1993): 215–22.

Freeman, Roland L. *A Communion of the Spirits: African-American Quilters, Preservers, and their Stories* (Nashville, TN: Rutledge Hill Press, 1996).

Glass, Barbara, ed. *Uncommon Beauty in Common Objects: The Legacy of African American Craft Art* (Wilberforce, OH: National Afro-American Museum and Culture Center, 1993).

Guy-Sheftall, Beverly, ed. *Words of Fire: An Anthology of African-American Feminist Thought* (New York: The New Press, 1995).

Hill, George, Lorraine Raglin and Chas Floyd Johnson, eds. *Black Women in Television: An Illustrated History and Bibliography* (New York: Garland, 1990).

hooks, bell. *Art on my Mind: Visual Politics* (New York: The New Press, 1995).

James, Joy. "Black *Femmes Fatales* and Sexual Abuse in Progressive 'White' Cinema: Neil Jordan's *Mona Lisa* and *The Crying Game*." *Camera Obscura*, 36 (September, 1995): 33–46.

——. "Radicalising Feminism." *Race and Class*, 40(4) (April, 1999): 15–31.

James, Joy and Ruth Farmer, eds. *Spirit, Space and Survival: African American Women in (White) Academe* (New York: Routledge, 1993).

James, Stanlie and Abena P. A. Busia, eds. *Theorizing Black Feminisms: The Visionary Pragmatism of Black Women* (New York: Routledge, 1993).

Keyes, Cheryl L. " 'We're More than a Novelty Boys': Strategies of Female Rappers in the Rap Music Tradition." In Jean Newlon Radner, ed. *Feminist Messages: Codings in Women's Folk Culture* (Urbana. IL: University of Illinois Press, 1993), 203–20.

King, Deborah K. "Multiple Jeopardy, Multiple Consciousness: The Context of a Black Feminist Ideology." *Signs: A Journal of Women in Culture and Society*, 14(1) (Autumn, 1988): 42–72.

Lubiano, Wahneema. "Black Ladies, Welfare Queens, and State Minstrels: Ideological War by Narrative Means." In Toni Morrison, ed. *Race-ing Justice, En-gendering Power: Essays on Anita Hill, Clarence Thomas, and the Construction of Social Reality* (New York: Pantheon, 1992), pp. 323–63.

MacDowell, Marsha L., ed. *African-American Quiltmaking in Michigan* (East Lansing, MI: Michigan State University Press, in collaboration with Michigan State University Museum, 1997).

Mazloomi, Carolyn. *Spirits of the Cloth: Contemporary African American Quilts* (New York: Clarkson Potter, Publishers, 1998).

Morrison, Toni. *Playing in the Dark: Whiteness and the Literary Imagination* (Cambridge, MA: Harvard University Press, 1992).

O'Grady, Lorraine. "Olympia's Maid: Reclaiming Black Female Subjectivity." In Joanna Frueh et al. *New Feminist Criticism: Art, Identity, Action* (New York: Harper-Collins, 1994), pp. 152–70. (Expanded and reprinted from *Afterimage*, 20(1) (Summer, 1992): 14, 15, 19.)

Simmonds, Felly Nkweto. "She's Gotta Have It: The Representation of Black Female Sexuality on Film." *Feminist Review*, 29 (May, 1988): 10–22.

Smith, Barbara. *The Truth that Never Hurts: Writings on Race, Gender and Freedom* (New Brunswick, NJ: Rutgers University Press, 1998).

Smith Valerie. *Not Just Race, Not Just Gender: Black Feminist Readings* (New York: Routledge, 1998).

Tobin, Jacqueline L. and Raymond G. Dobard. *Hidden in Plain View: The Secret Story of Quilts and the Underground Railroad* (New York: Doubleday, 1999).

Wallace, Michele. *Invisibility Blues: From Pop to Theory* (London: Verso, 1998).

Wilkerson, Margaret B. "*A Raisin in the Sun:* Anniversary of an American Classic."
   In Sue-Ellen Case, ed. *Performing Feminisms: Feminist Critical Theory and Theatre*
   (Baltimore, MD: The Johns Hopkins University Press, 1990), pp. 119–30.
—, ed. *Nine Plays by Black Women* (New York: New American Library, 1986).

Index